D1065271

Intelligence, Learning,
and Action

Intelligence, Learning, and Action

A Foundation for Theory and Practice in Education

Richard R. Skemp

Professor of Educational Theory,
University of Warwick

JOHN WILEY & SONS

Chichester · New York · Brisbane · Toronto

Copyright©1979 by R. R. Skemp

All rights reserved.

No part of this book may be reproduced by any means, nor
transmitted, nor translated into a machine language without
the written permission of the publisher.

Library of Congress Cataloging in Publication Data:

Skemp, Richard R.
  Intelligence, learning, and action.

  Bibliography: p.
  Includes index.
  1. Learning, Psychology of. 2. Intellect.
3. Emotions. 4. Education—Philosphy.
I. Title.
LB1051.S565   370.15'2   78–10827
ISBN 0 471 99747 1   Cloth
ISBN 0 471 27575 1   Paper

Typeset by Preface Ltd, The Malverns, Salisbury, Wilts
and printed in Great Britain at Unwin Brothers Ltd, The Gresham Press,
Old Woking.

To my wife
Valerie

Acknowledgements

In the writing of this book I have been greatly helped by discussion with many groups of people. These include my last postgraduate seminar group in the Psychology department at Manchester University, my first such group when I came to the Education department at Warwick University, and my colleagues in this department. Chapters 14 and 15 had the benefit of much discussion with a group of experienced teachers who were with me for their degree of Master of Education. Mr L. G. Buxton has read the whole book in manuscript and made many useful criticisms and suggestions. (He wishes, however, to dissociate himself from the views expressed in Chapter 15.) I am indebted to Dr S. R. St. J. Neill for many of the ethological examples; and to Mrs E. M. Beattie for much help in the final preparation of the manuscript. I am also grateful to the Sabbatical Leave Committee of Warwick University for a term's sabbatical leave—my first in twenty-one years as a university teacher—which made possible a period of uninterrupted writing at a time when it was particularly needed; and to the Social Science Research Council for a grant in support of the research mentioned in Sections 9.8 and 9.9.

My wife Valerie, herself a qualified teacher, has been a constant source of encouragement and good advice; and my son Peter has also helped in many ways.

Preface

Intelligence makes man educable; and our children's intelligence is our greatest potential wealth. At present this invisible asset is largely unrealized: for the current conception of intelligence, centred around 'I.Q.' and attempts to measure it in various ways, has led to its isolation from the main fields of experimental psychology and theories of learning. As a means to enlighten the daily activities of teachers and parents, it has proved of little value. As a consequence, education is still at a stage comparable with that at which medicine was before Pasteur, zoology before Darwin and Mendel, atomic physics before Rutherford. As was written many years ago: 'Theory is in the end . . . the most practical of all things' (Dewey, 1929), and until education has a theoretical foundation comparable with those which give such power in the fields of science and technology, teachers' efforts will not meet with the success they deserve.

An experienced teacher and head of department, one whom I much respect, wrote to me: 'Someone, somewhere is going to have to help us solve some of our problems. We seem to be unable to "see the wood for the trees".' The present book, which has been developed in close contact with practising teachers, is the outcome of thirty years as a teacher, university lecturer, and professor of education. It develops intelligence as a key concept for the understanding of human activities, and especially those dependent on the higher forms of learning (such as science and technology) and those characteristic of advanced cultures. And instead of offering to education students contributions from psychology, sociology, philosophy, history, to be put together as best they can, the present model of intelligence provides the core of a unified theory of education.

Although this is a theoretical book, its aims are mainly practical; in the same way as the main purpose of a map is to give practical help for walkers, motorists, campers, climbers, naturalists. This needs emphasizing, since books about theory tend to be read largely by other theorists, whose interests lie in such directions as comparing it with what has already been written on the subject, and discussing its merits relative to the contributions of other theorists. This is a useful and respectable activity, but it is not the way to obtain whatever practical benefit any particular theory has to offer. To give an analogy, there are two possible kinds of interest which people might take in bicycles. One—we might call it that of a bicycologist—studies the history of the bicycle from the early velocipede to the present day; notes important landmarks such as the introduction of pneumatic tyres, chain driven back wheel, the change from radial to tangential spokes; compares the merits of various makes and designs. He can do this without even buying a bicycle, though he may be in a position to give good advice to intending purchasers. The other—we will call him a cyclist—needs a bicycle as a practical help for his daily work and recreation, to get him where he wants to go as quickly, comfortably, and safely as possible: and these are the criteria by which he judges it.

I am by no means suggesting that these two interests are incompatible, still less that one is worthier than the other. Far from it: they are complementary, in the way that the interests and techniques of surveyors and cartographers are necessary and complementary to those of map users. The former have to satisfy the standards of their profession, and the latter are entitled to an assurance that this has been done.

Ultimately, however, bicycles and maps are for reaching destinations; and my hope is that the present theoretical model will be found of use by learners and teachers, to help them reach their goals more easily and reliably. This kind of interest will best be served by applying the model to the reader's own personal and professional experience.

What kinds of help might we reasonably ask from a model of intelligence? I suggest that these may fairly include at least some indications how to use better the intelligence we have: how to learn better, organize better the knowledge we have, plan better—how to achieve our aims in life, short and long term, individual and collective. These are ambitious aims for a theoretical model; but some of the current conceptions of intelligence have a history of seventy years and more during which they have not contributed noticeably to the above. Until we at least start aiming in the right direction, there is little chance of approaching any of these goals.

It is not only for professional teachers that I have written this book. Education is a lifelong process, and the ways in which each of us makes use of his own intelligence are a major influence on all our lives, individually and collectively. Much care and effort have therefore been taken to achieve a presentation which, in spite of the power and reach of the ideas, nevertheless make them accessible to a wide readership. With this in mind, may I conclude this preface with some information and suggestions?

This book needs to be read consecutively from the beginning—it is not suitable for 'dipping'. The first four chapters form an introduction and overview, and should be found reasonably easy to follow. Chapters 5 to 11 then develop the model in much greater depth and detail. This makes them necessarily more difficult: how much more, will depend on the background of the reader. For this reason, and also because different aspects of the model will appeal to the interests of different readers, my advice is not to make heavy going of any parts which prove difficult on a first reading, but to take from them what you can assimilate with enjoyment, and to read the rest lightly for the time being. (This is not only common sense: the model itself indicates this as the best way to proceed.)

Chapter 12 is a comparison between my own model of intelligence and others. It thus corresponds to the 'bicycology' part of the analogy offered earlier. Chapter 13 develops certain consequences of the model for social interaction, which lead in Chapter 14 and 15 to some of the many possible applications of the model to education. Chapter 16 is not a finishing-off chapter, and does not lend itself to a brief description.

There are two kinds of simplicity: that of naivety, and that in which, usually at a cost of much hard work, the essence of a matter is shown. The second kind is deceptive. So if, as I hope, you find that this book has rewarded your efforts in reading it once, may I suggest there is more which will only be gained by a second reading?

RICHARD R. SKEMP

Contents

CHAPTER 1

Survival, Evolution, and Learning

Billiard balls and human beings

1.1 The enterprise on which we, reader and author, are together embarking bears a close resemblance to the exercise of pulling oneself up by one's own shoe laces. We are hoping to use our own intelligence to explain the nature of intelligence; to understand what is understanding; to learn intelligently about intelligent learning. To the extent that we succeed—reader to comprehend, author to communicate—we shall have achieved something which cannot, by the nature of the task, be easy. As Dr Johnson said in a less appropriate context,[1] 'You are surprised to find it done at all.'

Nevertheless, I believe that it can be done; not only at the minimal level of being done at all, but to a level at which we can begin to make use of this new understanding. Moreover, the majority of the examples from which the necessary ideas will be built up are straightforward and from everyday life. This has the advantage that similar sources are available to every reader, both for verification and for amplification. Moreover, it is in everyday life (including our jobs) that we have to use our intelligence, not in the psychological laboratory; so ideas developed in this way can be more easily and directly put to work. To provide a much-needed new approach to our conception of intelligence, what is required (initially at least) is not new and sophisticated experimental data, but new ways of thinking about facts which are already widely known and agreed. And though the end-product will be new, the starting point is much closer to our common-sense ways of thinking than that based on concepts like 'stimulus' and 'response'.

1.2 Consider these two examples: (a) We have a billiard table, one billiard ball, and a cue. By striking the billiard ball suitably with the cue, we can cause the billiard ball to move across the table into a pocket. (b) We are in a room with a child who has agreed to co-operate in our experiment. There is a chair at the far side. We say 'Please go and sit on that chair', and the child moves across the room and sits on the chair.

Superficially the two events could be thought of as similar. We have 'caused' the child to go and sit on the chair, just as we 'caused' the billiard ball to move towards the pocket and enter it. It is this similarity on which the concepts of stimulus and response are based, by analogy with Newtonian mechanics. An object remains in a state of rest, or of uniform motion in a straight line, unless it is acted on by an external force. The child stays where he is until our words, acting like an external force (called a stimulus) on the child, cause the response already described.

But what a strange billiard ball it would be if, when we interposed an obstacle so that it could not get to the pocket by moving in a straight line, of its own initiative it made a suitable detour. The child will do this, with no change of 'stimulus'. Extend the obstacle right across the room, and the child will climb over it, or under it, or move it aside. Tie his legs together (having explained that this is part of the experiment) and he will get there by a series of jumps. Billiard balls will not vary their locomotion in any analogous ways.

It is this difference which sharply separates the present approach from those based on concepts like 'stimulus' and 'response'. The child's behaviour is *goal-directed*, and the actual movements by which he reaches his goal state (that of sitting on the chair) will not be exactly the same on any two occasions. The more the conditions vary, the more diverse will be the movements by which he reaches this goal.

If we want to know what someone is doing, we attach at least as much importance to their goals as to their outwardly observable actions. To say that I am riding my bicycle may be accurate, but it is incomplete. I may be going to my office, or enjoying recreation with my son, or checking the adjustment on my three-speed gear. And if I am seen to lean over to one side, what is equally important, though less obvious to a non-cyclist, is that I am maintaining my goal state of balance while rounding a corner. Sometimes, to know what is the goal of someone's behaviour is essential if we are to make sense of it at all. 'What are you doing?', we ask someone whom we see crawling around the floor on his hands and knees. We would regard 'I am crawling around the floor on my hands and knees' as a silly answer—we can see this for ourselves. But 'I am looking for a little spring, which jumped out of my ball-point pen when I was putting in a new refill' would be entirely acceptable as an explanation.

Our starting point is therefore that many human acts and activities are goal-directed.[2,3] Sometimes the goal is easily identified, and the acts by which it is achieved are fairly straightforward. Sometimes the goal is a distant one, and a person may strive towards it by complex processes for much of a lifetime.

This is not to imply that all human behaviour is goal-directed. When a child skips and dances instead of walking, or when we sing to ourselves while doing something we enjoy, these behaviours are expressive rather than goal-directed. So the ideas to be developed hereafter are not intended to apply to all human behaviour, but only to a large and important category. Nor does 'goal-directed' imply 'consciously goal-directed'. The function of consciousness is a separate matter, which will be discussed later at some length. All we need for a beginning is an acceptance that much of human (and animal)[4] behaviour is goal-directed; and that where this is the case, this feature is central to our understanding of what they do.

Properties of a goal state

1.3 This starting point immediately poses two questions:
(i) Why should goal-directedness be thought so important as to have been taken as the major difference between the movements of human beings (and, as we shall soon see, other organisms) on the one hand, and the movements of inanimate objects on the other?
(ii) Why are some goal states chosen rather than others?
By looking at some examples, we can see that the answer to both these questions lies in some property or properties associated with the goal state. In the bicycling example, three possible goal states were mentioned: being in my office, physical recreation with my son, and checking my three-speed gear. Among the properties of the first goal state are being physically in a good position for doing my job—having near me colleagues, students, a telephone, books, reprographic facilities—and thereby (among other things) earning a living. My salary enables me to pay for food, clothing, shelter; and without these, I would not long survive. Physical recreation with my son has health-giving properties for both of us, whereby we are both likely to live longer; and it is through our children that our families, our nations, and our species continue to survive when we do not. An efficient three-speed gear enables me to reach my destinations more easily, and so makes available more time and energy for other purposes—again, indirectly, with benefit to survival. Medium-term, long-term, and short-term, all three choices of goal state, and success in reaching them, have properties which contribute to survival.

Survival is a goal state on which all others depend. And for almost every goal state, we can find, once we are in the way of looking for them, properties which relate favourably to survival: be this state physical location, some other physical state such as temperature, or a mental state. Often these are interconnected. A person who is lost on the moors in winter (not in the mental state of knowing where he is) cannot reach a physical location where he will find shelter and warmth: and he may die as a result.

Consider the different possible locations of one's home. Associated with these, if one drives a car, are different probabilities of accident—differences reflected in one's insurance premiums. If one is buying a house or renting an apartment, there are differences in cost which affect one's remaining income, and this in turn affects how much one can spend on other contributions to survival such as food and clothing. Or consider the mental state of being able to read. For most of us, earning a living is dependent on having reached this state; while a child who cannot yet read is at risk through being unable to understand labels on medicines, or warning notices on insecticides.

As well as properties which relate to survival, any given state is likely to have other properties associated with it, and some of these may be so much more obvious to our notice that they appear as the important properties; while the properties relative to survival may escape notice altogether. Some states may possibly have no effect, one way or the other, on survival. But this is a hard world, in which every organism now living belongs to a species which exists today only because it has evolved, over millions of years, ways of bringing about goal states which contribute favourably to their survival. So more often than not, a connection can be found between goal states and survival if we seek long enough.[5]

By thinking about explanations for people's actions, we were led to the idea of goal-directed behaviour. This has the further implication of some kind of system which organizes and directs[6] these actions, which keeps things heading in the right direction until the goal state is reached. We are thus led towards the further idea of a *director system*.

1.4 In later chapters, these three ideas—goal state, survival, director system—will be developed in greater detail and more critically. The present purpose is to achieve an overview, within which the significance of these ideas can begin to be seen without an overload of detail. (And interestingly enough, the importance of having available the optimal amount of information for the job in hand—not too little, not too much—is itself one of the ideas which will be developed at some length in later chapters.)

1.5 Since an organism's director systems are so important for its survival, how do they come into existence?

We can distinguish two main processes: evolution and learning. In the first of these, the connections with survival are clear and close. In the second, the connections are less obvious and less direct, but the resulting contributions to survival are even greater.

Evolution by natural selection

1.6 The first of these processes is evolution by natural selection acting on a species as a whole. Most readers will already have a good general idea of the theory of evolution, but it will be useful to summarize the essential points here.

(i) All species reproduce themselves in greater numbers than would be necessary simply to replace those which die.

(ii) Within each generation there are small differences. Those individuals whose characteristics contribute more favourably to survival are more likely to reach maturity and to reproduce.

(iii) If these characteristics are genetically determined, they are passed on to the offspring of these individuals, and a greater proportion of the new generation both exhibit these characteristics themselves, and carry them in their genes.

(iv) Over a succession of generations, more and more of the individuals within a species come to possess these characteristics, which gradually become part of the genetic constitution of the species as a whole.

This process and its result can be seen most clearly in the physical characteristics of a species—those by which we can at a glance distinguish one from another. Thus the long neck of the giraffe, the protective colouring of the zebra, the powerful wings, beak, and talons of the eagle, are results of evolution by natural selection whose contributions to survival it is easy to see. But equally important for its survival are the behavioural characteristics of a species: which is to say, the complex of interrelated director systems by which its members reach and maintain their goal states. Of these eating, and not being eaten, are among the most obvious in importance and the easiest to see being pursued.

The director systems which become established in this way are those which, in the environment in which they have been selected, collectively optimize survival expectancy. Note that 'optimize' does not mean 'maximize'. The average lifetime of its individuals will affect how quickly beneficial mutations and recombinations of innate characteristics can be selected: so the longest possible lifetime for its individuals may not be the best for the survival of the species.

Evolution by natural selection is a process of adaptation of a species as a whole, by which its individuals are genetically equipped to be viable—able to achieve their goal states and thereby to survive—within that part of the environment which constitutes their habitat. In this, director systems and other physical characteristics all play their parts, and are closely interdependent.

1.7 The evolution of a species is influenced by two coexisting environments, which in some degree overlap.

(i) There is the physical environment, which changes either cyclically or randomly about some central or average condition. Tides ebb and flow, light alternates with darkness, seasons and weather change. The central condition may also change too. Open land is taken over by forest and vice versa, sea becomes land and land becomes sea, ice advances and recedes.

Cylic changes, within the lifetime of an individual, require a species to be viable under all the conditions of the cycle. Food has to be procured in winter as well as summer, in dry periods as well as wet. Changes in baseline conditions, when combined with these cyclic changes, may take the environmental conditions beyond the limits within which a species is viable. In this case it may find a suitable habitat in another location; or it may be able to adapt to the new conditions by the evolutionary process already described. If it cannot do either of these, it will become extinct.

(ii) This physical environment is shared by other species, which constitute an important part of the environment of each other. They compete for shared resources—food, water, living space. And they compete in the struggle to eat and not be eaten.

In this ceaseless competition, it is hard for a species to stand still. If its competitors become more viable by evolution, a species which does not do so is in great danger of becoming extinct. This is not inevitable: a few species have kept their present characteristics for a very long time. But the evidence of paleontology is that very many species have either become extinct, or have undergone great evolutionary changes leading to the forms in which they exist today.

1.8 Certain of the implications of the foregoing methods of adaptation—of achieving viability by a species—must now be considered which are particularly important in understanding the direction taken by the evolution of our own species.

The first is that the process of adaptation of these innate characteristics of a species, though often very effective, is a slow one. Haldane and Huxley (1927) have given a useful example from which we may get an idea of the time scale. Suppose that a mutation occurred in a particular species which gave a 1 per cent advantage to its possessor—in other words, on average 100 individuals with the new characteristic survived and reproduced, but only 99 without it. Suppose further that the new mutation existed in 1 per cent of the population.[7] Then they calculate that after 1658 generations, 99 per cent of this particular population would have this new and advantageous characteristic.

If we take a human generation as 25 years, this comes to 41 450 years: not long on the time scale of evolution, but a long time in terms of human history (41 000 years ago, Neanderthal man was still hunting woolly mammoths).

It was pointed out in Section 1.7 that if the environment changes faster than a species can adapt, the species will become extinct. Also, that the environment consists partly of other species, which are also evolving, and competing for food and other resources. In some cases these include predators, which are evolving more effective means of predation.

Under these conditions, one of the most valuable characteristics which a species can evolve is not a visible one, either physical or behavioural: but the invisible asset of adaptability. The more adaptable a species, the better it is able to keep pace with changes in its physical environment, and the more chance it has of out-pacing its competitors among other species.

Using hindsight, we might reasonably have predicted the evolution of a species which was selected largely on the basis of this particular characteristic, in combination with those others which help to make it most effective. We are that species: and the form of adaptability which we have in greater degree than any other species is called *learning*.

Learning

1.9 In evolution by natural selection, the less effective innate director systems are gradually discarded, over the generations, in favour of the more effective ones. By learning is meant the construction of new director systems within the lifetime of an individual. This is potentially much quicker, with the advantages already indicated. It has other advantages which we shall now consider.

Hereditary behaviours, like hereditary physical characteristics, have to be coded on to the chromosomes within the germ cells from which each new individual grows. These, in humans, are very small; and the chromosomes themselves are no more than very large molecules, just within the range of a good optical microscope. It never ceases to amaze me that, on top of the great complex of anatomical and physiological characteristics which together make up each new individual of a species, it is also possible to code genetic information which determines the innate director systems giving rise to its behavioural adeptness. Some of these behaviours are surprisingly complex: particularly those relating to courtship, mating, and nurture of the young. Nevertheless there is an upper limit to their complexity, and it is a low one compared with some of the things which we can do. Other animals dwell in nests, holes in the ground, caves: we build houses with electric light and central heating, running water, and sanitation. Other animals walk, or swim, or fly: we make railway trains, motor cars, aeroplanes, and ships. Other animals seek their food where they can find it: we create our own supply by planting seed and raising crops, and by breeding and raising animals. We have become such efficient predators that we no longer even have to hunt for our prey.

1.10 Other animals too can learn in some degree. There are different kinds of learning, and some of these we have in common with other species. A new characteristic does not appear on the evolutionary scene fully developed: and learning has 'made a start' in many species. Our own forebears had other characteristics, in combination with which ability to learn was particularly advantageous: notably prehensile hands, erect posture (which freed the forelimbs for manipulation) and opposed thumbs (which took manipulative ability a step further). These other factors set in motion a progressive evolution in the direction which has led to ourselves.

But we have so far outdistanced other animals in our ability to learn that I regard our species as an evolutionary breakthrough. It is not so much that we can do better than other animals at the same kinds of learning. At maze learning, for example, rats are better than humans. But we have available a more advanced kind of learning, which is qualitatively different from any of those available to other species. This will be explored in detail from Chapter 7 onwards, under the general description *intelligent learning*. One of the benefits it confers, which also increases its own power and effectiveness, is the ability to learn from the experience of others by symbolic communication. In Chapter 10 we shall consider what makes this possible. Here, let us look at some of its results.

Suppose that we want to go to some place where we have never been before. If it is quite near, we can ask a passer-by and he will tell us. If it is further away, and we want to drive, we can use a map. If it is still further, we can get a timetable and look up trains or air services. This sort of thing we do so habitually that we fail to realize what a remarkable ability this is. But is has taken about 3 000 000 000 years of evolution to produce an organism which can do this.

1.11 The potential conferred by this new kind of learning ability is enormous, and its consequences are far-reaching. Some of these are:

(i) Behaviour which will take an individual to a goal state he has never reached before can be learnt in advance of actually doing it. In the lower forms of learning, the new behaviour has to happen first, and it is chosen from among a number of other behaviours as a result of what happens *after* the behaviour has taken place—reaching a goal state, or getting away from its opposite, which in Section 2.2 we shall call an anti-goal state. This is called operant conditioning by psychologists, and trial-and-error learning by others. So if the right behaviour never happens, it cannot be learnt. But by symbolic communication we can set up in advance a set of directions which will take us from our present state to a goal state which we have never achieved before, and get there at the first attempt. The survival contribution of this may be very great, particularly if some of the alternative behaviours are dangerous.

(ii) *What* is thus communicated, however, has to be the result of someone else's past learning. And by symbolic communication behaviours which took months, years, a lifetime to learn for the first time, often by a specially gifted individual, can be acquired in a fraction of this time by others. Examples are:

the manufacture and use of penicillin (and medical techniques in general);

the design and construction of internal combustion engines (and technology in general);

methods of navigation, including the use of charts and navigational instruments (for ships and aircraft).

These were chosen as examples in which imitation and demonstration are not enough, in order to emphasize the function of symbols. Imitation is another important way of learning, less advanced than symbolic learning, but still making use of the experience of others.

(iii) Symbols in written and other permanent forms (maps, circuit diagrams, recorded tapes) make possible the storage of knowledge outside individual organisms.

The first evolutionary development, selection for ability to learn, bypassed the narrow bottleneck imposed by the genetic transmission of behaviours, and by changing the place of storage from the chromosomes to the brain increased the space available by a factor of, very approximately, 100 millions. It also made possible a further development. Having learnt the various symbolic systems by which knowledge can be communicated, stored and retrieved, we have been able to move the place of storage a second time. Knowledge is coded in the form of written descriptions, explanations, instructions, in words and by other symbols such as technical drawings, chemical formulae, mathematical equations. These are bound into books, the books collected in libraries and people's homes. The space now available for storage is almost limitless; and all the knowledge of previous generations which has been stored in this way accumulates, and is potentially available to each successive generation as part of their cultural heritage; who add to it in their turn.

1.12 The limiting factor is now how much of this vast store can be acquired and used by any individual. Five factors which affect this are:

(i) *Time*. An important characteristic of advanced cultures is that they allow their children and young people to spend a longer and longer proportion of their life-span in learning.

(ii) *Social environment*. Also characteristic of advanced cultures are the large number and variety of social institutions which exist solely for the purpose of passing on what has been learnt by past generations (schools, colleges, polytechnics) and for finding out new knowledge as well as passing it on (research institutions, universities).

Important also is the informal, non-institutionalized social environment. This will make a lot of difference to the degree to which children and others use the learning opportunities made available to them by these social institutions.

(iii) *Communications*. By this I mean all the processes by which knowledge is transmitted symbolically between individuals and between generations: beginning with the spoken word, and more recently printing, photography, radio, and television.

(iv) *Individual intelligence*. We still cannot use any of this vast external store of knowledge as a basis for our own behaviour until we have internalized it and made it part of our own director systems. This is a learning task, though a much easier one than finding out *ab initio*. And it is a learning task mainly of the more advanced kind mentioned in Section 1.10, namely intelligent learning.

(v) *Knowledge about the learning process itself*, and especially about intelligent learning: its nature and function, and how best we can bring it about in ourselves and others.

To lay some foundations of this knowledge is the central aim of this book.

1.13 The two main ideas to be taken forward from this chapter are:

(i) *The nature of intelligence is that it is a kind of ability to learn, which has reached its highest development in our own species, Homo sapiens.*

(ii) *Its function is the development of director systems more adaptable and successful than is possible either in innate director systems, or by other kinds of learning. In our own species, intelligence is central to the activities by which we survive.*

Notes for Chapter 1

1. From Boswell's *Life of Johnson*, 31 July 1763. 'Sir, a woman's preaching is like a dog's walking on his hind legs. It is not done well, but you are surprised to find it done at all.'
2. See Wiener (1948). The synthesis developed in the present book is largely based on cybernetic concepts.
3. It was, however, from an earlier publication that I first saw that teleology should not be rejected by psychologists as a scientifically respectable explanation. See Rosenblueth, Wiener, and Bigelow (1943).
4. It is also possible to construct machines which are goal-directed, and some simple examples of these will be described in Chapter 5.
5. There may, however, be a considerable time-lag between the achievement of a goal state and the pay-off in terms of survival contribution.
6. Originally I used Wiener's term 'control', but for use in a human context I decided that 'direct' was a more appropriate word. The term 'control' leads, if one is not careful, to ways of thinking such as are implied by terms like 'human engineering'.
7. Biologists will know that it is also necessary to suppose that the new mutation and the old condition are simple allelomorphs, and that the new mutation is dominant. Others may ignore these technical terms, which do not affect the main argument.

CHAPTER 2

Emotions and Consciousness

Emotional signals

2.1 In Chapter 1, we concerned ourselves only with the cognitive aspects of director systems and their functioning: aspects like information, perception, knowledge, learning. It is now time to remedy an important omission: for there has so far been no reference either to emotions or to consciousness.

Emotions play an essential part in human experience, which experimental psychology has had little success in bringing into a satisfactory theoretical framework. Some early psychologists, including William James, Lange, Freud, have made noteworthy contributions, as also has Darwin: but these beginnings have not been developed.

In everyday human activity and interaction, feeling and cognition are combined in varying degrees; and this close association between cognitive and affective experiences will follow as a necessary consequence of the theoretical approach which is being developed in this book. The dissociation of the two is I believe an artificial one, which has led to one-sided approaches in both psychological and educational theory.

2.2 First we need to expand the idea of an *anti-goal state*, which was mentioned briefly in Section 1.11. This is a state which we try to avoid or get away from, usually because it has a negative contribution to survival: such as being in deep water for a non-swimmer, or being in contact with a high-voltage electric cable for anybody.

An anti-goal state is not simply any state which is not a goal state. The difference is that between being in a room which is not warm enough for comfort, and being locked in a cold store; between not having as much money in the bank as one would like, and being overdrawn; between not being with one's friends, and being among enemies. So it is just as important for the survival of an organism to have director systems which take it away from anti-goal states as it is to have those which take it towards goal states.

2.3 If achieving and maintaining goal states are so important for survival, clearly it is equally important to know whether one is heading in the right direction: for without this knowledge, how could one direct one's actions so as to get there? And likewise, if avoiding anti-goal states is important, it is equally desirable to be warned if one is heading towards one of these. I propose therefore to regard emotions as providing just this kind of information.

From this starting point eight major categories can be defined, of which the first four are:

> *pleasure*, which signals changes *towards a goal state*;
> *unpleasure*, which signals changes *away from a goal state*;[1]
> *fear*, which signals changes *towards an anti-goal state*;
> *relief*, which signals changes *away from an anti-goal state*.

There is subjectively a marked resemblance between the first and the fourth of these categories, and also between the second and third. Nevertheless I think that the distinction is an important one. Certainly it could be argued that fear is an unpleasurable emotion, and that relief is pleasurable. But situationally, there is a difference between avoiding a state which is detrimental to our survival, and achieving one which is positively beneficial. And subjectively, the relief felt by a car driver after narrowly avoiding an accident is a different feeling from the pleasure he experiences while sitting down to a good meal at his journey's end.

The changes listed above are all-important to every organism, since cumulatively they determine its survival or non-survival. We might therefore reasonably expect the signals about these changes to be more insistent than other information which reaches consciousness: and perhaps of a different quality also, by which they are likely to stand out from the background of other information. This description, of a distinctive and attention-getting quality, applies very well to our personal experience of emotions; and explains it in terms of the present theoretical approach.

2.4 Since a state is a relationship between an organism and its environment, a change of state can as easily result from environmental changes as from activity by the organism. So far, therefore, we have no reason to distinguish between the pleasure we feel while approaching a goal state by our own efforts, and that resulting from our goal state being brought to us by external events.

But even more important to an organism than whether it is, at a given time, moving towards or away from goal or anti-goal states, is *whether it is able by its own efforts* to bring about these changes. The next four categories of emotion relate to ability/inability in this respect. These are:

> *confidence*, which signals *ability* to change *towards a goal state*;
> *frustration*, which signals *inability* to change *towards a goal state*;[2]
> *security*, which signals *ability* to change *away from an anti-goal state*.
> *anxiety*, which signals *inability* to change *away from an anti-goal state*.

Table 1

Changes		Knowledge of ability / inability to change	
Goal state — Towards	*Pleasure*	*Confidence*	*Frustration*
Goal state — Away from	*Unpleasure*	-	-
Anti-goal state — Towards	*Fear*	-	-
Anti-goal state — Away from	*Relief*	*Security*	*Anxiety*

Thus a skilled driver will feel both confident and secure. He knows that he can direct the powerful energies of his car so that they will take him to his destination (confident), and not to destruction (secure). If, however, his car's petrol pump develops a fault which he is unable to remedy, these feelings will be replaced by frustration. And if he is in the middle of the Yorkshire moors in mid-winter with night approaching and the temperature falling rapidly, awareness that motorists have been found frozen to death in these circumstances is likely also to lead to anxiety.

The eight categories of emotion which have been discussed, and the situations in which they arise, are shown in Table 1.

The four categories in the right-hand part of Table 1 are particular sub-categories of those on the left, since both confidence and security are experienced as pleasurable, while frustration and anxiety are unpleasurable. This is as it should be, on the hypothesis that pleasurable emotions in general are associated with states of affairs which are pro-survival, and unpleasurable emotions with those which are counter-survival.

Mixed emotions

2.5 Our felt emotions may fit clearly into one of the categories listed above; or they may be a mixture, particularly since at any time we are sure to have a number of director systems in operation. They may be stronger or weaker, depending on the subjective importance attached to the goal or anti-goal state, the perceived rate of change towards or away from these states, and perhaps other factors. Since changes of this kind are going on all the time, we would expect emotions to be as much a part of human experience as cognition.

Unpleasure from one source may be more than compensated by pleasure from another. One of the best children's dentists I have known is expert at this. His warm and frequently spoken approval of his young patients' courage, together with allowing them to play with some of his fascinating gadgets, are a great help to them in a situation involving both fear (of the anti-goal state of pain) and anxiety (since they are unable by their own efforts to prevent this). Another technique which has been used with success is giving patients a hand-held switch by which they can switch off the drill if it becomes too painful. The pain remains, but the anxiety is removed since this is now under the patient's own control.

The emotions on the two sides of Table 1 belong to different levels of function, in a hierarchy which we shall analyse in more detail later. Those on the left relate to ongoing changes of state. Those on the right refer to knowledge of the ability or inability of a director system to function successfully. So it is quite possible for different emotions to be aroused at these two levels.

A simple example is offered by a child who is trying to find the right place to put a piece of a jigsaw puzzle. When he succeeds he has a momentary feeling of pleasure. But if an adult offers unwanted help by pointing out where it should go, the child may well feel frustration at having been unable to achieve the goal state by his own director system.

2.6 An interesting consequence of the foregoing basic assumption, namely that the function of emotions is to provide information about progress towards goal states, can now be seen. It is that the emotions which we enjoy feeling—pleasure and relief, confidence and security—are likely to prove elusive if we set them as goals to be sought for their own sake. To seek pleasure as if it could be a goal is to mistake a signpost for a destination.

Novely and routine

2.7 If emotions are attention-demanding signals connected with changes relative to goal and anti-goal states, we now need to explain how it is that many of these changes are unaccompanied by any conscious emotion.

This question leads directly to that of the part played by consciousness itself, which is so difficult an area that many contemporary psychologists steer clear of it entirely. But I share the views of two early pioneers, William James and Sigmund Freud, that consciousness is one of the central issues of psychology: not peripheral, and not to be dismissed as some kind of non-question or epiphenomenon. So, tentatively, the following hypothesis is advanced.

Greater consciousness contributes to greater adaptibility of a director system; diminished consciousness is associated with routine functioning.

2.8 Routine actions and activities are done at quite a low level of consciousness. For example, many of the processes of our internal physiology are entirely automatic and unconscious. This is possible because our internal environment, within which these processes function, is very regular in its behaviour: not unchanging, but changing in a regular way. (Departures from regularity, such as indigestion, may however be signalled by unpleasure.)

The external environment is much more changeable, and increased consciousness in this direction helps us to master this variability: that is, it helps our director systems to extend their functioning into more widely differing situations.

It is especially when these are encountered for the first time that consciousness is heightened. As a director system gradually becomes more adept in a new situation, its functioning becomes more routine and less conscious. Level of consciousness, the amount and degree of novelty in a situation, and adaptability, are thus closely interdependent in a way which is summarized in Table 2.

If the initially novel compenents of a situation are encountered repeatedly, they gradually cease to be experienced as novel. Less conscious attention is then needed for the director system to function in what has now become a familiar situation.

Children and other learners may often be observed deliberately bringing about repetition of situations which were initially novel, until they have become routine. An important benefit of this can now be seen: consciousness is freed to make its distinctive contribution to adaptability in some other way.

Table 2

Situation contains (relative to individual)	Level of consciousness
No novelty	Low level of consciousness, routine functioning of directory systems
Some novelty	Heightened consciousness, adaptation (functioning of director system is extended to include novel aspects of situation)
Too much novelty	Beyond both present functioning of director system and ability to adapt. These situations are experienced as threatening.

The withdrawal or reduction of consciousness may also have some advantage to the director system concerned, relating to stability, and conserving what has been gained; leaving alone that which functions well enough. Routine skills (such as typing) function best, once mastered, if we do not think about how we do them.

2.9 The relations between situational novelty and consciousness may also be considered in the other direction, corresponding to the direction from right to left in Table 2. The heightening of consciousness in a routine situation, perhaps deliberately, may bring about more accurate direction of behaviour. Thus if we want to improve our driving, we must again direct our consciousness towards those activities which required our full attention when they were novel, but have become routine. And the lowering of consciousness associated with a situation regarded as routine may well result in the ignoring of some important non-routine element. The doctor seeing his twentieth influenza case of the day needs to be careful not to overlook some unusual symptom or sign; and the danger of lowered consciousness resulting from motorway driving at a monotonous 70 m.p.h. is well known.

To some extent, the relation between novelty and consciousness is self-regulating. Any change in a situation, even movement of what was previously still, is likely to attract attention. The more monotonous a situation, the less it holds our attention. The survival contribution of this is clear. Since it appears that our consciousness is limited in what it can cover at any particular instant, its most useful applications will be wherever novelty is greatest, and adaptability is therefore most required.

Failures of adaptation

2.10 A partial answer to the question raised in Section 2.7 has now been offered, in terms of novelty and routine. There is another aspect to be considered, which becomes important if we want to understand some of the reasons for failures in adaptation; that is to say, failures of the learning process.

Particularly in childhood, when our director systems are undeveloped, physically we are weak, and we are more subject to the wishes of those on whom we depend, there will be many occasions when we cannot attain our goal states. There may also be anti-goal states which we cannot avoid; for example, not all children like going to school.

Knowledge of inability to change towards a goal state gives rise to frustration, and inability to change away from an anti-goal state gives rise to anxiety (see Table 1). If the goal or anti-goal can be un-set as such, well and good. The director system is no longer vainly trying to achieve the goal state or get away from the anti-goal state, and the resulting frustration or anxiety cease. But some goals are too important to a child to be switched off, particularly those connected with love and care from his or her mother or parent figure. And the setting and un-setting of anti-goals, by their nature, we would expect to be even less under control of the individual concerned. In these cases a continuing state of frustration or anxiety is inevitable.

Such emotional states are hard to tolerate. They may also be counter-survival, for they are associated with non-functioning director systems, but compete insistently for consciousness with the emotional signals from other director systems and thereby interfere with their functioning.

Different individuals find different ways of defending themselves in these situations, which range from discomfort to intolerable mental pain. The exploration of these in all their detail and variety is outside the scope of the present volume. There is, however, one defence which fits well into the present discussion. This is simply the withdrawal of consciousness from the source of the offending emotion.

This source is the impotent director system as a whole, and when consciousness is withdrawn, although the frustration and anxiety are still there, we are no longer fully aware of them. A residual awareness may persist, and be experienced as 'tension'.

This withdrawal of consciousness is not likely to be deliberate, for volition would itself imply consciousness of the withdrawal, and thereby defeat its own ends. 'He who hides a secret must hide that he hides a secret.' I can offer no explanation of the process itself: but an important consequence may now be noted.

The hypothesis advanced at the end of Section 2.7 is that greater consciousness contributes to greater adaptability of a director system. It is a corollary of this that no further adaptation takes place in a director system from which consciousness is withheld. So once established, such a situation may be self-perpetuating, since a return of consciousness to this area is inseparable from a return of the experienced frustration and anxiety.

Sad examples of the foregoing are offered by young children who are long separated from their mothers (or parent figures), a frequent cause being that the child is ill and taken to hospital. Some of these have been recorded on film, others in writing; and there is considerable agreement about the stages which can be observed. At first, the child shows much grief and anxiety. After a time, this is followed by apathy. If the child is reunited with his mother before too long, the immediate result is a return of grief, sometimes accompanied by rejection of the mother. If, however, this restoration is too long delayed, not only may the former relationship with his mother never be fully restored, but there may be permanent impairment of his ability to form personal relationships.[3]

This hypothesis is also supported by experimental evidence from the field of hypnosis.[4] To a subject in a deep hypnotic trance is given the suggestion that he will perform a given act, in response to some signal or event after he has returned to normal waking consciousness. He is also given the suggestion that on waking he will not remember having been so instructed. The subject may in this way be caused to do something quite unusual, even bizarre, and not at all in keeping with his normal everyday behaviour. Denial of consciousness has prevented the subject from adapting, and he performs the act without voluntary control of whether he does it or not.

2.11 Many readers will already have realized that the processes described in Section 2.10 correspond very closely with those described many years earlier by Freud, particularly when the blocked director systems are sexual or aggressive. One of the reasons why people seek Freudian analysis (or other psychotherapy) is an eruption of the repressed anxiety, though still without consciousness of its source. Another is awareness that they are 'not their own masters': they find themselves behaving in ways which they cannot account for, and which are outside their ability to change or control.

This also raises the question whether one can have unconscious emotions. On the present hypothesis, the answer is that one can. Emotions are attention *seeking* signals. Sometimes, however, they relate to goals which are socially unacceptable, and are incompatible with the over-riding goal of keeping a good relationship with others. Particularly when young, these may be important others, such as parents, on whom survival depends. In such cases these unacceptable desires may (in Freudian terms) be repressed. This is an active repression, in contrast to the diminished consciousness associated with routine performance which was discussed in Sections 2.8 and 2.9. When, under the conditions of 'free association', the patient relaxes conscious direction of his thinking so far as he is able, these repressed desires gradually gain or regain consciousness, and this is one of the main techniques of Freudian therapy.[5] The therapeutic result is a direct consequence of the present set of hypotheses: namely that when these director systems become fully accessible to an individual's own consciousness, adaptability is conferred or restored.

2.12 In this chapter, beginnings have been made which are capable of further development in directions such as educational psychology, child psychology, psychopathology, and psychotherapy. In the present context, however, these must be kept subordinate to the main aim of the chapter. This has been to try to bring emotions into the present conceptual framework, to relate them to cognitive processes, and to suggest that any attempt to keep these separate is likely to hinder our attempts to understand either.

So far as the development of our new conception of intelligence is concerned, the main points of this chapter are:

(i) *Emotions are associated with the functioning of our director systems. They give information about progress, or ability to progress, relative to goal states and anti-goal states. They are therefore closely associated with survival.*

(ii) *Heightened consciousness is associated with adaptation*; *diminished consciousness with routine functioning.*

(iii) *Novelty, and the distinctive quality of emotional signals, both have the effect of calling conscious attention where it is needed.*

(iv) *The adaptive and integrative function of intelligence cannot take effect on director systems to which consciousness is denied by emotional difficulties.*

Notes for Chapter 2

1. The present explanation thus differs from that proposed by Freud, who wrote: 'We have decided to relate pleasure and unpleasure to the quantity of excitation that is present in the mind but is not in any way "bound"; and to relate them in such a manner that unpleasure corresponds to an *increase* in the quantity of excitation and pleasure to a *diminution.*' (Freud, 1922.)
2. This category is in broad agreement with that adopted by a number of psychologists. 'The general denotative definition of frustration which may be adopted is as follows: *frustration* occurs whenever the organism meets a more or less insurmountable obstacle or obstruction in its route to the satisfaction of any vital need.' (Rosenzweig, 1944.) My own usage emphasizes the emotional signal of this state of affairs.
3. See for example Bowlby (1953), and also Rutter (1972).
4. See for example Wolberg (1948).
5. Though the technique itself is well known, it may be of interest to read Freud's own directions for what he describes as 'the fundamental rule of the psycho-analytic technique':

> Whereas usually you rightly try to keep the threads of your story together and to exclude all intruding associations and side-issues, so as not to wander too far from the point, here you must proceed differently. You will notice that as you relate things various ideas will occur to you which you feel inclined to put aside with certain criticisms and objections. You will be tempted to say to yourself: 'This or that has no connection here, or it is quite unimportant, or it is nonsensical, so it cannot be necessary to mention it'. Never give in to these objections, but mention it even if you feel a disinclination against it, or indeed just because of this. Later on you will perceive and learn to understand the reason for this injunction, which is really the only one that you have to follow. So say whatever goes through your mind. Act as if you were sitting at the window of a railway train and describing to some one behind you the changing views you see outside. Finally, never forget that you have promised absolute honesty, and never leave anything unsaid because for any reason it is unpleasant to say it. (Freud, 1913.)

A therapist might well devise instructions similar to these directly from the hypotheses suggested in this chapter, even if he had no acquaintance with Freudian techniques.

CHAPTER 3

Actuality, and Inner Reality

Two realms of consciousness

3.1 This has been a difficult chapter to write. It raises matters which, if pursued far in certain directions, would lead us into difficult areas of metaphysics. But raised they must be, since they lie at the core of what follows in later chapters. The aim of the present chapter will therefore be to try to get clear as much as seems important for the purpose of this book, even if it means leaving unanswered—at least for the time being—some of the further questions which may come to mind as a result of what has been discussed.

3.2 In Section 2.7, I upheld the view that consciousness was one of the central issues of psychology: pointing out also that it was an area of much difficulty. One of the questions which must now be faced is: of what are we, or can we under suitable conditions become, conscious? To make a beginning in trying to answer this question, the reader is asked to join in the following very simple experiment.

Let us each look at some object in the room where we are sitting. Are we conscious of it? The simple answer is 'yes'. Now shut our eyes, and the answer is no longer so simple. We might reasonably say that we are no longer conscious of this object—closing our eyes has, at least for the moment, interrupted the process of vision by which we become conscious of it. But something remains—we still have some kind of conscious awareness of the object, through memory: and this can persist even if the object ceases to exist as such, like an extinguished flame or a burst bubble. In contrast, while our eyes are still closed, some one could bring a new object in front of us, but we would not be conscious of it. Similar experiments can be done just as easily with hearing or touching replacing seeing.

From these, a reasonable inference is that we can be conscious of external objects only indirectly, through our senses; and that we can be conscious of mental representations of these objects directly, even when the objects are not accessible to the senses. Nor are representations of physical objects the only kind of mental objects of which we can become conscious. Think of a large figure eight. Now imagine a long straight line drawn through its middle, where it crosses itself. It is most unlikely that either reader or author has seen the resulting diagram in the outside world, since it has been invented solely for the purpose of this paragraph. Yet we are both conscious of this diagram, in some kind of way, and can even agree on some of its properties. For example, most people will agree that the straight line must cut the figure eight either just once (at the intersection), or three times. No other number of intersections is possible. And this is but a very simple example of what can be imagined, visually and in other ways also.

3.3 Since they are by their nature inaccessible to independent observation, there are certainly those who would consider the existence of any kind of mental objects or activities to be an unwarranted assumption, and that something exists only if it is open to public observation. Others would take as starting point a conviction that our conscious experience is the one thing of which we can be sure, and point out the limitations of our senses and the ease with which they can be deceived. The present approach attempts to reconcile these two assumptions and to see them in relation to each other.

From the viewpoint of our individual consciousness, it may be difficult, and perhaps logically impossible, to prove the existence of an outside world—to demonstrate beyond all doubt that it is not a collective hallucination. Nevertheless, if we shut our eyes, whatever it is 'out there' appears not to go away. Though no longer seen, we still bump into it; and the moment we open our eyes, we see it again.

Hereafter we shall assume (what for most readers may indeed not be in question) that this common-sense belief is valid: that there is in fact an environment 'out there', which by our sense organs and nervous systems we perceive, and of which by various mental processes we each have an internal representation. This (hereafter assumed) environment in which our physical actions and activities take place we shall call *actuality*.

Our individual awarenesses of this outside world must differ because we are different persons, looking at it through different eyes, hearing it through different ears, touching it with different fingers. That these appear to resemble each other in many ways, so far as we can find out by communicating with one another, is one of the reasons why we believe that there is a world 'out there' which, though through different eyes, we are all looking at. In the process of granting existence to this outer world, it would seem strange to deny it to the individual experiences thereof about which we communicate—and which can indeed also take place independently of sensory input from actuality. To recognize the existence of this mental realm, but in a different way from that of the outside world, we shall describe it as *inner reality*. (When the usage of this term is well established, the word 'inner' will sometimes be dropped, particularly if it is implied by the context.)

We are thus contrasting, and giving equal importance to, two kinds of existence. We both direct our actions, and experience the results of these actions, within the limitations of our own inner realities. The actions themselves, and the objects of these actions, exist in actuality.[1]

The rest of this chapter is about some of the consequences of the distinction between actuality and inner reality as here defined: concentrating on those which contribute to our present purpose, which is the development of a new conception of intelligence, and leaving aside those which would lead us too far in other directions.

Mental models

3.4 The distinction which has just been made is not some pedantic piece of hair splitting. In its many applications, it is cumulatively a matter of life and death.

For our situation is very like that of the navigating officer of a ship at sea, out of sight of any land. On the bridge he has a chart of the sea area in which he is sailing; and somewhere on that chart is represented the present location of the ship. This may be a pencilled dot, an intersection of two lines; or (as in one ship I have been aboard) it may be a moving pointer controlled by the speed and course of the ship.

The navigating officer directs the movements of the ship by the use of this representation. He has no alternative, for he cannot directly observe the distant land, or the bottom of the sea. If the chart is accurate and complete, and if the spot on the chart correctly shows the ship's location on the ocean, the navigating officer will be able to direct the ship successfully to its destination. But if the chart is inaccurate (e.g. if it shows the island he wants to reach in the wrong place on the chart) or incomplete (e.g. it fails to show reefs or shoals in his path) then the ship is at risk; and likewise if he is mistaken about his present position.

The chart may be thought of as a two-dimensional model of a certain part of the earth's surface: and the assumption now under discussion is that, in very much the same kind of way, we each have an assortment of mental models, in each of which are represented certain features of the environment, and by means of which we direct our physical actions towards our various goals. We have different models of different parts of the environment—for example, of the neighbourhood of our home and of the city centre. And even of the same part of the environment, we use different models for different purposes and activities. A road map is not much help to a climber. A tailor and a medical doctor will be interested in different qualities of the same person; and even given the same doctor and patient, one can find by looking in *Gray's Anatomy* a wide variety of models for use according to whether the doctor is concerned with the patient's heart and circulation, his nervous system, his muscles or his skeleton.

3.5 Both the ocean and the ship on the one hand, and the chart on the other, exist in actuality and can be seen by outside observers. Our director systems cannot, however. Whatever may be their neural basis, the mental processes by which we direct our actions take place within the limitations of our own individual inner realities. But we physically survive, or fail to survive, by what happens in actuality.

Within the limited awareness of a child, coloured sugar-coated pills may be perceived as sweets, deadly berries as attractive fruits, a temporarily empty street as a good playground, a potential murderer as a 'nice man'. The mother's reality represents more closely the probable actual results of eating the pills or berries, playing on the road, accepting lifts from strangers. To the sophisticated reality of the medical profession, a poison in very small doses may be (as it is in actuality) a valuable medicine, and these same berries as sources of this.

These examples have been chosen in order to make the point strongly. As will be discussed at greater length later, survival is more usually not the all-or-none result of a single action, but the cumulative effect of a large number of actions. This does not reduce the importance of right action: it just spreads it over a longer period.

The examples just given all relate to the accuracy with which the goal state as represented within someone's mental model matches the actual consequences of achieving that state—of eating the pretty-looking berry, of having a car ride with the friendly man. Equally important for the successful functioning of a director system are the accuracy and completenesss with which are represented the paths (literal or metaphorical) by which the goal states are reached. On the accuracy depends whether the right state is reached (i.e. one which contributes positively to survival). On the completeness depends whether it is reached at all, and if so whether quickly and reliably, or otherwise.

As has been noted in earlier contexts, optimal does not necessarily mean maximal, and will depend on the function of the director system involved. This is easily seen in the case of completeness. For a ramble or a bicycle ride, the completeness of a 1-inch Ordnance Survey map is useful; for siting a house or laying a drain, a larger scale is required; while for a long car journey, we prefer a road map on a smaller scale which leaves out much of the detail represented in the other two. Optimal accuracy of representation is well exemplified by a map of the London Underground, in which neither distance nor direction is accurately represented, but which shows completely and accurately all the stations, their connections by rail, and the order in which they would be encountered by a traveller making a journey in actuality.

These are examples of external representations of actuality by symbols, in in this case maps, which in turn evoke the appropriate ideas in our minds. (For someone in whom they do not do so, e.g. someone who cannot map-read, they are of no use in directing his actions.) Here, different degrees of completeness and accuracy which are optimal for different purposes are embodied in physically different maps.

Our mental models are differently organized, in ways which enable us to retrieve and use for directing our actions just the right amount of information for the task in hand. On arrival at my local railway station I simply ask for a ticket to 'London', as if this were a single location. On arrival at London the mental map in terms of which I perceive my present location is enlarged to 'Euston station', and my goal location to (say) Waterloo tube station. For the final stage of my journey I retrieve still more of my available knowledge, and the mental map by which I direct my walking to the London Teachers' Centre (where I shall be discussing some of these ideas in relation to teaching) is more complex and detailed than either of the earlier two. The mental organization by which this sort of thing can be done at will is an important characteristic of intelligence. It will be explored in detail in later chapters, but the way in which it contributes to successful action in the present example can be seen here. It optimizes the internal representations in use for our present locations, goal locations, and the intermediate locations by which we get there, according to whether we are travelling by inter-city train, underground, or on foot. And it produces these out of a unified (but complex) overall mental model.

Concepts and conceptual structures

3.6 Our mental models differ in a number of ways from physical ones, apart from their inaccessibility to outside observation. One of these is that their elements nearly always represent not just one actual object or event, but what is common to a number of these. For example, when I get to London and go to the ticket office on the underground station, the mental representation which I use for directing my actions is not of just that particular ticket office, but of a class of places where, by giving money to the person behind the counter, I get in exchange a piece of paper or card which entitles me to ride on a train, or bus, or boat, or on a roundabout; or to enter a theatre and watch a play, to enter a concert hall and listen to a concert, to enter a stadium and watch a football match. A mental entity of this kind is called a *concept*; and by representing what is common to a variety of actual states, concepts enables us to act successfully in a variety of actual situations by means of the same director system. A mental model, which is made up of a number of interconnected concepts, is a *conceptual structure*. The process by which certain qualities of actual objects and events are internalized as concepts, while other qualities are ignored, is called *abstraction*.

3.7 Abstraction is not the only way in which concepts and conceptual structures are formed; others will be discussed later. The question also arises whether 'concept' and 'mental representation' mean exactly the same. This is not easy to answer in a few words, and recalls to mind the opening paragraph of Chapter 1. In the present exercise, we are trying to form a concept *of* a concept. So it is not to be expected that answers will be immediately forthcoming for all the questions which arise; nor that the answers which are found will necessarily be easy or complete.

The most important difference to be kept in mind, and which the terms in use must help us to remember, is that between innate and learnt director systems; or rather, since learning builds on what is innate, between director systems which are open to change by learning, and those which are fixed (or almost so).

From observation of the actions themselves, it would be hard to claim that the successful direction of my own journey from my home to the London Teachers' Centre is the result of intelligence, whereas the much longer journey of a swallow from its summer home (adjacent to mine) to its winter home in Africa is not. The difference is revealed by the sad little history, given by Erikson (1950), of the swallows from England who were imported to New Zealand by homesick ex-Englishmen. 'When winter came they all flew south and never returned, for their instincts pointed southward, not warmward.'

As was said in Section 1.6, the process of natural selection leads to the replacement, in successive generations, of those director systems which function less well by those which function better. We are now conceptualizing intelligence as an advanced kind of learning by which director systems are constructed and improved within the lifetime of the organism. So in the present context a distinctive quality of intelligence is not one which can be directly observed. It is one which has to be inferred from an organism's ability to construct new director systems, and to improve the ones it has.

If to a young child we hand a light pebble and then a heavy one, in the second case his hand and arm will fall. He will then compensate for the extra weight by increased muscular contraction, and the arm will come back to its former position. An octopus can do this too. But a child, as a result of repeated actions involving holding, supporting, lifting stones, gradually comes to compensate in advance, and thereby to hold his arm steady. An octopus cannot learn this. So we would say that a child can *conceptualize* varying weights as part of his mental models of pebbles of different sizes, and that an octopus cannot.

A cabbage white butterfly is sensitive to a particular chemical produced by members of the cabbage family. By its actions it shows itself able to discrimate between cabbages and non-cabbages: but not within the cabbage family. Nor is it able to learn to feed on other plants which, though good food, do not smell right. Effectively, the food-world of this butterfly consists of cabbage and non-cabbage, and it stays that way. In a similar kind of way, a baby at a certain age classes together nearly all adult males as 'daddy'. It discriminates between 'daddies' and 'non-daddies' but not within the former class. However, as time goes on, a child learns which particular adult male is its 'daddy'. It also learns what is meant by 'Andrew's daddy'; and that its own daddy and mummy both have (or had) daddies, who are its own grand-daddies. Much later it learns the biological significance of the word. It is this open-ness to change in the light of experience which distinguishes a concept from an innate mental representation.

This same distinction must therefore be extended to conceptual structures.

These we can now regard as learnt mental models: structures within our director systems which are not innate, but constructed by processes which we shall study in detail later. And this is the critical distinction between the instinctive basis of the swallows' direction of their migratory flight, and the various conceptual structures by which I direct my own travels.

But it is not only through experience that concepts and conceptual structures can come into being, develop, and change in other ways. Fantasies, hypotheses, plays and novels, musical compositions, are all sets of connected ideas, and therefore come within the description of a conceptual structure. While we may not at this stage want to explore these in any detail, we certainly do not want to exclude them from an overall conception—this would be to confine ourselves to much too narrow a view.

So the terms 'concept' and 'conceptual structure' will hereafter be used in a broad sense, for all those mental entities which are not wholly innate: and when particular kinds are under consideration, this will be shown by the use of different words (such as 'hypothesis', 'fantasy') and/or by the context. The concept *of* a concept and *of* a conceptual structure will thereby themselves satisfy the criterion stated earlier, namely open-ness to change in the light of experience: to which we must now add 'and possibly through other processes'.

For the moment we are concentrating on learnt mental models, by which we mean that they are not an innate part of a director system, but the result of learning by an individual during his lifetime. Not all learning is intelligent, however, and the distinction to be made between what we shall call intelligent learning on the one hand and sub-intelligent forms of learning on the other is one which we are not yet in a position to formulate. So the criterion for using the terms 'concept' and 'conceptual structures' will simply be that they are not innate. Later we shall explore differences between different kinds of learning, and as a result the term 'intelligent' will be seen as applicable to some kinds rather than to others.

3.8 The main points of this chapter are:
(i) *The physical world exists in actuality; our mental realm exists in reality.*
(ii) *Physical survival is in actuality; our director systems function within our own realities.*
(iii) *Our survival depends largely on the accuracy and completeness with which the mental models used by our director systems represent actuality.*
(iv) *Intelligent learning is one of the most successful ways of bringing these about.*

Note for Chapter 3

1. My terms 'actuality' and 'inner reality' correspond fairly closely to Karl Popper's 'world 1' and 'world 2', and I long hesitated whether to use the latter terms instead. So far as nouns go, there is much in favour of Popper's terms. But 'inner reality' gives us the verb 'realize' and the adjective 'real'. In future chapters both of these are given important technical meanings, closely corresponding to everyday usage.

For example, 'I did not realize that I was on the wrong road'; 'It was not real for me, although I knew it was actually happening.' These meanings cannot be well expressed in 'world 1, world 2' terminology. Another reason is that I do not at present wish to commit myself to acceptance of Popper's views about 'world 3', which usage of his terminology might be taken to imply. 'If we call the world of "things"—of physical objects—the *first world*, and the world of subjective experiences (such as thought processes) the *second world*, we may call the world of statements in themselves the *third world*. (I now prefer to call these three worlds "world 1", "world 2", and "world 3" . . .)' (Popper, 1976).

CHAPTER 4

Knowledge and Belief; Perception; Imagination

Reality testing

4.1 Among the important qualities of those conceptual structures by which we direct our actions are, as we have already seen, the accuracy and the completeness with which they correspond to the relevant parts of actuality. In this section we shall think about the former, and in particular about the ways in which we test this accuracy. This process, which we shall call *reality testing*,[1] has important implications for survival: of which some are already apparent, and others are still to come.

If on looking out of my study window I saw a pink elephant walking up the drive, probably my first action would be to call my wife and say, 'Do you see what I see?' If she then said, 'There appears to be a pink elephant coming up the drive', I might be reassured: or I might still suspect that this was a collective hallucination, and cast around for other ways to test whether there actually was a pink elephant there. An excellent method, if available, would be to take a photograph with a Polaroid camera. If the picture, available in a minute, also showed a pink elephant, I would begin to believe that it existed in actuality as well as in the realities of myself and my wife. My next action might be to telephone the police for advice. If I was then told that a pink elephant had escaped from a visiting circus, the matter would be both confirmed and explained: and I would await the arrival of a team from the circus to take my unexpected visitor away.

In this imaginary incident are exemplified the three chief modes of reality testing:

(i)   testing against expectations of events in actuality, which is the most basic and so has been put first;
(ii) testing against the realities of other people; and
(iii) testing for consistency with other knowledge and belief within our own realities.

'Do you see what I see?' epitomizes the second. Little elaboration is needed at this stage, beyond noting that if another person's reality *independently* confirms my own, the weight attached to their communication is much greater. Had I said, 'I see a pink elephant out there—do you?', my wife might reply soothingly, 'Yes, dear', to keep me calm while she summoned the doctor. A good hypnotic subject in a deep trance state will hallucinate nearly anything suggested by the hypnotist. And the social pressures to 'see what others see' must not be underestimated. The dependence of this method of reality testing on language (in its widest meaning) is also important to note, since this is the only way in which we can compare our own realities with those of other people.

In taking a photograph[2] of the elephant in question, I would be reality testing by mode (i), and reasoning along the following lines. 'Elephants which exist in actuality reflect light waves which can be focused by a camera lens on to a sensitive film, resulting in a latent image which can be developed to a visible one. Imaginary elephants do not have this effect.' It will not have escaped the reader that this method does not exclude the possibility of my hallucinating a picture of an elephant in the photograph. To check this, I might hand the photograph to an unprejudiced third party and ask him if he saw in it anything of interest. (Here I would be using the second mode again: testing my own reality against a report of someone else's.) And so on. That the elephant is indeed there in actuality seems impossible to prove beyond all doubt. Nevertheless there comes a time at which most of us are convinced, one way or the other, enough to direct our actions on the assumption that our own reality accurately represents actuality.

How long we continue reality testing in these two ways depends largely on the contribution from mode (iii), testing for consistency with our other knowledge and belief. I am already well aware that circuses have elephants, and that animals in captivity sometimes escape. The inconsistency which here raised my doubts was in the colour of the elephant. Had it been a postman whom I saw coming up the drive, this would have been so fully consistent with past experience that modes (i) and (ii) of reality testing would never have been set in motion. By mode (iii) I would have accepted my visual experience as caused by an actual postman without even thinking about it—unless the day were Sunday. Then an inconsistency would arise, for which I would begin to seek an explanation.

4.2 The somewhat fanciful nature of the above example was intended simply to call attention to a regular part of our mental activities, which goes on at all levels from everyday to advanced scientific research. The more unlikely an event, the more it sets in action our reality testing. By 'unlikely' we mean 'contrary to expectation', which is to say that it does not fit with the regularities which have been observed in past events. It is these regularities which are embodied in our concepts and conceptual structures: a concept is a (learnt) realization of some regularity in actuality.[3]

Different methods of reality testing may be more appropriate in different circumstances. For survival in the physical world, what matters most is testing against predicted events in actuality. That the ice is thick enough to skate on is best confirmed in some such way as by boring a hole, not by comparing opinions with other hopeful skaters. When Lorenzo de Medici lay on his deathbed, he was given by his physicians the 'hitherto infallible remedy' of a pulverized mixture of diamonds and pearls. That his physicians were agreed about the merits of this remedy was of little benefit to the patient.

For acceptance within a profession or social group, however, it is necessary to share their realities. Galileo's acceptance of the Copernican model of the solar system, although superior (as we agree today) in its representation of the actual movement of planets relative to the sun and to each other, did not save him from threats of torture and excommunication. And in general, for survival in our social environment, it is by comparison with those of other people that our realities are tested. The reasons for this will appear more clearly in Chapter 8.

4.3 Knowledge is the name we give to conceptual structures built from and tested against our own experiences of actuality. Beliefs are what we have accepted as facts for other reasons. These are frequently used in combination as the basis for the functioning of a director system. If, for example, we are making a journey by car to a place where we have never been before, we combine our personal knowledge of certain roads with beliefs about the existence and suitability of others, derived usually from maps but possibly from other sources such as verbal information. This is usually a perfectly satisfactory basis for action. In the process we are testing the believed parts of our mental model against actuality. If all goes well—that is, if the roads are as indicated by the map—some of our beliefs are changed into knowledge. Sometimes, however, we find when we actually arrive somewhere that a road is not as represented, that a new bypass has been made which is not shown on the map, or that a ferry no longer operates. In this case our own conceptual structure has to be corrected. If we then pass on this information to a friend, and if he believes us, he will change his conceptual structure accordingly.

In this way, reality building and testing often becomes a co-operative activity, whereby we help each other by making our shared realities more complete and more accurate.

It seems reasonable to talk about 'a body of knowledge', meaning a conceptual structure shared and agreed by a number of people, such that all of it has at some time been tested against actuality by someone. 'Agreed' also implies that every part of it has satisfied reality testing of the other kind, by mutual comparison between the realities of individual persons. Where these were not consistent to begin with, agreement may have been reached in various ways: for example, by appeal to actuality (experiment), or by arguments which show that certain beliefs are inconsistent with others. Both of these processes are dependent on agreement about criteria for evidence and inference, and these too are important characteristics of intelligence.

We often believe things simply because we have received this information from a source which we believe to be reliable. But it can happen that this person has not tested against actuality, and nor has anyone else. In such cases we should talk about shared beliefs, not shared knowledge: and the fact that such shared beliefs may be widespread is no indication of their accuracy.

Between persons whose systems for reality constructing and reality testing function in that particular way which we call rational, the criteria themselves seem to be agreed intuitively and without the need for discussion or argument. Though the negotiations between holders of conflicting realities may be hotly contested, the rules for conducting these negotiations on a basis of common rationality seem to be generally agreed between such persons. (Arguments about politics, in contrast, tend to be more polemical: for their chief concern is with power rather than with knowledge.)

The benefits of this co-operative building of shared knowledge structures may be seen in many areas, from the friendly exchange of information between neighbours to the development of scientific theories.

4.4 The more immediately reality can be tested (by action) in actuality, the easier the process of reality testing, and the more accurate and complete the reality is likely to be.

The more abstract—remote from that which is immediately testable in this way—the kind of reality, the more it depends on the two other kinds of reality testing: self-consistency, and comparison with the realities of other people. Neither by itself is entirely dependable: the inner reality of a mentally ill person may have a high degree of self-consistency, and the belief that the world was flat was for a long time agreed to be correct by everyone who thought about the matter at all. But these two processes, in combination with the first—testing against actuality—can be very effective. It is this threefold combination by which have been developed the scientific theories which give us so much power over our physical environment. (And it is the present lack of appropriate theories which accounts for our relative lack of success in such areas as management, government, politics, economics, education.)

Surveying and map-making offer an example which is less abstract than a scientific theory, but involves the same processes. Constructing an accurate map directly from on-the-spot observations of actuality, and checking these also for internal consistency, is a slow business. Charting the seas is even more laborious. But by combining many individual contributions, a shared knowledge structure has been built up which is available to all travellers for directing their journeys towards their chosen goals.

One often hears the term 'objective' used as if it meant the same as 'actual'. From the context in which the word is used, it appears to refer to some shared and agreed reality, with the implication that this may thereby be regarded as actual. By not exposing this implication, however, the use of 'objective' tends to be misleading. Any observation involves an observer as well as what is observed. If many observers agree, it is reasonable for them to decide that their shared reality is independent of the idiosyncrasies of a particular observer, and therefore corresponds well to something in actuality. But it is incautious to go beyond this and talk as if this widely agreed 'in here' *is the same as* whatever is 'out there'. Scientists in particular need to remember the provisional nature of the agreed mental models which form their theories.

Perception

4.5 Perception is the process whereby an individual becomes aware of present actuality, and in so doing classifies and structures it.

When a particular pattern of sensory input matches a particular concept, a process of recognition takes place whereby we perceive a pattern of light and shade as (say) a tree, or a camera; a pattern of sound as (say) a human voice or a musical instrument. Often the recognition takes place simultaneously with the sensory input, and these are fused into an experience of something 'out there' in which we do not distinguish between the two.

If recognition is delayed, however, we can become aware of sensory input and recognition as separate. When we see an everyday object from an unusual angle, or awake for the first time in a tent or the cabin of a small boat and wonder where we are, at the moment of recognition what we are looking at takes on a new appearance. From this we may deduce, since no change has taken place in actuality, that the change in our experience is due to a mental change whereby we now perceive 'what it is', 'where we are', and so on.

This can be explained by saying that a particular concept is *activated* by suitable input from the environment via our sense organs. The sensory input and the activated concept fuse into a perception of something which we *project* into the environment and regard as 'out there'. The term projection thus refers to our implicit (and often unconscious) assumption that the object of our perception is entirely in the outside world: whereas according to the view here taken, the object is external but our perception of it is internal. Thus, for example, the same tree may be perceived as something good for climbing, as an oak, or as potential timber; another object as a camera, a Leica, or as something worth stealing. To say the same in slightly different words, perception is our experience of actuality as it is *construed* by our concepts and conceptual structure. It is actuality as it is filtered by, shaped by, represented within, a particular inner reality.

Realizing

4.6 The special meaning which has been assigned to 'real', 'reality', enables us now to use the word 'realize' with a meaning which is basically the same as its everyday meaning, and to increase our understanding thereof. We might say something like: 'and then I realized I was talking to a policewoman, not an air hostess'. By this we would mean that we had wrongly perceived the person to whom we were talking, by construing our visual input in terms of the wrong concept. In an airport, the concept of an air hostess is more easily activated than that of a policewoman. This accounts for the failure to perceive what are in fact easily noticeable differences in the uniform.

The importance of correct realization becomes apparent when we remember that the director systems, on whose successful functioning we depend for survival, have no direct access to actuality. They depend on the mental models by which actuality is represented; and it is by activation of the appropriate concept, and thereby of the rest of the conceptual structure to which it is connected, that the right mental model is brought into use. Without both of these—availability of the model and its activation—director systems cannot function.

The railway system of the British Isles exists in actuality, equally for a dog, a human child, and for all adults. Physically, all are well able to climb aboard a homeward-bound train. But a dog, having only an incomplete mental model of the system, is not able to direct his actions aright. A child, or a person newly arrived from the Amazonian jungle, whose models of the railway system included being carried to their destination but did not include high-voltage electricity and its effects, might easily fail to survive because their models were not complete enough to direct them away from these lethal anti-goals.

So far as our survival is concerned, and also our further development, existence in our personal realities is just as important as existence in actuality. Things may have been in the world for thousands or millions of years which we have been unable to make use of because we did not know enough about them. Men were dying of fevers which a decoction of the bark of the cinchona tree would have cured. But until the actual physical effects of quinine were matched within our mental models, and until we had the conceptual apparatus whereby to categorize this species of tree in an unusual way, we were unable to direct our actions in such a way as to make use of the medicinal properties of quinine.

Another example. Someone is alone in a house at night and hears an unidentified sound. Until he realizes what it is, he is uneasy. This uneasiness is due to an intuitive awareness that until the noise has been identified (i.e. classified by means of an available concept), a person does not know whether he should do something about it, and if so what. The present usage of 'realize' explains this intuitive awareness, and makes it accessible to further discussion.

In the sense with which we are here using the word, realization maps or images actuality within an appropriate conceptual structure, and thereby makes it usable by a director system. There is, however, another everyday meaning of 'realize', which appears to be almost the opposite of this: namely to convert one's hopes, plans, ambitions, into actuality. Whether a place for this meaning can be found in the present formulation will be considered towards the end of Section 4.7.

Imagining; three modes of reality testing

4.7 Having emphasized at some length the importance of having conceptual structures which correspond well to actuality (or rather, by a process of abstraction, to certain features of actuality), we shall now make a change of direction in which other kinds of conceptual structure will be considered. This will begin to remedy what would otherwise be a one-sided view of intelligence.

Section 3.7 began: 'Abstraction is not the only way in which concepts and conceptual structures are formed: others will be discussed later.' These other ways in which new concepts and conceptual structures come into existence within a personal reality for which nothing (or nothing as yet) exists in actuality include different varieties of the process which we describe as *imagining*. Fantasies, hopes, ambitions, designs and plans (including those of a technical, professional, or scientific nature), have in common that they are all products of someone's imagination. Have they anything else in common? And in what ways do they differ?

A detailed examination of these matters would require a book to itself: and deserve it too, since what we are now initiating is an exploration of the creative activities of intelligence. The present aim is a more restricted one: that of suggesting that these questions can be well formulated in terms of the present ideas, with good hope that a more extended investigation along these lines will be time well spent.

Any kind of imaginative activity implies a partial suspension of reality testing, so it may be as well to begin by reminding ourselves of the ways in which we do this; and also by giving them for convenience shorter names.

Mode (i) reality testing is by comparing expectation or prediction[4] of what would be encountered in actuality by taking certain actions, if a particular model correctly represented actuality, with the actual results of these actions. This is not as complicated as its sounds. Example: 'If my mental map is correct, by going along this road I should soon come to the railway station'. This is the method of *experiment*.

Mode (ii) reality testing is by comparison with the knowledge and beliefs of other people. This is essentially *social*: *discussion* is often an important feature. Example: 'Is this the right way for the railway station?'

Mode (iii) reality testing is by *internal consistency*. Example: 'I think that this is the London train. I also think that London is roughly South from here, whereas this train is heading in the opposite direction. So these cannot both be true.'

What is important in all imaginative activity is to know just which of these is in suspense, and to what degree. Plans of a house will look much the same whether it is of an actual house which we have just bought, or one which we would like to have built. In the latter case, we do not apply the reality test of whether the house actually exists. We know that it doesn't, so we do not try to move in. Other tests still apply: e.g., by consulting the knowledge and beliefs of an architect, we decide whether it could be built like this in actuality.

In this kind of exercise, we are using our existing conceptual structures to construct models for which no counterpart as yet exists in actuality, but which we have good reason to believe could so exist. In their early stages, the best models to work with may have quite a low degree of accuracy and completeness. Thinking it a good idea to have a separate study, near the kitchen for convenience in making frequent cups of tea, but away from the children's playroom for quietness, an early plan might look simply like Figure 1.

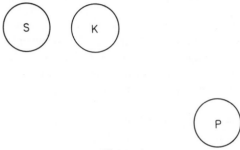

Figure 1

Similarly, for many purposes Figure 2 is a suitable plan for a hi-fi installation.

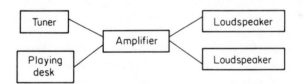

Figure 2

From an assortment of models one may choose a particular one to bring into actual existence; after which the chosen model will be developed with increasing accuracy and detail, and also with increasing application of appropriate kinds of reality testing.

This corresponds to the second everyday meaning of the word 'realize', already mentioned at the end of Section 4.6: that of realizing a plan or wish. In this process too we are matching reality and actuality: but in this case by changing actuality. This difference is too important to take the risk of overlooking it which is involved in using the same word for both. So we shall hereafter use 'actualize' for the second meaning. Thus we might *actualize* the plans of our dream house; or *realize* that this house, which we were viewing, was just what we were looking for.

There are other imaginative constructions which are never intended to be brought into actual existence. Nevertheless there are still reality criteria to be satisfied, notably consistency. Persons with no actual existence must still behave in character. The unexpected turn of events which makes a good story must not involve cheating. The 'Sherlock Holmes' stories offer a superb example of this: so much so that he and Dr Watson—not to mention Billy the page boy and Moriarty the arch criminal—have become more real to generations of readers than many a person whom we know to exist in actuality. Pure mathematics is another example of a widely shared reality based on internal consistency and agreement by discussion within a particular group.

4.8 In thus moving from conceptual structures which represent actuality as it is to the invention of an unlimited number of conceptual structures, within which we conceive and choose goal states which we then bring into actual existence, human intelligence takes a great leap forward. Instead of accepting the world as it is, we shape it in accordance with our imaginative constructions.

And here is the beginning of an answer to a question which may by now have begun to shape itself in the minds of some readers. So far almost every discussion has been related, in one way or another, directly or indirectly, to survival. One may well ask: is this all that life is about? Has the human species evolved to its present level only the better to survive? Was survival the only reason for the civilizations of the Nile, for the artistic and scientific achievements of Renaissance Italy, for the symphonies of Beethoven, the plays of Shakespeare, the novels of Tolstoy? Do we as individuals advance our knowledge and understanding only to stay alive?

These are questions of a kind to which everyone has to find his own answers. They do not deal with matters of fact, nor of rational inference from accepted facts. Certainly our progress as a species, and as individuals, is dependent on survival as a prerequisite; and competition must be seen as a major influence on certain kinds of progress. But whether we progress in order to survive, or survive in order to progress, are not questions which a book of this kind can be expected to answer.

Yet it would be even harder to deny that for many, they are the most important questions of all; and while it may not be possible to answer them, this does not require that we ignore them. By the end of the last chapter, a viewpoint will have been reached from which some at least may feel that they can see in what direction answers might be found. Meanwhile, any who seek to know my personal viewpoint will find it well expressed in an old Chinese proverb: 'If you have a loaf, sell half and buy a lily.'

4.9 In this chapter, we have seen that:

(i) *The accuracy and completeness of our conceptual structures are tested in three ways*:

   (a) *by experiment*;
   (b) *socially, and particularly by discussion*;
   (c) *by internal consistency*.

(ii) *Knowledge is the name we give to conceptual structures built from and tested against our own experience of actuality. Beliefs are what we accept as true for other reasons.*

(iii) *In perception, inner reality and actuality fuse into a combined experience in which each is modified by the other.*

(iv) *Imaginative activity makes possible the construction of new conceptual structures which do not necessarily match actuality, by the partial suspension of reality testing. And instead of accepting the world as it is, we can sometimes shape it the way we want.*

Notes for Chapter 4

1. I have taken the term 'reality testing' from an article by Nathan Isaacs, which I read a number of years ago and am now unable to trace. 'Inner reality' is always implied.
2. Polaroid has the advantage of immediate processing, but of course any system would do.
3. Since I have on occasion been accused of being a 'naïve abstractionist', and also a 'naïve realist', may I again emphasize that it is not only by experience of actuality that concepts and conceptual structures are formed and developed.
4. Here, by 'expectation' I mean an intuitive expectation, not necessarily even fully conscious—though the contradiction of an expectation by events is likely to attract consciousness. By 'prediction' I mean an expectation which is consciously formulated. This may involve reflective inference, which is a mode (iii) activity. These are discussed in Chapter 11.

CHAPTER 5

First Steps towards a Model for Intelligence

Advanced mental models

5.1 The idea of a mental model was first introduced in Chapter 3. During the rest of that chapter and in Chapter 4, we began to realize the importance of our mental models, and to consider some of the ways in which they contribute to success in achieving our goal states.

The more inaccessible to direct perception are the features of actuality with which we are concerned, the more necessary is an appropriate model; but also, the more difficult it is to construct. For finding our way about the near neighbourhood of our home or place of work, it would not take us long to make a sketch map for ourselves. The model used by the navigating officer for directing the course of his ship (Section 3.4) represents far shores which he cannot see at the time, and depths of the ocean which he never sees. The charts which he uses combine the results of many years of patient survey.

Here are two examples of models used by chemists. The first represents a simple chemical reaction, the second a benzene molecule.[1]

$$NaOH + HCl \longrightarrow NaCl + H_2O$$

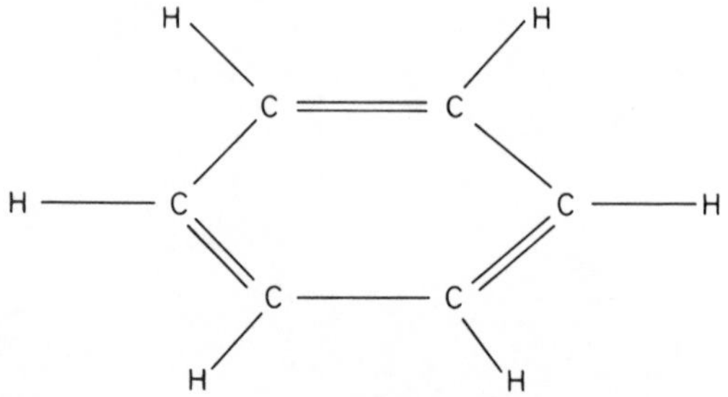

Figure 3

Below is a model which represents a vibrating system acted on by an external periodic force, internally damped by a force proportional to the velocity. This model takes the form of a differential equation, and the solution of this equation explains the phenomenon of *resonance*. The latter is a key concept in acoustics, radio and television, and many other fields in which vibrations play a major part.

$$\frac{d^2s}{dt^2} + 2k \frac{ds}{dt} + p^2s = a \cos \omega t$$

The development of models like these has required the cooperation of many able persons over a long period.

Though the foregoing have been called models, it needs to be remembered that this is a shorthand description. More accurately, they are groups of symbols which, for navigators, chemists and electricians respectively, elicit the mental models which they use in their particular domains. For those who cannot attach the right meanings to both the individual symbols and the ways in which they are related, the symbols get them nowhere. But for those who can, these models are an essential and powerful contribution to their expertise; and evidence of the high level of present expertise in these, and in other fields of science and technology, is all around us.

It follows that in our present exploration, where the field of enquiry is such that our thinking needs all the help we can give it, a suitable model will certainly be necessary. The basic ideas needed have been introduced in the first four chapters, which were introductory. For further progress to be made, the next step has to be the more detailed development of a model which can support and guide our thinking about intelligence itself. The one now to be described is (to the best of my belief) new,[2] and unlike any of the existing models of intelligence. The reader is therefore recommended for the time being not to try to relate it to any existing ideas about intelligence; for as Ross Ashby (1956) writes, in his very clear *Introduction to Cybernetics*: 'The new point of view should be clearly understood, for any unconscious vacillation between the old and the new is apt to lead to confusion.' A critique of other models, and a comparison with that offered in the present book, is given in Chapter 12.

5.2 Before beginning this task, there are a few general points which need to be borne in mind.

(i) A model is always a simplification. This is one of the ways in which it helps us to cope with the unthinkable complexity of actuality. It is a good model to the extent that it represents those, and only those, features of actuality which are important for the task in hand; and thus helps us to take account of these and ignore the rest. In this way, good models reduce cognitive strain and improve mental efficiency.

(ii) Our starting point will, however, be a simplification of another kind. Just as a beginning student of chemistry is not introduced to the subject of molecular structure by means of complex examples like the second one above (benzene), but with simple examples like H_2O, so we shall begin with models much simpler than are needed for thinking about intelligence, and build on these.

(iii) Like the models already given as examples, what we shall be building is a mental model, with the help of symbols. The latter are indispensable both for communicating the ideas involved, and for our own thinking. But without their associated meanings, the symbols are useless; so model and symbols must progress together.

Symbols take the form of diagrams and words. The latter include technical terms, which are indispensable in any field of study. Rightly used, they express our meaning more briefly and accurately than would be possible otherwise; and a glossary of the technical terms used in this book will be found at the end of the book. Jargon, in the derogatory sense, refers to the unnecessary use of technical terms in ways which obscure meaning by using them when everyday words would do the job better. I have tried to avoid this.

(iv) New ideas can most easily be acquired initially from an assortment of examples, rather than from abstract and formal definitions. The simplest everyday embodiments of the ideas to be developed happen to be physical ones. These are simply being used as aids to thinking, and without any implication about the underlying physical basis of intelligence. We shall be concerned with what intelligence does, not what it is made of.

This last sentence needs to be emphasized, since statements will sometimes be made of the form 'Intelligence is a . . .'. There is no inconsistency in this. If I say 'This is a bottle opener', or 'This is fertilizer', I am describing the object or substance by its function. I am leaving aside whether the bottle opener is a twisted spike or a hollow needle attached to a compressed air pump. I do not say whether the fertilizer is composted stable manure, dried seaweed, or ground-up bones. Similarly, when I say 'Intelligence is a . . .', this will describe one of the ways in which it functions.

(v) This raises the question: is the present approach mechanistic? My answer here is 'Yes and no, more no than yes.' Any model has to be in some degree mechanistic, or it could have no predictive ability. But this does not necessarily mean that what it is a model *of* is mechanistic—only that it is in certain ways regular, non-capricious. It is these regularities which are embodied in the model.

(vi) Those who are familiar with the concepts of cybernetics will recognize that some of the ideas used here are directly borrowed from that source, as has already been acknowledged. In a new context, however, both words and ideas acquire new meanings, and attempts to translate the conception of intelligence here put forward into the separate discipline of cybernetics may well lead to a distortion of meaning.

Models of director systems

5.3   We begin with two quite simple examples of goal-directed systems.

(a) a thermostatically controlled electric oven; and
(b) the steering mechanism of a ship.[3]
(*If you are one of those who 'switch off' at the mention of a thermostat, or any other electrical or mechanical device, before continuing please read note 4 at the end of this chapter.*)

(a) To save us the trouble of constantly watching the oven temperature, and switching the heat on and off as required, the ovens of almost all electric cookers today are controlled by a thermostat. The cook sets a dial to the desired temperature, and the thermostat switches the current on and off in such a way that it brings the oven interior to this temperature and then keeps it there. (Gas cookers have similar devices, as also do electric irons, central-heating systems, incubators, etc.)

(b) On small craft, the rudder is moved to its required position by the muscular power of the helmsman, and kept there in the same way. On larger vessels, the rudder is too big and the forces on it are too great for this to be possible. Instead, the rudder is moved by a small steering engine to whatever position the helmsman chooses by his setting of the steering controls.

In each of these examples, we can distinguish three main parts.

(i)   That which is changed from one state to another and kept there. In (a), it is the interior of the oven, which is brought to the desired temperature and kept there. In (b) it is the ship's rudder, which is brought to the desired position and kept there. We shall call this part of the system the *operand*. Sometimes the operands are our own bodies, as when we walk from one location to another, or change our position from sitting to standing.

(ii) That which actually does the work of changing the *state* of the operand (the temperature of the oven, the position of the rudder) from its initial state to the state chosen by the cook or the helmsman. In both of these examples there is a source of energy, which in (a) takes the form of electrical energy and in (b) might typically take the form of steam under pressure. There is also some kind of converter, which in (a) consists of a heating element and in (b) could be a small steam engine. This converts energy from the form in which it is available to the form in which it is required for changing the state of the operand: heat energy for the oven, mechanical energy for the rudder. This part we shall call collectively the *operators*.[5]

(iii) That which directs the way in which the energy of the operator system is applied to the operand so as to take it to the required state and keep it there. For the oven, this is the thermostat itself. For the rudder it is a valve mechanism still to be described. This part we shall call the *director system*. It is particularly with the functioning of director systems that we shall hereafter be concerned.

5.4 To act in the way described, a director system must have the following component parts.

(i) A part which is sensitive to the relevant aspect of the present state of the object. In the thermostat, it is a special kind of thermometer. In the steering mechanism, it consists of gears or levers connected to the rudder which register the angle between its present position and the central position. We shall call this a *sensor*.

Note that one of the requirements of a sensor is that it selects, from the many aspects of the object's present condition, that which is important for the particular purpose served by its director system. So in the oven, the sensor is sensitive to temperature; in the steering mechanism, to position. A position-sensor would be useless for the oven thermostat, and vice versa.

(ii) A part by which the *goal state* can be set. The cook turns a dial to the required temperature; the helmsman brings a pointer to the required angle of deflection, port or starboard. Here the important concept is the goal state itself, as represented within the director system.

(iii) A part in which is represented the difference between the present state of the operand and its goal state. This we shall call the *comparator*. In the examples given it is a little difficult to identify physically, since basically it is embodied in the gap between the positions of (i) and (ii). What is important is the information it gives: whether the oven temperature is too low, too high, or at the goal temperature; whether the rudder position is to port of its goal position, to starboard, or in its goal position.

(iv) A *plan* which determines what happens when the object is not in its goal state, and also when it is. In the case of the oven, this is embodied in an electrical on/off switch, suitably connected, so that it switches on the current when the comparator registers 'below goal temperature', and off when it registers 'at or above goal temperature'. In the earliest kind of ship's steering mechanism there was a valve which in one position (e.g. when the comparator registered 'rudder to port of goal position') admitted steam which rotated the steering engine in one direction, and in the opposite position (rudder to starboard of goal position) admitted steam into a different pipe which rotated the steering engine in the other direction. When the rudder was in its goal position, the steam to the steering engine was shut off.

These are both very simple plans. But is is worth noticing that, in the case of the thermostat, if the on/off switch were wired the wrong way round the thermostat would then work according to the opposite plan.

This would switch the current to the heating element *off* when the oven was too cold (useless), and *on* when it was too hot (disastrous). However, if the thermostat were fitted to a refrigerator or freezer, this second plan would be the right one. So the plan is an important part of a director system, and even such a simple plan as the above must be the right way round.

5.5 It will be useful to clarify a few points of detail before continuing.

(i) When we refer to the present state and the goal state of an operand, we mean its state with respect to a particular quality (or qualities, as we shall see later) in which we are interested. In the case of the oven, by 'state' we mean its temperature (and that of its contents); not its position or whether it needs cleaning. For the ship's rudder, 'state' means position; not temperature, or the state of its paint.

(ii) Both present state and goal state are determined relative to (selected qualities of) the environment. Oven temperature is determined relative to 0° and 100° Centigrade, the temperatures of melting ice and boiling water. The position of the rudder is determined relative to the axial plane of the ship. *'State' means a relationship*.

(iii) The oven is kept not at an exact temperature, but within a few degrees either way. Similarly the ship's rudder will come to rest not exactly in, but sufficiently close to, the specified position. And in general a *goal state is an interval* which may be large or small, according to the requirements of the situation which in turn determine the accuracy with which the mechanism is constructed.

(iv) The term 'goal-directed' applies appropriately to the operand which is taken to its goal state, to the operator whose energies are directed by the director system, or to the two together. It can also be used to describe the activity.

For the system as a whole—director system, operator, and operand—the term *goal-seeking* is often used.

5.6 Our major interest in this book is in director systems of various kinds. By 'various kinds' is meant, not different physical embodiments, but different functions. Moreover, our interest is not in what they are made of, but in what they do. If there is intelligent life elsewhere in the universe, its physical embodiment is likely to be very different from ourselves. That it is intelligent will be characterized, not by its particular anatomy and physiology, but by an abstract and complex set of qualities which it is our present purpose to identify and conceptualize.

Because these ideas are abstract and complex, it is necessary to approach them first by way of relatively concrete and simple examples, such as the two which have been used already. It must therefore again be emphasized that I am *not* introducing mechanical models for intelligence. A mechanistic conception is neither implied nor, for that matter, excluded: the age-old problem of free will is not one on which I wish to embark at the present stage. Our aim is to be as clear as possible about certain basic ideas, by finding them first of all in fairly simple situations, before using them in the much more difficult enterprise described in Section 1.1.

5.7 Let us now consider two slightly more complex examples:

(a) a dinghy with one sail being sailed single-handed; and
(b) a car together with its driver.

We shall regard the dinghy and the car as operands, while the director system is within the dinghy sailor or car driver. The operators consists of the muscles and bony levers of the sailor or driver, together with certain parts of the boat or car.

The greater complexity lies mainly in the fact that we now need several items of information for a satisfactory description of the state of the operand.

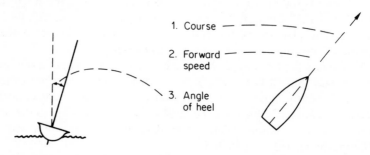

1. Course
2. Forward speed
3. Angle of heel

Figure 4

(a) For the dinghy, these might be

    1. course (i.e. direction in which it is pointing);
    2. forward speed;
    3. angle of heel.

(b) For the car, these might be

    1. direction;
    2. forward speed;
    3. lateral position on road;
    4. distance from other traffic going in the same direction;
    5. distance from other traffic going in the opposite direction.

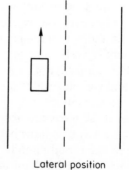

Lateral position
Figure 5

In each of these examples, the goal state is achieved and maintained by processes which are functionally analogous to those described in Section 5.3. The dinghy sailor or car driver receives information about the present state of dinghy or car through his sense organs, particularly but not exclusively his eyes. He compares its present state with the goal state (of which he has a mental representation), and by means of a suitable plan he directs the energy available to the operators in such a way that the operand is taken thereby to its goal state.

A typical goal state for the dinghy might be:

1. pointing towards a certain shore mark;
2. a forward speed as great as possible, and certainly greater than zero;
3. angle of heel between zero and 30° away from the wind.

A typical goal state for the car is given later, in Section 5.9.

For our present purposes it will not be helpful to become over-involved in a discussion of just where and what are the physical means by which these processes take place. The forward speed of the car is controlled by pressure of the driver's foot on the accelerator pedal (assuming that he doesn't change gear) and on the brake pedal. Whether we also include the mechanical linkage from these pedals to the carburettor and brakes as part of the director system, or of the operand (car) is at this stage a matter of detail. What does matter here are the plans involved, and we may note that opposite plans are used for the accelerator and the brakes. For the former, the plan is (viewed superficially): if too slow, depress pedal further; if too fast, raise pedal; if within goal speed, keep where it is. For the latter, the plan is approximately the opposite. Going beyond this, the functions of these two plans are respectively to vary the amount of energy used by the two different effector systems: engine, and brakes. It is on this, rather than on the mechanical details, that we want to concentrate for the present discussion, which is about intelligence. Oven thermostats, steering engines, dinghy sailors, car drivers are simply being used as convenient examples from which to derive certain concepts.

This emphasis on 'does' rather than 'is made of' by no means implies that the mechanical, electrical, or physiological details are never important. They matter very much, for example, when it comes to designing and constructing. But even here, function has to be considered first: one cannot even begin to design or construct any part of a system until one knows what it has to do. And our present emphasis on what various director systems have in common implies a corresponding lack of emphasis on those differences in their physical embodiments which do not affect their functions.

Goal-directed machines, and organisms

5.8 Since we have now used both non-living and living examples of goal-directed systems for developing our concepts, we need names to distinguish between these two kinds. The former we will call *goal-seeking machines*, and the latter *organisms*—we do not need to say goal-seeking for these, since as we have seen no organism remains alive unless it is goal-seeking. There are also many situations in which an organism and a goal-seeking machine work together, thus forming a system which as a whole is also goal-seeking. A helmsman and a ship's steering mechanism work together in this way, and if a car has power steering so do the driver and the car's steering mechanism.

Sometimes director system, operators, and operand are permanently joined together (as with the oven and its thermostat); sometimes the connection is temporary, as between sailor and dinghy, car and driver; and sometimes the physical connection is remote and of the slightest, as in the case of radio control. But this attenuation of the connection can only happen between the director system and the effectors, not between effectors and operand. We shall see in Section 8.2 why this is so.

5.9 Just how many items of information we need for an adequate description of the state of the operand, and which these are, depends on what we are currently interested in. Three have been suggested for the dinghy, five for the car: implying that we are not for the moment considering the state of the dinghy's varnish and paint, or the degree of corrosion in the car's body, though for some purposes these are important.

These separate items of information, which collectively specify the *state* of the operand, we shall call *components* of the state. Sometimes we need to think of the state as a single 'package'; sometimes we need, as it were, to take off the wrapping and think about the separate components. There is nothing new in this way of thinking: we do it all the time.

(*There now follows a more detailed discussion of the meaning given to the word 'state'. If desired it may be taken lightly at a first reading, and referred back to as necessary.*)

In everyday conversation, by 'temperature' we can mean one of two things. We can mean this observable quality of an object, as against its colour or its weight. Or we can mean a particular value of this quality, say 15 °C as against 7 °C or 32 °C. Similarly for 'position'. We can use the word in general, to describe a kind of relationship between an object and its surroundings (as against, say, electrical potential). Or we can use it to refer to a particular position. Usually the context makes it clear which meaning is intended. In Section 5.3 by 'present temperature' (of the oven), and 'present position' (of the rudder), we clearly meant a particular temperature or position: that at the time referred to as 'present'. And by 'goal temperature', 'goal position', we meant any temperature or position within a particular interval. (See Section 5.5 (iii).)

These were used as examples of states of objects—of observable qualities in which we were interested. In this chapter the idea of state has been expanded to mean a collection of observables, which we think of together in describing a present or a goal condition of some operand. So 'present state' means the present values of these observables, taken all together. Thus for the dinghy, the present state might be (South-west, 3 knots, 20°), using parentheses to show that we regard these as contents of a single package.

Throughout this book we shall continue to use the term 'state' in this particular sense. *A state is a set of values of certain chosen observables*.

The word 'state' will take its meaning from the context, which will also determine the number of components. Here are some examples of typical states.

Oven: (80 °C)
Rudder: (Port 15°)
Dinghy: (S.W., 3 knots, 20° of heel)
Car: (parallel with the direction of the road, 70 m.p.h., nearside lane, more than 80 yards, more than 5 yards)

The possible meanings of 'state' is often clear from the context. When we want to be more explicit, however, we specify a *universe of discourse*, which is simply the set of all states currently under consideration. Thus the universe of discourse for the example of the oven thermostat is the set of temperatures from (say[6]) 0 °C to 350 °C. In this universe, 'state' means a particular temperature of the oven. For the dinghy sailor, the universe of discourse is the set of all values of (direction, speed, angle of heel) where direction can have any value in the set of points of the compass, speed can have any value from (say) -10 knots to $+20$ knots, and angle of heel can have any value from $-180°$ to $+180°$ (if the dinghy turns turtle). In this universe of discourse, 'state' means a particular set of values of these three components. The reader may find it useful to repeat the above exercise for the rudder and car examples.

5.10 By those who like diagrams, the following have been found helpful for thinking about the various component parts which have been distinguished within a director system.

Starting with the operand and its environment

Figure 6

we draw lines to represent relationships
between these two

and circles to represent sensors which abstract
these relationships.

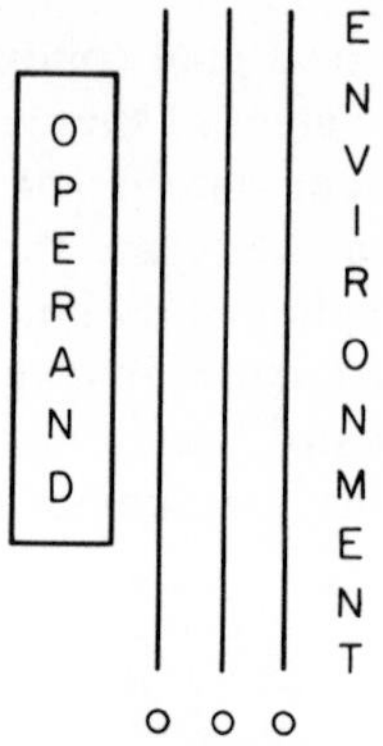

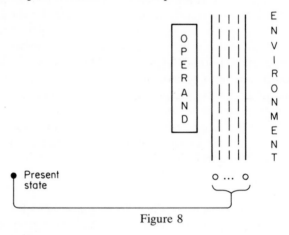

Figure 7

Here three lines and circles are shown, representing a state with three components (such as the dinghy example). To represent the car example specifically we would use five; but in general it is convenient to use dots to represent an unspecified number of components.

Figure 8

A bracket leading to a single dot shows that the components collectively specify a single state.

For a one-component state (e.g. the oven temperature) the goal state would be represented by an interval on a line. The present state would be shown by a point on this line, and the set of all points on the line would represent all the conceivable states of the system.

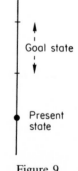

Figure 9

For a multi-component state, a single point still represents the present state of the operand. A goal state is now shown by a set of points within a region.

Figure 10

The comparator, shown like a large C, compares present state and goal state.

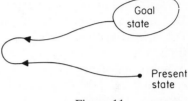

Figure 11

and the plan converts this information into appropriate action by directing the energies of the operators, acting on the operand, in such a way as to bring the operand to the goal state.

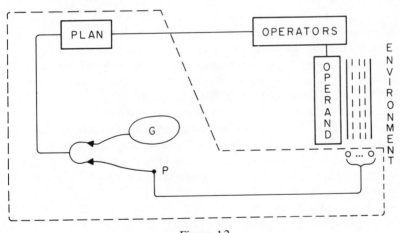

Figure 12

In Figure 12, the director system as a whole has now been enclosed by a dotted boundary line.

5.11 For a one-component director system, the plan may be quite a simple one. This was the case in the two examples used in Section 5.3 (oven thermostat, ship's steering mechanism). But when a number of components are involved, interaction effects may become important. If the dinghy sailor hauls in his sail or lets it out to get the greatest possible forward propulsion from the wind, this affects the tendency of the boat to heel over, and he will need to shift his weight to keep the dinghy in its goal state with respect to the angle-of-heel component. Likewise, he will need to adjust the position of the rudder, since the action of the wind on the sail also affects the steering.

In the five-component state of the car, the interaction effects are more complex. Suppose that on a country road a driver has set the following goal state. {Direction: parallel to that of the road. Forward speed: between 45 and 50 m.p.h. Position on road laterally: within the left-hand half (in Great Britain), and more than 1 yard from the edge and the centre line of road. Distance from other traffic going in same direction: 20 yards or more. Distance from other traffic going in opposite direction: 2 yards or more.} He then comes up behind a farm tractor. At once the second and third components of his goal state become incompatible, due to the change in environment. His plan under these circumstances will normally be to overtake, but this requires a change in goal state of the second component taking him over to the right-hand half of the road. At once the minimum value of the last component, distance from oncoming traffic, must increase very greatly.

The first and third components, direction and lateral position, are so closely interdependent that the lateral position is maintained for most of the time by changes of direction. When he comes to a cross-roads, however, there is a choice of directions, each of which is consistent with the goal states of the other components. An appropriate plan at this stage will normally be related to a less immediate goal state, namely his ultimate destination.

In human activities, multi-component goal states are the rule and not the exception: and the interaction effects are such that a successful director system has to be more than a simple juxtaposition of several one-component control systems. These have to be co-ordinated, and the diagram developed in Section 5.10 does not include anything which explicitly represents this co-ordinating activity. An approach to this problem will be made in Chapter 8. For the present, what is important is to remember the importance of co-ordination whenever multi-component goal states are involved. In this connection, it is interesting to note that studies of gifted children have shown that they are above average in physical co-ordination as well as in their higher mental activities. The integrative function of intelligence shows itself at many levels.

Open goal states

5.12   Sometimes a goal state is clearly and specifically represented in our mental models, but sometimes it is more open. We recognize it when achieved, but do not know in advance exactly what it will be like: a present for a friend, a melody to fit a particular poem, somewhere to live in our next job. This simply means that the concept representing the goal state is of a more general kind. Without having a specific example in mind, we know whether what we have arrived at fits the concept or not. This won't do; this is just what we wanted—although we did not know in advance that this is what it would be.

To be able to distinguish between examples and non-examples is the criterion for having a concept. So open goals of this kind are simply those represented by more general concepts than the goal states in our introductory examples.

Open goals of another kind are those in which the interval itself is open on one side—the greatest possible bank balance, the fastest possible racing car, the finest possible performance of a piece of music.

Open goals of this kind also fit the general model, in that 'as far as possible in a given direction' is a concept which can be set as a goal state. Though we do not know whether or not the maximum so far reached can be exceeded, this does not prevent a director system from functioning. The comparator can always register whether things are changing in the desired direction, but the director system does not 'switch off'. Implicit in the concept of any open goal state is that each improved state is treated as a sub-goal on the way to further progress.

In such examples, though the upper limits are not parts of the person's own conception of the goal states, there are always situational constraints. Bank balances are limited by constraints such as legality, competition, taxes; racing cars by engineering factors and the abilities of their drivers; musical performances by talent and the difficulty of the work. Other constraints are contained in the fact that overall resources in time and energy are limited, and those which are spent in pursuit of one goal are not available for another. So 'maximum' is not always the same as 'optimum'. How an individual deploys his resources is largely a matter of personal choice and judgement, taking into account both his own inclinations and the situations in which he finds himself.

5.13 The main ideas of this chapter are:

(i) *The more inaccessible to direct perception is the system which we are trying to understand, the more we need to support our thinking by the use of appropriate models.*

(ii) *Intelligence is a quality of those higher mental processes by means of which we become able to direct our activities towards goal states favourable to survival.*

(iii) *We may therefore hope to understand it better with the help of the general model of a director system which has been introduced in this chapter.*

Notes for Chapter 5

1. For chemists, this offers a simple example for mode (iii) reality testing: internal consistency with respect to valencies.
2. Many of the constituent ideas have of course been around for some time, and I have done my best to acknowledge their sources. It is the synthesis which I believe to be new, and within which existing ideas have acquired new significance.

3. This example is taken directly from Wiener (1948), pages 13–14. I chose it partly for its clarity, but partly also for its historical significance; since on page 19 of the same book, Wiener writes: 'We have decided to call the entire field of control and communication theory, whether in the machine or in the animal, by the name '*Cybernetics*, which we form from the Greek κμβερνητησ or *steersman*.'

4. This model of a director system is essential as a starting point for what follows. To introduce it I needed a very simple example, and one with which a majority of people are familiar: so I chose that of a thermostat. However, a group of three intelligent women with a gap in their scientific education, who read this book in draft form and gave me the benefit of their comments, told me that they found this example a real stumbling-block; since they automatically reacted to anything mechanical or electrical with a deep mistrust of their own ability to understand it. It is for others like them that this note is written.

A thermostat is a very simple gadget. You probably have several in your home, since they are used to control electric and gas ovens, electric irons, refrigerators, freezers, central heating systems, tropical fish tanks, and anything which you want to stay at or around a given temperature. The commonest kind has as its basis a bi-metal strip, which is to say, a strip made from two different metals which expand and contract by different amounts when heated and cooled. A strip of this kind, if it starts flat, will bend one way when heated and the other way when cooled. If it is coiled into a spiral, with the outer end fixed and the inner end joined to a rod, then when heated or cooled the spiral will coil more, or uncoil slightly, and in so doing will cause the rod to twist one way or the other. By joining the other end of the rod to an electric switch, we now have a special kind of thermometer which can be used to turn a switch on and off at the desired temperature. And that is all there is to it.

After receiving the above explanation, one of the group, a professional singer, wrote:

> I shall never again regard mechanical things with the same hopelessness as I did in the past. I now know how a thermostatically controlled oven works—I've overcome a mental block and fear of mechanical things. It took effort and involved second, third readings of this particular chapter; but the fascination of the other chapters made it so very worth while, and in so doing I've killed two birds with one stone.

5. Whether we restrict the term 'operators' to whatever acts directly on the object concerned (i.e. to the heating coils and the steam engine), or whether we include the back-up source of energy, is open to choice; and this choice may vary from person to person, example to example. If we take the latter approach, it is hard to know where to stop. Do we also include the whole of the electrical system, the ship's boilers and the source of heat for these . . . ? It therefore seems best to use the term with the first, more restricted, meaning.

6. The exact limits chosen are not important, provided that all temperatures likely to be actually encountered are included. For a potter's kiln the upper limit would be higher than for a domestic oven.

CHAPTER 6

Development of the Model

Survival in relation to habitat

6.1   A very important feature of goal-seeking machines, and of organisms, is their ability to achieve and maintain goal states in the face of environmental changes. The oven thermostat does this in spite of changes in kitchen temperature, small fluctuations in mains voltage, or somebody opening the oven door and putting in cold food. The ship's steering mechanism does this in spite of the action of Atlantic rollers and the motion of the ship. The dinghy sailor does this in spite of changes in wind direction and force, and waves and currents in the water.

Nevertheless, there is a limit to what they can do. The oven thermostat cannot maintain the desired oven temperature if there are power cuts, or even if the mains voltage drops excessively. The dinghy sailor cannot sail in a flat calm or in a gale, and he avoids such conditions.

So there is an important relationship between on the one hand a goal-seeking machine or an organism, and on the other hand the set of all the environmental conditions within which its director system and operators, working together, can bring the operand to its goal state and keep it there. To express this relationship we shall say that the organism (or goal-directed machine[1]) is *viable* in this environment, which we shall call its *habitat*.

This meaning for the word 'habitat' is consistent with, but a slight enlargement of, everyday usage. The *Concise Oxford Dictionary* defines habitat as 'natural home of plant or animal', thus relating it to the locations in which the organism is normally found. We have taken this meaning a little further in two ways. First, by referring to environmental conditions rather than to the locations where these conditions exist naturally, we have allowed for the fact than an organism can come to be out of its habitat for other reasons besides a change of location. A child who cannot swim may fall in the river (change of location); but in times of flood, many people find themselves out of their habitat in this more general sense, while still located in their own homes. Second, having seen from earlier chapters that the ability of an organism to reach and maintain its various goal states is what enables it to survive, we have shifted the emphasis in our thinking about habitat from where an organism lives to why and how it lives there. Organisms which find themselves outside their habitats sooner or later fail to exist as such (unless some outside agency restores them). So we come back to habitat as the natural home of an organism, having deepened but not basically altered the original meaning.

6.2 We tend to use the word 'survival' with the implied meaning 'bare survival'. But as was pointed out in Section 1.7 (ii), even the requirements for bare survival of a species are closely associated with its evolution; and a similar argument applies to individuals. A changing environment, and more effective competition from other species or individuals, both impose the necessity for continual improvement, even to keep pace with situations as they are met.

But it is even better to be ahead of these demands: not merely to have the minimal requirements for viability in the present habitat, and change as and when confronted with new situations, but to have something in reserve. This is the positive aspect of survival, leading to the concept of an *expert*. Such an individual does not wait to be overtaken by events, but puts himself ahead of them by developing his abilities beyond the minimal requirements for viability. As a car driver, by developing his skills beyond the minimum necessary to pass the driving test, he is more likely to emerge safely from an emergency. As a dairy farmer, he constantly seeks to improve the milk yield of his herd. Another quality typical of an expert is foresight. Such a person does not wait for the winter before building his woodpile.

The term 'viability' thus covers a wide range. It extends from bare survival ability on the one hand (and always remembering that viability is relative to a habitat) through survival with a margin, to mastery over the environment, to foresight and the pursuit of excellence—in short, to expertise.

6.3 By survival, we mean continuing in existence as such. This does not necessarily mean in exactly the same form. A baby who survives becomes a child, and then an adult. An adult who survives is continually changing the substance of his body. Biologically, the important unit of survival is the species: and the individual organisms which collectively make up the species are continually dying and being replaced. This is also true of the individual cells of which our own bodies are made. What is meant by survival is continuity of existence, not absence of change: and what we choose to regard as the unit of survival may vary.

There is also an implied time dimension. Thus a ten-year-old, and an octogenarian, are both surviving. But the future life expectancy of the ten-year-old is considerably greater than that of the octogenarian. And although we cannot say what these expectations are for particular individuals, insurance companies have tables which give their values on a statistical basis: namely, the period of survival which has occurred with greatest frequency in the past, and to which we therefore attach the greatest probability in the future, on the assumption that future events will follow the same overall pattern as in the past. They also attach greater life expectancies to certain categories of individuals than to others—greater to non-smokers than to smokers, greater to doctors than to deep-sea divers. Here once again we observe a connection between state and survival, first pointed out in general terms as early as Section 1.3. It is now time to examine this in more detail, and in relation to the model newly introduced in Chapter 5.

Survival contributions

6.4 The relationship of some states to survival is obvious and direct. If for the dinghy sailor we specify a one-component state having only two values, head above water and head under water, only the first of these has the property of keeping him alive: so his choice of this for goal state needs no elaboration.

In general, however, the relation is less obvious, and probabilistic rather than directly causal. If he can swim, a dinghy sailor can keep his head above water after a capsize for some time, even without a lifejacket. But he can do so for longer if he is in the state of wearing a lifejacket than if he is not. And if he is wearing one, the effects of cold water are such that the time he can survive in the water after a capsize is a matter of hours or even minutes compared with his normal life expectancy of years. So if we consider the four possible values of the state whose first component is wearing/not wearing a lifejacket, and whose second component is capsized/not capsized, the state defined by (wearing a lifejacket, not capsized) has the greatest survival value, and that defined by (not wearing a lifejacket, capsized) the least.

We can see a fairly direct relationship between the foregoing, and the goal state described earlier for the dinghy sailor (Section 5.7). As long as his angle of heel is between 0° and 30° he will not capsize. A forward speed greater than zero is necessary for a dinghy to answer the helm, without which it is less manageable in a gust. Without a forward speed greater than zero, he cannot (unassisted) get back to shore—a necessity for food and sleep, which are themselves necessary for survival.

It is instructive to trace the relationship between goal states and survival in other examples. This will help to consolidate the fundamental ideas that in a goal-seeking machine or organism for which there are many possible states:

(i)   an important property associated with each state is its effect on the survival expectancy of the machine or organism while in this state; and

(ii) that a frequently found explanation for selection of goal states is that they optimize this property, in comparison with other states. I have said 'optimize', rather than 'maximize', in order not to prejudice the question whether the longest possible survival period is always the best. For example, although most of us would hope to live to 70 or 75 rather than die at 40 or 45, would we like even better to live to 100 or 150? Clearly other factors are also involved. But in the case of the dinghy sailor, 'optimize' clearly means 'maximize', since we are only taking into account the effects on his survival expectancy of the states under discussion.

Whatever it is that we are trying to understand, it is necessary to limit our attention to certain observables in order to make our task thinkable. The concept of a state helps us to do this. We collect together the values of all the observables under consideration, and call this set of values a state. The associated property of each state will have an effect (in which we will include zero effect, to take care of all possible cases) on the overall survival expectancy of the organism or goal-directed machine.

To know this overall survival expectancy is clearly beyond our ability, since we cannot know all the states which have an effect thereon. Even if we did, we could not process all the information. What is both possible and useful is to examine the effects on survival of the properties of particular states. These effects we shall call the *survival contributions* of these states.

These contributions do not necessarily have numerical values — of the many variables we are considering in this book, some have numerical values, but many do not. For most purposes we simply need to know whether survival contributions are better or worse than each other. In Figure 13, states are represented by single dots as in Chapter 5, and the written words describe the associated survival contributions.

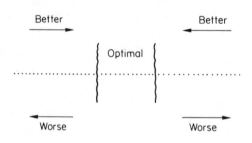

Figure 13

Occasionally, survival contributions are sharply distinguished; for example, those attached to the two values of the state of the dinghy sailor, head above or below water. Other examples are easy to think of, such as touching or not touching a 10 000-volt electric cable. More often, different state values simply make small improvements or deteriorations in survival expectancy. But, as a Scottish teacher of mine used to say in quite a different context, 'Many a mickle mak a muckle'; and the cumulative effect of many small changes in survival contributions can be considerable.

Prohabitat

6.5 Positive contributions to survival come from reaching a large variety of goal states, simultaneously or at different times. These range from relatively simple ones like being warm and well-fed to complex ones like having a job and being credit-worthy. They may be independent, or some may be prerequisite for others; and indeed, some may compete with others if they call on the same resources in time and energy. This further emphasizes the point made earlier, that 'optimize' does not mean 'maximize'. A man who sets as his goal state to be as rich as he possibly can, ignoring all else, may work himself into an early grave or end up in prison. Some people in fact do one or other of these.

Most organisms thus have a wide variety of director systems, loosely combined with an assortment of operators. The same person may act sometimes as a car mechanic, sometimes as a swimmer, sometimes as a gardener. These activities relate to different features within his (total) habitat. He can survive in a garage, and in a swimming pool, and in a garden, and in many other places too. But he cannot achieve his goal states as a gardener while he is in a garage or in a swimming pool.

So we need a distinguishing word by which to refer to that part of an individual's habitat within which, and only within which, a particular complex of goal-seeking activities can take place. This part may be physically within the total habitat, in the way that a swimming pool is within a person's home town. Or it may consist of certain features which he attends to within his environment, ignoring those which are not relevant to the activity in question: as when a car driver attends to traffic lights or road signs, but ignores (for purposes of driving) neon advertising signs.

As was indicated in Section 5.2 (iii), when working with new ideas (which may sometimes be new syntheses of existing ideas) one needs symbols by which to refer to them in communication, retrieve them from memory, and manipulate them. Sometimes one can find an existing word which is suitable, sometimes it is necessary to invent a new word. The present case is one of the latter kind; and I propose that we use the term *prohabitat* for those features of an individual's habitat which are relevant to his activities within a given category. A prohabitat is an aspect of our environment with respect to which we are 'at home'.

A person can *be* a mechanic, a swimmer, and a gardener all at the same time—and indeed, when he is not with a car, or in a swimming pool or a garden, but sitting watching television. To *be* one of these means that he has the necessary director and operator systems available, at levels which may range from marginal viability to expertise. But the contributions to survival which result from reaching the related goal states can only be obtained within the appropriate prohabitat. The pay-off comes from actually achieving these goal states—a car which runs well, a healthy body, a productive garden—not just from being able to gain them. To *act as* a car mechanic, a swimmer, or a gardener, a person has to be in the appropriate prohabitat: for it is in actuality that our physical survival takes place.

Survival in inner reality

6.6 Remembering now the distinction between actuality and reality which was discussed at some length in Chapter 3, an interesting question arises. Is there any way in which it is meaningful to talk about a person's survival in his own inner reality?

I think that there is. To be, say, a (professional) comic means to be able, by performing on stage, television, or film, to make people laugh. It is to be able to bring about certain goal states (laughing) of certain operands (paying audiences), given the necessary prohabitat: which includes these, and also theatres and studios, agents, script writers, ticket sellers, etc. A comic can continue to *be* a comic outside his prohabitat, and can even increase his adeptness, e.g., by rehearsing with a mirror or tape recorder, by increasing his repertoire of jokes. And though he can only *act as* a comic within his prohabitat (and thereby get cash contributions to his actual survival), he can still continue to *be* a comic even if he gets no engagements.

But suppose now that he does get an engagement, and that nobody laughs at his jokes. Suppose further that this happens a number of times in succession. He is no longer able to achieve the goal states (laughing, or at least a mental state of amusement) of the appropriate operands (the paying audience—it doesn't matter about the ice-cream sellers). Then he ceases to be viable as a comic, and can no longer conceive himself as such. Within his own reality now, as a comic he has failed to survive; and it is no empty metaphor that professionals in an situation where, despite their best efforts, the audience remains indifferent or hostile, sometimes refer to it as 'dying the death'.

How much a failure of this kind matters to the person will depend on a number of factors, including the importance of the goal to him and how much of his total self-confidence depends on its achievement. Restriction of consciousness to a particular prohabitat also leads to an intensification of feelings in this context. This is in general advantageous, since it improves functioning where adaptability is most needed. But in particular cases it may be disadvantageous, in that failure is experienced as complete and utter. Depending on factors such as these, in analogous situations persons such as teachers, politicians, lovers, and all who depend for their self-conceptions on the reactions of others, when they find themselves unable to bring about the desired reactions, experience feelings ranging from loss of confidence to personal disaster.

The remedy is for the person concerned to try to expand his consciousness beyond this particular prohabitat — deliberately to realize that there are other areas of life besides that within which the failure has taken place. This redeployment of consciousness is another example of its importance for adaptability.

We must also recognize wide differences in vulnerability to such situations, and the existence of persons whose inner realities are resistant to such disappointments. Most of the possible sources of this inner strength (which can be found also in fanatics) lie beyond the scope of the present enquiry, in the field of personality. But we may note that a high degree of internal consistency within a particular reality is one factor which will make it less dependent on external support. Some other factors are touched on in Chapter 16.

6.7 In Section 5.5 (ii), we noted that in our present model, 'state' means a relationship between the operand and its environment. In the diagram developed in Section 5.10, this operand is shown separately from both the organism itself and the environment.

Often the operand is part of the environment, and what is being changed is the relationship between this operand and the rest of the environment: as when someone puts food from the kitchen table into the oven (change of location), whereby its temperature is changed to a goal temperature optimal for cooking.

Sometimes, however, the operand is the organism itself, as when we change our own location by walking or driving. In this case we use Newton's third law of motion, that to every action there is an equal and opposite reaction. In walking, our direct action is to push the ground backwards with alternate feet, whereby the ground pushes us forward with equal force. Because of the huge mass of the earth in proportion to our own mass, we go forwards more than the earth goes backwards. It is different when diving from a small boat.

The term 'state' can also be used more generally to mean a social relationship. In many such cases a similar argument applies: if we want to achieve certain states, we have to act towards others in ways which result in their taking us towards these states. If we want (legally) to own more money, we have to act towards others in ways which result in their giving us money. To be famous, we have to act in ways which cause other people to talk or write about us, invite us to appear on radio or television, etc. Before a girl, however beautiful, can become a model, artists or photographers or costumiers must paint or photograph or display their new fashions on her. There are, however, important differences between the physical reactions described in the previous paragraph, and these social reactions. The latter are less predictable, and may take longer.

Domain of a director system

6.8 As was pointed out in Section 6.1, for any contribution of director system and operators there are environmental conditions in which they can together take the operand to its goal state, and other conditions in which they cannot. The oven thermostat cannot maintain oven temperature in the face of power cuts, or excessive drops in mains voltage. The dinghy sailor cannot sail in a flat calm or a gale, nor can he sail directly against the wind.

If a goal state cannot be achieved, it is useful to be able to distinguish between failures of the director system, and those of the operators. During a power cut, the oven thermostat keeps the switch between mains and heating coils on, but there is no energy to give power to the heating coils. The director system is doing the right thing, but the operators are ineffective. In a gale, the dinghy sailor may be doing the right thing but come to grief because his strength and weight are not sufficient.

In contrast, a novice sailor may capsize because he has not learnt, in a gust, to correct excessive heel by spilling wind from the sail as well as by shifting his weight. This is a failure of the director system; if he knew what to do, he could do it. A drunken driver is another good example of a faulty director system — he is physically capable of making the right movements, but his co-ordination has deteriorated.

So let us now consider separately the contributions of the two main parts of a goal-directed system, beginning with that of the director system; and assuming for the time being that there is full support by the operators. For any director system there will be a set of states within which it can take the operand to its goal state and keep it there, and outside which it cannot. If the dinghy starts going backward (i.e. the second state-component has a negative value), few dinghy sailors will be able to keep their craft on course. If on a wet road his car starts pointing in the wrong direction, an expert driver will be able to correct the skid, a beginner will not.

The set of states within which (and only within which) a director system can take the operand to its goal state and keep it there is so important that it needs a special name. We shall call it the *domain* of the director system. Like other technical terms, the word 'domain' has been introduced because once acquired it helps us to say what we want briefly and clearly. The one word 'domain' replaces the twenty-five words 'the set of states . . . keep it there'. We shall also often want to say: 'brings the operand to its goal state and keeps it there', and for this we shall use the single word *functions*.

Briefly, then, a director system functions within its domain, and not outside it.

In Figure 14(a), which corresponds to the lower left-hand part of the full model at the end of Section 5.10 (Figure 12), each point represents a state. Only a few typical states in each set are represented: there are of course many more. The small letter f stands for 'functions'. The arrows starting at points within the domain end at points in the goal state, indicating that the director system functions for these initial states. The arrows outside the domain, without an f, do not end on marked points to show that we do not know to what state the operand will change.

This diagram suggests an alternative formulation for the concept of domain. If (as shown) P is a typical point representing a present state, and G a goal state, then P is within the domain of a director system if it can take the operand to another point such as G.

We would normally expect G also to be within the domain, but this does

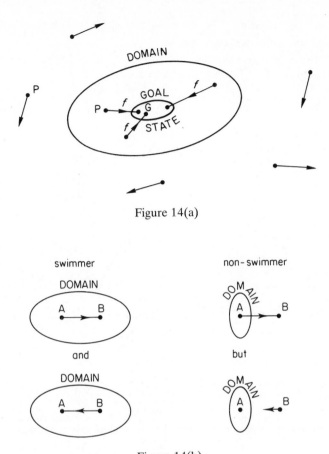

Figure 14(a)

Figure 14(b)

not necessarily follow. For example, a child may climb half way up a cliff, but be unable to get back. To take care of this we can extend the formulation as follows. Two points A and B are both within a domain if and only if A can be a present state and B an achievable goal state, *and vice versa*. Thus, for a swimmer, A can represent a location on the surface of a pool, and B somewhere on the bottom at the deep end. But this is not the case for a non-swimmer, who can get from A to B but not from B to A (Figure 14 b). So an important feature of an expert is that he knows the boundaries of his domain, and avoids actions which may take him beyond.

Capacity of operators

6.9 We now turn our attention to the activity of the operators: briefly, because our main interest is in director systems. If, given the right direction of their energies, the operators can bring the operand to its goal state, we shall say that they are *capable*. The set of states within which the operators are capable we shall call their *capacity*.

The relations between domain (of the director system), capacity (of the operators), and prohabitat, are shown in Figure 15.

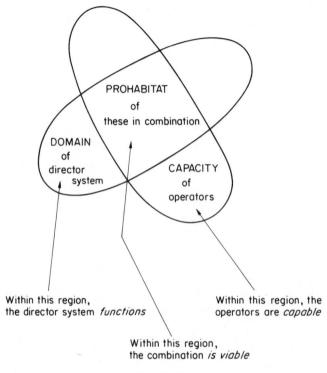

Figure 15

The prohabitat is that region which is within both the domain of the director system and the capacity of the operators. Using swimming again for an example, a non-swimmer is outside his prohabitat if he is in deep water, not because of lack of muscular strength but because he cannot make the right movements. He is within the capacity of his operators but outside the domain of his (relevant) director system. A good swimmer caught in an off-shore current is also outside his prohabitat but for a different reason. He can make the right movements, but cannot swim powerfully enough to reach the shore, or he cannot keep it up for long enough. So he is within the domain of his director system, but outside the capacity of his operators. Both are non-viable because they are outside their prohabitats; but for different reasons.

Universe of discourse

6.10   The domain of a director system is represented by a region

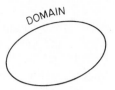

within   which   the   director   system functions

and outside which it doesn't.

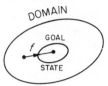

Figure 16

These outside points also represent states, however; and the meaning of 'state' depends on what we are talking about at the moment. If we are talking about ovens and thermostats, 'state' means temperature. If we are talking about rudders and steering mechanisms, 'state' means degrees to port or starboard. At other times 'state' means a package, as we saw in Section 5.9. So all these points in our diagrams, whether inside or outside the domain, represent not any states whatever, but a particular set of states for which we need a name. Since it depends on what we are talking (or thinking) about, the philosophers' term *universe of discourse* is appropriate.

So a domain is that region (represented by a set of points) inside a given universe of discourse within which a director system functions, and outside which it does not.

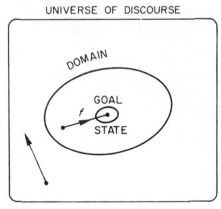

Figure 17

Frontiers

6.11   The boundary of a domain we shall call its *frontier*, which is simply to expand the metaphor already in use when we talk about 'the frontiers of knowledge'. So far this frontier has been represented in our diagrams by a line, suggesting a sharp distinction between those states from which as starting points the director system can take the operand to its goal state, and those from which it cannot. This may sometimes be the case; but often the frontier would be more accurately represented by a zone. Beyond this zone the director system cannot function at all, and in those parts of the domain which are not in the frontier zone the director system functions with complete dependability. Within this frontier zone, the director system also functions, but less reliably and efficiently. Using our swimming example once more, imagine a good swimmer and one only just able to swim, both pushed backwards from the side of a pool into deep water. From this initial state, the former will achieve the goal state of a normal swimming position quickly and reliably. The latter will do so only after a struggle: possibly he may not even manage it at all, and need rescuing. Or take another universe of discourse, one involving mental activity, say arithmetical problems. For every individual there will be some kinds which he cannot do at all, and some kinds which he can be sure of getting right. But there will also be some kinds which he can make a good attempt at, with a fair hope of success, but not certainty. These constitute his frontier zone, within that universe of discourse.

We expand a domain by turning part of its frontier zone into *established domain*: that is, the region within which the director system functions with complete dependability. This brings into existence a new frontier zone, beyond the former one; and this may in its turn be changed into established domain. Learning is thus an activity which may benefit greatly from protected conditions, in which the learner can make mistakes without too serious consequences.

While the above diagrams are helpful as a support to our thinking, they may be misleading in one respect. By representing the domain as a region surrounded by a single boundary line, there is an implication that all points within this boundary lie in the domain. This is not the case. All points in the domain lie within the boundary: but there may also be points within the boundary which do not belong to the domain. An arithmetical example shows this clearly.

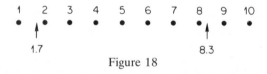

Figure 18

Imagine a young child who knows only the numbers from 1 to 10. His present domain may be represented by a set of points in a line, as in Figure 18. Outside this domain are not only the numbers greater than 10 and less than 1, but also all the numbers between 1 and 2, all those between 2 and 3, and so on. Two of these are indicated by arrows.

We need therefore to bear in mind that frontiers may be not only at the outer boundary of a domain, but also within it. At an everyday level, when visiting a new town, one may soon become familiar with the main thoroughfares in the central area, but still become lost (at least temporarily) in side streets between these.

6.12 The more numerous and the more extensive our prohabitats, the better is our overall chance of survival. Increasing these in both ways, though at a more complex level than those considered so far, is (or should be) a major task of education.

A given prohabitat can be enlarged in two ways: by extending the domain of the director system, or increasing the capacity of the operators. Figure 15 shows, however, that these are not entirely independent. An enlargement of the domain of the director system is only useful where it is within the capacity of the operators, and increased capacity of the operators needs to be within the domain of the director system—the extra power must be controllable.

For example, if instead of a domestic oven we want a kiln hot enough to fire pottery, it is necessary to extend the domain of the thermostat by using a thermometer which can register much higher temperatures. But this is not sufficient: heating coils of much greater capacity are also required, otherwise the higher temperatures will not be achieved.

Someone whose goal state is to drive a car at 100 m.p.h. may for that reason acquire a car with engines of greater capacity than his former one. But he should also take care that he improves his ability to control it.

Successful adaptation will be greatly helped by knowing whether it is the director system or the operators which needs to be improved: whether more knowledge and skill, or more physical power, are required, or perhaps both. In the case of the ship's steering mechanism it could easily be either. The director system could be too insensitive or slow, or the engine itself could be too weak to move the size of rudder under ocean-going conditions. In our own case, the director system is usually the more important factor. The chief differences between a concert pianist, a surgeon, and an airline pilot—all expert within their own prohabitats, but not each other's—lie in their available director systems, not in their operator systems. Any enlargment of the domains of their director systems is likely to be within the capacity of their operators (arms, hands, fingers, muscles).

In later chapters we shall give much time to considering ways in which domains can be increased, but there is one simple way which can be mentioned here. This is by increasing the range of the sensors. If our dinghy sailor has now capsized and a rescue boat is searching for him, the look-out is likely to extend his range of vision with the help of binoculars, and thereby to extend the region within which he can bring the rescue boat to the goal state of zero distance from the capsized craft. Radar, echo sounders, microscopes, stethoscopes, television cameras are all means of increasing the range of our own sense organs. So are instruments such as voltmeters and ammeters, whereby states which our sense organs cannot perceive at all are converted to those which we can perceive, in these examples locations of a needle on a dial.

Even when the deficiency is on the operator side, the means whereby this is remedied are usually via an improved functioning of our director systems. If we want to lift things which are too heavy for us, we are more likely to use levers, pulleys, fork-lift trucks, cranes, than we are to start doing exercises to strengthen our muscles. Both the construction and the operation of these is within our physical capacity: what we increase are our knowledge and skill.

Abstraction

6.13 A goal-directed machine will probably have a single prohabitat, for which it has been specifically designed and constructed. That of a ship's steering mechanism consists of all ships for which this particular mechanism is of suitable accuracy and power. In any such ship, the steering mechanism will be viable—it will take the rudder to its goal state and keep it there.

Most organisms however, and particularly we humans, have many director systems which share the same operators (our voluntary muscles acting mostly on the bony levers formed by our skeletons). Thus the same person may be an excellent cook, a talented musician, and a gifted teacher. Her prohabitat will differ according to which of these director systems is actively functioning. This will be the case even when her physical surroundings remain the same. Within the same city, the prohabitats of a car assembly worker, a secretary, and a school child *as such* will be different and will not overlap; while as father, mother and child their prohabitats will have much (but not everything) in common. This imposes a new requirement on our director systems: that of abstracting what is relevant from the available sensory input.

The sensor of an oven thermostat is sensitive only to oven temperature. That of the ship's steering mechanism, though a position sensor, only registers the position of the ship's rudder, and not that of any other part of the ship. But our eyes are sensitive to everything within view, our ears receive sound from far and near. From the enormous sensory input, our director systems have to select what is relevant and ignore the rest. A car driver, at night, has to attend to traffic lights, and ignore the multiplicity of other coloured, often flashing, lights in his total environment. A mother can hear her baby crying when no one else does, selectively from among the other sounds which are reaching her ears.[2] Simply to distinguish an object from its background is a feat of visual discrimination. In a crowded room, we can attend to the conversation in which we are engaged and ignore the rest.

This *abstractive ability* of an organism's director system, appropriate to the current universe of discourse, is a major contributor to the higher mental processes characteristic of intelligence. It will be discussed at greater length in Chapter 9.

6.14 (*This is a tidying-up section. It does not affect the main argument, and may be taken lightly, or omitted, at a first reading.*)

In Chapter 3 the distinction was made between reality and actuality; and all that has followed has related to these in one way or another. Some of the concepts which have been introduced in the last few sections now need to be examined in relation to this basic distinction. These are: state, domain, prohabitat, universe of discourse. For the question now arises whether these refer to actuality or to inner reality.

So far as 'state' is concerned, the answer appears to be both. The physical survival of an organism is dependent on its actual state, whereas the basis for the functioning of its director systems is its conceived goal state (which is part of its inner reality) and an ongoing comparison between present states (as perceived) and goal states. So we need to use the term 'state' with all of these meanings, according to context.

Another category of states refers to those states represented within a director system which are neither (perceived) present states, nor (conceived) goal states, but which one can nevertheless imagine. Such as these may be called *conceivable states*; and both a perceived present state, and a conceived goal state, are particular states within this overall category.

A universe of discourse can now be reformulated as a set of conceivable states, together with all the other concepts by which these states are connected, and also all those which are generated by this conceptual structure. It consists of a *set of related concepts which can, or which could in principle, form the subject of an utterance.*

It is time for an example. The present location of my car is the car port attached to our house. (So in the present context 'state' means location.) Easily conceived goal locations include the car park near my office at Warwick University, that at my local railway station, and (say) a hill top where my son and I enjoy flying our kites. These become actual, perceived locations at such times as my car is there and I can see it there. Conceivable locations are infinite in number. These are connected by roads, and otherwise related by (e.g.) distance, or direction; out of which arise a variety of other concepts such as velocity, time of journey, or petrol consumption. All of the latter concepts belong to the *universe of discourse* within which I can imagine, discuss, and if necessary direct, actions in relation to all conceivable locations and changes of location of my car.

The use of 'conceivable' merits a little further consideration. Is (say) the roof of my house a conceivable location for my car? Certainly: I could not write or even talk about it if I were not first able to conceive it. But equally certainly, I would be very surprised to perceive my car as (apparently) there in actuality, and reality testing as described in Chapter 4 would come into action. 'Conceivable' does not imply that it is likely to become actual.

But unless and until a state has been conceived, whether as possible, improbable, or impossible, it cannot form a goal state for a director system. And when it has been conceived, there may be surprises in store; as when some engineering students at Cambridge University did in fact, one night, put a small van on the roof of the senate house.

Whether the domain of a director system should be taken to refer to a set of actual states, or states as they are represented within a mental model, must now be considered. This is not at once obvious. Looking at the Glossary, we read: '*Domain*. The set of states within which (and only within which) a director system can *function*, i.e., can take the operand to its goal state . . .'. Actual, or perceived? The survival of the organism depends on the right actual state being reached. But this in turn depends on a correct perception of the actual state being registered within the director system, this requirement having already been discussed at some length.

This solves the problem, and somewhat neatly too. The domain of a director system can only include those actual states which can be correctly represented within (or construed by) the mental model used by the director system: so within the domain of a director system, all actual states are correctly matched with real states, and the term domain is appropriate for both.

With this amplified meaning for 'domain', the original meaning of 'prohabitat' still holds good, and needs no further elaboration at this point.

There is one other point to be tidied up which may not have passed un-noticed. This came in Section 6.9, and more specifically in Figure 15. It arose out of the superimposition of a region representing the domain of a director system on one representing the capacity of its associated operators to show that their common region was the prohabitat of the organism or goal-directed machine. What was not pointed out at the time, in order to avoid distraction from the main points of the discussion, is that two universes of discourse are here involved. That of the director system, within which is the domain, consists of a set of states. These are relationships between the operand and its environment such as temperature, location, speed, or sets of these taken together. But the capacity of the operators is determined by relationships of a different kind, typically between the amount of energy the effector system has available and can use, and the form taken by this energy; and that to be overcome by nature of the job to be done—oven to be heated, girder to be lifted, piano keys to be depressed, surgical scalpel to be manipulated. So the two regions shown as overlapping really belong to different universes of discourse.

The problem was avoided in Section 6.9 by not including any universe of discourse in the diagram. If in future discussions we are considering director and effector systems at the same time, then we can formulate a universe of discourse which includes both. For the most part, however, we shall be concentrating our attention on one of these at a time, usually a director system. And for these purposes, as in general, it helps our thinking to include only what is relevant for the system under discussion.

6.15 The present chapter may perhaps have been found a little difficult on a first reading, in view of the number of new ideas which have been introduced, ogether with their corresponding technical terms. The first four chapters gave a bird's-eye view of the subject matter as a whole. At the beginning of Chapter 5 we saw how the ideas thus far developed, applied to the present task, made evident the need for a model. The building of such a model was begun in Chapter 5, and in the present chapter it has been developed in ways which enable it to represent more accurately and completely situations of the kind we are trying to study. This, in turn, will help us to realize better what is going on, and thereby (it is to be hoped) eventually to function more successfully. In the next chapter the model will be applied to the learning process itself.

The main points made in this chapter are:

(i) *An organism is viable within only part of the total environment. That part we call its habitat. The term 'viable' covers a range of meaning from bare survival ability to expertise.*

(ii) *Survival is the cumulative result of the combined activities of a number of director systems. These are not independent, but it helps our thinking to concentrate on one at a time by specifying a universe of discourse.*

(iii) *A single director system relates only to certain features of the habitat, and these features constitute a prohabitat. To be viable within a given prohabitat, an organism requires a director system which functions, together with capable operators.*

(iv) *The set of states within which, and only within which, a director system functions is called its domain.*

(v) *The most important ways in which man as a species, and especially men in advanced technological cultures, increase their viability are those which improve the functioning of their director systems.*

Notes for Chapter 6

1. The word 'habitat' may be thought less suitable for goal-directed machines than for organisms. Our chief interest is certainly in the latter, machines being used as examples only to help our thinking. Since we are for present purposes concentrating on the similarities, it is convenient to use the same word for both.
2. What is more, a married student tells me that in a maternity ward a mother can be asleep and wake at the crying of her own baby, but not at that of others. What a feat of abstraction! Its value for survival is twofold. A mother's director system is oriented primarily towards the nurture of her own baby. And if these mothers all woke when any baby cried, none of them would get much sleep.

CHAPTER 7

Learning

The state of a director system

7.1   In Chapter 1, at the end of Section 1.8, appears the following passage.

Under these conditions, one of the most valuable characteristics which a species can evolve is not a visible one, either physical or behavioural: but the invisible asset of adaptability. The more adaptable a species, the better it is able to keep pace with changes in its physical environment, and the more chance it has of out-pacing its competitors among other species.

Using hindsight, we might reasonably have predicted the evolution of a species which was selected largely on the basis of this particular characteristic, in combination with those others which help to make it most effective. We are that species: and the form of adaptability which we have in greater degree than any other species is called learning.

In Chapter 6, we noted that viabity within a given prohabitat is a product of a functioning director system together with capable operators. In both these spheres, and with respect to almost any feature which one cares to name, we are surpassed by other species. In the muscular power of our operators we are exceeded by elephants, boa-constrictors, bears, to name only a few. Eagles have more acute vision, dogs keener scent, bats more sensitive hearing. Many species have better director systems for the co-ordination of skilled movement; and all the more advanced species are innately endowed with complex director systems by which they are viable within their respective habitats.

That we have in many ways outdistanced them all is due almost entirely to our advanced ability to learn: to construct director systems complex beyond whatever can be coded on to the chromosomes within a germ cell; adaptable to new habitats more swiftly than is possible by the slow process of evolutionary change; and adaptable in a new dimension, by shaping our environment into a habitat of our own choice rather than by shaping ourselves to fit the environment. By these advanced director systems we amplify the power of our operators, extend the range of our sensors, and even in some ways assist our own mental activities.

It is this ability to learn with which the present chapter is concerned. Reminding ourselves (Section 5.1) of the power contributed to our thinking by a suitable model, the aim is now to help ourselves towards a better understanding of learning itself, by formulating it in terms of the basic model introduced in Chapter 5. (Before continuing, it will be helpful to re-read Section 5.13.)

(Initial formulation.) *Learning is a change of state of a director system towards states which make possible better functioning.*

7.2 This formulation implies that at least some director systems can have different states. (Note that we are now talking about *states of a director system*, not of its operand.) To function in some degree is a property of every state, or we would not call it a director system. But in those director systems which can have different states, it is to be expected that their functioning will be better in some states than in others; and it is those changes towards states associated with better functioning which constitute learning.

One of the benefits of a good model is that it helps us to see what questions we need to ask next. In the present instance, these are:

(a) What do we mean by 'state' when applied to a director system?
(b) What do we mean by 'better' when applied to its functioning?
(c) What are the connections between its different states, and better or worse functioning of a director system?

These are far-reaching questions which, in one way or another, will occupy us for the rest of this book. But a beginning can be made right away.

(a) The term 'state', applied to a director system, describes:
    (i)   the extent of its domain;
    (ii) the accuracy; and
    (iii) the completeness of the conceptual structures by which actuality is realized within, or mapped into, the director system;
    (iv) the skill with which it actualizes plans (i.e. translates plans into actions).

We are here distinguishing four components of the state of a director system. Later we shall consider others.

(b) 'Better', applied to the functioning of a director system, means:

    (i)   that it can function within a larger domain;
    (ii) that the conceptual structure it makes use of is more accurate; and
    (iii) more complete;

(iv) that the director system can take the operand to the goal state more quickly and reliably. (This is the meaning with which we shall hereafter use the term 'more skilfully'.)

For a director system to be better in each or all of these ways means that it can contribute more to the survival of the individual.

The connections between (a) and (b) can best be seen with the help of examples. Consider first a child finding its way home. The importance of this as a goal location needs no emphasis, for here he finds shelter, food, protection, and other forms of nurture. The universe of discourse is here a set of locations in the neighbourhood surrounding his home. The domain of the system by which he directs his footsteps homeward is simply the set of locations from which he can find his way, and the operand is his own body. If his legs are also capable of carrying him, the domain coincides with his prohabitat. (Reminder: a prohabitat is always with reference to some particular universe of discourse, stated or implicit.)

(i)   For a young child, this domain is likely to be quite small. As he gets older, its extent becomes greater by exploration and learning.

(ii) Within the outer boundary of this domain, there may be inaccuracies: a path which he thinks is a short-cut, but which actually ends up in someone else's backyard. By learning, this inaccuracy is corrected.

(iii) Within this outer boundary there may also be a wood having many paths which twist and turn, branch and join. A young child, once off the main path, may be unable to find his way back because his mental representation of the wood and its tracks is incomplete. With learning, there are more and more locations within the wood which connect with his existing mental map. So without increasing the extent of a domain, its interior can become more detailed and better connected, and thus contain more locations which form part of the domain.

(iv) Two children dwelling in the same house which for one was his home, while the other was a visitor, might well differ in a fourth component of their 'homing' director systems. From a given location each might be able to find his way home without getting lost. But one would do so better in the sense of 'more skilfully'. At each choice point, both would know which direction to take. But one would not know till he got to it, whereas the other, through greater familiarity, could anticipate and take the right direction without thought or hesitation. Another aspect of skill is greater reliability: fewer wrong turns. So assuming the two to be equally fleet of foot, nevertheless in a race home the child with greater familiarity would win.

Given the same plan, greater skill means putting it more efficiently into action, which means that less time is spent reaching the goal state. This means in turn that less time is spent in states of lower survival-contribution. Reverting briefly to our dinghy-sailor example, suppose that his operand is now the boat's painter (mooring rope), and that his goal state is for this to be securely tied to a mooring buoy. Both a novice and an adept may know the right knot for this purpose: but the latter can tie it more quickly and also with less chance of mistake, and so he spends less time in a state where his boat, and him in it, are not yet secured.

For our second example, take a car mechanic. The operand is now any car, and the universe of discourse is all the possible states which relate to its mechanical efficiency and roadworthiness. (So we exclude social components such as whether it is taxed and insured, or who owns it.)

(i)   A reasonable meaning here for the extent of his domain is the variety of cars which he knows how to service. 'Knows how to' is likely to coincide fairly closely with 'is actually able to': but not identically, since some cars may need special tools which he does not have.

(ii)   Clearly if his knowledge of a particular car is inaccurate, he will think he knows what to do when he doesn't, and will make mistakes which could be costly.

(iii)   If his knowledge is incomplete, he will not know what to do—but will be aware of this.

(iv)   A novice may know what to do, but an adept mechanic will still do it better, meaning more skilfully. In the present context, this means more smoothly and efficiently, with a more sensitive feel for the materials, an ear more attuned to the right engine sound. The skill component again refers to the plan-into-action stage. Its independence of the first three can be seen by imagining a competent mechanic encountering an out-of-the-way situation—for example, a car I once owned on which the securing nuts for the off-side wheels had left-hand threads. Though it was I who suggested that this might be what was holding up progress, once he realized the situation correctly my friend the mechanic finished the job much more quickly and smoothly than I could have done.

A new kind of director system

7.3   We have now conceptualized learning as a change of state of a particular class of entities, namely director systems; and changes of a particular kind, namely towards states in which these function better. 'Better' here means the same as it did in earlier chapters: contributing better to the survival of the organism.

Can changes of this kind be accounted for by any of the parts or processes within our present model of a director system as represented by Figure 12? It seems clear that they cannot. These changes are not random, but goal-directed; and they differ from the examples of goal-directed changes so far encountered only in one important particular:

the operand is itself a director system.

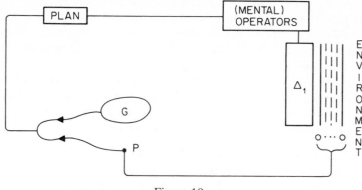

Figure 19

Figure 19 represents learning as now conceived. The triangle within the rectangle representing the operand is a Greek capital delta, signifying from now on a director system. We call it delta-one (Δ_1) because it is a *first-order* director system whose operand is something in the physical environment—something in actuality. The director system shown in detail in Figure 19 is the *second-order* system delta-two (Δ_2). Its operand is delta-one, and the function of delta-two is to take delta-one from a present state in which it does not function optimally (which includes not functioning at all) to a goal state in which it functions optimally.

What meanings should we assign to the other parts of this diagram? Some can be found right away, others will have to wait. Three of the lines representing relationships between delta-one and its environment represent components (a) (i), (ii), (iii) of the state of a director system as already described in Section 7.2. A possible interpretation of the circles O . . . O will follow later, in the section on reflective intelligence in Chapter 11.

The comparator of delta-two thus has at least three comparisons to make between the present state of delta-one, and the goal state. These correspond to components (i), (ii), (iii) already discussed; and can be seen to be subdivisions of the first mode of reality testing as discussed in Chapter 3. Where the second and third modes of reality testing come into the picture relates to the subject matter of Chapter 8 (co-operation between individuals) and Chapter 11 (reflective intelligence). Mode (ii) reality testing compares a person's own reality with those of others. A goal state of full consistency between these may often be set, but by no means always, particularly when there is disagreement with the results of modes (i) and (ii)—remember Galileo's famous remark 'Eppur si muove'. Mode (iii) reality testing compares relationships within a conceptual structure, particularly those of implication (e.g. if A is true, then B must also be true). The goal state is complete self-consistency within a particular universe of discourse. Modes (ii) and (iii) thus relate to other components of the state of a director system than those listed as (a) (i), (ii), and (iii) in Section 7.2.

The box marked PLAN in delta-two refers to whatever means are employed to bring delta-one towards states of better functioning, in the light of information from the comparator. Different kinds of plan thus distinguish different kinds of learning. These range from the most primitive, such as the conditioned reflexes investigated by Pavlov, through the learning of simple behaviours to satisfy basic physical needs around which the behaviourist school have centred their researches, to the formation of concepts and conceptual structures, the learning of language and learning mediated by language, and those higher forms of learning which we characterize as intelligent. Some of these kinds of learning can be found in quite primitive species, as well as in ourselves. Others are special to our own species, *Homo sapiens*, and constitute the evolutionary breakthrough mentioned in Section 1.10. It may be possible one day to subsume all these varieties of learning within a single model. But this is a task beyond the scope of the present book, and we shall here concentrate on the development of a model to support our thinking about intelligent learning.

While wishing to keep to a minimum the introduction of new terms, we do need a way of distinguishing between fixed director systems, and those in which those changes which we call learning can be brought about. This can, however, be done without introducing a new technical term, and I propose that we call these *teachable*. Most of the director systems concerned with the maintenance and repair of our bodies are innate, involuntary, and either unteachable or almost so. But the director systems by which a child finds his way, speaks, washes and dresses himself, solves mathematical problems, are all highly teachable. Learning thus involves the action of a delta-two system on a teachable delta-one system. Intelligence is a particular case of this—an advanced kind of learning. So far no assumption has been made about whether this delta-two is itself teachable.

These terms—learning and teachable—have now been given technical meanings which on the one hand are fully consistent with everyday usage, but on the other hand go far beyond this by formulating them in terms of special kinds of director system. The importance of this is that unlike some technical terms which separate our everyday from our scientific thinking, these form a bridge between the two.

Improved functioning not always due to learning

7.4   To learn is to become able to function better, but the reverse is not necessarily the case. Improved functioning may also result from a wide variety of other conditions, which we would not call learning. Two categories of such causes can be identified: there may be others.

(i)   Removal of hindrances to functioning: for example, rest after fatigue, removal of distractors such as noise, of internal distractors in the form of competing director systems. These, however, are not changes in state of the director system itself, and are already excluded by the initial formulation at the end of Section 7.1.

(ii) We will also wish to exclude changes in a director system which result from maturation, either of the sense organs or of the nervous system. By this is meant that the changes are genetically determined, but do not make their appearance until the individual reaches a certain age. Bird song in certain species comes into this category: though in others, the mature form of the song is partly innate and partly learnt.

This is not to say that the appearance of the behaviour is necessarily independent of the environment. Nest building, for example, necessarily depends on the availability of materials. But given these, the behaviour will appear in a form typical for the species, and is independent of the particular life history of the individual. In other words, the environment may influence whether or not the behaviour occurs, but not the form it takes. Against this we may contrast the wide variety of human dwellings. Within the same species, these range in design and material from igloos made from blocks of snow, tepees made with poles and stretched skins, to skyscrapers of concrete, steel, and glass.

Assumed environment

7.5 A more serious difficulty arises when we come to think about behaviour which shows every sign of having been learnt, yet which subtracts from rather than adds to the overall survival potential of the individual.

Here we must distinguish between two categories:

(i) There are learnt behaviours which are generally favourable to survival, but not on a particular occasion. For example, a person takes his usual train home, but on this occasion it crashes. He opens a can of soup for his dinner, but this one is tainted. His doctor gives him an antibiotic, but it is one to which he is allergic.

(ii) Some behaviours are such that on the one hand one cannot explain them on any other assumption than that they were somehow learnt; and yet it is equally difficult to explain them in terms of improved contribution to survival. A little boy, when given a biscuit, used to hold it above his head between bites. He himself did not know why he did it; but his father, who was a psychologist, traced the behaviour back to a dog belonging to a family they had been friendly with on holiday. This dog also liked biscuits, and it was necessary to hold one's own biscuit out of its reach.

By choosing examples of increasing strangeness, or striking lack of survival contribution, we would soon require a third category: that of neurotic and psychotic behaviours. But we are here concerned with normal functioning, not with psychopathology. The purpose of the present discussion is not to try to explain malfunctioning and breakdowns, but to test the present formulation of learning by seeing how it stands up against what appear to be counter-examples within the sphere of normal, everyday life.

For this we need the help of a concept borrowed from ethology, that of *an assumed environment*.

Nestling thrushes, when their mother appears above them with a worm, tilt up their heads and open wide their beaks: which makes good sense to us. But Tinbergen (1951) has demonstrated that they will also do so if a human hand, or even a stick, is held above them; which benefits them not at all. This particular behaviour, which is innate, is still pro-survival for the environment in which it evolved: namely, one in which moving overhead objects are more often worm-bearing mother thrushes than hands or sticks belonging to ethologists. We saw in Section 1.6 that an innate characteristic only has to be pro-survival more often than not to be selected, and this applies equally well to innate director systems as to innate physical characteristics. Once it has been selected, it is pro-survival (in the statistical sense) only *for an assumed environment*: one sufficiently like that in which it evolved. If this assumption is invalid, as it was in the example described earlier (Section 3.7) of the swallows imported to New Zealand, the director system may no longer take the operand to states which are pro-survival.

Learning always takes place within, and therefore relative to, an environment; and the resulting director systems will function successfully only (a) more often than not, and (b) for an assumed environment, which is not too different from that in which the learning took place. Looking back now to the examples in category (i) at the beginning of this section, we see that the behaviours are entirely appropriate to an assumed habitat in which trains seldom crash, canned soup is almost always wholesome, and patients allergic to a particular antibiotic are in a small minority. And the actions of the little boy used as an example for category (ii) seemed odd only because his parents were initially unable to relate them to the environment in which they had been learnt, and because the child had not noticed that his assumptions about the environment no longer held good in an important detail.

Both categories of the difficulty raised at the beginning of this section have thus been removed by seeing that the functioning of both innate and learnt director systems is to be understood in terms of probable success rather than certainty, and always relative to an assumed environment. Further understanding can be gained by taking this same line of reasoning a step further, and applying it to the processes by which, in terms of the present model, we explain learning. These too can only be innate, or learnt, or a combination of the two: so we must expect learning itself to result in better functioning not invariably, but once again, only probably. And the learning process itself will be appropriate only to an assumed environment.

The swallows already referred to have an innate director system for their winter migrations, assuming a northern hemisphere as environment. In contrast, indigo buntings, which navigate by the pole star, do not have an innate ability to recognize it. Instead they have an innate learning ability to learn which is the pole star. They identify it as the one which stays still, and about which the others rotate. This is appropriate to their natural environment. But if they are raised in a planetarium in which the (simulated) stars rotate about Betelgeuse[1] they will identify this as the pole star: and their subsequent outdoor navigation will lead them astray. (Emlen, 1975.)

The nestling thrushes which we have also used as examples have an innate method of identifying their mothers which, as we saw, is very primitive. In contrast to these, greylag goslings have an innate method of learning which animal is their mother, which in its way is equally primitive. Whatever living object they first see after hatching they identify as mother, and thereafter they will follow it. (Lorenz, 1952.) This assumes an environment in which this object is indeed, more often than not, the mother greylag goose. If, however, it is a human, he likewise will be treated as mother, and the goslings will direct their movements towards following him wherever he walks.

The assumed environments to which these two learning processes are appropriate are easy to distinguish: respectively, one in which the stationary star is the pole star, and one in which the first moving object seen is the mother goose. Since, however, it is intelligent learning in which we are primarily interested, the purpose of the foregoing discussion has been to lead up to the question: what is the assumed environment for which intelligent learning is appropriate?

The difficulty of answering this question lies in the apparent absence of assumptions about the environment: for an intelligent person can learn to direct his actions appropriately in polar regions and in the tropics, on land and sea, at the bottom of the ocean and even on the surface of the moon. So it looks as though part of the answer is just this: that the value of intelligent learning is that it can build appropriate director systems for survival almost anywhere, and is not restricted to any particular assumed environment.

This is, however, only part of the answer. Another part, as will continue to emerge from Chapter 9 onwards, is that certain qualities of the environment are indeed assumed: namely, that future events, though not identical with past, will follow similar patterns; that the universe is lawful and not capricious. The assumption that we live in a consistent universe is implicit in all efforts to find out what these consistencies are, whether by an eminent scientist or by a young child exploring the small world of his own house.

The concept of an assumed environment has been used in relation to three different kinds of director system; so before leaving the present section, it will be useful to review these. They are as follows:

(i)   Innate director systems, such as that of the nestling thrush. This assumes an environment in which moving objects which appear overhead are usually a food-bearing parent. Systems of this kind are not teachable.

(ii) Director systems which are (wholly or partly) the result of learning, such as that of the indigo bunting. This assumes an environment in which the star which appears stationary can be used as a pointer for the north. Systems of this kind can be taught either the right thing or the wrong thing, relative to the environment in which the organism will have to survive thereafter.

(iii) The systems which bring about learning. In the case of the indigo bunting, this assumes an environment in which the star which appears stationary while the bird is young, and that which does so when the bird is old enough to migrate, will be (a) the same star, (b) the north star.

The question of whether these last systems—those which bring about learning—are themselves teachable has not yet been discussed: nor are we assuming that all of them fit the model of a higher-order director system acting on a lower-order director system introduced in Section 7.3. This model has been introduced to help our thinking about intelligent learning, which is the subject of this book; and discussions of sub-intelligent kinds of learning are for this same purpose. Among other ways, they help us to see that many forms of learning, like innate director systems, are highly species-specific; and by contrast, to see that though it has made a beginning in other species, intelligent learning has reached its fullest development so far in man. So let us finish this section with examples appropriate to ourselves.

(i)   Sucking is an innate behaviour in human babies. It assumes an environment in which objects inserted between its lips are, more often than not, milk-yielding.

(ii) The *result* of learning to speak assumes an environment in which people in general speak the same language as that learnt within the family.

(iii) The *process* of learning to speak assumes an environment in which people speak, and that there are regularities of meaning and grammar.

Nurture

7.6   In Section 1.10 the beginning of the progressive evolution which has led to ourselves was ascribed to the early appearance of learning in combination with other characteristics with which it was specially favourable. Prehensile hands, erect posture, and opposed thumbs were mentioned. Many writers have stressed the importance of tool using, and others have taken the further step of suggesting that tools for killing were of particular importance. To my knowledge, few have emphasized nurture as an innate characteristic which would particularly favour natural selection for learning.

For the evolution of our advanced innate learning ability has been at the expense of other innate director systems. A baby crocodile, having hatched from its egg in the hot sands of the Nile, may never see its mother and never needs to. It is equipped with a complete set of director systems by which it is viable from the start. The young of many other species are not able at first to survive without nurture by one or both parents, during which time they develop both physically and behaviourally to a state of independent viability. Human young are physically helpless for longer than any other species, relative to total life span. Behaviourally too, they are initially less viable; but during their long childhood, they reach higher levels of expertise than any other species. By the process described in Section 1.11, each new generation uses the knowledge and skills accumulated by earlier generations to build up, under the direction of delta-two and of external teachers, its own complex of director systems.

Total viability now comes from two sources. We still have left some innate director systems, which together constitute the genetic part of our inheritance. That non-genetic inheritance which provides the rest of our total viability is what we call a culture.

This change in emphasis, from genetic to non-genetic inheritance, has implications which are too many and too far reaching to follow in the present volume. There is, however, one which is important, can be stated briefly, and is perhaps specially relevant here. The genetic characters of a species are carried in the germ cells of each individual. They are thereby safeguarded against loss in much the same way as would be a book of which copies were kept in every home. But a culture, particularly an advanced one such as our own, is widely divided among many individuals, none of whom possesses more than a fraction of the whole. A culture could be lost in a single generation. To see that it is not lost is one of the tasks of education, formal and informal: which is to say, the direction of learning in ways which ensure the continuance of the culture. The more advanced and complex the culture, the more carefully its members need to study the processes by which it is transmitted.

Emotions in relation to action and to learning

7.7 In Chapter 2, hypotheses were offered which related emotions and consciousness to the functioning of director systems. These were summarized at the end of that chapter (Section 2.12) and it will be helpful to review them before continuing. The next step is to relate these hypotheses to the model introduced in Chapter 5 and developed in Chapter 6 and the present chapter.

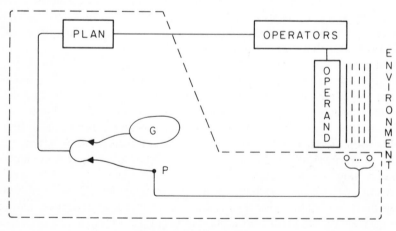

Figure 12 (repeated)

Looking at the above representation of a director system, emotions of pleasure and unpleasure, fear and relief, can now be formulated as outputs from the comparator signalling changes, towards or away from, goal states or anti-goal states. And having introduced the concept of a prohabitat as that part of the environment relative to which an individual can reach the goal states set by a particular director system, confidence and security are now signals to the organism that it is within its prohabitat, frustration and anxiety are signals that it is outside it. Table 1 (Section 2.4) may now be updated to show these connections with the model, as shown in Table 3. Within a prohabitat, a person feels both confident and secure; outside, he feels frustrated, or anxious, or both. (The difference here is because a prohabitat is a region within which a person can both achieve his goal states and avoid his anti-goal states; whereas he may be outside this prohabitat because of inability to do either, or both.)

The major hypothesis of this chapter is that intelligent learning[2] can be explained in terms of a second-order director system, delta-two, acting on a teachable first-order director system, delta-one. The first and simplest prediction from this hypothesis is that successful learning will be experienced as pleasurable in itself, since it signals that the operand delta-one is changing towards 'better' states, that is, states which contribute more favourably to the survival of the individual concerned. This is in accordance with our everyday

Table 3

	State perceived as changing	Signals from comparator	Knowledge of ability to change state	
			ability	inability
Goal state	Towards	Pleasure	Confidence	Frustration
	Away from	Unpleasure	-	-
Anti-goal state	Towards	Fear	-	-
	Away from	Relief	Security	Anxiety
			Signals that organism is	
			within	outside
			prohabitat	

experience. 'Better' here includes having more extensive domains; having available for use conceptual structures which are more accurate and complete; and possessing greater skills in putting plans into action. Again, everyday experience confirms that improvements of any or all of these is signalled by pleasure; and Papousek (1969) has clearly shown that infants as young as two or three months show behavioural signs of pleasure and joy from success in problem solving, without any material reward.[3]

An interpretation of what might be meant by anti-goal states, in the context of learning, must be postponed until Chapter 9, where we shall see that in certain learning situations, delta-one has to 'get worse before it gets better'. These worse states, in which temporarily it may be unable to function at all, evoke the emotional signals related to anti-goal states and can be a serious obstacle to learning.

Since two director systems are involved, delta-one and delta-two, we need to consider separately the emotional signals from each. These may be alike or different.

For an example of pleasurable emotions signalled at both levels, we have only to watch a child practising some new physical skill, such as riding a bicycle or diving from a springboard. Each time he succeeds in maintaining balance, or diving at all, he is achieving a goal state at one level; while each time he does this more skilfully, he is progressing towards a goal state at a higher level—a state of better functioning of his cycling or diving director systems. This double pleasure offers an explanation why the repeated practice so often observable in children is pleasurable for them and not boring There is pleasure at delta-one level from moving towards a goal state, and pleasure at delta-two level from progress towards greater expertise. And even if he falls off his bicycle and hurts himself, or his dive is a belly-flop, the unpleasure from the lower-order system is usually controlled by the pleasure of progress in learning.

Such mishaps do, however, call our attention to an important characteristic of every learning situation. As we have already seen (Section 6.11), these take place in frontier zones. They involve setting goals which the learner is not sure he can achieve. What is more, he is not sure that he can *learn* to achieve them. Risk is involved, which may be physical (e.g. trying to learn a new kind of dive), or to self-esteem (failure may make him both look and feel stupid). Confidence or frustration, security or anxiety, will now be signalled from two levels, delta-one and delta-two. In the next section we shall try to disentangle the emotions, often conflicting, from these two sources.

7.8 Consider an intellectual task at the delta-one level: say, translating an unseen prose passage from French into English. Since the learner has not seen this particular passage before, he cannot know for sure that he will be able to do so. His confidence cannot have the strength of knowledge, but only that of belief, derived from previous success at similar tasks. The more similar the tasks, and the easier the success, the stronger will be this belief. Success at the new task will reinforce this belief; a single failure will weaken it, probably not permanently; but repeated failure will sooner or later destroy the learner's confidence and replace it by frustration. How long he goes on trying, if the prose passage proves to be a difficult one, will depend on the degree of confidence he brings to the task initially. His chance of success, too, will depend partly on how long he goes on trying. So a good level of initial confidence tends to be a self-fulfilling prophecy: the learner is more likely to succeed because he believes he can. This piece of folk wisdom is explained in terms of the present model by saying that the temporary absence of pleasure, from the left-hand side of Table 3 (little or no progress towards goal state) is made up by a positive contribution (confidence) from the right-hand side. The table suggests further, that where there is a negative contribution from the left-hand side in the form of fear of failure (anti-goal), confidence will be replaced by frustration more quickly if success is not achieved. At this stage there is only one sure way to end the feeling of frustration, which is to un-set that particular goal and stop trying. But this is at the cost of further weakening the learner's confidence in his ability to succeed in tasks of this particular kind.

We now transpose this whole argument one stage up, to the delta-two level. The tasks at this level are not just doing, but learning to do. Pleasure (from the left-hand side of the table) signals that learning is progressing towards this goal state. Unpleasure signals that the delta-one system seems to be getting worse, not better. Confidence now relates to a belief by the learner that he can bring delta-one to a state of being able, in the present example, to translate passages of a new level of difficulty. Prohabitat refers to the intellectual regions within which a delta-two functions—brings delta-one systems to better states. So an academic, confronted with the task of learning to function as an administrator, may well perceive the situation as taking him outside his prohabitat, and experience frustration, or anxiety, or both. If, however, someone happens to speak some French, and wants to learn a little Italian, these prohabitats are sufficiently alike for the confidence gained in the former to be applied to the latter.

As at the delta-one level, this confidence is half the battle; and the successes it helps to bring about further reinforce this same confidence, in the way already described. Continued failure will have similar results, of the opposite kind. Processes at the delta-two level will again parallel those at the delta-one level, but with more lasting consequence for better or worse. For what is here involved is whether, for emotional reasons, effective (as against potential) learning ability is increased or decreased. Pleasure in learning, confidence in ability to learn, are pro-survival signals which result in the student pushing outwards the frontiers of his director system's domains, and improving their internal qualities. Frustration and anxiety have opposite effects, and lead not only to giving up trying to do certain tasks, but to giving up trying to learn to do them, and even to not attempting to learn to do other tasks which appear similar.

That strong emotions are often involved in learning situations is abundantly confirmed by experience. Those who need convincing should read John Holt's book, *How Children Fail*. (Holt, 1965.) The management of these emotional factors is an important part of the teacher-learner relationship which a few good teachers seem to have learnt intuitively, but many not at all. The difficulties are likely to be greater where the tasks are not self-chosen, but externally imposed, as is the case most of the time for younger pupils undergoing compulsory schooling. Having recognized that the learner's emotional vulnerability is a risk inseparable from many learning situations, what is much needed now is a systematic body of theory and practice whereby learners may be given the emotional support they need. With the help of the present model, it is hoped that these may be developed in future publications.

7.9 The insecurity connected with a learning situation is related to that particular universe of discourse, and it both can and needs to be compensated by feelings of confidence and security from other sources. This corresponds, in emotional signals, to the fact that our survival is the cumulative result of contributions from many prohabitats. So when the contribution from one of these is reduced by the individual being on the fringe of this particular prohabitat, or even outside it, the contributions from other sources must be fully assured and if possible increased.

In the case of children, who are still learners in so many of their prohabitats (and have also not yet fully developed their physical capacities), these contributions have to come from outside sources. This takes us back to the importance of nurture for the actualization of human potential, but adds a further requirement. Studies of children in institutions where all their physical needs are provided for, but with little personal attention, have shown them to be backward in physical development, in speaking and walking, and more susceptible to illness. (See for example Spitz, 1945.) It is now generally accepted that what is lacking in such cases is love. Cuddling, talking and listening to, playing with, and other actions which tell the child he is loved, provide the emotional signals by which a child gains from outside the confidence and security which he is as yet unable to achieve from his own limited mental and physical resources.

Poets, song-writers, sweethearts, and mothers, as well as some (though not all) religions, have long known the importance of love. Yet in a 700-page introductory textbook on psychology which I have beside me, deservedly regarded as a good one, the word 'love' does not appear in the index. Nor have I been able to find in the body of the text, by reading what was written under headings such as 'affect', 'emotion', any reference to it at all. So I must confess to some personal satisfaction that the present model offers the beginning of a bridge between our everyday experiences of personal relationships, in which love and liking, affection and goodwill, play an important part, and our scientific thinking about personal relationships, in which as yet these concepts play no part at all.

Nurture and teaching

7.10   As well as nurture and learning, nurture and teaching are also related. Adequate nurture must include not only enabling a child to survive while he learns and grows, but also teaching him some of the many things he must know, and be able to do, for survival outside the family. And the younger the child, the greater the element of nurture which a teacher needs to contribute.

Teaching is also an activity independent of nurture; and the learning model introduced in this chapter indicates that it is a more complex activity, involving more complex relationships, than is generally realized. In the past, one of the chief errors was in failing to take account of the self-directed learning of the student, and assuming that vigorous teaching was what was wanted. More recently there has been a shift of emphasis towards so-called 'discovery learning', in which the main contribution of the teacher is to provide suitable materials from which the student learns in his own way.

Neither of these approaches is based on an adequate theory of the teacher-learner relationship; nor, in my view, does such a theory yet exist. At least four director systems are involved: two in the learner, and two in the teacher. There is the teachable delta-one system of the learner, to which only the learner's own delta-two system has direct access. This makes teaching an indirect activity, in which part of the teacher's task is to collaborate with the learner's delta-two system, not to confuse or disrupt it by the wrong kind of intervention. Also involved is the teacher's own delta-two system, of which the main function in the present universe of discourse is to direct his own learning and planning of how to teach.

We shall return to this problem in Chapters 14 and 15, after further consideration of the interaction of director systems and of the learning process itself.

Open learning goals

7.11   In 5.12 we noted that:

> Sometimes a goal state is clearly and specifically represented in our mental models, but sometimes it is more open. We recognize it when achieved, but do not know in advance exactly what it will be like: a present for a friend, a melody to fit a particular poem, somewhere to live in our next job. This simply means that the concept representing the goal state is of a more general kind. Without having a specific example in mind, we know whether what we have arrived at fits the

concept or not. . . . To be able to distinguish between examples and non-examples is the criterion for having a concept. So open goals of this kind are simply those represented by more general concepts than the goal states in our introductory examples.

This applies equally to learning goals. Sometimes these can be clearly and specifically conceptualized: to learn bricklaying, to speak Italian, to solve second-order differential equations. Sometimes the goals are very general: to enlarge a particular domain, or improve its internal quality. Goals of this kind may never be reached.[4] Sometimes the learning goal lies somewhere between the specific and the very general, such as the solution to a problem. We do not know in advance what the solution will be, nor even for sure how to find it. Nevertheless, we know whether we have it or not, by whether or not it satisfies certain criteria—removes the background noise when tape recording, reconciles the two parties in a dispute, cures the common cold.

This answers the question: how do people know what they are trying to learn, until they have learnt it? It is true that until they have reached their learning goals, they do not know in full detail what these will be like, and their beliefs about how they can get there may be accurate and detailed, or vague. (Here is where a teacher can help.) But this is not to say that people do not know what they want to learn. So far as the particulars are concerned, they may not know: but at a more general level of conceptualization, they do.

Meta-learning

7.12 If it is accepted that teaching is an indirect activity, more complex than is usuall supposed, and if we also remember that learning is a natural activity from the earliest day of life onwards, independent of whether or not teaching is also involved, then we shall not be surprised to find that other things are learnt besides what is taught. Here is an example (Biggs, 1972).

A six-year-old said to me the other day: 'Give me a number and I'll double it for you.' I gave him 37 (he was calculating in his head). He said 'Two thirties that's sixty, two sevens that's fourteen, seventy-four.' He continued, 'Don't tell my teacher.' I asked why not since his method was a good one. The boy answered 'She makes me write it down and I don't understand her method, so I do it in my head and then I write it down her way and I always get my mark, so don't tell her.'

In the article from which this was taken, the above was quoted for a different reason. I give it here to introduce the concept of meta-learning. Without much help from his teacher the child had *learnt* how to double two-digit numbers; and he had also *meta-learnt* both how to keep intact the method he understood, and how to keep his teacher satisfied with him by not revealing that he was not using her method, and thereby to 'get his mark'. Quite good for a six-year-old!

The meaning of the term 'meta-learning', implicit in the foregoing, may be formulated as follows. Suppose that a person is consciously learning X. Also, that as a result of the learning situation of which X is a part, he also learns Y. Then we shall say that he meta-learns Y relative to X.

By 'relative to X' I mean more than just 'in addition to X'. While attending a lesson on a particular topic, pupils will learn the names of the textbooks used, where to sit, and much else which does not have any influence on the present or future learning of this topic. This is incidental learning rather than meta-learning. The meta-learning of Y relative to X means that the learning of Y influences the present or future learning or performance of X, in spite of Y being in a different universe of discourse from X. Here are some more examples.

Some years ago, at a summer camp, I was demonstrating to a group of boys a way of propelling a canoe without using a paddle, which they had not seen before. Known as 'hooching', it consists of standing near the stern of the canoe, and causing it to move forward by alternately half-crouching, and then swinging the body forward and upwards. (This is easier to demonstrate than to describe.) By watching and then imitating me, they could have learnt to do this themselves: but they would not even try. Then, after a while, one boy made the attempt, and soon succeeded. Within half an hour (since they had to take turns with the canoes) they were all doing it. What the first boy had demonstrated was not how to do it—this they had already seen—but the fact that one of themselves could easily learn to do it. Not until they had meta-learnt this were they willing even to attempt the learning of the new canoeing technique. They had the necessary physical skills (such as balance) and learning ability, as evidenced by the fact that some of them could soon perform this trick better than myself. But initially, they were not in a state of mind whereby they could use these abilities. The universe of discourse X was here that of canoeing; Y was the related, but different, one of their own learning ability for skills of this kind.

An important category of meta-learning thus relates to a person's conception of his own learning abilities, relative to learning goals of a particular kind. It is thus closely related to confidence, the effects of which were discussed in Section 7.8; and more generally, to the development of a person's self-image.

Another possible category relates to the learning methods themselves. If a child learns to read by the 'look and say' method, on meeting a written word he has never seen before the ways available to him are to ask somebody else who knows, or to guess. If on the other hand he has learnt phonically, he may well be able to work it out himself, either letter by letter, or by recognizing it as like a class of words he already knows. To the extent that he is thereby learning either to seek help when he doesn't know, or alternatively first to try to puzzle things out for himself, this is meta-learning. Unfortunately English spelling is often so irregular that the latter approach may prove fruitless. It would, however, be easy to use some cueing system (such as different colours) to tell children which new words are phonic, and which are irregular. From this, children would learn something about the nature of English spelling in general—that it is partly regular, partly irregular. This, and other higher-order generalities about the nature of this or other subjects, are important and affect future learning. Whether or not one describes them as meta-learning will depend on whether one regards them as belonging to the same universe of discourse as the subject itself—on how one defines one's universe. But if, from the colour-coded readers, children also learn that there are different kinds of learning, associative learning and learning with understanding, and that these are both necessary and are appropriate to different learning tasks—if they learn this, it is meta-learning of a valuable and far-reaching kind.

7.13 Meta-learning is explained in terms of the present model by noting that almost any object or event can be conceptualized in more than one way, which is to say in more than one universe of discourse. So progress towards a goal state in one universe may also entail progress towards, or away from, a goal or an anti-goal in a different universe. Examples: a child giving a right answer, and his teacher being pleased with him; a child showing interest in his work, and classmates calling him a 'licker' or a 'teacher's pet'. Similarly, the achievement of particular learning goals may be conceptualized in more than one universe of discourse. One of these is likely to be conscious, and if teaching is also involved this will be overt: the others may be unconscious. The conscious learning goal could be conceptualized within a universe of discourse of some academic subject, such as mathematics, French, geography; or it may be some physical skill such as turning a cartwheel, skateboarding. But simultaneously, success or failure may be conceptualized as being clever or stupid, agile or clumsy. This double conceptualization does not necessarily always take place, but given the importance of these other universes, it is likely that it happens more often than we are aware of; and it is especially when it happens unconsciously that meta-learning can take place which has long-term effects.

The ways in which the model can help are two. In the case of young learners, possession of this concept of meta-learning can enable parents, teachers, and other adults who have the care of children to realize when it happens or is likely to happen; and so to make conscious and intentional, favourable kinds of meta-learning, and to try to prevent unfavourable kinds. In the case of mature learners, it can enable them to look for and identify earlier meta-learning in themselves which may be hindering their progress in some learning task of their own choice. Either way, the effect will be to make accessible to consciousness, to intelligent consideration or reconsideration, and to a person's own intention and choice, areas of learning which have hitherto remained unconscious and thereby involuntary.

7.14 In the present chapter, learning has been conceived as a goal-directed activity by which director systems are changed towards states which make possible better functioning, and thus increase the viability of the organism. In the course of the chapter the preliminary formulation, though remaining basically unchanged, was modified in two ways. The first was to exclude maturation—the appearance of characteristics which, though genetically based, were not apparent at birth or in early life. It was also necessary to take account of the evolutionary process by which both delta-one and delta-two systems have reached their present form. This has resulted in director systems which function successfully, that is, take the operand to the goal state in actuality, 'more often than not'. Only if the environment were completely unchanging, so that future patterns of events were identical with the past, would a 100 per cent success rate be possible. 'Optimal' now takes on a new meaning when applied to a director system: namely, that of 'best fit' between its functioning and the only partially predictable environment, leading to the greatest achievable success rate.

This averaging process can also be seen at work in the way a delta-two system builds up the functioning of the delta-one system on which it acts. Clearly, it is non-adaptive to learn on the basis of a single event. A balance is needed between learning as fast as possible, and learning on the basis of a large enough sample of actuality. This brings into relief the importance of early learning, and in particular:

(i) that it should be a true sample of situations which will be encountered in later life; and

(ii) as will be seen in Chapter 9, that it leads to the construction of sound conceptual foundations on which to build more advanced learning.

7.15 In this chapter, we began by recalling one of the main points of Chapter 1. This is that our own species has been naturally selected for one characteristic above all, that of adaptability. Innate director systems, largely predetermined for the lifetime of an individual, have been replaced by an ability to learn which has been conceptualized in this chapter in terms of the model of a director system introduced in Chapter 5. From this beginning, the following are the chief ideas which were developed:

(i) *Learning is a goal-directed change of state of a director system towards states which, for the assumed environment, make possible optimal functioning.*

(ii) *Intelligent learning is now conceptualized as a process involving two director systems. These are:*

   (a) *a director system delta-one, whose state can be changed in this way. Such a director system is described as teachable.*

   (b) *a director system delta-two, whose operand is the director system*

> described in (a), and whose function is to take it towards states which make possible optimal functioning.

(iii) The emotional signals described first in Chapter 2 operate in both systems, and must be understood as an important feature of the process of learning.

(iv) While an individual is learning relative to a particular prohabitat, he needs to feel greater security relative to other prohabitats.

(v) Since a child is learning relative to many prohabitats, he needs from others the actual support of physical nurture, and the emotional security of knowing himself to be loved.

Notes for Chapter 7

1. Betelgeuse is a bright star in the constellation of Orion.
2. And possibly other forms of learning too. I am not excluding these from possible applications of the model, but only from the present part of this enterprise.
3. Having first learnt to turn on a light by moving his head to the left, an infant can learn successively to turn the light on by a head movement to the right, then left followed by right, and in some cases as complex a sequence as right, right, left, left. Once each new learning task is mastered, interest falls until a new one is presented. A fuller description of this and related experiments may also be found in Bower's valuable book, *Development in Infancy*. (Bower, 1974.)

4. Yet all experience is an arch wherethro'
   Gleams that untravelled world, where margin fades
   For ever and for ever when I move.

   (From 'Ulysses': Tennyson, 1885)

CHAPTER 8

Interaction between Director Systems

Supporting, inhibiting, co-operating, co-existing

8.1   We are now in a position to examine further the differences between the two examples which were used at the beginning of Chapter 1 (Section 1.2) to illustrate the major difference between the 'stimulus–response' way of thinking and the present approach. The interaction which takes place between the cue and the billiard ball is that of a physical force. That between the experimenter and the child is *an interaction between two director systems*.

8.2   Before going any further, it may be useful to consider the possible argument that the sound waves produced by the experimenter act like a physical force on the eardrums of the child. This is true in a way: but the force involved is so much smaller that a difference in size becomes a difference in kind. The energy of the sound waves is infinitesimal compared with that which would be used by the experimenter if he physically lifted up the child, carried him across the room, and put him in a seated position on the chair. Even a small fraction of the latter energy in the form of sound waves would be painful and injurious to the eardrums of both experimenter and child.

   The essential component of what passes between these two is not physical force or energy, but *information*. Though some kind of physical basis is necessary as a carrier for the information, the energy levels involved are very low compared with those necessary for the physical movement of the child, either by his own operators or those of the experimenter. And in general, director systems use relatively very small amounts of energy to determine the manner of application of the much larger amounts of energy used by the operator systems on which they act. An important characteristic of their sensors is their ability to derive information from very small physical changes, at very low energy levels. (This explains the point raised at the end of Section 5.8.)

8.3   The environment in which we, and all organisms, have to be viable in many ways if we are to survive is made up of objects which are not in general[1] goal-directed; and living organisms, especially our fellow human beings, which are.

As might be expected, the nature and properties of the former are much easier to understand. Our collective knowledge of these is embodied in sciences such as physics, chemistry, electrical and mechanical engineering; and their application through modern technology has given us considerable mastery of the inanimate part of our environment. Because the ways of thinking developed for these purposes have been so successful, it has been easy to make the mistake of using the same kinds of mental model for the second category.

But if A, B, C, D, ... are persons who are all parts of each other's environment, then everything which A does in the process of moving towards his goal states changes the environments in which B, C, D, ... are moving towards their goal states. So although these goal states may remain the same, the activities are likely to vary, and so in turn to affect what A does. Now apply this argument simultaneously to B, C, D, ... and it is easy to see that the complexity of all the possible interactions is likely to be far beyond the reach of our presently available techniques of thinking. What becomes surprising is no longer the generally low level of success of governments and management, but the fact that they have any success at all.

At a more general level, problems of this kind come into the fields of politics, sociology, economics, social psychology, etc., and as such are outside the field of the present volume. But there is an old Chinese saying, 'A journey of a thousand miles begins with a single step'; and it is my hope that the mental model here offered will take us a step or two in the right direction. It can help us to ask at least some of the right questions: the main ones being (in this chapter), 'What are the conditions for intelligent interaction?'; and (in Chapter 13), 'In view of the aforesaid complexity of possible interactions, how do we manage even as well as we do?'

8.4 If A is part of B's environment, a change by A towards A's goal state must have one of the following results.

(i)   B is nearer B's goal state.
(ii) B is further from B's goal state.
(iii) B's distance (in a general sense) from his goal state is unaffected.
('Nearer' can include the goal state being reached; 'further' can include it being impossible.)

In the first case, an increase in the probability of A's reaching his goal state brings about an increase in the probability of B's reaching his goal state (and this is what we mean by 'nearer'). Loosely, we might say for short 'A helps B'. But this might be taken as implying intention on the part of A, which goes beyond the original formulation. Compare these two examples.

(a)   A bee collects nectar from my apple trees, and thereby pollinates their flowers, which increases the probability that the trees bear apples.
(b)   A mother buys food from a grocer, cooks and serves it for her family.

These have something important in common, in that the activity of the former (bee; mother) is favourable to the survival of the latter (species of apple by producing seed and myself by eating the apple; the family). There is also an important difference. The mother intends to improve the survival probability of her family; but (to the best of our knowledge) the bee is quite unaware of the benefits to other organisms of its nectar-gathering.

Whenever an activity of A results in an increased probability that B reaches a particular goal state, we shall say that this activity of A *supports* B. If A intends this, we shall say that A *helps* B. With this usage, the bee's activities are *supportive* for the propagation of the tree and/or for my eating of its apples; and the mother is *helping* her family to eat.

Supporting, and helping, can be direct or indirect; and we may also include in their meanings activities of A which help B to avoid anti-goals. So the activities of a fireman in putting out a fire in my house are helpful to me and my family; and supportive to the birds nesting under my eaves, of whose existence the fireman is unaware.

Turning now to the second of the results listed at the beginning of this section, we need corresponding terms for the general case and for that in which there is intention. For these we shall use 'inhibits' and 'obstructs'. Thus we would say that the noise made by workmen outside while doing their job *inhibits* my own efforts to give a lecture, and those of my students to learn from it; and that a heckler who interrupts a political speech with the intention of impeding the speaker's efforts to communicate is *obstructing*.

We often encounter cases in which A helps B, and also B helps A. This reciprocal help we shall call *co-operation*. Reciprocal obstructing we shall call *conflict*. And finally, the third state of affairs in which neither one supports or hinders the other (intentionally or otherwise) we shall call *co-existing*.

8.5 Supporting and inhibiting, helping and obstructing, co-operating and conflicting, refer to particular goal-directed activities and therefore to specific universes of discourse. The goal states themselves may be the same for A and B, or they may not.

Suppose that my wife and I are shopping together. We go first into a food shop, then into a photographic shop. In the first, my wife and the shopkeeper co-operate, I and the shopkeeper co-exist; whereas in the second, it is the other way round. In neither case is the goal of the shopkeeper the same as ours. His is to acquire money, ours is to acquire food or a camera film. On the other hand, if my wife is helping me to back our car into a narrow parking space, both the operand (the car) and its goal location are the same for both of us.

Within the same overall situation we can often distinguish more than one universe of discourse: and there can be co-operation in one, conflict in another. Though the shopkeeper and ourselves are in co-operation over their wishes to sell us their goods, ours to buy, there is some degree of conflict where the actual price is concerned. Their goal is to obtain the highest price they can, ours is to pay no more than we have to. Or we may recall the example of a child doing a jigsaw puzzle. He may have two goals simultaneously: to put a particular piece in its right place, and to do this unaided. So an adult whose thinking is confined to the first universe may find that what he intends as help is construed otherwise by the child, in the second universe. Whether the adult's intervention is regarded as inhibiting or obstructing will depend on how the child also construes the adult's intention.

Freedom

8.6 We must now consider two major differences between the simple mechanical examples of goal-directed systems we began with, and the human examples which are our main interest.

The goal state of an oven thermostat is set by the cook; that of a ship's steering gear is set by the helmsman. These are designed and constructed to fulfil as efficiently as possible the intentions of cook or helmsman: they are not capable of setting their own goals.

But living organisms in general, and humans in particular, can and do set their own goals. We have also seen (Chapter 1 onwards) that a very general factor underlying the choice of goals is that the properties of these goal states contribute favourably to the survival expectancy of the organism or species. The organism may or may not be conscious of this: the bee gathering nectar is not, the housewife buying food is if she cares to think about it. But whether we are specifically aware of it or not, the selection and achievement of our individual goal states, is, for each one of us, related to our own survival.

So it is hardly surprising that being able to choose and pursue our own goals is itself a goal state which is widely sought. We call it *freedom*. Wealth, power, and status[2] are sought after largely because they have attached to them the important property that their possessors are more able to choose their own goals, and also those of others.

The is the first difference between the mechanical and human examples; and the second is closely related to it. The goal states of an oven thermostat or a steering mechanism are set physically from outside by turning a dial, setting a pointer on a scale, or the like. But in our own case, no one but ourselves has direct access to our own mental processes. So to talk about A setting B's goal state, when B is a person and not a machine, could never be more than a shorthand for an indirect and often complex process. Since it would be easy to forget this, and since the difference is an important one, we shall not risk losing sight of it by any such abbreviation.

This is not to say that A cannot influence the working of B's director system; but rather to emphasize that what passes between their director systems can only be information. This may be information relevant to a goal chosen by B; and if it is also accurate, and is construed by B as accurate and relevant, then A is helping B. This is one of the commonest ways in which we help each other. If it is inaccurate, then A is inhibiting or obstructing B by distorting the functioning of B's director system, often for A's own ends. Propaganda in warfare, and the 'hidden persuaders' of Vance Packard (1957) are examples of the latter.

Another kind of information which A can give refers to the probable result if B sets and pursues a particular goal. If, moreover, A is himself in a position to bring about this result, then A is in a power relationship towards B. Under such conditions A may seem to set B's goal states. According to the present model, however, A is *choosing* these goal states; but it is still B who is *setting* them, albeit with diminished freedom as a result of inducements or threats from A.

Table 4

	B has more important (to B):	
	(a) *goals*	(b) *anti-goals*
which A can:		
1. *unilaterally* (e.g. by control over B's environment, physical or social; by superior physical force; by possession of a weapon).	*provide for B,* or *allow to B* (by not obstructing)	*impose on B*
2. *by agreement*	*help B to reach*	*help B to avoid*

These conditions will be effective if and only if B knows of, or believes in, them.

Four main categories can be distinguished, in which B sets his goal as a result of information from A, and these are set out in Table 4. Here is an example of each category.

1(a) (A is a parent, B a school child.)
'If you finish your homework by 7.30, you can watch "Startrek"'.

1(b) (A is the local authority, B is a motorist leaving his car at a parking meter.) 'If you overstay your time, a fine will be imposed.

2(a) (A is a medical practitioner, B is a patient.) 'Take one of these capsules 3 times daily after meals'.

2(b) (A is the writer of an instruction manual which comes with a calculator I have just bought, B is myself.) 'CAUTION. Before recharging, check to make sure that the switch on the charger is set at the line voltage corresponding to your AC outlet.'

Notwithstanding the wording, 1(a) and 1(b) are power relationships. A commands, B obeys. And in spite of the appearance of an order, 2(a) and 2(b) are relationships in which A helps B. It is because people usually dislike receiving orders that we commonly take care to avoid the appearance of this by the use of phrases like 'Please (short for 'If *you* please'); 'It might be a good idea if you . . . '. Identifying which are in fact orders, however politely given, and which are genuine suggestions, is part of the process of learning in a particular culture or sub-culture.

Setting one's goals as instructed by someone else always implies some loss of freedom, which will be accepted only for power reasons 1(a) and (b), or for goal reasons 2(a) and (b). The former cannot be ignored, and understanding is an intelligent person's best defence against misuse of power, whether he be in the position of A or of B. In the context of the present volume, however, our main concern is with the second pair of categories: which is to say, with helping and co-operation.

The positive-sum principle

8.7 If B accepts help from A, we may suppose that he does so because he believes that he is thereby better able to reach his goal state, and this outweighs the reduction of freedom involved. We shall also come upon examples where the help received from A does not involve B's allowing A to set his goals.

It is not so easy to see, in terms of the present model, why A should help B, since while he is doing so, A may be less able to pursue his own goals.

The explanation to be offered is based on what I call 'the positive-sum principle'. This term is an adaptation of one found in games theory, 'zero sum'. The latter is used to describe a game in which *A wins* implies *B loses*, and A's gain is equal and opposite to B's loss. In the absence of sales tax, value-added tax, and the like, the financial side of shopping is a zero-sum transaction: the amount by which the shopkeeper is richer is equal to that by which the purchaser is poorer. Value-added tax turns it into a negative-sum transaction: the money retained by the shopkeeper is less than that spent by the purchaser. If as part of a sales promotion the shopkeeper accepts a coupon as part payment, afterwards receiving cash from the manufacturer in exchange for the coupon, then so far as purchaser and shopkeeper are concerned it is a positive-sum transaction.

A simple example of a positive-sum helping situation can be found whenever A gives and B receives information useful to B in reaching his goal. If I ask the way somewhere, the time spent by a passer-by in telling me may be less than a minute: the time saved by me in not having to search for the place myself, may be more than an hour. Telling someone how to do something is a simple extension of this idea. It should also be noted that while in the examples just given gain or loss may be quantifiable, this is not always the case.

Even though B's gain is greater than A's expenditure (in money, time, or any other contributor to survival), we have not yet fully explained why A should be willing to incur this expenditure. A very understandable reason would be that, at the same or a future time, B will reciprocally help A. If the second situation is also positive-sum, then overall both are better off than they would be if neither had helped the other. This may seem rather calculating: the next paragraph will make it less so.

It would be an oversimplification to say that one person helps another only in the expectation that the other will help him, at the same or a future time. Though this may sometimes be so, it is quite as often the case that the one who has received the help has a friendly desire to reciprocate; or at the lowest, feels under an obligation to do so.

Where more than two persons are concerned, it is not necessary for the giver of help to receive it reciprocally from the receiver. If A helps B, who helps C, who helps . . . , who in turn helps A, we still have a positive-sum situation overall. And more generally, all we need is a group of people, who over a period of time help each other in an assortment of positive-sum situations. For such a group as a whole, the resulting interactions will over this period of time be positive-sum. The long-term nature of this process is worth emphasizing. The kind of help which is most needed will vary greatly between individuals, and from time to time. The person best able to help, and who is available to do so, will vary likewise. So if a group of people are, in many different ways, helpful to each other as and when needed, then over a long period the total interactions are likely to be positive-sum to a high degree. For this to be successful, however, there must be precautions to exclude cheaters: i.e., those who accept help but do not give it. These precautions, in a large group, take the form of rules (explicit or otherwise) with means such as shame, punishment, and guilt to enforce the rules.[3] We can see the same principle at work in complex culturally determined exchanges of benefit such as trade and the use of money.

Organisms and organizations are both complexes of interacting goal-directed systems. What these have in common is that their total interactions are positive-sum. While they remain together, their collective survival expectation is increased, and so is the average for its members.

In the case of an organism, all the parts are physically connected; whereas in an organization, the members are connected by the passage of information. This is one major difference. Another is that the physical structure of an organism is genetically determined, and so to a large extent are the relationships between the director systems—though in man, learning also has a part. In organizations, the structure is for the most part learnt by its individuals (though there may be innate contributions). An organization usually relates to a particular universe of discourse, and is positive-sum specifically with respect to goals within this universe. Both the goals, and the rules which govern the behaviour of the members, are often made explicit in written form.

So the resemblance between organizations and organisms should not be pressed too hard. It is an analogy, not a homology.

A general discussion of organizations would be inappropriate to the present volume, and would also take us too far afield. Here, our main concern is to relate the present model of intelligence to the inescapable fact that in the course of our lives we all belong to a number of organizations, and to various other human groups ranging from families to nations and beyond. The implications of this fact are in three main areas. The first of these, which will be followed up later in this chapter, is consideration of the elementary conditions necessary for interactions between individuals to be positive-sum. The second, which will be developed further in subsequent chapters, is consideration of interactions between intelligences—the conditions under which these are positive-sum. And the third, which can here be no more than mentioned, is the developmental aspect: the ways in which family, school, and other social influences affect the actualization of the potential conferred by innate intelligence.

Co-operation considered further

8.8 What are we going to call an organization? Unless it is positive-sum, it will not survive as such, so this is a necessary criterion; but not sufficient, or the term becomes nearly all-embracing. A swarm of bees and an apple orchard are positive-sum in their interactions, but we would not call this combination an organization. The relation is mutually supportive, but not co-operative since we cannot attribute intention to either the bees or the trees. Such a system in a complete form we call a *mutualism*. Suppose now that a smallholder deliberately sets up a hive of bees in his orchard. I propose that we do call this an organization, on the grounds that the smallholder is intentionally bringing the organisms concerned into a positive-sum interaction. These are his operands, and the goal state which he has conceived and brought about is that the bees should fertilize his fruit trees while gathering nectar, thereby also providing him with honey. If the bees die, he will deliberately replace them. This does not happen in a mutualism.

More generally, for a complex of goal-directed systems to be regarded as an *organization* I propose three criteria.

(i)   It is positive-sum.
(ii) There is at least one director system (which will be called an *organizer*) whose operands are these other goal-directed systems, and whose goal state is a positive-sum interaction between them.
(iii) The organizer intends this.

We can now talk about 'the organization of behaviour' for both organisms and organizations, meaning simply that there is some kind of direction which keeps these in a positive-sum relationship. This direction may be innate, or learnt, or a combination of both. It may be done by a single organizer, or by several, or shared among all. In an organization there is intention to organize; within an organism there may be, or not.

A mutualism comes into existence, and survives, because of the mutually supportive interactions between its member organisms. Lacking an overall direction which has brought these into such a relationship and keeps them there in the face of internal and environmental changes, a naturally occurring mutualism does not meet our criteria for an organization. (But a similar system set up and maintained by a biologist would do so.)

Some of the social systems to which we belong are more like mutualisms than organizations. The members are mutually supportive, but more as a result of an overall settling-down process, a mutual shaping of behaviour, than by an overall direction. There are systems of this sort which seem to work very well, and show considerable ability to adjust their internal relationships in the face of change: for example, a family as the children grow older; a city as the style of living changes. Others, however, seem able to adapt either not at all, or only at a cost of hardship and suffering to some or all of their members: for example, the marriages and families which do break up; the cycle of boom and slump which industrialized nations seem unable to avoid. The kind of knowledge we need if we are to make any progress in solving problems of this kind is what may be called social intelligence: that which helps pairs and groups of individuals intentionally to *direct* their interactions in ways conclusive to 'the greatest good of the greatest number'. General goodwill, a desire to help other people and put society to rights, is good as far as it goes, but is not enough. To help persons who are ill, a little benevolence plus a lot of medical knowledge is more successful than any amount of benevolence by itself.

With this in mind, even a small beginning—just a toehold—in understanding what are the conditions for intelligent social relations would be worth while. And while working on this, we should recall that as here conceived, intelligence is not only a cognitive activity. Emotions too are involved.

The kind of co-operation required when two people together move a heavy object—say a chest of drawers from one room to another—is so simple that we hardly think about it. By thinking about it in terms of the present conceptual model, however, some useful general points can be made.

The operand and its goal location must be the same for both persons; and the process by which this agreement was reached may have been simple, or may have involved discussion and negotiation. At first it might appear that both must be using the same plan. So far as successive states of the operand are concerned this is so—for example, whether to take the drawers out before moving: it would not be mutually helpful if one tried to do this while the other tried to start lifting. But there may well be differences in the ways in which the two have to direct their muscular energies. One may need to pull while the other pushes, or to walk backwards while the other walks forwards. Vertically, their energies must be in the same direction and roughly the same in amount. So the individual plans must be (i) compatible, (ii) complementary. This takes the positive-sum principle a step further. By 'complementary' is meant that whatever the two plans add up to must be a unified overall plan which enables the combination of director systems to *function*: to take the operand to its goal state. We remember also that this depends on adequate *capacity* of the operators. In the present example the whole object of the co-operation is to do a job which is beyond the muscular capacity of one person. There is also *intention* to co-operate, and some kind of overall *direction* which maintains the positive-sum relationship: in this case, probably informal and shared. If the object is heavier and more persons are involved—say, a boat to be moved—the overall direction is more likely, by general consent, to be taken over by one person. And even when only two persons are concerned, much the easiest way to reach a unified plan and follow it successfully may be for one person to plan and direct the operation.

A slightly more complicated example is provided by the co-operation of two persons in backing a car into just the right position for hitching on a boat trailer or a caravan. The operand here is the car, and moving it as required is beyond the capacity of muscular power; so mechanical energy is put to work. Here the problem is to direct it accurately enough, a function which neither person can perform alone. The one in the driver's seat has a clear mental representation of the goal location of the car, but he cannot see the present location of the part which matters—the towing hitch. If his range of vision could be suitably extended (e.g. by a mirror) he could function unaided. In practice, however, he and his helper are likely to couple their director systems together. The kind of way in which this may be done is by the co-driver saying, 'Left hand down . . . now right hand down a little . . . keep as you are now . . .'. If the car is now moving in just the right direction, the co-driver may then say, 'Two yards . . . one yard . . . six inches . . . that's it'.

Two different kinds of coupling are involved here. At the last stage, when the car is backing straight on, the contributions are as presented in Figure 20a. (For a reminder of what the parts of these diagrams represent see the whole of Section 5.10.)

Since the driver cannot see the towing hitch, his vision is not contributing to the combined function and so no sensor is shown in his diagram. He also has no representation P of the present location of the operand, and although he has a clear conception of its goal state he cannot compare present state and goal state. His comparator is thus also inoperative, and is therefore not shown in the diagram. So the most useful information for the co-driver to give him at this stage is comparative information, and this is shown in the arrowed dotted lines pointing out of the co-driver's director system and into the driver's. What connects the two is not shown in the diagram: it is the verbal information 'Two yards . . . one yard . . . etc.'. This emphasizes that another requirement for the coupling of two director systems is a method for the giving and receiving of information: a shared coding and decoding system. By using the information which comes from the co-driver's comparator, the driver can put into effect his own simple plan: which is roughly 'If some distance from goal location, back at a moderate speed. If near goal location back very slowly. If at goal location, stop.'

At the earlier stage of the operation, when direction as well as distance from the goal location have to be taken into account, the comparative information required by the driver would be harder to give and receive though still possible. Experience has shown that it is easier to bypass the driver's plan and use that of the co-driver, so that the driver turns the wheel to right or left just as the co-driver would do if he could reach it. The coupling is now as shown in Figure 20b.

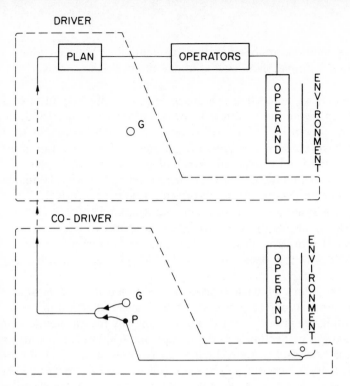

Figure 20a

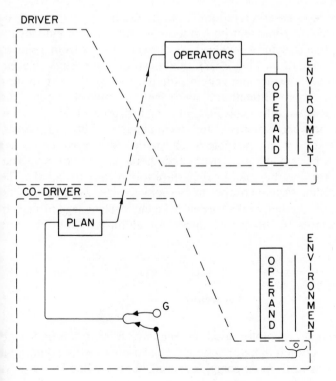

Figure 20b

In both these methods of co-operation, compatibility between plans is arranged by using a simple plan, located in one director system only.

8.9 In Section 8.7, we noted that if a group of people are helpful to each other as and when needed in a variety of ways and over a long period, the total interactions are likely to be positive-sum to a high degree. And in Section 8.8 we have noted that minimal requirements for co-operation are that the goal states of individuals are compatible, and that their plans are complementary. Also, that there has to be a shared coding/decoding system by which information can pass between the director systems concerned.

In the long-term situation even these minimal requirements are not best met if they have to be set up anew for each co-operative situation. And compatibility is not transitive. That A's plan is compatible with B's, and B's plan is compatible with C's, does not imply that A's plan is compatible with C's.

If, however, the plans of each individual are based on widely shared conceptual structures, a long step has been taken in the direction of overall compatibility within the group. This helps to explain why (as was pointed out in the last paragraph of Section 4.2) for acceptance within a profession or social group, it is necessary to share their inner realities. Those who do not will perceive actuality differently, and co-operation will be more difficult. The greater the number of persons involved and the greater the variety of situations in which co-operation is required, the greater becomes the need for a shared reality which is consistent both internally and between individuals. Where the conceptual structures involved are derived directly from a shared actuality (as in the case of backing a car), this consistency is easily achieved. As they become more abstract and general, the techniques of reality testing by mode (i) become more difficult and specialized; but the same principle, appeal to experiment, is still involved, and a high degree of co-operation remains possible between scientists and technologists. Where, however, mode (i) reality testing is not possible at all, myths, ideologies, and other forms of shared inner reality take over; and there may be strong social pressures against 'rocking the boat' by departure from orthodox beliefs. The shared coding/decoding system now becomes a common language: such as the common language of a nation, or the specialized technical language of a group of scientists, adherents to the same religion, or enthusiasts for the same sporting activities.

Hierarchies

8.10 The two simple examples used in Section 8.8 were of brief and informal couplings between director systems. The co-operative working of a big ship by her crew is vastly more complex overall, but is suitable for our next example for several reasons. The operand is still easily identifiable—it is the ship itself. We can separate out one set of couplings for consideration: that involved in its navigation. We have used this example before, so we can continue where we left off. And perhaps surprisingly, the nature of the couplings involved is simple.

We recall that a ship, like a large car, has powered steering. The helmsman sets the goal position for the rudder, so the universe of discourse for the steering mechanism is the set of possible angular deflections of the rudder.

For much of the time, the navigating officer simply tells the helmsman what course to steer. The helmsman compares the present direction in which the ship is pointing with the goal direction set by the navigator, and via an appropriate plan sets the goal positions for the rudder so as to turn the ship to the goal direction and keep it there. (We may note in passing an extension of the helmsman's sensors by the ship's compass. Out of sight of land, the helmsman cannot see whether the ship is pointing towards Southampton or New York.) The universe of discourse for the helmsman is the set of possible courses for the ship.

The navigator (as such) functions in a third universe of discourse, namely the set of possible locations to which the ship can be taken in safety. His goal location is set by some higher command—the captain, the owners, or (if a naval vessel) someone in the admiralty.

So a person at this top level in the chain of command only has to decide 'New York' or 'Gibraltar', and the three director systems of the navigator, the helmsman, and the steering mechanism, coupled together so that they function as one complex director system, will direct the powerful energies of the ship's engines in such a way as to take it there.

The coupling involved here is of the simplest possible kind. Each director system unilaterally decides the goal state of the next: either literally, as in the case of the helmsman who physically sets the pointer which determines the goal position for the rudder, or in the indirect sense of Section 8.6. For short, we say that one *commands* another. So far as the navigator and helmsman are concerned, we are simply giving a more precise meaning to an everyday word. If we also say that the helmsman commands the steering mechanism, this simply recognizes that the two relationships are effectively the same. The inverse relationship is, of course, *obeys*.

An organization whose members are related in this way is called a *hierarchy*. A hierarchy has the great advantage of simplicity, and the more numerous the members whose functions have to be co-ordinated, the greater becomes the need for this. Two persons moving a chest of drawers can afford to discuss where to put it, and ask politely 'Do you prefer to carry the upper or the lower end on the stairs?' A crew of several hundred cannot afford this. In terms of our present formulation, the combination would not function as a unified director system: it would not be positive-sum.

We can see more clearly why this is so by counting the number of possible interactions. Where four director systems, A, B, C, D, are coupled in strict

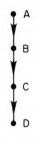

Figure 21

hierarchy, the number of interactions possible is only 3 (see Figure 21). Rearrange these so that two-way interaction is possible between any pair, and the number of possible interactions is 12 (see Figure 22).

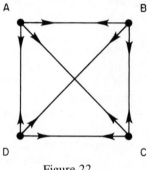

Figure 22

In practice hierarchies are not quite so simply organized as in Figure 21. A more likely sort of arrangement is shown in Figure 23. As before, an arrowed line from one dot to another means 'commands'. Here we have 10 such lines. But if every dot were connected to every other dot by arrowed lines in both directions, there would be 110.

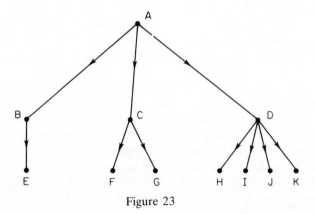

Figure 23

The difference is even greater than appears from this comparison. An arrowed line in a hierarchy means commands/obeys, and the result is predictable. But in a 'free-for-all' interaction, it simply means that information passes, and the result is much less predictable until the nature of the coupling has been agreed.

A hierarchy is simpler both to understand and to operate. Having told the helmsman what course to steer, the navigator can turn his attention to other duties. Having decided the destination of a particular ship, the high commander leaves to the navigator the detailed directions by which the ship is taken there.

8.11 Corresponding to the hierarchy of command, there is another hierarchy of goal states. The helmsman chooses a goal position of the rudder which will bring the ship's direction to the course ordered by the helmsman. He chooses it because of the boat-turning property of this position of the rudder, and chooses a particular position which optimizes it—not too fast a turn, not too slow, and not to overshoot the desired course. So the goal position in the lowest universe of discourse, that for the steering mechanism, is chosen because of its properties in the next universe above, that of the helmsman. Likewise the course which the navigator chooses at various times will be that which best takes the ship from its locations at those times to its destination. The destination chosen by the ship-owner or the admiral will be so chosen because of some property associated therewith—lucrative passengers or cargo, strategic considerations. In this way, although the various director systems (mechanical and human) function in different universes of discourse, the relationships between these universes are reasonably easy to understand.

The higher up in the hierarchy, the more extensive are these universes likely to be, in space, time, and interactions with other organisms and organisations. The helmsman only has to think about the ship's present course; the ship-owner or the admiral must base their decisions on world-wide economic or strategic considerations.

8.12 In any strong hierarchy (meaning one in which the majority of interactions are of a command/obey nature, with serious consequences for disobedience) the constraints on individuals are also strong. Every member, except possibly the one at the top, must set his goal states in accordance with commands from those of higher rank or status, and their own commands to subordinates are also indirectly determined by those received from above. So for every human, membership of a strong hierarchy involves considerable loss of freedom. Another disadvantage is that the benefits arising from the positive-sum character of the organization are often unevenly distributed: the greater share going to those at or near the top. This may be legitimized by a pay structure; or those with greater power due to their position may simply direct more into their own pockets. Those in the upper strata not only use their power to stay there: they try to put their children there too.

The hierarchic form of organization has thus great advantages, and great disadvantages. We saw in Section 8.8 that successful organization requires that individual plans and goal states must be (i) compatible, and (ii) complementary. In a hierarchy, compatibility of plans results from the fact that each director system functions within a different universe of discourse. (This was not the case for the two examples of Section 8.8.) Both complementarity and compatibility are ensured if goal states in one universe are chosen because of their properties in the next universe above. So the simplicity and efficiency which hierarchic organization confers are great, and this is even more apparent when compared with the complexity and unpredictability of free-for-all interaction between any but a very small number of director systems. In situations such as national defence, where efficiency is a prime consideration, we find strong hierarchies: navy, army, and air force. The disadvantages to individuals within strong hierarchies can also be great (though they do not have to be). So it is not surprising that throughout history we find conflict between supporters of hierarchic and of egalitarian forms of organization; and the emergence of various forms of compromise.

Here we are on the borders of sociology and political theory, and to follow this line further would not help the present line of enquiry. The object of following it this far has been to demonstrate the versatility of the model which has been developed in earlier chapters, and its potential for bridging some of the gaps between disciplines within the social and behavioural sciences. In the next section we shall apply it to a term which belongs to psychology.

The concept of motivation

8.13   The term 'motivation' has so far been avoided because as generally used it leads to confusion. Suppose we ask, 'What is Smith's motivation for lunching always at that café? Is it because the food is good, or because it is near his job, or does he like that pretty waitress?' What we want to know is what goal state is achieved by his lunching at that café. We are not enquiring whether what moves him there is his legs, or a bus, or his car. The kind of observation which would help to answer our question is what Smith does if the food gets worse, or his office moves to the far side of town, or the waitress in question leaves.

The question which is really being asked is, 'What sets Smith's legs moving (a) at all, (b) in the direction of that particular café?' In both cases the answer is his own director system. When an organism has a goal state which is not its present state, then (provided there are no more important requirements) its director system sets into action the available operators to take it to its goal state. So the term 'motivate' as generally used confuses the motive power in actuality (Smith's legs, or the car or bus engine) with that in Smith's inner reality which initiates and directs its actions. For the former we are now using the term 'operators' and for the latter 'director system'.

Another sense in which the term motivation is used is in connection with wants and needs. A want refers to a goal state which has been set but not yet achieved; a need refers to a particular object or action which is necessary for the achievement of a goal state. Thus, 'I want a cup of tea' means that I am away from a goal state which would be achieved if I had a cup of tea. Such a want may well set in motion actions such as putting the kettle on, or a suggestion to my wife: and to use the term 'want' in this way is fully consistent with the present model. When a comparator registers a gap between present state and goal state, this brings into action an appropriate plan. So to say 'I have put the kettle on because I want a cup of tea' makes good sense. It makes less good sense to say 'I am motivated to put the kettle on by wanting a cup of tea': for how can something one has not got provide motive power? Food and drink can only motivate, if this word is to be used accurately, by providing energy for muscular activity: which is to say after they have been both ingested and digested.

Output from a comparator which signals being away from a goal state (or being in an anti-goal state) has the distinctive and attention-calling quality which we call emotion. The particular emotion which signals a want or need, we call desire. Want and desire are so often associated that although want is a lack, a state of being without, while desire is an emotion, the words are often used interchangeably. So it also makes good sense to say 'I have put the kettle on because I desire a cup of tea.'

8.14   The object of the foregoing discussion was not an exercise in pedantry, but with a view to answering the question, 'Can one person motivate another?' For there is a widespread assumption that this is possible. Teachers, for example, are now told that children should not be made to work by threat of punishment: it is part of the teacher's job to 'motivate' them. What might this mean?

Clearly it does not mean 'provide motive power'. Directly, any motive power comes (in the teaching example) from the children's own muscles. And as regards the back-up energy, that which is provided by school meals provides muscular power indifferently for playing leapfrog, making mischief, or learning arithmetic.

The general sense in which 'A motivates B' is used means, roughly, that A gets B to do something which A wants B to do, and which B would not otherwise have done. With this is an implication that the action by A is intentional, and unilateral. If B agrees to co-operate with A, the situation is more accurately so described. The phrase 'which B would not otherwise have done' is necessary in order to exclude the release by some action of A of activity by B towards some already existing goal: for example, a policeman who beckons a motorist to proceed, a teacher who says 'You may go out to play now'.

What can A do whereby to bring about the action which he wants B to do? A can command or threaten, strongly or mildly, explicitly or implicitly. He can request or persuade, again strongly or mildly, explicitly or implicitly. These appear as direct approaches. He can change B's environment in a way that will bring about the desired action by B. This appears to be indirect. But in fact, all are indirect. A has no direct access to any of B's director systems. A can only get B to do something by making a change in B's environment which sets in action one or more of B's own director systems. Among these changes are giving B certain information. And the differences listed in Table 4 are differences in the kind of change.

Are there any of these changes which it is more accurate, or more useful for any other reason, to describe as motivation? I have been unable to find any. If a thief points a gun at a bank clerk and demands money, the clerk is then in a dangerous situation from which he will take action to escape, by obeying the thief, and/or treading on the alarm button. If the bank is on fire, the clerk will also take action to escape. In both cases, the motive power comes from his own muscles, and the direction of this power from his own director systems. The situation is in no way better understood by saying that the thief motivates the bank clerk by threatening him with a gun, or that the clerk is motivated to escape from the fire.

An experimental psychologist can impose upon a rat an environment without food, and thereby after a sufficient time ensure that the rat wants (lacks) food. Given the opportunity, the rat will then, in a familiar situation, do whatever actions bring him to food (e.g. run through a maze) or bring food to him (e.g. press a bar). In an unfamiliar situation, it will gradually learn what to do to get food. In both cases it is performing goal-directed activity: in the first case muscular, taking it from a state without food to a state with food; and in the second, an internal activity called learning, which takes it from a state in which it can get food only slowly and unreliably to one in which it can get it quickly and reliably.

Or using again the example of Smith and the café, suppose that one says 'Smith is motivated to go to the café. What would this mean, more than that Smith is now going, or will, given suitable circumstances (e.g. lunch hour) go, to the café? If we want to explain further, this can best be done by referring to: (a) the goal state (girl, food, or minimal exertion); and (b) the director system which takes him there. In this case, to say that some other person has motivated Smith to go to the café could only mean something like persuade (e.g. the café owner by providing good food or engaging pretty waitresses), or threaten (e.g. Smith's employer by telling him there will be trouble if he takes a minute beyond one hour for his lunch).

I have been unable to find any class of situations to which the terms 'motivates' or 'is motivated' can be applied, which cannot be described more accurately and informatively in another way.

8.15 From observable behaviours, it is always difficult and may be impossible to infer the mental processes which give rise to and direct them. We

:an only set up models, and test these in ways which were described in Chapter 7. When, as we are now, we are thinking about mental models of mental activities, the degree of difficulty is multiplied by itself.

Mental models are made up of concepts, and structures of concepts. When people have become accustomed to using a particular concept, they cannot be expected to give up doing so without good reason. And the concept of motivation' has become well established: so what reasons can be offered for its abandonment?

It has already been suggested that there appears to be no class of examples, to which the term 'motivation' is commonly applied, which cannot be described more accurately and informatively in some other way, which also is no more difficult. This is because in general, the term motivation confounds four factors which need to be distinguished. These are:

(i)   the motive power itself—physical energy for the activity;
(ii) the system which directs this energy in one way rather than another;
(iii) the goal towards which the activity is directed;
(iv) environmental changes which, by changing an organism's relationship with the environment (or the relationship of some other operand), bring into action a director system which was previously inactive.

A description that states clearly which of these factors is involved will necessarily be more helpful to our thinking than one which does not.

A reason of importance to all who are professionally concerned with influencing the behaviour of others, such as teachers, social workers, managers, is that they will find their task easier if they stop thinking in terms of motivating, and begin thinking in terms of co-operation. The problems with which I am myself best acquainted are those of teachers. Learning under threat of punishment has, in my view rightly, been (for the most part) abandoned. Instead, teachers are expected to 'motivate' the children to learn. The confusion surrounding this concept makes their task difficult. (And the present lack of a coherent educational theory increases their difficulty often to impossibility.)

But most of all, the trouble with the concepts of motivation and motivating is that they lead to thinking in terms of what is done *to* an individual rather than what is done by him. Applied to others, this way of thinking leads to what a student of mine has well called 'the thingifying of people'. The bank clerk under threat from an armed thief has a choice, which 'things' do not. He values his life more than money. In other circumstances, he might well put his life in peril because he valued something else more highly. And applied to oneself, to think that other persons can motivate us independently of our own choice similarly underestimates our own degree of freedom.

There is, however, an apparent contradiction here. Although it has been emphasized that only a person himself can set the goal states for his own internal director systems, there are certainly times when A seems not only to choose but to set B's goal states. And this may seem to be so, not only to an outside observer, but to B himself, who obeys A's commands as if he has no choice. The apparent paradox lies in the fact that B's ability to decide whether or not he will do as A tells him depends on B's realizing that he has this power to decide.

The paradox disappears when the above is seen to be a particular case of the principle discussed in Section 4.6, namely that unless a person realizes that something is the case, he cannot make use of it. So a person who is unaware that he has a choice, effectively has not: in the same way as a prisoner, the door of whose gaol has been unlocked, is not free until he realizes that he is.

8.16   In Section 1.2, the following example was used. We are in a room with a child who has agreed to co-operate in our experiment. There is a chair at the far side. We say, 'Please go and sit on that chair', and the child moves across the room and sits on the chair. In Chapter 1, the stimulus–response model was rejected as not being appropriate for explaining this; and the burden of Section 8.15 is that it will be no help to our own understanding to say that our request *motivates* the child to go and sit on the chair. Earlier, it was pointed out that no one but the child himself can set his own goals: so why would we confidently expect the child to do as we request—in terms of the present model, to set his goal state in accordance with our words?

We have seen, in the earlier part of this chapter, that a co-operative relationship between two persons is a positive-sum interaction: that is, that it increases their overall survival expectation. (It may be well also to recall that this is a probabilistic statement; and that the probable increase may be large or small. But an organism's overall survival expectation results from the summation of many small such contributions: and their cumulative effect is considerable.) In other words, a co-operative relationship is a state of value in itself: so we would predict from the present model that the achievement and maintenance of such a relationship will be a goal state which both individuals, in the situation described, will direct their activities towards achieving and maintaining. On the child's side this will involve, for example, sitting on the chair when so requested. On our own side, we would not tie his legs together without having first explained that this is part of the experiment.

So the behaviour described is predictable from the present model. And whereas a physical push towards the goal location does cause our inanimate billiard ball to move there, our model also predicts that it would for many children have quite a different effect.

A long-term, positive-sum relationship of great importance is that between parent and child; and it will be of much interest, when opportunity allows, to analyse the ways in which their director systems are coupled, and also those by which each contributes to the achievement and maintenance of the relationship.

Another such relationship is that between teachers and pupils. Learning is a primary process, and much learning can and does take place without a teacher. In Chapter 7 this was explained in terms of innate second-order

irector systems, whose function is to take the director systems on which they
ct to states of greater expertise. The coupling between these two kinds of
ystem within the pupil, and another director system belonging to a teacher, is
ne of much greater complexity than is generally thought. It is the present
writer's belief that no one yet understands it well, or even adequately.

Internal and external organization

.17   In the present chapter we have moved from a consideration of director
ystems within individuals to how those of different individuals interact, and a
eginning has been made in considering social organizations such as
ierarchies.

Within our total environment, some of our most important prohabitats are
made up of our fellow humans, and other organisms. If we want to improve
ur ways of interacting, both individual and collective—and a glance through
he newspapers is enough to show how greatly this improvement is
eeded—then it will be a first step in the right direction if we can understand
more about how our director systems function and interact in the
chievement of individual and collective goals.

Also, in trying to make our internal mental organization accessible to our
wn thinking, it may be helpful to consider external organizations which are
y their nature more accessible to observation, and which can therefore serve
s tentative models: remembering always the important difference that within
n individual there may be direct access by a higher-order director system to a
ower. Though our understanding of the organization of behaviour within an
ndividual is still in its infancy, it seems highly probable that it is a composite
irector system, made up of many interacting ones, both innate and learnt.
Among the latter, both sub-intelligent and intelligent learning will have been
nvolved: and the self-knowledge of an intelligent person must also include
wareness of his own irrationality.

Given that our survival results from the cumulative contributions of many
oal states, at any one time there are likely to be many director systems in
ction. These can interact in any of the ways described in Section 8.4,
upporting and helping, inhibiting and obstructing, or co-existing. If the
verall interaction is to be positive-sum, there has to be some kind of overall
irection and co-ordination. Much of this is certainly innate, such as that by
which our uvula closes when we swallow, to prevent food going down our
windpipe. At the higher levels there will be conscious choice, integration,
udgement. Everyday usage would include these in the concept of
ntelligence; whereas the present model reserves this term for a particular
ombination of director systems—a delta-two system for constructing director
ystems, and the teachable delta-one system which is thereby developed.
ntuitively, one would expect judgement and wisdom on the one hand,
ntelligence on the other, to be related; but everyday experience tells us that
ighly intelligent persons can also display notable lack of judgement. To

questions such as these the present model does not yet offer an answer: but i does suggest the kind of concepts in terms of which answers may be found namely a complex organization of interacting director systems.

Finally, there is evidence from developmental psychology in support of the view that this internal organization is in some respects modelled on influential external relationships in childhood. And these in turn may act as the mental models which structure our perception of certain external relationships Inter-personal and intra-personal relationships are more closely related than is generally realized.

8.18 We have now begun to see the great complexity of the task involved in trying to understand what goes on when director systems interact, especially when their number exceeds two. In the general case, the task is beyond our presently available techniques of thinking. (This is not the case for large numbers of inanimate objects: e.g. the kinetic theory of gases succeeds very well in dealing with the interactions of very large numbers of molecules.) The lines of thinking which have been offered as possible beginnings are:

(i) *Both organisms and organizations are conceived as complexes of director systems which interact in ways which are positive-sum: that is, such that the change in overall or collective survival expectations due to these interactions is positive.*

(ii) *Intelligent organization (in contrast to mutuality) is conceived as the result of a high-level organizer, whose operands are director systems and whose function is to bring these to an optimal positive-sum state of interaction and keep them there.*

(iii) *Minimal requirements for co-operation are that the goal states of individuals are compatible, and that that their plans are complementary There must also be a shared coding/decoding system.*

(iv) *Long-term co-operation among a group of individuals requires an overall positive-sum set of relationships between their goals, and widely shared conceptual structures within the universe of discourse involved. The shared coding/decoding system now becomes a language.*

(v) *A kind of organization which greatly reduces the complexity of interactions is a hierarchy.*

Notes for Chapter 8

1. That is to say, except for a small number of goal-directed machines such as thermostats, homing missiles, auto-pilots.
2. The term 'status' is used here in a general sense, including prestige, location in a system of social relationships or social network, and authority of two kinds: power, and knowledge.
3. For a fuller discussion, see Trivers (1971).

CHAPTER 9

Concepts and Schemas

Vari-focus and interiority

9.1 In Chapter 3, the importance of our mental models for our survival and progress was explained and discussed at some length. Among the main points were that we each have an assortment of these mental models, on which we are entirely dependent for the direction of our actions towards goal states which favour survival (Sections 3.4, 3.5). We can also imaginatively conceive new states which neither we nor anyone else has previously brought about. Some of these can be set as goal states, and we can also devise plans for actualizing these (Sections 4.7, 4.8). Our conceptual structures are thus a major factor of progress too.

Their success depends on a variety of factors, which were discussed in the earlier part of Chapter 7 as a preliminary to the formulation of learning in terms of the present theoretical model. These include the extent, accuracy, and completeness with which they represent actuality (Section 7.2): or rather, by a process of abstraction, those qualities of actuality which are relevant to the functioning of particular director systems (Sections 3.6 and 6.13). Three kinds of reality testing, by which the accuracy of a conceptual structure is checked, have been discussed (Sections 4.1, 4.7, and 7.3).

This chapter will concentrate in greater detail on these conceptual structures themselves: how they are built up, and how they become more extensive in space and time, more accurate, and better organized. Various other points which were introduced briefly in earlier chapters will be taken up again and developed further: particularly the abstractive process (Section 6.13).

9.2 It will be convenient from now on to use the shorter term 'schema' for a conceptual structure. This term was introduced into psychology by Bartlett (1932), and has since come into general use among psychologists with meanings which, though varying slightly between individuals, are basically similar to that which has just been assigned (with the exception of Piaget, who uses it somewhat differently). Its use has the advantage not only of brevity, but also of emphasizing its unified character, and thereby reminding us that when a number of distinct elements are suitably connected, the resulting structure may take on new properties of its own. (For example, by suitably connecting transistors, condensers, inductances, etc., we get a radio receiver whose properties could not have been predicted from a knowledge of the properties of the individual components only.) Some of the properties of schemas will be discussed in Chapters 10 and 11.

Up till now, the terms 'concept' and 'conceptual structure'—or as we shall now usually say, 'concept' and 'schema'—have been used as though they described two quite different kinds of mental entity. This distinction, while it will still often be helpful in simplifying our thinking, turns out to be less clear-cut than has hitherto been revealed. Almost any concept, if we look at it closely, can be seen as containing within itself other concepts. Thus the concept vegetable includes beans, cabbages, peas, potatoes, broccoli, ... That is to say, vegetable is itself a conceptual structure: a schema. Does this mean that the distinction between concept and schema is invalid? For a time, I had begun to think so. But after further thinking, what had at first appeared as an inconsistency and source of potential confusion revealed one of the most important ways in which intelligence contributes to the better organization of our knowledge.

Let us continue the vegetable example in two directions. Cabbages includes Primo, Winter Monarch, Jupiter, January King, . . . (from a current seed catalogue). Beans includes Crusader, Goliath, Kentucky Wonder, Romano, ...

So each of the examples given of the concept vegetable turns out to be itself a concept. And so again for each of the latter: Goliath beans include (say) those on my plate, those on your plate, those still in the freezer, those at the supermarket, etc. In the opposite direction, vegetable, together with meat, sugar, eggs, . . . belong to the concept food. Food, together with postage stamps, creosote, sewing cotton, yesterday formed part of the category shopping. And so on upwards. Among all these, which shall we regard as concepts, and which as schemas?

We have already seen, and shall often have cause to remind ourselves, that how best to categorize something depends on what we want to do with it. And this is equally true of mental objects, such as those we are currently using for examples. Sometimes it is more helpful to think of vegetable as a concept, sometimes as a schema. Our ability to do this in almost every universe of discourse means that we have a data storage and retrieval system which enables us to handle the maximum of information with a minimum of cognitive strain. We can bring into use as much or as little information as is useful for a particular purpose.

In earlier writings I have used the term 'conceptual hierarchy' to describe this kind of organization. But hierarchy is a method of government, and so while it is appropriate to refer to a hierarchy of director systems (such as that in Section 8.10), it is not quite the right analogy for this kind of conceptual

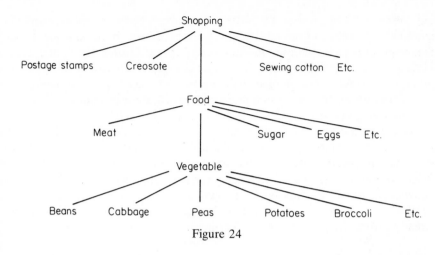

Figure 24

structure. When diagrammed as in Figure 24 we get a 'tree' diagram which is often useful for putting on view a particular set of concepts and their connections. But this does not do so well for examples in which the connections are not tree-like, such as the 'London' one (Section 3.5). Especially, it does not do justice to the way in which the same mental entity can be expanded into a schema of great detail, or contracted into a single concept and treated as one among many, just as London can be represented by a detailed map covering a large wall, or as a small dot on a map of Europe.

What expands or contracts in the 'London' example, however, is not the city itself but the way we view it, related to a particular purpose: the routing of a fire-engine from brigade headquarters to a particular house, or that of an airliner from one capital city to another. So my next analogy is an optical one. Sometimes we look at things closely, through a magnifier, or a microscope using a low- or high-powered objective. Sometimes we move back to normal viewing distance; sometimes from still further away we take in a bird's-eye view.

As a further development, imagine that instead of having to change the viewing distance we have a vari-focal instrument (like the zoom lens on a camera, with close-up facility as well) by which, at will, we can bring into consciousness either a small part of what is available, in great magnification and detail, or a much larger part but diminished in size and detail. This is the best analogy I have been able to find for helping myself and others to realize this quality of intelligence.

'Vari-focal' is useful for helping to think about the different ways in which a particular concept or schema can be viewed. But we also need a word to describe the corresponding quality of the concepts and schemas themselves, for it is no good viewing a smaller part at greater magnification if this does not enable us to see any more. Magnifying the picture on a television screen does not show us any more detail: it only magnifies the blur. Likewise for some of our concepts. These, if we try to enlarge our view of them, reveal only areas of ignorance. Others, when we do this, reveal a wealth of interior detail. Sometimes within each detail there is available still further detail, like a nest of Chinese boxes. This quality or dimension of a concept I shall call its *interiority*. Thus for one person the concept of a colour film will have much interiority, while that of a china plate will have little. For another, it will be the other way about.

These two qualities of intelligence, vari-focal consciousness and concepts having interiority, are used in much of our thinking, and it would be useful for the reader to pause at this stage and consider further examples within his own fields of knowledge. One advantage offered by conscious realization of knowledge which has hitherto been used unconsciously is that we can then begin to use an appropriate model deliberately; and this vari-focal model has already proved helpful in guiding research discussions.

Abstraction considered further

9.3 'We cannot step twice into the same river.' The present experiences from which (sometimes) we learn become part of our past, and will never be encountered again in identically the same form. But the situations in which we need to apply what we have learnt lie in the future as it becomes present, or as by anticipation we bring it into our present thinking. It follows that if our mental models are to be of any use to us, they must represent, not singletons from among the infinite variety of actuality, but common properties of past experiences which we are able to recognize on future occasions. This once again emphasizes the importance of the abstractive process which is such a central feature of concept formation. Concepts represent, not isolated encounters with actuality, but regularities abstracted from these. It is only because, and to the extent that, our environment is orderly and not capricious, that learning of any kind is possible. A major feature of intelligent learning is the discovery of these regularities, and the organizing of them into conceptual structures which are themselves orderly.

Though actuality is the ground from which these regularities are abstracted, this contains infinitely more than is embodied in the conceptual structure of any individual. This raises a very large and general question: why are some concepts formed rather than others? While making a start with the development of an explanation, we shall confine our attention to concepts whose origins can be traced back to sensory input from actuality.

Repetition is certainly one important factor in determining which features of actuality are abstracted rather than others. For this, a pleasing analogy has been provided by one of the earliest pioneers of psychology, Sir Francis Galton. He photographed the faces of a number of persons on one photographic plate, taking care to get the main features in the same positions on the plate, and giving on each occasion an exposure which was insufficient to produce an image by itself. The result was a composite photograph showing only the resemblances between the persons concerned for which the successive exposures had a cumulative effect. The more general the resemblance, the more clearly it was shown in the photograph; while details peculiar to single individuals did not register at all. (Galton, 1883.)

This procedure required careful positioning in the camera's field of view of each successive contributor to the composite image. But in our daily experience, even the same object on different occasions will be seen from different angles, at different distances, against different backgrounds and under different conditions of lighting. So to recognize it as the same object each time, constant in size and shape, requires a more complex process of abstraction than that which Galton's camera was able to do.

Galton's analogy also tends to make the process of abstraction seem too passive, whereas in the present model, learning is an active and indeed a goal-directed activity, with reality testing mode (i) (the testing of events against expectations) as an important feature from very early days.[1] If we conceive the goal to include the formation of concepts which are most likely to be useful in the future, the model as developed so far suggests that initially one kind of regularity has as good a chance of being abstracted as another. A certain neutral, generalized receptivity (as distinct from passivity) is necessary so that the concepts formed can be genuinely representative of actuality as it is found by an individual in his environment, whether this be the arctic tundra of Alaska, the arid deserts of the Sahara, the rain forests of the Amazon, or the urban surroundings of a capital city. Social environments differ in equally important though less obvious ways. Without some degree of neutrality of this kind, the advantages of the learning process would be lost, since what is needed is to adapt to the actual environment without presupposing what it is going to be, as do innate director systems. (What is presupposed, as has been discussed earlier, is that it is orderly and not random.)

Nevertheless, it is hard to conceive of any such learning system which would be equally successful in abstracting every kind of regularity, whatever this might be.

Given any particular sequencing of events, some of the recurring features will be more quickly learnt than others. Bower, Broughton, and Moore (1971), in experiments with young infants, have shown that if a baby sees an object disappear behind a screen and re-appear, it shows signs of noticing changes in some of the properties of the object sooner than others. For example, if the object disappears while moving at one rate and reappears moving at a different rate, this is noticed quite early. But if it goes in as one object and reappears as a different object, this is not noticed until later.

Object-concepts

9.4 The very basic kind of concept by which we recognize an object as being (or not being) the same thing that we have seen before, we call an *object-concept*. Most of our own learning of everyday object-concepts took place before we can remember. This process has been described in detail by Piaget (1955), to whom we owe much of our realization of its importance. That one has to learn even so basic a concept as that of one's mother has been nicely demonstrated in an experiment by Bower (1974). An arrangement of mirrors was used whereby a baby saw several images of its mother at the same time. Young babies, who had not fused the various separate appearances of their mothers into unified concepts of a single mother, were not disconcerted by this. Older ones, however, aged over 5 months, showed distress. Persistence of a mother concept dichotomized into a 'good mother' and a 'bad mother' may be found in many a fairy tale. These are personified in such ways as a cruel stepmother who has replaced the true mother, or as a witch and a fairy godmother.

Perceptual learning

9.5 The ability to distinguish between examples and non-examples of a class, which is acquired by learning the appropriate concept, can also be provided by innate mechanisms. One of the differences between these two—between concepts, and what ethologists call 'innate releasers'—has already been discussed: open-ness to change as a result of experience. Another is in the basis of discrimination. Lack (1943) has shown that a male robin distinguishes between examples and non-examples of the class 'other male robins' by the presence or absence of the red feathers on its front. A tuft of red feathers, bearing no other resemblance to any kind of bird, will be attacked by a male robin if he sees it in his own territory: whereas an otherwise lifelike model lacking only this red marking will be ignored. From this and other examples (a good source is Tinbergen, 1951), a general characteristic of innate releasers is seen to be crude discriminatory power only, often on the basis of a single characteristic.

The same robins can, however, learn to discriminate between their own mates and all the other very similar birds of the same species and sex. This difference is a much subtler one than could possibly be transmitted genetically: nor, indeed, could any innate discriminatory process 'know' in advance which particular other robin would be its mate.

This kind of learning consists of the formation of a concept which is fused with incoming sense-data and projected on to an external object. This process, which results in increased subtlety and discrimination of perception, we call *perceptual learning*. Much of our own perceptual learning took place so early in our lives that we cannot recall it: but examples of it in adult life can be identified as part of the learnt expertise of many professions. Medical colleagues have told me that as students they could hear through their stethoscopes the two sounds characteristic of a normal heart-beat without difficulty from the beginning; but that it was some time before they could hear the different sounds resulting from faulty closure of the valves. That this is a matter of perceptual learning and not of sensory acuity can be deduced from the fact that these same sounds were easily audible to much older colleagues whose hearing was in general likely to be less acute, not more. The changes are not the result of improvements in our sense organs themselves, but in development of concepts which sensitize us to new qualities in our sensory input.

Other examples are offered by tea and coffee tasters, and sherry blenders, whose livelihood depends on their well-developed sensory discrimination. Once we have the concept of perceptual learning, we can begin to recognize examples in our own experience. One which recently took place in myself followed the purchase of new hi-fi equipment. After about six months, I found myself much more aware of differences in quality of recording, though the records and equipment were still the same. I also began to notice differences between broadcasts: especially between studio broadcasts, and outside broadcasts over land-lines of less than excellent electrical characteristics. Whatever his profession or hobby, the reader who cares to look there for examples of perceptual learning has a very good hope of finding them.

Another learning process, which fits better into the category of perceptual learning than elsewhere, is that which results in our perceiving in an object three-dimensional qualities, and others such as hardness, texture, which from past experience we know them to have. These are not derivable from the immediate sense data, but are activated by it and then projected into the object. It is from past strokings that we 'see' a cat as warm, soft, and velvety.

Higher-order concepts

9.6 So far we have distinguished between innate discriminatory processes and concepts, but not between the kind of concepts which can be learnt by other animals as well as ourselves and the kind which give us our much more advanced mental abilities. To some of these differences we now turn our attention.

One of the most important is in our own ability of successive abstraction: that of repeating the process of concept formation at a higher level; based now, not on regularities as experienced directly from actuality, but on the discovery of higher-order regularities among these regularities. In other words, having formed various concepts directly from sensory input, these concepts can then be used from which to form further, higher-order, concepts. To these statements, themselves highly abstract, interiority will now be given by examples:

From concepts of particular objects which are alike in some way we may derive a class concept; e.g., from seeing a number of different chairs, we abstract certain regular features from which we form the concept *chair* (as against this or that particular chair). In the same way we form other class-concepts such as *bookcase, desk, bed*.

Continuing the process, by abstracting certain features common to *chair*, *bookcase, desk, bed,* . . . , we can form a new concept, *furniture*; and from concepts such as *furniture, cameras, gardening equipment, motor vehicles,* we can derive another concept: *consumer durables.* And so on.

The individual experiences from which a concept is formed we shall call its *contributors.* These may vary from person to person, even for the same concept. Thus, while it is very probable that both reader and author have the same (or almost the same) concepts to which we have attached the labels 'chair', 'bookcase', etc., it is very improbable that these concepts were derived from the same actual chairs, bookcases, etc. Once we have a concept, what were (for us) contributors become *examples,* and we can recognize, seek out, and even create new examples.

Whether the concepts just mentioned are the same for two persons could most easily be verified by indicating an assortment of objects, and asking each other 'Would you call that a chair?', etc. These objects should be chosen from the same universe of discourse as chair. We might sensibly point to a stool or a bench, as well as to an easy chair and an upright chair, but not to a teacup or a dog. This is the most basic criterion for knowing whether people have the same particular class-concept, namely whether they include and exclude the same examples and non-examples. Given this they can co-operate. Definitions as an alternative method will be discussed in Section 10.7. Meanwhile we may note:

(i)   that the possession of a concept can be evidenced in this way, namely by distinguishing between examples and non-examples, before a person is able to define it verbally;

(ii)   that animals can also demonstrate that they have learnt concepts of the simpler kind this way, e.g. by always choosing a door marked with a triangle in preference to that marked with a square;

(iii) that some concepts (e.g. mathematics, justice) appear to defy definition, even by those who are in considerable agreement about examples and non-examples.

In this section we have confined our attention to class-concepts, these being the easiest to think about. There are other kinds of concept also, such as relational concepts (e.g. larger than). A job waiting to be done is a taxonomy of concepts: or if this is too difficult, then a preliminary working classification. Also, the relations between these and our existing classification of words into nouns, adjectives, verbs, etc.

9.7 Early in the process of successive abstraction which has just been described, there comes an important difference in the kind of contributors from which the new concepts are formed. Concepts such as chair (or cat, or hot, or sour) can be formed directly from sensory experience of actuality. These I call *primary concepts.* Concepts such as gardening equipment (or consumer durables, or scientific method) are derived from other concepts, as may be seen both from typical contributors and from the kind of examples we would use to verify agreement. ('Would you include fertilizers in garden equipment?' Fertilizers is itself a class-concept.) These are *secondary concepts*.

Primary concepts represent regularities as they are directly encountered in actuality. Secondary concepts represent regularities among these regularities, and by repetition of the abstractive process, successively higher-order regularities. We may therefore want to talk about 'more abstract' or 'higher-order' concepts. The term 'deep' is also sometimes useful, meaning remote from the surface; deep as against superficial.

Any particular concept enables its possessor to map some feature of actuality into one of his available schemas, which is a major step towards appropriate behaviour. This is true even of primary concepts. Not until we know what something is, meaning to what class-concept it can be mapped, do we know what we can do with it. The more abstract the concept, the greater the number and variety of situations to which it can be applied, and so the more extensive the domain of the director system of which it forms part. This is part of the reason why present-day scientific theories gives us such power to explore and shape our environment. Another reason appears to be that as our concepts become deeper in the sense described earlier, we penetrate more nearly towards the essential nature of the universe itself. Many of the concepts used in this way are so abstract that it takes twenty or more years of a lifetime even to acquire those which are already known. But once mastered, and formed into appropriate schemas, they enable their possessors to do such marvels as transmit images around the world, to make aircraft which fly faster than sound, to insert electronic pacemakers into tired hearts. Our present task is now to develop concepts and schemas whereby we can begin to explore and understand the much more complex regularities of our own nature.

Concept formation

9.8 Since conceptualization is so central a feature of the learning by which we become more expert in our behaviour, any progress we can make in identifying the factors which affect concept formation will have widespread value for setting up conditions favourable to intelligent learning.

One of these is time interval. The shorter the time interval between similar experiences, the more likely they are to become contributors to a concept. If these contributors are physical objects, it may be possible to group them together spatially and thereby enable them to be seen (or otherwise experienced) almost simultaneously. The likenesses between the contributors can be further emphasized by contrast with non-contributors. Contrast also heightens consciousness (Section 2.8) and this may be another way in which it contributes to concept formation. Clearly the physical-grouping method can only be used to help in the formation of primary concepts, and then only in a limited number of cases. Where concepts themselves require to be grouped together to form a new secondary concept, the most reliable method is by the use of words and other symbols. If the concepts involved are of a high order of abstraction, it is probably the only way. 'What is meant by "invisible exports"?' 'Insurance, banking, tourism—these are examples of invisible exports.'

Naming is clearly a powerful way of bringing concepts together, with minimal time intervals, in a person's mind, with the aim of enabling him to use them as contributors to a new secondary concept. Contrasting non-contributors can again be introduced in this way. And for the formation of primary concepts, where it is not practical to group objects together by changing their locations in space or time, naming is also helpful. In this case it is object-*concepts* which are grouped, in substitution for the objects themselves. A similar method is possible for other experiences. And when naming is not deliberately employed as a teaching device, simply talking about what is seen and done will have much the same effect, though more slowly, by bringing into consciousness memories of similar sights and events in the past.

How can we account for concept formation in the absence of such help? In other words, how can someone group together the necessary contributors from which to form a new concept, if no one does it for him, and if he doesn't know himself what to group together because he hasn't the concept? The question is an important one, since this is how many or most of our concepts are formed, in the absence of a teacher, under the informal learning conditions of everyday life.

When I first became aware of the need to explain this, I formed the hypothesis that an intermediate stage could be provided by a process of matching. Concentrating, to start with, on class-concepts at a primary level, I thought it possible that objects could be seen as being in some way alike before there was awareness of what was the quality which they had in common. In this way they could be grouped together, mentally or physically; after which their common property could be abstracted in the manner already described.

The testing of this simple hypothesis provided unexpected methodological difficulties, the problem being to find a criterion by which the experimenter could be reasonably sure whether a child was sorting by matching, or by the use of a superordinate concept. This is to say,

whether like this: O — O — O — O

or like this:

Much time was therefore spent initially in observational studies, and in developing materials suitable to children of various age groups. From detailed records of the behaviour of children aged 7–11 years, it was found that these tended to move rather quickly to the second of the two modes of sorting used above. Careful observation of younger children, however, convinced the experimenter that these were clearly sorting by matching; and that they stayed at this level.

This offers an explanation of how some children become more knowledgeable than their elders within universes of discourse which interest them. Long before he reached double figures, my own son could identify fourteen different kinds of butterfly while I still confused a Peackock with a Painted Lady. One of his friends was equally expert on motor cars: and as a child I myself, when not much older, was able to recognize at a glance almost any camera on the market. Perceptual matching, often based on a salient feature such as wing marking, makes possible the abstraction of a class-concept. To this an appropriate name may afterwards become attached, for example, by looking it up in a book; but this is not an essential feature of this particular process of concept formation. When a naturalist has identified some new species, it is at this stage without a name, and cannot be found in any book.

Noise

9.9 An important factor which influences the ease or difficulty of concept formation is the amount of noise present in the contributors. The term 'noise' is here used in its generalized sense, meaning everything which does not provide information relevant to the universe under consideration. Thus a splatter of white dots across one's television screen is noise relative to the programme one is watching, though it may inform us that someone is using an unsuppressed electrical apparatus. The ringing of the telephone bell is noise relative to the fourth symphony of Brahms which we are listening to on our hi-fi, though it informs us that someone is calling us. And conversely, the symphony itself becomes noise if, having answered, we are trying to hear our telephone caller during a loud passage.

Noise is thus irrelevant input which has to be ignored in relation to the functioning of a given director system. It is always relative to a universe of discourse. For students, the activities of the window-cleaner are noise relative to those of the lecturer; and in student seminars, the low-cut blouses of some of the girls have been experienced as noise relative to the academic discussion.

In the present context of concept formation, the noise we are most concerned with is that which is combined with the conceptual properties in each contributor. For example, the individual colour and markings of each individual cat are noise relative to the concept cat. At a much more abstract and difficult level, the melodies, harmonies, and instrumentation of any individual musical work are noise relative to the concept sonata form.

Some noise is therefore inseparable from concept formation, since a zero-noise contributor would be the concept itself. The important questions are: against how much noise can a concept be formed and used, and is there an optimal noise level for concept formation?

As a beginning to research in this area, I formed the following related hypotheses:

(i) that in the early stages of formation of a particular concept, low noise levels are optimal;

(ii) that the better formed a concept, the higher are the noise levels in which it can still function (this is perhaps less a hypothesis than an explanation of what I mean by 'well formed');

(iii) that as the formation of a concept progresses, the higher are the optimal noise levels for its further strengthening; since it is in these conditions that an individual increases his ability to differentiate concept from noise.

Hypotheses (i) and (iii) taken together have been verified by several experiments of similar design but using different material. Two groups of subjects were given the same set of contributors to a given concept, these contributors having noise of many different levels. For one group, the order of presentation was random; for the other group, the contributors were presented in order of increasing noise, from low to high. The prediction that the second group would form the concept better, as tested against a new set of examples, was confirmed in every case. Since the former (random) condition is the one normally encountered in everyday life, here is another factor which a teacher can manipulate to make concept formation easier.

Another hypothesis not yet tested experimentally but which seems plausible is:

(iv) that the higher the noise level, the closer together in time do the contributors need to be for concept formation to take place.

The view is sometimes put forward that a new concept can be formed from a single contributor. This may be possible in particular cases, e.g., where all the examples are so alike that 'when you've seen one, you've seen the lot'. This is nearly the same as saying that not only each contributor, but all the examples which will afterwards be encountered, contain very little noise, nearly all the qualities belonging to the concept itself. My own view is that if all the contributors are so alike, then what is happening remains at the level of matching as described in Section 9.8. In that case, classification is taking place without concept formation, of which abstraction is an essential feature.

Influence of goal states on conceptualization

9.10 Of the many factors which may affect concept formation, the one which has so far received least attention—but to which the present model points strongly—is the goal state of the individual during the situations from which the concepts are formed. Hollands (1972) describes how a bright seven-year-old solved some of the hardest problems from a set of work cards in arithmetic. Two of these were: 'John had 22 marbles and his brother had 35 marbles. How many marbles did they have together?'; and 'Seven children had six sweets each. How many sweets were there altogether?' For the latter problem, in the child's own words: 'This one's a "times" because I've done things like six times seven and these are hard cards so it wouldn't be six add seven, or a "take away" sum.' And for the question about the marbles: 'We haven't done "timesing" big numbers so it can't be that. It must be an "add up".'

One of the regularities of a school-based learning situation is that by giving correct answers, a teacher's approval is gained; and another is that problems are set in gradually increasing order of difficulty. These were the concepts which, to a greater degree than mathematical ones, the little girl was intelligently bringing to bear on her task. Unfortunately, they do not hold good for the world outside school, nor do they offer a good foundation schema for the further development of understanding in a mathematical universe of discourse. In the present case it is good to know that the child herself was not satisfied. 'I know how to do them but why did I have to add in this one and times them in that one?' If it is accepted that not every child would have been aware that her understanding was incomplete, and approached the visitor for further explanation, then we must face the likelihood that the problems which many children are using their intelligence to master are not those which we intend. They are, however, the problems with which situationally we often face them.

Updating of concepts and schemas

9.11 Earlier, and particularly in Sections 1.8, 3.7, and most of Chapter 7, it has been emphasized that a major difference between conceptual and innate director systems is the open-ness of the former to change as a result of experience. In this section and those which follow, we shall examine how concepts and schemas keep up to date, and the limitations on their ability to do this.

The main features of this process are:

(i) realization
(ii) assimilation
(iii) expansion
(iv) differentiation
(v) re-construction

Picking up from Section 4.5, we begin by reminding ourselves that (in terms of the present model) one of the ways in which individual concepts are activated is by particular inputs from the environment, via our sense organs. They thus map present actuality into whatever schema this concept is part of: a process we call *realization*. Concepts thus sensitize us to actuality, but selectively. This emphasis in our experience of actuality towards what is like our existing concepts is called *assimilation*. The interaction is, however, two-way. Each new experience which we realize in terms of an existing concept becomes a contributor to the concept, which thereby *expands*, little or much. We also form new classes within existing conceptual groupings, a process called *differentiation*. All these changes can take place fairly smoothly. Our schemas grow by expanding existing concepts and by forming new ones. They also enable us to realize new distinctions of which we were previously unaware, by differentiation. The domains of the director systems in which these schemas are used extend continuously, and there is no disruption of their functioning. Confidence is not shaken.

Sometimes, however, we may encounter a situation for which we have a schema which is relevant, but not adequate. Attempts to realize the situation in terms of this schema give such a faulty representation of actuality that our director system cannot function. If possible we avoid such situations, for they are outside our prohabitats. But if we cannot, then we have no choice but to *re-construct* our schema. Since this necessarily involves first taking it partially or completely to pieces, this is disruptive, unwelcome, and difficult: because while this is going on, we are unable to use our schemas effectively for directing our actions. Nevertheless, it is sometimes necessary.

Having outlined the overall process, and indicated the relationship between its main features, we shall now consider these with greater interiority and bring them to life by the use of examples.

9.12 Let us imagine that a child has formed a simple object-concept: that corresponding to the family cat. The contributors to this concept were the various appearances of the cat itself, in different positions and seen from different angles. At this stage his concept of cat is restricted to this particular animal: it does not represent a class of animals, as it does for an adult. His next step is to expand this concept to include the cat next door, the one down the road, and any others which may be encountered. This involves becoming aware of their similarities and, so far as this particular concept is concerned, setting aside their differences. The family cat may be of a marmalade colour and pattern, the one next door black and white, the one down the road a smoke-grey Siamese which emits quite a different sound. The concept to which we attach the word 'cat' represents the characteristics held in common by all these animals, and does not include their differences *as part of this concept*.

Awareness of these differences is not however lost. It remains, but embodies in different concepts: those of the individual cats. And within the same object-concept, perception tells us the position, activity, and location of the cat we are presently looking at.

For different purposes we need to use concepts at different levels of abstraction. Upwards, the concepts include more general likenesses and ignore more differences; downwards, the reverse. To help us to find the right level, verbal labels are often attached. At the supermarket we buy cat food: for cats not goldfish, but for all cats and not just ours. But we do not give this food to all cats: just to our own, which being a marmalade cat we call 'Cooper'. The other families use different names for theirs: 'Kitty' for the one next door, 'Mahar-Shal-Al-Hashbaz' for the aristocratic Siamese. The following remarks and replies to them thus make use of two levels of conceptualization: two groupings of likenesses and differences. 'There's a cat at the window, mewing to be let in.' 'If it's Cooper, let him in and give him some cat food.'

Further expansion of the concept cat has taken place when a child is able to accept lions and tigers as members of the cat family: and to classify in this way new examples, such as cheetah, puma, caracal. The differences through which similarities have to be perceived are now greater: and are for some purposes more important than the similarities. Incautious visitors to Safari parks have found this to their cost: another example of the importance of using the right concept at the right level of generality for the direction of our behaviour. Here, 'wild animal' is a more appropriate concept.

A particularly powerful way of expanding a concept is by *generalization*, or *reflective extrapolation*. Since this involves reflective activity, which has not yet been discussed, we shall return to it in Chapter 11.

This simple set of examples is typical of the ways in which new experiences both change and are changed by concepts which have already been formed. Every time some new encounter with actuality is recognized as an example of an existing concept, this interaction takes place. On the one side, the concept structures the incoming sense-data. On the other side, the concept itself may be changed by new experience. Once a Siamese or a Persian has been accepted as an example of the concept cat, this concept itself is no longer quite the same as it was before. The former process, structuring the incoming data, is what (following Piaget's terminology) I call 'assimilation'. The latter I now prefer to call expansion, rather than using Piaget's term 'accommodation', which so far as I can tell does not distinguish between expansion and re-construction. It has been seen that assimilation by a concept, and expansion of a concept, are closely related. Sometimes one of these predominates over the other, sometimes the processes are balanced.

A particularly clear example of predominance of assimilation over expansion is offered by an experiment of Piaget, since often replicated.

128

Young children, shown a glass of liquid first in

this position:

and then tilted, when asked to draw what they have seen draw it

like this:

and not like this,
as we would:

This low-noise example of complete assimilation (because containing no expansion) also shows well the stability of a concept in the face of incoming sense-data. Without this stability, concepts could not embody any regularities of actuality since they would be continually changed by new sense-data. But without the ability to change, no new regularities could be embodied.

For an example of re-structuring, we move from children to famous scientists: since it is hard to think of a better example of this than the famous conflict between the Ptolemaic model of the solar system, in which the sun and the planets revolved around a stationary earth; and the Copernican, in which the sun was conceived as the stationary centre about which earth and the other planets revolved. The hostility which proponents of the latter model encountered, notably Galileo, is well known; and typical of many such situations, both historical and in the lives of individuals.[2]

9.13 We have now examined a number of factors which affect the process of concept formation and the progressive development of schemas. A person who has already acquired particular concepts can manipulate these factors in ways which will greatly help others to acquire them too, if he knows how. What is difficult is to form these concepts for the first time without such aids, under conditions such as are encountered in everyday life and in scientific research: high noise; random encounter at irregular and often long time intervals; not knowing which experiences belong together as contributors; high level of abstraction; and often too a shortage or absence of others who have enough knowledge in the same area to engage in useful discussion. The difficulties and dangers involved in reaching a new summit for the first time are not likely to be fully realized by those who follow along a well-mapped route. Yet even for the latter, the climb can be long and steep; and it may take twenty years or more.

Functional equivalence

9.14   In the description of the formation of concepts of successively higher order by repeated abstraction (Section 9.6), a new kind of similarity was introduced which we must now consider in more detail. This is that of *functional equivalence*.

Whatever our goal state, the actual object or situation by which it is achieved is hardly ever unique. If thirsty, we want a glass of water, not that particular glass containing that particular bit of water. Probably the class which will satisfy our needs is larger still: a glass, cup, mug, tankard, beaker, . . . containing water, tea, beer, lemonade, ...

To buy a ticket on the underground, we need a 10p coin. Any 10p coin will do, and so also will an old two-shilling piece, which not only has the same monetary value, but is the same in size and weight as a 10p coin, or it would not work the automatic vending machine. It does not matter which particular 10p ticket we have; and we do not wait for one particular train driven by the only man who will take us to our destination—we board the next south-bound train.

Almost every goal state to which we direct our actions, and the sub-goals from which we choose our paths, can be achieved within an equivalence class which usually offers more than one possiblity: often many more. The examples used to introduce this concept of functional equivalence are equivalence classes of objects. A goal state is however a relationship (Section 5.5), and further examination will reveal these relationships, and how the objects make possible the relationships. On the underground train, I travel as a fare-paying passenger, which is a contractual relationship between myself and London Transport. This relationship is established by change of ownership of a coin, and evidenced by my physical possession of a ticket. Ownership and physical possession are themselves relationships, the one legal, the other spatial. And so on. Each of these relationships[3] defines an equivalence class: the class of coins which entitle me to ride from Euston to Goodge Street, the class of journeys I may make for the same money, the class of fare-paying passengers, and so on.

Once again we find classification to be a central feature of what concepts enable us to do. This time the emphasis has changed: from bringing together regularities in our own experiences of actuality, to equivalences in how we use them to fulfil our needs, and how they are related to the functioning of our director systems. These two aspects sometimes meet, sometimes diverge. They often meet at the perceptual level: when we want *an* apple (as against *that* apple), we identify members of this equivalence class by their physical resemblances to each other. At the functional level, the two aspects mentioned may diverge. The second bottle opener described in Section 5.2 (iv) is functionally equivalent to a corkscrew though perceptually different. The man behind a window in the ticket office, and the coin-in-the-slot machine, are even more different perceptually. Their functional equivalence is recognized by the class-concept ticket-vendor. Physical similarity and functional equivalence come together again in examples like spare parts for a car. These will only be functionally equivalent if they are carefully manufactured to be almost identical physically.

Activation of concepts

9.15 In any system for the storage of information, retrieval is an important part of the overall organization. We all have large stores of conceptualized information, so the next question is: what are the conditions which change these from a latent to an active state, in which they are available for use?

As we have seen, one situation in which a concept may become active is when one encounters an example of it. (Or a potential example: we may decide it isn't a such-and-such after all.) We then become conscious simultaneously of the new experience and of the concept it evokes: the two together forming a percept. This is clearly a useful mechanism for bringing low-level concepts out of store into use, in environmental conditions where they may be needed. But there is more to it than this. Not only do different people have different stores of concepts, but in the same person, different concepts may vary in threshold (ease of activation) at different times. So, as has often been demonstrated both experimentally and clinically, the same (or identical) physical objects may be perceived differently by different people, and differently at different times by the same person. This underlines the inconsistency of the usual concept of a stimulus. A certain letter box is for me a 'stimulus' to stop and post a letter on some occasions, while at other times it produces no response. Another letter box is a 'stimulus', when I am driving a car, for preparing to turn down the inconspicuous side-road where I live. Other drivers ignore it. So one may well ask, 'When is a stimulus not a stimulus?'

In terms of the present model, the explanation offered is that concepts have different thresholds according to a person's current needs. Schemas which serve the latter become more active as a whole—for we must regard active/latent as a continuum, not a dichotomy—and concepts belonging to them have their thresholds lowered. We both notice and perceive objects in terms of our present needs and interests. Examples abound. Two have just been given: here is another. One glorious summer day, I was walking down a ot city street full of exhaust gases and thinking that this was a day for being n the water. Above a shop window I noticed, with slight surprise, a onspicuous sign 'OUTBOARD MOTORS'. Looking more carefully, owever, I saw that the actual letters were 'OXFORD MOTORS'. Though I ad in fact been thinking about sailing, a general activation of my boating chema had brought about distorting perception of what I saw. 'Freudian slips' can also be explained in terms of the present model.

.16 It is thus only a short step in the development of our concept of a chema, and in agreement with available data, to bring in the idea of *onnections between concepts* to account for the fact that activation of one oncept can activate, or lower the threshold for, others. Those more closely onnected will be more activated than more distant ones. This idea can be lustrated by analogy with a net—not a regular one like a fishing or garden et, but more like a network of roads or electrical connections. The knots epresent concepts, the lines connections between concepts.

Now imagine that this net lies on the floor, above which there is a layer of nist so that we cannot see the net at all. This represents a schema which is atent. Activation of a particular concept brings it right to the surface. Others o which it is connected come nearer the surface: the closer the connections, he nearer the surface. This will happen whether the concept is evoked by ncounter with an example, or by the utterance of a symbol for the concept. he schema as a whole is brought nearer to the surface either by current eeds, or by a symbol (such as a word) for the schema as a whole. Thus two uite different concepts will be evoked by the word 'bat' according as I first ctivate, by appropriate words, a cricketing or baseball schema on the one and, and a wildlife schema on the other.

The net analogy is also helpful in distinguishing between denotative and onnotative meanings of a word (or other symbol). Its denotative meaning is ts attached concept. Its connotative meaning is this together with the network f connected concepts which are also evoked by the word. The latter are likely o be more personal and individual than the former. Scientists and lawyers (as uch) tend to use denotative meanings, to minimize ambiguity, while onnotative meanings are important in poetry.

A resonance model

.17 The net analogy is quite a simple one; and in the difficult task of onstructing and thinking about models of the model-making-and-using rocess itself, this simplicity is useful for getting us started. But when we list ome of the ways in which a concept can be active, we see that the net analogy loes not offer any explanation of how the concept does what is described. These ways include:

i)   enabling a person to distinguish between examples and non-examples;
ii) contributing to a higher-order concept;

(iii) selectively sensitizing perception, as a result of a need;

(iv) becoming an object of reflective thought and/or communication.

We shall now develop a model based on the idea of resonance, which though more difficult has also greater explanatory power.

Resonance is one of the most widespread of effects in the physical sciences. While it is particularly important in radio and television, resonance also explains such diverse phenomena as the dark bands in an absorption spectrum and Caruso's ability to shatter a wine-glass by singing the right note. The reader who is not already familiar with the concept can acquire it quite easily, to a degree sufficient for our present purposes, by performing one or two simple experiments for himself.

The first requires some sort of simple pendulum—a weight on a string, or even a suspended light-fitting. The object serving as a weight should be quite heavy, and the natural time of a single swing somewhere between half a second and five seconds. If you blow at the weight once the effect will be quite small; and likewise even if you continue to blow as hard and long as you are able. But if instead you puff at it regularly, watching the swing and timing your puffs so that you blow whenever the weight is moving away from you, you will find that you can gradually build up quite a sizeable amplitude of swing. Though the force exerted by each of the single puffs is small, by matching their frequency to the natural frequency of swing of the pendulum their effect becomes cumulative. Any one who pushes a child on a swing uses the same method.

For the next experiment, you need a piano. First lift the lid. Find a note which you can sing easily, and press down the piano key for that note slowly so that the note is not sounded but the damper is lifted from the string. Now sing the note for a second or two, stop and listen. You will find that you have without touching or striking it, set the string vibrating audibly. The reason is basically the same as before, except that the natural rate of vibration of the string is much faster (for middle c, 256 complete to-and-fro cycles in every second), and the accurately timed puffs are provided by compression waves of air originating from your vocal cords.

Next, repeat the experiment as before, but instead of raising only the damper for the note sung, raise all of them by pressing the right-hand pedal. Now you will hear a number of other strings vibrating: particularly the octave above the note sung, but also a number of other notes. Part of the explanation for this can easily be found if we think back to our pendulum experiment, or to a child on a swing. If we push, not once for every swing of the child, but on alternate swings, the amplitude will still build up, although more slowly. Likewise if we push at every third, fourth, . . . swing. Here we have kept the natural frequency of the swing the same, and varied the frequency of the applied force. But the effect would be similar if we kept our applied frequency the same, with swings of twice, three, four, . . . times this applied frequency; and this in effect is what is happening on the piano. Strings with frequencies wo, three, four, . . . times as great as the one sung will be heard as one octave higher, an octave and a fifth, two octaves, etc. For middle c these would be c′ frequency 512 cycles per second), g″ (768), and c″ (1024).

The other part of the explanation is that the vibrations produced by the voice, vibrating strings, and indeed most audible vibrations, are not pure wave forms consisting of a single frequency only, but complex wave forms in which, additional to the slowest or fundamental frequency, there are superimposed an assortment of higher frequencies. These higher frequencies, called harmonics, are at 2, 3, 4, 5, 6, . . . times the frequency of the fundamental note. So when we sing into the piano, the fundamental note which we sing causes the vibration of the string having the same natural frequency; while the harmonics, being of higher frequencies, set into vibration the corresponding strings on the piano.

The next experiment is quite striking, and if a piano is not immediately available it is worth taking a little trouble to obtain access to one. Choose a note; raise all the dampers as before, and then sing any vowel sound, say AAH. Repeat with others, lowering the dampers in between: say EEE, OHH, OOO. Experiment with others, including the short sounds Ă, Ĭ. In each case the piano will mimic the sound of your voice with surprising closeness.

Part of the explanation for this can be derived directly from the schema which has just been built up. The harmonics in the vowel sound which is being sung set into vibration the various piano strings having the same frequencies as these harmonics, and these afterwards give back the same harmonics as were present in the complex wave form produced by your voice.

The rest of the explanation depends on the correspondence between the actual physical vibrations and what is experienced in the reality of the hearer.

The amplitude of the vibrations received by our ears determines how loud it sounds; the fundamental frequency determines what we experience as pitch; and the harmonics present, their frequencies and relative amplitudes, are collectively perceived as the quality of the sound. This last, also called its timbre, is changed by changing the vowel sounds voiced while singing the note. More generally, it is by their individual timbre or quality that we distinguish between sounds of the same pitch given out by different musical instruments, and by different singers.

9.18 The effect described in the last section is called *resonance*. Though the term originates from examples in the field of sound, such as those already given, the term is used by physicists for a wide variety of effects in which some structure or system having a particular natural frequency is caused to vibrate by some outside agency which vibrates with the same frequency. Resonant circuits are particularly common in electrical instruments of all kinds. Two important features of resonance have already been seen in particular examples, and they are quite general. The first is the cumulative effect. A force (or its analogue in the system concerned, e.g. electromotive force) which is so small as to be quite ineffective if applied singly, irregularly, or a a frequency other othan the natural frequency of the system to which it i applied at this natural frequency. The second feature results directly from th first. Since a system resonates only to a particular frequency, it can be used t select this from a mixture of frequencies applied externally to it. It is in thi way, by varying the natural frequency of electrical circuits within a radio o television set, that we can selectively receive electromagnetic vibrations o just one frequency from among the many to which our aerial (antenna) i exposed. In brief, and again using a term originating from accousti resonance, we 'tune-in' a desired station.

9.19 Nothing in the section just completed is hypothetical. Everything ther described is well known to physicists, who have developed both the theor and applications of resonance to an advanced level. Among the resonan structures studied are electrical circuits, vibrating strings and air columns molecules, bridges, automobile suspension. What now follows is a menta model of a more hypothetical kind. It uses the ideas of resonance to construc a model by which to support and give more power to our thinking abou concepts and schemas, but it has not yet been tested by mode (i).

The starting point is to suppose that conceptualized memories are store within tuned structures which, when caused to vibrate, give rise to comple wave patterns. (Imagine a set of piano strings corresponding to the vowe sound AAH vocalized at a steady pitch of middle c.) Sensory input whicl matches one of these wave patterns resonates with the corresponding tune structure, or possibly several structures together, and thereby sets up th particular wave pattern of a certain concept.

And in terms of our resonance model, this is how we explain the activatio of a concept by sensory input. The cumulative effect which is one of the mai features of resonance also explains why information of this kind can b carried at such low energy levels (Section 8.2).

This particular mode of activation is experienced as recognition. A matcl between a pattern in present actuality, and a conceptual pattern stored withir an individual's reality, gives rise to a sudden increase in amplitude o vibration within a particular tuned structure; and something 'out there' i suddenly perceived to correspond with something 'in here'.

Concept formation requires the additional hypothesis that repeatec excitation of particular tuned structures increases their sensitivity for future occasions. The closer the time interval, the more quickly this sensitivity build up. Initially, all the tuned structures are equally sensitive. This corresponds tc the 'generalized receptivity' referred to in Section 9.3. But with repetition the structures which correspond to regularities of the environment become more sensitive—more easily activated by subsequent input of similar wave patterns. They now exhibit the selective sensitivity characteristic of all tunec structures, and which has already been described in some particular cases. It i this quality by which we explain the ability of someone having a concept (sc ar at a simple level only) to distinguish between examples and non-examples. Examples activate the wave pattern of a particular tuned structure, non-examples do not. This selective sensitivity also emphasizes the structuring effect of our existing schemas (conceptual structures) on sensory input.

.20   Suppose now that we ask a woman, a man and a boy to sing the same note which we have just sounded on the piano: choosing a note within the compass of all three. We will have no difficulty in perceiving whether each of them is actually singing the right note. We will also be able to tell which person is singing. The concept by which we recognize the note itself consists of the fundamental frequency only. The timbre or quality of sound, by which we distinguish between the three voices, is determined by which harmonics are present, and their relative amplitudes. This depends in turn on the vocal cords and resonant cavities of the particular singer. The same timbre can be recognized at different pitches: if our three singers were to sing consecutive parts of the same melody, we could easily perceive when it was the same singer and when they had changed over.

There is, however, an important difference between recognition of a particular frequency, and of a particular quality. The harmonics which give the same timbre to different notes are themselves different in frequency from note to note. So what is it that stays the same?

In this case two things, both of them proportions,[4] remain the same (or almost so) between notes. Taking a simple case, suppose that the main harmonics present have frequencies of 3, 5, 7, 9 times the fundamental. These are called the 3rd, 5th, 7th, 9th harmonics, the first harmonic being the fundamental itself. If the note sounded is c, the actual frequencies heard would be (for this example):

256   768   1280   1792   2304

or the note g, the actual frequencies would be:

384   1152   1920   2688   3456

But both of these sets of four frequencies are *in the same proportion as*:

1   3   5   7   9

and it is the proportion, not the actual frequencies, which we are able to recognize as remaining the same. This is the first part of what we recognize as timbre.

The second part is the relative amplitude of these harmonics, which determines their relative loudness to the ear. These will stay in the same proportion (or nearly so) whether the note is sounded loudly or softly, and again it is the proportion which we are able to recognize as staying the same. Otherwise, we could not tell whether two notes, one loud and one soft, were on the same or different instruments.

Putting these two parts together, our recognition of timbre depends on ou ability to recognize the same proportions of frequencies and of thei amplitudes, although the actual frequencies and actual amplitudes may differ It is these proportions which can be manipulated on an electronic synthesizer to vary the timbre at will.

The importance of proportionality does not stop here. How is it that if one person sings or plays a tune, and then plays it again starting on a differen note, we can recognize the tune as the same though all the notes are different? Again, what we recognize consists of two proportions, one of frequencies relative to the key-note, the other of durations relative to the starting note. I to these we add another proportion, that of relative amplitudes (determining relative loudness), we have now included much of the expressive quality.

It is clear from the foregoing that an ability to recognize the same proportion, in a variety of different examples, is a central feature of the kinds of conceptual activity which we have been discussing. And it is these same kinds which are embodied in the recognition of speech (the same word spoken at different pitches and with different timbres) and of speakers (different words at different pitches with the same timbre). The rise and fall of the voice also convey shades of meaning, and emotional content. The wave patterns of consonants are more complex than those of vowels, and the successions of wave patterns in words are more complex than those of melodies; but the basic requirements for recognition are the same.

Our model as developed so far can recognize, by selective resonance particular wave patterns. How can we now expand it to be able to recognize different sets of wave patterns which are in the same proportion?

9.21 The key to the next step is a mathematical one; the idea of a logarithmic scale. In order not to lose the non-mathematical reader, I shall include only as much about logarithms as is essential to follow the argument; so what follows is accurate in outline, but not complete in every detail. I shall also assume that the reader has come across logarithms before, so that we are not starting entirely from the beginning.

A logarithmic function is one which converts equal *multiples* into equal *differences*. Here is a simple example, in which the arrows mean 'is converted by the logarithm function (base 10) to . . . ':

$$
\begin{array}{rcl}
1 & \longrightarrow & 0 \\
10 & \longrightarrow & 1 \\
100 & \longrightarrow & 2 \\
1\,000 & \longrightarrow & 3 \\
10\,000 & \longrightarrow & 4 \\
\text{etc.} & & \text{etc.}
\end{array}
$$

Here, multiplying by 10 down the left-hand column is converted to adding 1 down the right-hand column. Equal multiples, say from 1 to 100 or 10 to 1 000, are converted to equal intervals, in this case from 0 to 2, or 1 to 3.

A piano keyboard is logarithmic in character, if we regard the distances between keys as measuring differences between notes. Going left (lower notes) and right (higher notes) from middle c, we have:

Table 5

Frequencies				
64	128	256	512	1024
c''	c'	c	$c^{'}$	$c^{''}$
Notes		(middle)		

This lower, logarithmic scale corresponds to how we experience these notes in reality. The differences in pitch between any two adjacent Cs are all experienced as equal intervals, namely one octave. Likewise for intermediate notes: for brevity, only two are shown.

Table 6

Frequencies												
64	80	96	128	160	192	256	320	384	512	640	768	1024
c''	E''	G''	c'	E'	G'	c	e	g	$c^{'}$	$e^{'}$	$g^{'}$	$c^{''}$
Notes						(middle)						
Logarithms (base 2) of frequencies												
6	6.32	6.58	7	7.32	7.58	8	8.32	8.58	9	9.32	9.58	10

Logarithms (to base 2) have now been added, showing now more precisely how equal multiples of frequencies are transformed into equal differences between logarithms.

An interval from C to G is called by musicians a fifth. At different octaves, the actual frequencies will be (writing them in pairs as ratios[4])

$$64 : 96 \qquad 128 : 192 \qquad 256 : 384 \qquad 512 : 768$$

But all these ratios are equivalent to each other, and to the simpler ratio 2 : 3. And this interval is experienced as the same, in whatever octave it occurs. Likewise for the interval from C to E, called a major third. Wherever it occurs, the frequency ratio of the two notes is equivalent to 4 : 5, and the interval is experienced as the same wherever it occurs. Looking now at the logarithms, these two ratios correspond to logarithmic intervals of 0.58 (a musical fifth) and 0.32 (a musical third).

All our model therefore requires to explain our ability to recognize proportions is the assumption that it can respond logarithmically. Not only logarithmically—we can conceptualize individual notes as well as intervals between them, and we can recognize difference in the pitch at which they are played as well as samenesses of melody. So our model requires two levels of response and thus of recognition, one 'as it comes' and one logarithmic.

9.22 We have now explained, in terms of the model, our ability to recognize the same intervals, though the notes themselves may be different. Once our model includes a way of perceiving proportionality, this can be used to explain all the other perceptual abilities which were seen in 9.20 to depend on this: timbre, melody (relative pitch and relative duration), expressive quality, leading on to the recognition of speech and of speakers.

The same principle can also be applied to visual perception. Unfortunately, to do so here would take us too far afield: but the reader who is able to consult Gibson's (1950) elegant analysis of visual perception will recognize the close analogy with the introductory outline of auditory perception which has here been presented. Gibson deals (among other things) with our perception of the constancy of shape when an object is seen at different angles, of size when an object is seen at different distances, and also of distance itself. From his work it can be clearly seen that our perception of these is dependent on our ability to recognize not only ratios which are in the same proportion, but also proportions between proportions, and rates of change of these.

9.23 Our resonance model now offers an explanation, albeit for simple cases only, of (i) in Section 9.17: namely the ability of persons having appropriate concepts to recognize examples, and to distinguish between these and non-examples. Again at a simple level, the model has also shown itself able to explain (ii); since timbre and melody are both higher-order concepts than pitch and duration. If vibarations within the model also resonate with each other, bearing in mind the logarithmic property, there is the beginning of an idea how higher-order concepts could arise spontaneously within the model, and in particular the discovery of analogies. These beginnings cannot be taken any further for the present, for a more important addition to the model awaits attention. This is to relate it to consciousness, and to wants and needs.

In Section 9.17 the basic feature of the resonance model was introduced: tuned structures which resonate selectively to wave-forms representing particular concepts. Up till now we have considered the effect on these of sensory input—and also, the structuring and selective effect *of* these *on* sensory input. Now let us imagine that there are also internal inputs to these conceptual structures, of a very general kind which we will call 'excitation'. This excitation will have the effect of setting the tuned circuits vibrating, each at its own particular frequency. For an experimental illustration, gently depress the piano keys for G, B, D, g, so as to raise the dampers without hitting the strings. Now bang the woodwork, clap hands, or in any other way mit a sound of mixed frequency. Each string will select from this general excitation its own particular frequency, and respond to this.

We now have an analogy for lowered and heightened consciousness, the sleep and waking states. This only requires the supposition of a general excitation of all the resonant structures of small or zero amplitude during states of diminished consciousness and sleep, and of greater amplitude in states of heightened consciousness. The various resonant structures will hereby be set vibrating, each in its own characteristic way. (It is as though nobody is now singing into the piano, but it is vibrating all over of its own accord, as a result of which certain patterns of strings are in continual gentle vibration.) This will have the effect of making them more or less sensitive to sensory input, according as they are already in vibration to a greater or lesser amount.

Wants and needs of a particular kind will also have this excitatory effect, but localized now to concepts, representing particular goal states, or to schemas representing particular domains. This selectively sensitizes perception towards objects relevant to the satisfaction of these wants, and also for paths, literal or metaphorical, towards those objects. We now have an explanation, in terms of the resonance model, of the 'letter box' example in Section 9.15. If the reader will briefly refer to that section, he will realize that the concept of a stimulus has now been put into reverse. It is not that the letter box is a stimulus for action, but that a need or goal state selectively sensitizes one's perception so that one picks out a letter box from among the multitude of objects within the range of one's vision.

In Section 9.19 it was suggested that the more frequently particular tuned structures are activated into vibration, the more easily activated they become. If we now combine this increased sensitivity with the generalized excitation from within, which has just been described, there will come a stage when many of one's concepts can be sufficiently activated in this way alone, without sensory input, to be accessible to consciousness. We now have the state of affairs described in Section 9.17 (iv), in which concepts can be objects of reflective thought and/or communication. Both of these aspects will be taken up again later.

9.24 Given that we all have a wide assortment of schemas by which present incoming sense data, or symbolic communications, might be construed, are they all activated simultaneously, or are they in competition? And if in competition, what are the factors that determine which particular schema takes over?

On the medium and long wavebands of a radio receiver, if several transmitting stations are close together in frequency, we hear them all however carefully we tune. The most powerful comes in loudest, and this may or may not be the one we want to hear.

In our mental resonance model, want selectively sensitizes perception;

either by activating as a whole the schema of a director system which could lead to the satisfaction of the want, or by first activating a concept representing a goal state, and thereby subsequently the schema of which it forms part. Whether I perceive a department store as a place to buy something, somewhere to shelter from the rain, or where I may hope to find a toilet, will depend on present goal or anti-goal states. Schemas are also activated from within, and are thus more likely to respond to some particular input, by a current universe of discourse or occupation. We hear the word 'wash' one way when talking about clothes, and in quite another when talking about boats. This is clearly pro-survival—we realize input by concepts belonging to the director system appropriate to our present goal state. But if, as in the radio example, the others persist as background noise, this is still a distraction. So far as goals are concerned, it would be an advantage if we could shut out these interferences: though always remaining alert to signals from anti-goals.

Radio engineers have solved this problem in two ways: frequency modulation (FM) and automatic frequency control (AFC). Leaving aside the technical details, the effect of frequency modulation is that once the correct station is accurately tuned, sensitivity to other input drops and background noise is reduced almost to zero. Automatic frequency control is a goal-seeking mechanism by which, when a station is approximately tuned, one's receiver homes in on that station, which acts as an attractor.

Both of these are examples of what we may conveniently call a capture effect, using a term borrowed from radio engineering. This effect is stronger than that of an attractor: there may be several attractors, but only one of these actually captures. If mechanisms for proving this can be provided within a man-made system of resonant circuits, clearly they could in principle have been evolved as part of the complex electrical circuitry of our brains. So by adding this to the resonance model already outlined, we can provide the beginning of an explanation of the process by which a particular schema, having successfully claimed our attention, gradually takes over almost the whole of our consciousness for the time being. Current input is then either construed in terms of this schema, or fails to reach consciousness at all.

And although we are as a matter of policy concentrating on the ways in which intelligence functions rather than on its physical basis, nevertheless it is reassuring to know that the model is entirely compatible with what is known about brain function as a complex of rhythmic electrical activity.

9.25 Although the resonance model which has been described in Sections 9.17 to 9.24 is not an essential part of the overall theoretical model which is being offered in the present volume, it will be found a useful adjunct. Especially to those who are already familiar with the accoustical phenomena described, or who care to perform the simple experiments suggested, it offers a concrete analogy which is helpful in thinking about the very abstract concepts which are involved; and the reader who cares to review the earlier part of this chapter will find that the resonance model assimilates to itself, and thereby draws together, a number of the matters which have been dealt with.

Another merit of the resonance model is that while it would be too much to claim that it explains creative mental activity, it is certainly more open in this direction than more mechanistic kinds of model. If one has a number of tuned structures, which are kept in continual vibration by general excitation from within, then other tuned structures will tend to respond to proportions between these; becoming more sensitive by being excited over a period of time (Section 9.19). So after a while, two ideas will interact to produce a third and new idea. Moreover, which of these are more continually in vibration will depend not only on our history of past sensory input, but on emotional factors—our needs, and personality. So mental creativity will be a very individual process.

A further interesting feature of the resonance model is the importance it attaches to our ability to perceive the equivalence of ratios, and of ratios between ratios. It could be—which is not to say that it is so—that by building on this, we might move towards an understanding of rationality itself, which is one of man's highest attributes.

These last two paragraphs are much more speculative than what has gone before. But speculation itself, provided we know which modes of reality testing are in temporary suspense, plays a more important part than is usually acknowledged in the expansion of scientific thinking into new areas. Imagination is as necessary to a creative scientist as logical and methodological rigour.

9.26 The main points of this chapter are:

(i) *Concepts and schemas are not distinct kinds of mental entities. Sometimes one classification is better, sometimes the other, according to purpose. A schema can be thought of as a concept with interiority.*

(ii) *Primary concepts are those which have been abstracted by direct sensory experience from actuality. Secondary concepts are those which are derived from other concepts.*

(iii) *Among the factors which affect concept formation are frequency of contributory experiences (which includes their number and the time intervals between them), noise, and the availability of necessary lower-order concepts. Matching can act as a precursor of abstraction. These factors are random in everyday life, but they can be manipulated by a teacher who understands them.*

(iv) *For the successful direction of action it is necessary both to possess and to use the right concepts.*

(v) *A resonance model is offered as helpful for thinking about concepts and schemas, and provides possible explanations for selective perception, formation of higher-order concepts, reflection, and creativity. A connection can be seen with the idea of rationality itself.*

Notes for Chapter 9

1. This reality testing seems evident to me from the actions described by Piaget (1955) as 'secondary circular reactions', which he observed in children aged less than 6 months.

2. This process is discussed in greater detail in Skemp (1971), pages 43–46. (At that time I was using the term 'accommodation' for what I now call 're-construction'.)

3. To the mathematical reader, it must be made clear that these relationships are not equivalence relationships. The term 'equivalence class' as here used is, however, consistent with its mathematical use, and the relationship between any two members of the same equivalence class is an equivalence relation in the mathematical sense. See Skemp (1971), the beginning of Chapter 10.

4. A proportion is a set of equivalent ratios. For example the ratios $1:2$, $2:4$, $3:6$, $10:20$, $45:90$, all belong to the same proportion. The triple ratios $2:3:7$, $10:15:35$, both belong to the same proportion.

CHAPTER 10

Understanding

10.1 We now come to the important but difficult topic of understanding, which is central to the present conception of intelligence.

Subjectively, we usually think we know whether we understand something or not. We also feel that it matters. Just what it is that happens when we do understand but does not happen when we don't, few can say: nor what are the obstacles to understanding, and how to overcome them. Nor do we know whether it has the importance which subjectively we feel it has, and if so why.

First as a teacher, then as a psychologist, and now as an educationist, this problem is one which has confronted me for many years. A first step towards trying to answer these questions was taken in the context of mathematics (Skemp, 1971), where the contrast between understanding and non-understanding shows particularly clearly, and where the mental discomfort of not understanding is a source of grief to many children. Using hindsight, this was a good place to start, since mathematics offers low-noise examples (see Section 9.9) of many of the concepts needed to understand understanding. At that time, however, the present model had not been developed. We are now in a position to make further progress.

We have already seen that the functioning of each one of our director systems depends on the use of a variety of schemas (conceptual structures) within which can be represented a present state, a goal state, and other states from which we can construct paths between any two states, provided that both are within this structure. To support our thinking in this difficult area, diagrams such as Figure 25 have been found helpful. This is an expansion of that part of the general diagram (Figure 12, Section 5.10) which represents present state and goal state.

To start with, this may be thought of as a road map, so 'state' here means location. P is as usual the present state (location), G the goal state, and from the map one can find several paths by which to direct one's actions so as to get from P to G.

The next step is to generalize the diagram by thinking of it as a cognitive

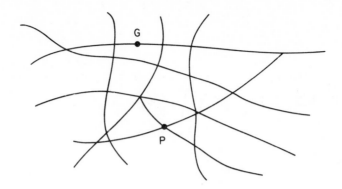

Figure 25

map. Though this term seems to be employed mostly as a useful metaphor, it can be made more precise by thinking of it as representing any set of states within the same universe of discourse. A single point represents some particular state, and points connected by lines represent states such that the operand can be taken from one to the other. As a two-dimensional universe of this kind, think of an operand for which state means (temperature, pressure). Under given conditions, these may well be interdependent, in which case only particular points and paths will appear in the diagram.

Finally, when confidence has been gained, these diagrams may be thought of as representing schemas. Each point now represents a state of an unspecified kind, and some of the points may themselves have much interiority. Movement along a line represents change from one state of the operand to another, and the lines and their connections show the possible ways of taking the operand from one state to another. This generalization includes the original idea of a road map as a particular case, by giving 'state' the particular meaning of location; and when thinking at a high level of abstraction becomes difficult, it is often a help to drop down to this level for as long as necessary.

Our schemas are at the core of our viability, in any universe of discourse: be it literally finding our way to the place we want to be, or the complex and abstract paths by which we move from awareness of a problem to its solution. But suppose now that a concept is activated into consciousness which we find is isolated from any appropriate schema (Figure 26).

At this stage, P can be anywhere. We do not even know in which direction it literally finding our way to the place we want to be, or the complex and such situations we are mentally lost, just as surely as if we were physically in unknown territory. And this, in general terms, is our state of mind when confronted with some object, experience, situation, or idea which we do not understand.

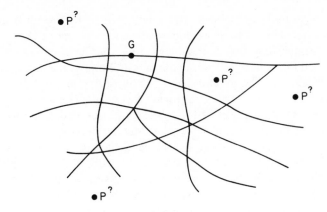

Figure 26

The achievement of understanding makes connections with an existing schema, as shown in Figure 27.

The new state has now been brought within the domain of a director system. We now know that in such a state, we could cope. Metaphorically (and in particular cases literally), we know where we are, so we can find a way to where we want to be. And referring back to Table 3 (Section 7.7), we can now recognize the emotions which signal not understanding as frustration and anxiety, and those which signal understanding as confidence and security.

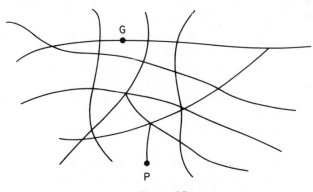

Figure 27

10.2 The generality of the above formulation has both advantages and disadvantages, as will be seen more clearly when explanation itself has been connected with the present model. In the present section we shall consider five categories within the above general description, with examples of each category: in each case contrasting non-understanding with understanding.

(i) We encounter an object or event which we cannot adequately categorize. This is what we mean when we say, more loosely, that we 'don't know what it is'. Someone gave me for Christmas an object which consisted of a sharp hollow needle, about 2 mm in diameter, attached to a polished handle in two parts which slid telescopically apart and together. Beautifully made, but what was it for? The foregoing concepts, activated by perception of this object, did not enable me to connect it with any goal-directed activity. Fortunately there were also instructions in the box. By reading these I was able to classify the object as an opener for wine bottles, to be used by piercing the cork and pumping the handle until the air in the bottle was compressed sufficiently to force the cork out. When I *realized* what it was, (see Section 4.6), i.e., when it activated concepts within my wine-bottle-opening schema, I understood what I had been given and how to use it.

Next time I saw one of these, on a shelf at the back of a bar, recognition was immediate. In such cases, and whenever we encounter familiar objects and events, we are less likely to think of the experience as one which involves understanding. The difference here, however, is not between presence or absence of understanding, but in the attention we give to it. Familiarity and routine functioning take place at low levels of consciousness (Section 2.8); so we only become aware of this process called understanding when novelty both enhances consciousness, and delays or prevents the achievement of understanding. Nevertheless, I think that the continuous realization of new experience by an existing schema has to be accepted as within the present conception of understanding. It is one way in which what is newly encountered becomes connected with an existing schema; and if in some instances these connections are easily and quickly made, this is not sufficient reason for withholding the description of understanding.

(ii) Realization does not necessarily bring understanding, however, for there are some states which we can correctly classify by an available concept, and for which we have an appropriate schema; but we cannot make the necessary connections between the two, so we cannot construct any path from these states to chosen goal states. My tape deck provides an example. On playback (not on record) it sometimes enters a state in which it receives foreign radio stations and feeds this into the amplifier. No one with whom I have discussed the matter has been able to explain it, or even to offer a plausible hypothesis. Though we fully realize what is happening, we cannot relate it to our existing schemas about tape decks and radio reception, probably because these schemas are not sufficiently extensive. Correct realization is thus necessary, but not sufficient, for understanding.

More serious examples are offered by those medical diseases which have been identified, but for which no cure is yet known. Here the operand is the patient, and both his present (medical) state and his goal state are known. What is not yet known is how to take him from one to the other. Understanding, in this case, will involve making the necessary connections with an existing body of medical knowledge.

(iii) In the first and second categories, those concerned know that they do not understand. But a five-year-old not only does not understand Ohm's law, relativity theory, and photosynthesis: he does not know he doesn't understand, since they have no existence within any of his realities. In the complete absence of an appropriate schema, not only can there not be any understanding at all, but there may be complete unawareness of its absence. Before Faraday, Marie Curie, Röntgen, Marconi, it was this kind of non-understanding which was universal with respect to electromagnetic phenomena, radioactivity of molecules, X-rays, and radio waves. In cases of this kind, whole new schemas have to be built up before there is an appropriate schema at all, by connection to which understanding would be possible. And it is only when our schemas are far enough developed to sensitize us to some of the more abstract regularities of nature that we know that there is something to understand. This also explains why the more we know, the more we realize how much we don't know. It was a genius, Isaac Newton, not an ignorant person, who said:

> ... to myself I seem to have been only like a boy playing on the sea-shore, and diverting myself in now and then finding a smoother pebble or a prettier shell than ordinary, whilst the great ocean of truth lay all undiscovered before me.

(iv) We may mis-understand, meaning that we think we understand something when we do not. This may be because we connect it wrongly to an appropriate schema; as in the case of a friend of mine who, for some time after he had a job in London, continued to think that Oxford Street ran into Piccadilly Circus, and wondered why he got lost. Or we may connect it to an inappropriate schema. There are still those who attribute bodily illness to the influence of malevolent spirits. If we mis-construe an event, by realizing it in terms of the wrong concept, mis-understanding will also result. A little boy kept hitting the back of the newspaper which his father was reading over breakfast. Initially his father reproved him for ill behaviour, but no improvement resulted. He then realized that his son wanted him to pay attention to him rather than to the newspaper; after which he was able to act more appropriately to satisfy both their needs.

Activation of the wrong concept can also happen at a perceptual level, as when we mistake chocolate sauce for gravy. It also happens when the same word has several meanings, and we attach the wrong one.

The ways in which we may discover a misunderstanding all fall into one or more of the categories of reality testing described in Chapter 4.

Our actions do not lead to the expected result in actuality; we find that other people understand things differently from the way we do (i.e. in terms of different concepts and schemas); or we find inconsistencies.

(v) There is rather a special kind of understanding, which applies to words and other symbols. To understand one of these means to associate the symbol with an appropriate concept. So to mis-understand means to associate it with an inappropriate concept, and not to understand at all means to be unable to associate it with any concept. Even to recognize it as a symbol within some known category, for example, a word in a foreign language, constitutes understanding of a kind which is far from useless, since it enables us to take the appropriate action of looking it up in the right dictionary.

All these five kinds of understanding come within the general description given in Section 10.1. This will now be formulated concisely, after which it may be found helpful to re-read Section 10.1 and the present section.

To understand a concept, group of concepts, or symbols, is to connect it with an appropriate schema. To understand an experience is to realize it within an appropriate schema. A state of understanding is one within the domain of a director system, which can therefore function. Not understanding means the opposite. Understanding is therefore crucial to the achievement of our goal states, and thus to survival.

The achievement of understanding is thus itself a goal state of great importance and generality, and the present model predicts that its achievement will be accompanied by the pleasurable emotions of confidence and security (see Section 7.7, Table 3). There may be exceptions to this, since understanding may sometimes bring with it awareness that the situation is beyond one's present power to remedy. But at least one knows what would have to be done to achieve the desired goal, which is a step in the right direction. So as a generalized goal, understanding is certainly pro-survival more often than not; and it is on this basis that natural selection has operated, giving us an innate curiosity to understand the universe in which we live.

Knowledge and understanding

10.3 Finding ourselves in a state of non-understanding, there are various choices open to us. Much will depend on how high we rate the importance of this particular universe: for our well-being depends on the total contributions which result from successful functioning of our respective director systems within many different universes of discourse. Much will also depend on how much the achievement of understanding is likely to cost, in time and effort. It can be a long and difficult struggle; so if we set this as a goal state within one universe, it has to be in small or large degree at the expense of progress in other universes. We have only limited resources, particularly in time.

Knowledge and understanding are so closely connected that the terms are often used interchangeably. But they are not quite the same. A particular area of knowledge is a schema, tested against actuality in the ways already discussed in Chapter 3. The greater the extent and depth of a person's total knowledge, the more of what he encounters or thinks about will he be able to understand. So knowledge is one of the major contributors to understanding. It is not the only factor, however. The other one is ability to apply it—to realize the new task in terms of one's existing knowledge, and find ways of achieving the desired goal state.

Once someone has achieved new understanding in this way, by the enlargement of his own knowledge, its benefits can be shared in two different ways. One is by the exchange of expertise. We all rely on the help of those who have spent much time increasing their knowledge in fields such as motor engineering, electronics, medicine, law, cooking—a long list could be extracted from the 'yellow pages' of a telephone directory. No great understanding on our part is required to enable us to couple our director systems to theirs. It includes being able to identify the appropriate universe of discourse: whether it is medicine, motor engineering, or electronics. It also includes compatibility between our own schemas and those of our chosen expert. Another way in which we can use the expertise of others is by buying its results; as embodied in motor cars, washing machines, refrigerators, cameras, television sets, etc. Much less knowledge is needed to use these than to make them.

The other way of sharing the benefits of understanding has already been mentioned, in Sections 1.10 and 1.11. Knowledge slowly achieved by previous generations, and by contemporary experts, can be made available to others by symbolic communication. This is one of the functions of education, including self-education; and it is hoped that the present model will prove to be a useful one within this major universe of discourse. For the schemas built up by education can form a major contribution to our powers of understanding.

We can now see how a positive-sum system of relationships of great value can develop within a community where there is a suitable balance between the achievement of completely new understanding the hard way by particular individuals; the building up of knowledge by learning from those who already know; the exchange of expertise in many ways; and the raising of our overall level of general knowledge. These processes together provide a collective level and extent of knowledge, and thereby potential for understanding, which is one of the major differences between advanced and primitive cultures.

Symbols

10.4 The use of symbols for the communication of concepts is an essential feature of such a system, and to this process we now turn our attention.

Concepts are personal to each individual, and cannot be directly observed by any one else (Indeed, they can be elusive and inaccessible even to their possessor.) A symbol is something which is observable, mentally connected with a concept. If person A wishes to communicate certain ideas to person B, this appears to be quite easy. All A has to do is talk to B, or write to him, or show him certain mathematical, chemical, or electrical symbols on paper, blackboard, screen—actions which collectively we will call *uttering* these symbols. But this appearance is deceptive. The ideas which come into B's consciousness have not been put there by A. At a first approximation, they have been evoked from B's own concept store by their connection with the symbols uttered by A. This presupposes first, that the concept is available in B's store. Second, that the same symbol is connected to this concept in the minds of both A and B. So the next approximation to what happens is that the concept in A's mind activates this symbol, which A utters; which B receives; which activates the same symbol in B's mind; which activates a concept in B's mind like that in A's mind. This chain of events is represented by Figure 28.

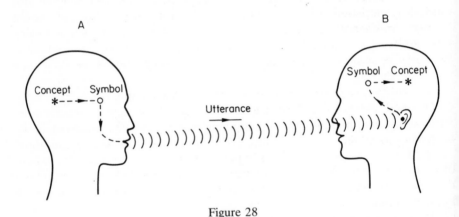

Figure 28

The term 'activates' has just been applied, twice in the same sentence, to the term 'symbol'. As originally introduced, 'activate' referred to concepts; and the recent statement that concepts are private, while symbols are publicly observable, may well have suggested that symbols are different from concepts. This must be clarified.

Symbols too are concepts of a kind. A particular word will be not pronounced exactly the same by any two people; and very differently, say, by a child from one part of a country and an old person with a different regional accent. Handwriting and typography also differ. That we can recognize different utterances as examples of the same symbol therefore implies a simple kind of conceptualisation. And a familiar word spoken with a strongly different accent may not be recognized by the hearer until his concept of this ymbol has been somewhat expanded. So each individual symbol is itself a rimary concept, with these properties:

i) a fresh example can be produced when we want, by speaking, writing, drawing, projecting on a screen, or otherwise uttering;
ii) it activates and is activated by another concept, which is its meaning;
iii) for communication it is also necessary that the symbol activates the same concept (so far as one can tell) in the utterer and the receiver.

This is not the end of the matter, for what has to be communicated is not only the set of concepts themselves, but their inter-relationships, or structure. To this we shall return in Section 10.11. Meanwhile it may be emphasized that the aim of the foregoing has been, not to complicate a simple and everyday activity, but to reveal the complexity behind what only appears as simple, partly because we do it every day. Once we have realized the tenuousness of the links, we shall be less likely to make the mistake of assuming that we are communicating when we are not. We should indeed be surprised, not that we sometimes fail to understand one another, but that we succeed as often and as well as we do.

Co-operation of any complexity depends on successful communication. This in turn requires both a common coding/decoding system, and matching schemas. How well two invisible objects match is necessarily a matter of some uncertainty, whatever they may be; and this uncertainty applies with particular force to concepts and schemas. Where these are of a fairly low order of abstraction, a shared environment makes the assumption of matching schemas not too unreasonable. Where high-order abstractions are concerned, is a different matter.

Communication at a high level of abstraction has advantages as well as disadvantages. Among the advantages are low noise, high information content, great generality: and above all, the fact that these high-order regularities are hard to discover for the first time. Some of the disadvantages are directly related to these advantages. Too little noise initially may cause difficulties subsequently, when the concepts need to be used in noisy situations. High information content often results in underestimation of the time required for assimilation, by both communicator and receiver: so both are liable to go too fast. Great generality may result in lack of interiority of the concepts; and it may therefore be difficult to find the way down from general concepts to particular cases. Both communicator and receiver can help to reduce these disadvantages: the former by not only using these high-order abstractions, but also giving examples which provide content for categories, offer paradigms for finding other examples by the matching process described in Section 9.8, and reduce the concentration of information. This combination is what I have tried to provide throughout the writing of this book: a recent example of such an attempt being in Sections 9.11 (abstract level of communication) and 9.12 (examples).

Ten functions of symbols

10.5 Though communication is one of the most conspicuous functions of symbols, there are a number of others. So far I have been able to identify ten in all, which though related are sufficiently distinct to be considered under separate headings. These are:

(i)   *communication*;
(ii)   *recording knowledge enduringly*;
(iii)   *the communication of new concepts*;
(iv)   *making multiple classification straightforward*;
(v)   *explanations*;
(vi)   *making possible reflective mental activity*;
(vii)   *helping to show structure*;
(viii) *making routine thinking automatic*;
(ix)   *recovering information and understanding*;
(x)   *creative mental activity*.

These will be taken one at a time in the next nine sections, the first having been discussed already.

10.6 *Recording knowledge enduringly.* Ideas remain highly perishable so long as they exist only in the reality of one individual. By spoken communication, they become less vulnerable, because they no longer perish with the death of a single person; and if they are repeatedly handed on in this way, they can become part of the tradition of a particular social group. But there are still severe limitations on what can be conserved in this way, imposed by the limited memories of individuals. By carving symbols in stone, incising them on clay which is then baked, writing them on parchment, the conceptual world has gained a durable foothold in actuality. With printing this has, as we first saw in Section 1.11, become ever more extensive. Instead of being limited to what can be stored within individual minds, and passed on by the spoken word, the space available for storage is now limited only by how many books we print and how many libraries we build.

What can be stored in this way, however, is not the knowledge itself, but something which can, given the right conditions, be used to gain knowledge. A coded map of a treasure island is not wealth in itself. The code has to be understood, latitude and longitude must be translated into position on the earth's surface, and to arrive at this location it is necessary to have knowledge of navigation. Likewise, the enormous potential conferred by what we call for short 'recorded knowledge' can only be used by those with the prerequisite knowledge by which they can attach the right meanings to these symbols. When these are understood, individuals can use the resulting schemas to direct their actions in ways they could never in a lifetime have found out for themselves. Ideas without symbols are transitory, but the potential value of symbols to which we cannot attach the right meanings remains neither realized nor actualized. Linear A is still undeciphered.[1]

10.7 *The communication of new concepts*. The first two functions of symbols presuppose that the symbols used by the communicator are connected with the same concepts, or rather with matching concepts, in the mind of the receiver. But if no such concept is there, what then? How can symbols be used by one person to bring about, or at least hasten, the formation of a new concept by someone else?

One of the most commonly used, and also mis-used, ways of trying to do this is by giving them a definition. This works (when it does) by relating together classes already know to the hearer. From where I sit to write this chapter (it is the summer vacation) my window overlooks an estuary frequented by yachts. In conversation a visitor asks 'What is a ketch?' 'A ketch is a sailing boat with two masts, the main mast in front and the smaller mast (called a mizzen) behind.[2] The sails on both masts are fore-and-aft'. All these terms have meanings for the visitor, which is to say that she has concepts attached to them. By relating these together in ways corresponding to the structure of the sentences, she can now form the class-concept *ketch*.

For some readers, however, the words 'fore-and-aft' may not have a clear concept attached. It might be possible to communicate this by another verbal definition, but in this case a pair of drawings is easier (Figure 29). This assumes familiarity with an assortment of different kinds of sails. What these drawings aim to do is to enable a person looking at them to differentiate two main classes, and to attach the words 'fore-and-aft' to one, and 'square rig' to the other.

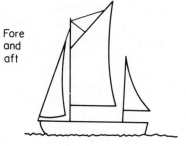

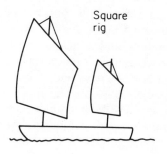

Figure 29

It is important for the communicator to know that definitions work only from higher to lower levels of abstraction or generality, and where the new concept can be formed by relating existing classes. In the foregoing example, ketch is less general than sailing boat; sailing boat is less general than boat; main mast is less general than mast; and so on. Definitions are at their worst for communicating new concepts when these are of a higher order of abstraction than the relevant ones which the recipient already has. Most of the concepts used in everyday life are relatively low in degree of abstraction, and so the prerequisites for the kind of approach exemplified by the 'ketch' example are satisfied. Communication succeeds at these low levels of abstraction more by luck than by knowledge. But in the teaching of subjects in which a major part of the learner's task is the formation of increasingly abstract concepts, communication fails without either side knowing why. This happens particularly widely in the teaching of mathematics, and is one of the reasons why so many persons come to grief in trying to learn it.

How mathematical concepts can best be communicated has been discussed at length elsewhere (Skemp, 1971). The principle has already been mentioned in Section 9.8, in which we saw how symbols could be used to bring together lower-order concepts in a person's mind with the intention of enabling him to abstract their common properties and thereby to form a higher-order concept. The other requirement is that the necessary lower-order concepts shall be both present, and activated, in the mind of the learner. This requires a careful analysis by the communicator to find out exactly what these contributory concepts are, and what are the contributors to these, and so on. Although the principles are straightforward, they are widely ignored; and their application involves extensive re-thinking of existing approaches. The successful communication of mathematical concepts is so demanding a task that the more one begins to realize all that is involved, the better one understands why so many find it a problem subject.

10.8 *Making multiple classification straightforward.* 'What is this?' 'It's sandstone veined with green copper ore, with an embedded fossil'. 'It's an interesting piece of rock which I'm polishing for a paperweight'. 'Don't look—it's going to be your birthday present'.

In these three possible replies, the same actual object has just been classified in three different ways, with the help of three different groups of symbols, and in relation to three different goal states or possible goal states. So frequent is it that a single object belongs to several categories at the same time—indeed, so seldom is it that an object can only be usefully categorized in a simple way—that an appropriate reply to the question 'What is this?' cannot be given without assuming a particular universe of discourse, or knowing what is the purpose behind the question.

By 'appropriate' is meant that it enables the hearer to relate the object to an appropriate schema: that is, one by which he can direct his actions towards his goal state. Or rather, one of his goal states: for our survival is the cumulative result of achieving and/or maintaining a wide assortment of goal states of a great variety of operands, animate and inanimate. We function simultaneously in several at a time, and move quickly from one to another. Though many of these switches are routine, words and other symbols contribute greatly to the versatility of our behaviour by bringing into activity, at the right moment, some particular one out of our many available concepts. This is particularly useful when an important way to classify, realize, and thereby use to direct actions is not one that is obvious to perception. 'Careful, this plate is hot.' (He can see that it is a plate, but by the time his senses tell him it is hot he has either dropped it or burnt himself.) 'I did not realize how strong the sun was.' ('Dangerously high in ultra-violet content' was the category he should have used here, as well as the sensuous pleasure of warmth penetrating his skin.)

We also need to bear in mind that alternative classifications may be used to disguise the goals of the speaker, and make them appear more like our own. A 'free offer' is usually also a selling device. 'Packed flat for easy transport' means also 'You have to assemble it yourself'. There is no need to be manipulated if one accepts that the other party to any commercial transaction will surely have goals of his own. Putting them into words for oneself is a useful device for keeping these in view, as well as one's own goals.

There is a well-known passage by Eddington (1928) in which he refers to his 'two desks'. One is the desk of everyday experience, solid, opaque, stationary; and the other is that of the atomic physicist, a cloud of tiny particles with more space than solid matter, transparent to X-rays, with each molecule in constant motion. These are two realizations of one and the same physical object, each as valid as the other, made possible by two different schemas. Which is appropriate to use at a given time depends on the activity and purpose in which one is engaged. And whereas the everyday use of our desks hardly needs symbols to bring it to our consciousness, the second kind of realization is impossible without.

10.9 *Explanations.* An explanation is a conceptual bridge which, by forming connections with an appropriate schema, makes possible new understanding. This includes the kind of explanation which a person constructs for himself unaided; but in the present section we shall concentrate on those given by symbolic communication from others. Often words and diagrams are used together to evoke the bridging concepts, and show how they relate to each other.

The kind of explanation needed will vary according to the kind of non-understanding which is the present mental state of the person to be helped. Realization of this state by the explainer is therefore necessary for success. Here are some examples, corresponding to the same categories as were used in Section 10.2.

(i)   'What is this?'

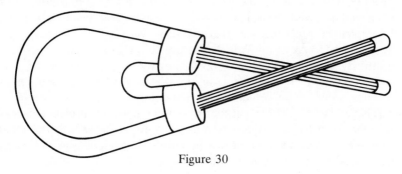

Figure 30

Meaning 'I cannot categorize this appropriately.' Explanation: 'It's a knife sharpener.' (Evokes category already available to hearer.)

(ii)   (a) 'How do you use it?'. Meaning 'I am now able to categorize it, but I cannot connect it with my existing knife-sharpening schema which is based on rubbing the blade on a carborundum stone.' 'You pull the blade between those two prongs, pressing it in firmly. Be careful you don't cut yourself.' This explanation builds a conceptual bridge between an existing schema and the new gadget. This enlarged schema also brings its user within risk distance of an anti-goal which was absent from his previous knife-sharpening schema, so it was also appropriate to call attention to this.

(b) In some cases the conceptual bridge needed to connect the new concept to an appropriate existing schema may be a longer one. Example: 'What is an achromatic lens?' For many adults the necessary connecting concepts will probably be available (refraction of light, spectrum, Newton's experiments with prisms, etc.); so the explainer only needs to evoke these in a suitable sequence by the use of symbols, verbal and visual.

(c) If the necessary concepts are not all available, then a full explanation becomes a much longer teaching situation. A partial explanation may often be preferable, and will depend for its success on knowing for what purpose the explanation is needed.

The teaching task will thus vary according to whether the new concepts which the learner has to form are of the same or lower order as those to which it has to be connected, or higher. If a child asks 'What is a steam locomotive?', this is fairly easy to explain. But 'What is entropy?' is not. The conceptual bridge needed for a full explanation requires knowledge of the integral calculus, so both of those concerned would usually have to be content with a partial explanation, such as 'It is a mathematical way of expressing the amount of disorder, or randomness, in a system.'

(iii) Explanations in this category must first create their own market. Until we know a little, we don't know that we knew nothing: and the kind of problem which leads us to seek an explanation does not exist for us, until it can be realized, however dimly, by one of our available schemas. Examples of problems on a grand scale were given in part (iii) of Section 10.2; here is one which was put to me in a single sentence. 'If moths fly towards a light, why don't they fly towards the moon?' I was able to give only a partial explanation, that unless they had some innate mechanism which prevented them from doing so, the species would long ago have become extinct. (Can anyone tell me what this mechanism is?) But the need for an explanation could only be felt when the schema representing certain regularities in moths' behaviour was sufficiently developed in the mind of the questioner.

(iv) An explanation for correcting a mis-understanding is usually sought or offered when something has gone wrong, in one or more of the three categories already mentioned for reality testing: failure to achieve the desired goal in actuality, disagreement or failure of co-operation between persons, inconsistencies within or between schemas of the same individual.

(a) 'Why don't I ever get any apples on my tree, although I always have good blossom?' Explanation (having ascertained that it is a solitary tree): 'Apple trees aren't self-fertile—they have to be cross-pollinated with a different variety.' With this explanation, action leading to success becomes possible.

(b) Sometimes actions which, from a parent's point of view, are necessary for a child's good, are construed by the latter as interference with his freedom of choice. 'Why am I never allowed sweets?' The explanation, that they are a major contributor to dental decay, may or may not be fully satisfying since the short-term pleasure of eating a sweet is realized more vividly than the distant unpleasure of dental decay.

(c) Here is an inconsistency for which I still seek an explanation. Raising the temperature of water increases the amount of soluble solids which it will dissolve, but drives dissolved gases out of solution. How can these both be the case? The inconsistency here is between two generalizations which cannot co-exist within my present, rather simple, schema for understanding the way one substance is dissolved by another. One of these generalizations applies to solids, the other to gases. When an explanation—for which I shall be grateful—reaches me, though I do not know what it will be, I can be reasonably confident that it will be communicated symbolically. Also, that it will result in an overall expansion of my present schema concerning the ways in which molecules arrange themselves in the spaces between one another, and the forces which govern these arrangements.

(v) Visiting Italy for the first time, a person turns on a tap marked 'caldo' and the water comes out first cold (as expected), and then (contrary to expectation) hot. The explanation here is not in the irregularity of foreign plumbing, but in his having attached the wrong meaning to the word 'caldo'. So the purpose of an explanation would be to help him attach the right meaning to 'caldo'—the meaning which in English is attached to the word 'hot'. In the present example the connection could be strengthened by a suggestion to think also of the English word 'scald'.

10.10 *Making possible reflective mental activity.* This will be explored at greater length in Chapter 11. The present section will concentrate on how symbols help to make it possible.

Concepts and schemas are invisible, inaudible, intangible. Even by their possessor, it is questionable whether they can be observed directly: for our sense organs are directed outwards, towards actuality. So perhaps we should be surprised, not at the difficulty of reflecting our consciousness inwards and becoming aware of our own thought processes, but rather that we can do so at all.

The process of making a concept accessible to reflective consciousness seems to be closely connected with associating the concept with a symbol. Symbols, as we have seen, are primary concepts, and are thus the least abstract kind of concepts we have. This offers a possible explanation why these are more accessible than the others: and it may be that secondary concepts are not directly accessible to reflection at all, but only indirectly by having become connected with symbols. The symbols then act as both handles and labels, by which concepts are identified, activated (which is equivalent to retrieving them from memory store), and manipulated.

Verbal symbols are the easiest to utter aloud; and in children, one can observe transitional stages between this and internalized speech, which is one form of verbal thinking. When it comes to reading, however, mentally forming the sounds of the words is unnecessary for activating their associated concepts, and is a hindrance to rapid reading.

The processes of communicating one's ideas to other persons by the use of symbols, of putting one's thoughts on paper, and of becoming conscious of them oneself, are so closely related that one might almost regard thinking as a way of communicating with oneself.[3] The benefits of thinking out loud, with an interested and patient listener, are great when one is trying to clarify one's thinking in a new area. So it is a pity that this benefit is particularly concentrated in one kind of symbolism, that which can be spoken aloud (which includes not only words but algebraic symbols, and the simpler kinds of chemical formulae). Elsewhere (Skemp, 1971, Chapter 6) I have discussed at some length the uses of visual symbols, and have suggested that verbal symbols on the one hand, and visual symbols on the other, may serve complementary functions. Briefly, the suggestion is that verbal thinking concentrates our attention on one part of a schema at a time, and is mainly analytic; whereas visual symbolism is better at showing how the parts relate to each other, and is mainly synthetic. Also, words sound much the same to speaker and hearer, whereas a visual image is much more personal and harder to externalize. So verbal thinking is more socialized, visual is more individual. Add to this the fact that a succession of words can be produced much more easily and quickly than a succession of diagrams and pictures, and it emerges as a strong possiblility that our present predominantly verbal symbol system is causing an imbalance in the kinds of thinking we are good at.

10.11 *Helping to show structure*. In earlier sections, we have been thinking mainly about the connections between individual symbols and concepts. But what has to be both communicated by an utterance, and brought to consciousness in reflective thought, is not only individual concepts but their inter-relationships. For this we need not just a collection of words (or other symbols) but a language.

A language is a set of symbols, with their associated concepts, such that for certain relations between the symbols there correspond certain relations between the concepts. In a verbal language, the relations between symbols include order of words, punctuation, and inflections. So the concept 'meaning of a word' can now be expanded to 'meaning of an ordered and punctuated group of words and their inflections'. Other examples of symbol-systems are electrical circuit diagrams, engineering and architectural drawings, maps, and the symbol systems of mathematics and chemistry. It is an interesting exercise to make explicit the correspondences between the symbol structure and the conceptual structure of some symbol system with which the reader is familiar. Non-verbal systems are mostly easier: here are three fairly straightforward examples.

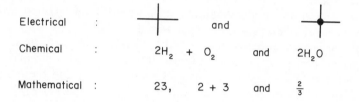

Electrical	:		and	
Chemical	:	$2H_2 + O_2$	and	$2H_2O$
Mathematical	:	23, $2 + 3$	and	$\frac{2}{3}$

10.12 *Making routine thinking automatic.* Thinking is hard work—just how hard is not appreciated by those who do not make their living by it. Once a particular process has been mastered, it is a great advantage if it can be repeated on subsequent occasions without having to devote our fully conscious attention to it. The reason for this was first suggested in Sections 2.7 and 2.8, namely that greater consciousness contributes to greater adaptability of a director system; diminished consciousness is associated with routine functioning. Though the discussion then was about sensori-motor activity, with objects in the external environment as operands, the argument is quite general. The more difficult the task, the more do we need the help which comes from routinizing that which can be routinized, so that as much as possible of our consciousness is free to concentrate on the new and problematic aspects of the situation.

One of the ways in which this is done, when the task is a mental one, is to allow the symbols to become detached from their concepts, and manipulate these without attention to their meanings according to well-formed routines. A proof-reader correcting an error, a doctor writing a prescription and simultaneously saying 'I want you to take one of these three times a day after meals', an air-hostess requesting passengers to fasten their seat belts, a bank clerk rapidly summing the entries on a paying-in slip—on most occasions they manipulate the symbols automatically, with little or no attention to their meanings. Some of these activities can indeed be taken over by machines, as when a recorded voice says 'Stand clear of the gates', or the routine courtesies of a business letter are delegated to a programmed typewriter. The difference between what I here call automatic and mechanical processes is however an important one, whether at physical or purely mental levels of activity. Machines cannot become conscious of what they are doing: we can. The machine which mechanically emits the sound 'Stand clear of the gates' cannot make allowance for a passenger in a wheel chair; the air hostess can and does, and likewise whenever some novelty signals a departure from regularity in the environment, and by bringing to bear consciousness, changes her behaviour from routine to adaptive.

10.13 *Recovering information and understanding.* If thinking is hard work, the acquisition of new information and the achievement of new understanding for the first time are even harder. The forefront of our consciousness and our quick-access memory store are limited in what they can hold, and are occupied by schemas in active and non-routine use. So how can we recover the information and understanding which we so hardly gained last week, month, or year, when next they are required?

Symbols, again, provide part of the answer. Because these can be externalized and given actual existence, the written notes we make or the words we record on tape can be stored where we can find them again. By reading the notes or playing back the tape, the symbols re-activate their associated concepts and schemas.

As well as this long-term storage and recall, symbols also support our thinking short-term while we are in process of 'putting our thoughts on paper'. Quotation marks are used here because it is, of course, not our thoughts but the associated symbols which we are putting on paper. When our present thoughts have moved on to a later stage of the argument, exploration, or formulation, we can back-track and see how it is all fitting together much more easily by running our eyes over what we have written than we could be searching in our memories.

10.14 *Creative mental activity.* We shall return to this topic in Chapter 11: here we discuss it briefly as yet another example of the contributions of symbols to our mental processes.

Much of what goes on in creative mental activity is unconscious and cannot be brought under voluntary control. There is, however, considerable agreement that an essential preliminary is a period of mental concentration on, or preoccupation with, the problem. During this period, all the data which might be relevant to the solution of the problem are internalized, and considered from many angles and in various combinations. For these receptive and reflective parts of the activity, symbols are essential; for it is by symbols that we acquire the raw data of the problem, and by symbols that we reflect on and manipulate the ideas, first in one way and then in another.

After this, there usually follows a period when conscious work on the problem comes temporarily to an end. During this period, however, it would seem that activity concerned with the problem continues at an unconscious evel. For suddenly, if one is lucky, a new insight, perhaps even what seems to be a complete solution of the problem, jumps into consciousness.

This is, however, by no means the final stage, nor the end of the hard work. For the new insight has to be formulated before it can be shared, and verified by one or more of the three methods of reality testing already described. In this last stage as in the first, symbols are an essential aid to the formulation of experimental hypotheses (mode (i)), the discussion of the new ideas (mode (ii)), and the process of mental reflection by which one tests them for consistency with one's own existing structure of knowledge (mode (iii)).

Symbols as an interface

0.15 Symbols thus make a unique contribution to the fulfilment of the potential conferred by intelligence. Many have taken the view that it is our use of language which most distinguishes us from other animals, and that without language an individual does not become fully human. It is therefore natural to wonder whether there is something special about symbols which enables them to do this. An answer is offered by the present model.

Symbols have a dual status, existing simultaneously in both actuality and reality. Their use for communication would be impossible if they could not be heard, seen or otherwise received by the sense organs of the listener, reader, or viewer. By uttering symbols we give them existence in actuality, and thereby make possible a number of other functions which have already been discussed. But symbols are also concepts of a simple kind, as we saw in Section 10.4; and they are connected to other concepts, which are their meanings. These meanings may be simple, or highly abstract and with great interiority. Some of the functions of symbols thus result from their being accessible concepts by which one can activate and manipulate less accessible concepts.

Symbols can now be seen to act as an interface, in at least three different ways: between inner reality and actuality; between two or more persons' realities, as in communication; and between the presently conscious and unconscious levels of one's mind, as in mental reflection, and in retrieval from memory. Freud (1913) and Jung (1964) have taken this last function of symbols further. In their theorizing, dream symbols in particular play an important part in making accessible to consciousness, in some degree at least, those parts of our inner realities which, though unconscious, nevertheless influence our behaviour and personalities. And finally, by serving so many functions, symbols also act as links between these various functions.

Before moving on, it is important to note that the full development of symbolic functions depends also on a corresponding development of concepts to a degree when they can be used independently of any exemplar or embodiment. In Section 9.17 we saw that one situation in which a concept becomes active is when one encounters possible examples, and uses it to distinguish between examples and non-examples. But the lower animals too can form and use concepts in this way. All the functions of symbols which have here been discussed depend on their attached concepts having become sufficiently well formed to be activated by encountering, or even thinking of the symbol. It is only in this way that way that we become able to direct our present actions by the use of schemas extending far beyond what is presently perceived, both in space and in time.

Reality construction, and the construction of theories

10.16 Among the most powerful kinds of schema for penetrating beyond the easily observable aspects of our environment, and directing our actions in ways which far outstrip common sense and everyday experience, are scientific theories. The rest of the present chapter will be given to a discussion of these as a particular application of some of the ideas which have been developed in this book.

When we are constructing something in actuality, such as a wall or a transistor radio, building and testing are used in combination. In the case of the wall these alternate—whenever we have built a few more bricks into the wall, we test for alignment and verticality. For the radio, definitive testing is not possible until building has been completed: we then switch on, and hope to receive a broadcast. In these and similar cases the operands are physical objects, existing in actuality; and it is a delta-two system which is involved.

The term *reality construction* refers to a similar combination of building and testing at the delta-two level, in which the operands are the concepts and schemas used by delta-one in its functioning. Three kinds of reality building and three kinds of testing have been distinguished, and these are brought together in Table 7. In this process of reality construction, one, two, or three modes of reality building can be used in combination with one, two, or three modes of reality testing.

The more difficult and complex are the observations by which a particular schema is constructed (built and tested), the smaller is the part of it which a single individual can contribute. It is fairly easy for someone to make a map of the streets around his home. It is harder to make a chart of the waters in the estuary where he keeps his boat, since observations of the depths and nature of the river bed are more lengthy and difficult, even with modern echo-sounding equipment. To make a chart of the waters surrounding the British Isles is probably beyond the scope of any single individual.

Likewise, certain kinds of shared conceptual model are beyond the capacity of a single individual to construct, because of:

(i) the difficulty of making the observations themselves (technical difficulties);

(ii) the difficulty of making inferences from them (difficulties of interpretation).

Astronomy, and atomic physics, offer examples of both kinds of difficulty.

Table 7

	REALITY CONSTRUCTION	
REALITY BUILDING		**REALITY TESTING**

REALITY CONSTRUCTION

REALITY BUILDING	**REALITY TESTING**
Mode (i)	*Mode* (i)
from our own encounters with actuality: *experience*.	against expectations of events in actuality: *experiment*.
Mode (ii)	*Mode* (ii)
from the realities of others: *communication*.	comparison with the realities of others: *discussion*.
Mode (iii)	*Mode* (iii)
from within, by formation of higher-order concepts, by extrapolation, imagination, intuition: *creativity*.	comparison with one's own existing knowledge and beliefs: *internal consistency*.

Accurately to observe the successive apparent positions of what ancients called 'the wandering stars' is difficult enough. To interpret these observations, made from another such 'wandering star' which is also rotating on its axis, and to deduce from these a model of the solar system complete with the size and shape of each orbit, is an intellectual achievement of the first order. Likewise with regard to the tracks in cloud chambers from which other scientists are building up knowledge of sub-atomic particles. In such areas, our only hope of getting an adequate conceptual model is by a high degree of co-operation among a number of people, extending over what may be considerable periods of time.

We have already seen that the minimal conditions for any kind of co-operation are:

(i)   a shared schema, within which people realize the particular parts of actuality relative to which they are co-operating;
(ii) a shared, or compatible, goal structure;
(iii) a shared language.

In the development of a body of scientific knowledge, these become:

(i)   a shared theory;
(ii) a common goal, to increase knowledge in this field, together with individual goals which even when in competition, e.g., to be among the leading contributors, are compatible within the overall common goal;
(iii) the particular shared symbol-system of that science.

So a scientific body of knowledge can be seen as a shared schema whic exemplifies a highly positive-sum relationship between individua intelligences, since:

(i) it is the result of much co-operation in building it up;
(ii) it makes possible much further co-operation
    (a) in using it;
    (b) in further developing it.

(By 'shared' I mean here that all scientists within a particular discipline hav some of it, not necessarily that they all share all of it. But where there overlap, there has to be agreement.)

In constructing such a body of knowledge, all three of the modes of realit building and reality testing summarized in Table 7 are used in variou combinations. In using modes (i) and (iii) together, we work on th assumption that actuality is regular, not capricious: though the regularitie may not always be easy to abstract. So if we extrapolate from our existin conceptual structures (reality building mode (iii)) in ways which are internall consistent (reality testing mode (iii)) we expect that the results will accuratel model other regularities of actuality. Sometimes this is confirmed (mode (i) in exciting and powerful ways, as when predictions derived from Maxwell' electromagnetic wave equations were confirmed, eight years after Maxwell' death, by Hertz's discovery in actuality of what we now call wireless waves

10.17 We accept other people's contributions to our own conceptua structures (reality building mode (ii)) on the assumption that these othe people have tested their contributions in the same ways as we would hav done so ourselves. On this assumption depends the co-operation within discipline by which individual contributions are accepted into the collectiv body of knowledge. It presupposes knowing what these tests are, appropriat to the particular discipline; and a reasonable level of expertise in applyin them. So we can now begin to see much sense in the hurdles which are set u for entrants to a profession or discipline, both in required content c knowledge and in accepted criteria for its validity. Now that we have a clea criterion by which to judge them, some of the hurdles may no longer be see as sensible ones. But we can now understand better the need for th certification function of universities, and of other professional and technica bodies, even if in particular cases the certificate-awarding-and-collectin process appears to have been carried to excess.

What are the appropriate criteria for working within a discipline will vary i detail between disciplines: and disciplines may also differ in their relativ emphasis on testing by modes (i), (ii), (iii). Pure mathematics relies heavily o mode (iii), in varying degrees on mode (ii), and not at all on mode (i) Following Popper (1974), however, I propose that we reserve the tern *scientific* knowledge for that which has been tested by mode (i), agains actuality. The present formulation also accords with Popper's often-quote criterion of falsifiability (or testability or refutability), but with a different emphasis. Though a coherent explanation of diverse past events is satisfying, the survival value of any model lies in its ability to help us direct our actions aright on future occasions. This requires that it can be used to make predictions, and predictions can be false as well as true. So predictive ability implies falsifiability, though as I see it the former is what matters most.[4] Too many false predictions would certainly be strong ground for rejecting a particular model. One would not, however, reject a model which was successful in the vast majority of cases, and which was the best currently available, on the basis of a single false prediction.

10.18   As this discussion has progressed, increasing emphasis has been put on the internal coherence of the model, and on the extent and variety of its application. These are the chief qualities, in addition to those already discussed, which a model needs to satisfy before we call it a scientific *theory*. In the earlier part of the present discussion, the emphasis was on the value of a shared schema for co-operation in building up and using a body of scientific knowledge. The agreed model used as starting point may also itself have been a co-operative effort, but this has seldom been the case historically, and seems intrinsically less likely. A penetrating, coherent and far-reaching synthesis is unlikely to take place unless the contributory ideas are all in the mind of one person.

It is, however, also unlikely that this same person himself gathered all the ideas at first hand. This does not detract from the importance of the creative synthesis by one individual which gives birth to the theory. It merely emphasizes the work which has to precede this, both by earlier scientists whose knowledge is made use of—though often transformed in its significance—and by the originator of the new theory in first making this knowledge his own. It was Newton who said: 'If I have seen a little further than most, it is because I have stood on the shoulders of giants.' One might add that it would be difficult to stand on the shoulders of more than one giant at a time unless one were also a giant oneself.

10.19   The main points of this chapter are:

(i)   *The process which we subjectively experience as understanding is conceived, in terms of the present theory, as making connections with an appropriate schema.*

(ii)   *The importance of understanding is that it brings new experience into the domains of our director systems. Understanding is an essential contributor to their functioning, to the achievement of our goal states, and thereby to survival.*

(iii)   *Symbols make a unique contribution to fulfilling the potential conferred by intelligence. They act as interface between reality and actuality, between the realities of two or more persons, and between the conscious and*

166

unconscious levels of one's inner reality. Ten different functions of symbols have been distinguished.

(iv) *A theory is a particular kind of schema, often beginning as a creative synthesis by one individual and subsequently developed by co-operation within a discipline. A scientific theory is one tested against actuality, and is particularly powerful in directing our actions in relation to qualities of the environment which are inaccessible to simple observation.*

Notes for Chapter 10

1. Linear A is a script used in Crete from about 1700 to 1600 B.C. Scholars have not yet been able to decipher it, and even the language written in Linear A is not known for certain.
2. Experts will point out that the mizzen has to be forward of the rudder-post, otherwise it is a yawl.
3. The relationship between language and thought has been extensively explored by a number of writers, notably Vygotsky (1962).
4. This is not to say that a scientific theory can only be tested against predictions of events which have not yet happened. If by using only information which was available at a particular time, it is possible by using a theory to predict events which happened at a later time, then this is a fair test of a theory.

CHAPTER 11

Knowing That, Knowing How, and Being Able

Plans, plan making, and plan using

1.1 In this chapter we shall be largely concerned with the relationships between knowledge and action; about how the knowledge embodied in a schema may be translated into effective action, and what are the factors which influence success or failure. Clearly an appropriate schema is necessary, but not sufficient, for successful action. *Knowing that, knowing how*, and *being able to*, are different, though closely connected. It is the nature of these connections which we shall now explore.

The present model also reminds us that we must not, in our thinking, restrict the term 'action' to that which takes place at the physical level, directed by delta-one systems. Equally important for survival is the mental activity, directed by delta-two systems, in which delta-one systems are the operands.

1.2 *Knowing that* is represented in the present model by the possession of an appropriate schema; and the qualities of this schema, both in content and in organization, are one set of influences on the know-how which can be derived from it.

A schema is a highly abstract concept, and in Section 10.1 a diagram was introduced as a support to our thinking (see Figure 31).

This can be interpreted at three levels of abstraction:

i) As a road map. Here the state represented by each point is a physical location.

ii) As a cognitive map. Here each point represents a specified state within some universe of discourse. It will only be a flat map or graph for a two-dimensional universe, and clearly the shape will not always be like the above.

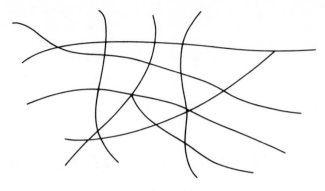

Figure 31

(iii) As a generalized schema, in which each point represents an unspecified state.

At all three levels, a *path* is a sequence of states; and a *plan* consists of:

(i)   a path from a present state to a goal state;
(ii) a way of applying the energies available to the operators in such a way as to take the operand along this path.

Some plans are 'wired in', either literally as in the case of the oven thermostat (Section 5.3), or metaphorically as in the case of the system which regulates the level of carbon dioxide in the blood. (If the level is too high, we breathe faster, and so on.) In both these simple cases, the state is unidimensional and the path is a sequence of temperatures or CO_2 levels connecting present state and goal state. All innate behaviours are in this category, from simple reflexes to complex director systems such as those involved in bird migration. These function only in the assumed class of environments in which they evolved.

The next simplest kind of plan is a *habit*. Habits are learnt, not innate, but with repetition they become so automatic that one might almost think of them as 'wired in', in this case not at the factory but by the user. They form an essential sub-structure of our daily life, since they free our conscious attention for the non-routine and problematic. Thus, I can write this chapter only because the formation of each letter, the spelling of each word, and to a great extent the grammar and punctuation, are all taken care of by well-established habits; and for a similar reason I cannot type it, though I can type routine letters which require little thought. But once established, habits are very difficult to change, as was noted many years ago in a well-known passage by William James.[1]

In situations where faulty habits are likely to be disadvantageous, therefore, it is very desirable that so far as possible they be set up consciously and deliberately. An individual cannot do this unaided until he has formed an appropriate schema, out of which good plans can be formed by the process of reflective plan-making to be described. Until then, he will need the guidance of an expert teacher, who possesses such a schema as an essential part of his expertise: or he is in danger of forming faulty habits which will be difficult to un-learn.

11.3 If we think of Figure 31 at the lowest level of abstraction, that of a simple road map of part of a town, then an innate behaviour corresponds to a fixed plan taking the operand along a predetermined path, as in Figure 32.

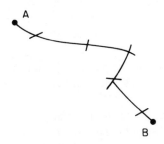

Figure 32

One may think of this as a tram route. A bus route is much like it, once it has been set up. The difference is that the bus driver has to learn his route initially, whereas the tram-driver's route is determined for him by the tram-lines (assuming that there are no points on the route).

The greatest adaptability of behaviour is made possible by the possession of an appropriate schema, from which a great variety of paths can be derived, connecting any particular present location to any required goal location. This corresponds to the case of a taxi-driver. His knowledge *that* is represented by his mental map of the town (Figure 33).

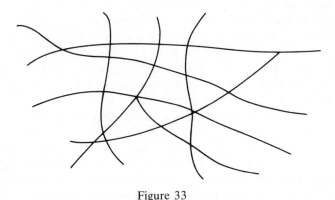

Figure 33

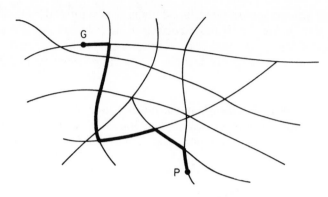

Figure 34

The first part of his knowledge *how*, on each particular journey, consists of his ability to derive from this a path between the present location of his taxi and the goal location.

From P to G in Figure 34, there are many possible paths. The one shown thickened might have been chosen to avoid the six-road junction and the five-road junction. The second part of his knowledge *how* consists of the actions necessary to take the taxi along this particular path: particularly at the choice-points encountered on route. (Start with a U-turn, left at the first cross-roads, left again at the next, first right, and so on.) From his general knowledge *that*, the taxi-driver can produce, as required, a large number of separate knowings-*how*, each one consisting of a plan for a particular journey. In this, choosing the path is the part where the adaptability comes in most strongly. The rest of the plan is simply to keep the taxi heading along the path in the right direction.

This, at a concrete level, illustrates the differences between innate behaviours, habits, and the adaptability of action made possible by schematized knowledge. Prerequisite for the production of these plans is understanding: the realization of present state and goal state within an appropriate existing schema. This implies the existence of one or more paths between these states, but it does not guarantee that this path can be thought of. Most of us have heard the story of the person who was asked how to get to a place, not too far away, and after several attempts to explain he gave up and said 'If I wanted to get to X, I wouldn't start from here'. This is the essential feature of a problem situation, in contrast to a routine task: how to find a way to achieve a desired goal when one has no existing plan which would enable one to do so. When we do succeed in finding such a plan, we know that we have done so, but would usually be unable to say with any degree of clarity how we did it. That is to say, we have no conceptual model of the problem-solving process itself; and with the exception of Polya's (1945) book on problem solving in mathematics, there is little in the literature to guide us. In the next section, the plan-finding process will be formulated in terms of the present model; and this may take us a little further towards conscious realization of how we can improve our problem-solving abilities. The new development of the model will centre mainly on the path-finding part of the activity. Once a suitable path has been found, the process of taking the operand along this path is nearly the same as that already described.

Intuitive path finding

11.4 In the section leading up to the resonance model described at the end of Chapter 9, the idea was introduced (Section 9.16) of *connections between concepts* to account for the fact that activation of one concept can activate, or lower the threshold for, others. Those more closely connected will be more activated than more distant ones. Path finding at an intuitive level can be explained in this way. In Figure 35, the thin lines represent the schema as a whole; the thicker lines radiating from P and G represent the activation of neighbouring concepts resulting from heightened consciousness of present state and goal state.

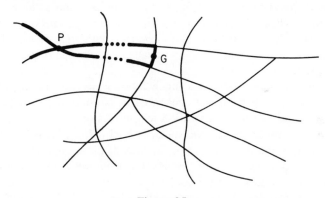

Figure 35

If these neighbourhoods connect, then one or more paths from P to G will result. This represents path finding at an intuitive level. Under some conditions, simply by activation of the concepts represented by P and G, a path from one to the other reaches consciousness. And this may be interpreted at two levels: as an actual example at a concrete level, and as a metaphor or analogy for what goes on at more abstract levels of mental functioning.

A direct inference from this model is a widely held piece of folk wisdom, namely that if one wants something and thinks about it a lot, one will achieve it in the end. This can be derived from the explanation just given in combination with two other parts of the model which were mentioned earlier. One is 'that repeated excitation of particular tuned structures increases their sensitivity for future occasions' (Section 9.19); and the other (Section 9.24) is that 'want selectively sensitizes perception; either by activating as a whole the schema of a director system which could lead to the satisfaction of a want, or by first activating a concept representing a goal state'. So given a strongly and continuously held desire, even if a path to its achievement is not immediately obvious, over a period of time a path may slowly reach consciousness, and continue to develop until the way becomes clear. And also, features in the environment will be noticed and used as contributors to a path which in the absence of this strongly held desire would have been overlooked. Sometimes, in contrast, eruption into consciousness may be sudden, giving rise to the 'Eureka' effect. In either case, the model not only leads us to believe that the folk wisdom may well have a sound basis (though overstated: men wanted to fly for centuries before the Wright brothers succeeded), but also suggests some of the processes by which the result may come about.

Reflective planning

11.5 The further apart, either literally or metaphorically, are the present state and the goal state, the less likely it is that the neighbourhoods of activated concepts surrounding P and G will connect. A possible method then is to start off in what is hoped to be the right direction, until one arrives at a present P whose neighbourhood does connect with that of G. This too is unreliable; and intuitive path finding always has this weakness, that it does not always perform to order.

The planning function becomes much more powerful and reliable if the schema as a whole can be made accessible to consciousness. If this can be done, and if P and G can be identified within this schema, it is then often a relatively simple matter to find and specify a path. How much simpler, can be realized by comparing in imagination the task of planning a journey by road over terrain which one knows only moderately well, under two conditions: the first purely 'in one's head', and the second with a road map open before one's eyes. What the map does in this case is to make the whole network of roads available for scanning, to make all one's *knowledge that* fully and simultaneously conscious as a basis for deriving whatever *knowledge how*, or plan, is required at the time. (In other cases, a map does more than this by enabling one to join one's own local knowledge to a body of knowledge built up and tested by a team of surveyors. But in these cases also, one still has to make one's own plan, since the knowledge symbolically communicated by the map has the form of a schema, not a predetermined route.)

And what a road map does at a concrete level is but a special case of what a theoretical model (including the present one) does more generally and at a more abstract level: to make accessible to reflective thought a structure of connected concepts within which can be represented a variety of present states; and thereby to understand past events, to predict outcomes in actuality, and sometimes to set these as goal states and bring them about.

Even when an appropriate schema is available, to devise from this a good plan for a particular task may be a slow and difficult matter when done for the first time. Next time it is much easier, since one only has to remember how one did it last time. So in any given universe of discourse, be it mathematics or car mechanics, the most generally useful mental organization is a combination of knowledge-that and knowledge-how. One needs a set of ready-to-hand plans for jobs which one does often, distinguished from habits by being derived from a schema with which they maintain their connections. This gives the advantages of routine functioning in routine situations, while keeping open the possibility of forming new plans as and when required. In terms of the diagram, we want something like Figure 36, in which the thick lines represent ready-to-hand plans, and the thin lines the integrating schema.

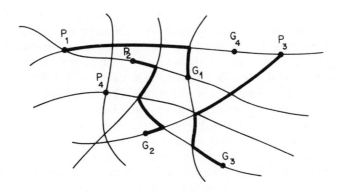

Figure 36

Given this schema, new plans can be produced if required, say, to get from P_4 to G_4. If necessary, parts of two plans can be linked, say, to get from P_1 to G_3.

Full schematization also requires reversibility of scanning, so that one could get from G_2 to P_2. This offers a good criterion for distinguishing a pure habit from a plan within a schema: can you write your name backwards, sing backwards some tune you know well forwards, or reverse this simple operation to find its starting point?

Figure 37

When particular plans are over-practised, their connections with their integrating schema may weaken past recall. The advantages of routinizing may then be outweighed by lack of adaptability, since all that is left is a set of fixed habits (Figure 38).

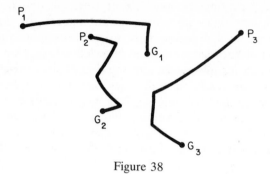

Figure 38

At the opposite pole from this is problem solving, and though there is still much to be found out about how we do this, the foregoing makes it clear that one requirement is the ability to set aside existing pre-formed habits and make equally available for use the whole of an appropriate schema.

For the present discussion, the road-map example has the advantages of being familiar to everyone, of being easy to follow at a low level of abstraction, and of suggesting more abstract applications. When one seeks specific examples of the latter, however, the difficulty arises of finding more abstract universes of discourse which are familiar to both author on the one hand, and almost every reader on the other. Mathematics offers a particularly good field of application for the foregoing ideas, and indeed for most of this book: but examples in this universe of discourse would appeal only to a minority of readers, the majority having been put off by bad teaching.

One possible example is offered by music. What a musical performer has is a repertoire of pieces which he can play well—sequences of notes and chords which he can run off according to ready-to-hand plans, together with a basic schema by which he can quickly learn new pieces as required. These new pieces are sequences of notes and chords already devised by a composer, and communicated symbolically by musical notation. The performer needs a schema within which he can realize the intentions of the composer: in contrast to a child who has learnt to play just two or three tunes by heart. The composer has the more difficult task of originating these. What is of interest here is the fact that one can often identify with some confidence the composer of a work one has never heard before: which is to say, one recognizes the parent schema from which a particular musical pattern was derived. This implies an ability to become aware of regularities of a degree of abstraction such that even those of us who can do so would for the most part be unable to formulate or explain.

Intuitive and reflective functioning of intelligence

11.6 The discussion of these two kinds of planning, intuitive and reflective, provides an introduction to the more general consideration of these two levels of functioning of intelligence.

When the subject of consciousness was first introduced, in Section 2.7, it was suggested that greater consciousness contributes to greater adaptability of a director system; diminished consciousness is associated with routine functioning. Since here two levels of director system are involved, we now need to distinguish between two levels of consciousness: consciousness *in* the delta-one system *of* whatever is its operand in the environment, and consciousness *in* the delta-two system *of* the delta-one system on which it acts. It is consciousness at the first level, *in* one's driving director system *of* road and traffic, which may diminish dangerously while driving at 70 m.p.h. under monotonous conditions on a motorway, so that one fails to perceive and react quickly enough to an approaching hazard. It is consciousness at the second level, *in* one's self-observation *of* one's driving director system, which may realize that this happening and do something to keep oneself alert.

This ability to make one's own mental processes the object of conscious observation, and to change these intentionally from a present state to a goal state, introduces such new powers and dimensions to our abilities that it must be distinguished by a separate name. Following Piaget (1950) we will call it *reflective intelligence*; noting also that my model is not the same as Piaget's, and that the beginning of the present conception derives from Bartlett (1932), who referred to the ability of persons to turn round upon their own schemas. The next five sections will be given to considering some more of the functions which may be attributed to reflective intelligence, and to the additional mental powers which result; starting with further consideration of reflective planning.

11.7 An immediate consequence is the possibility of separating the activity of thought from physical action. This not only allows the preparation of plans in advance of action: it also makes it possible to construct several possible plans for the achievement of a particular purpose, to consider their respective merits, and to settle on that which seems to be the best; then, either immediately or at a later time, to put this plan into action. In terms of the present model the three phases are:

i) Delta-one ceases to direct action. Effectively, it is disconnected from the operators between the box in the diagram (Figure 12) marked PLAN and that marked OPERATORS.

ii) Delta-two acting on delta-one takes it from a state in which delta-one has no plan for the achievement of some specified goal state, through states in which there is some kind of plan, to a goal state in which there is an optimal plan.

iii) Delta-two goes out of action, delta-one stabilizes with the plan chosen, and then directs sensori-motor activity by the use of this plan.

This separation also makes possible much more effective correction of errors. Failure to achieve the set goal state suggests that one's plan may have been wrong. Ability to reflect on one's plan makes it possible to realize just where one went wrong, and either to correct this plan as necessary or to replace the plan as a whole with a better one. Once might also decide that the plan was a good one, and that it was in putting it into action that things had gone wrong. Without this ability to identify and correct errors, trials are random and errors may be repeated. By the use of reflective intelligence, trials and the correction of errors become contributors to a goal-directed progress towards optimal performance.

Reflective problem-solving

11.8   The initial state here is an awareness of a problem. This can be of two kinds: a goal state in actuality which can be imagined, but to which one can as yet construct no path; or experiences which have been conceptualized, but which cannot yet be explained in terms of an available body of knowledge. The initial state here is an awareness of a problem—a goal state which can be imagined, but to which one can construct no path; or experiences which have been conceptualized, but which cannot be explained in terms of an available body of knowledge.

How can we re-fasten the lead on our boat's twin keels with the tools and other apparatus currently available to us, given that we have no crane or hoist, that the boat weighs ¾ ton, and that it is resting on these keels? What makes an intelligent adult confess to feelings of anxiety amounting to panic when confronted with a simple task in mathematics? These are two of the problems which currently occupy my own mind: the former on and off for the past week, the second at intervals for many years. (The reader is invited to think of some of his own.) A solution of the first problem will make possible the achievement of a physical goal state, the operand being our family boat. A solution of the second problem will make possible the avoidance of a mental anti-goal state by the persons concerned. In both cases, a path to the set goal state can be completed only by a conceptual bridge not yet in existence; but on which, in each case with one collaborator, I am hard at work. The location of this bridge-under-construction is my own mind; so the only possible fabricator is my own reflective intelligence, helped also at the intuitive level by the processes described earlier.

11.9   Our ability to collaborate, in the two examples given, also depends on the reflective process described above. The requirements for co-operation in a physical task were discussed in Sections 8.8 and 8.9, and summarized at the end of Chapter 8. Minimal requirements are that the goal states and plans of the individuals involved are both compatible and complementary. There we were talking about first-order director systems acting on a physical operand. Now that the operand is itself a director system, there is an additional requirement that each of the collaborators keeps the other informed of the present state of his thinking, and of whatever progress he is making. There are indeed two operands, the schemas in the minds of the two collaborators: each inaccessible to the other, and only accessible to its owner by the reflective process now under discussion. Co-operation thus depends on a combination of reflection by each on his own schemas and plans-in-progress, together with utterances about these. Though the utterances of each appear to be for the information of the other, they are also an important part of the reflective process. Consciousness of our own schemas is not always easy to achieve, and the process of communicating them is also one of thinking aloud, which helps to heighten this consciousness.

This combined process both requires better organization of the schemas, and facilitates it: requires, because communication imposes the necessity of talking sense rather than nonsense so far as one is able; and facilitates, because the more conscious one can become of one's schemas, the more one becomes aware of where they need improvement, and the better chance one has of finding out how to do so.

In the boat-maintenance example, the schema and derived plans are of a concrete nature, involving only low-order concepts, many of them primary concepts. In the 'mathephobia' example, the schemas involved are highly abstract, and prolonged reflection is involved both in their formation, and before they can be got into a good enough state to be communicated.

Our situation in such cases is rather like that of two persons in different buildings, connected only by telephone. Each is trying to construct a similar model with the help of ideas also from the other, so they have to keep each other informed of what they are doing. This is not too easy, because also they are working in the dark, except for what light is afforded by a small flashlight which they can shine on only part of their models at a time. So they scan their models with their torches, describing what they see; whereby each helps not only the other, but himself, to become aware how it fits together, and how it might be improved and further developed.

Objectifying our knowledge; inference and prediction

11.10   This change from the sensori-motor and intuitive to the reflective mode of intelligence is equivalent to mentally standing away from our own schemas, treating these (so far as we can) as objects which we observe and on which we act. This opens up the way to a more advanced form of the tidying-up activity already mentioned. By objectifying one's schemas one also makes them accessible to discussion; to criticism including self-criticism; to consciously making and testing inferences; and other forms of theorizing. This fits in with the position taken by Popper (1974): 'And by an objective theory I mean a theory which is arguable, which can be exposed to rational criticism, preferably a theory which can be tested.' So here we shall return briefly to the subject of theory and theorizing, already discussed in Sections 10.16 to 10.18.

First, there is an important distinction to be made between inference and prediction. *Inference* (the verb) is a logical process within a particular schema by which, if we know that A is true, we are confident that B is also true.

Example:

A	B
Today is Saturday.	Tomorrow will be Sunday.
The number of this page is prime and greater than 2.	The number of this page is odd.
This wire is copper.	This wire conducts electricity.

An inference (noun) is a statement derived in this way from another statement. In itself it says nothing about whether A or B accurately represents present actuality—about what day today actually is, about what is actually the number of this page; about what this wire is actually made of.

But if it is an accurate model—if we have correctly represented actuality within an appropriate schema—then from an inference within the model we can make a *prediction* about events in actuality. If this prediction is correct, the use of this model in these circumstances is confirmed, and we are encouraged to use it on similar occasions in the future. If it is incorrect, we have to decide whether we have picked the wrong use for a perfectly good model: '2 + 3 = 5' is a good model for putting 3 apples into a bowl which already contains 2 apples, but not for putting 3 blobs of mercury into a bowl which already contains 2 blobs of mercury, nor for putting water at a temperature of 3°C into a bowl which already contains water at 2°C. Or we may have been at fault in the inferential process, e.g., we have got our sums wrong. Or we may decide that this is altogether an unsuccessful model, as when the phlogiston theory of heat was replaced by that in terms of molecular kinetic energy.

Inference is a reflective process, taking place entirely within a reality. Prediction is a projection of the result into actuality: a sophisticated kind of expectation, the latter also being possible by intuitive processes not involving reflection. Testing a theory involves testing both the inferences and the predictions which it makes, but the consequences for the theory of a false inference and of a false prediction are quite different. A single false inference invalidates a theory, at least in the given form; whereas a single false prediction does not, for the reasons already given and for other reasons which will follow. Popper is sometimes inaccurately quoted on this important issue, as having said that a single false prediction refutes a theory. But he writes (Popper, 1974):

> no test of any theoretical statement is final or conclusive, and . . . the empirical, or the critical, attitude involves the adherence to some 'methodological rules' which tells us not to evade criticism but to accept refutations(though not too easily). These rules are essentially somewhat flexible. As a consequence the acceptance of a refutation

is nearly as risky as the tentative adoption of a hypothesis: it is the acceptance of a conjecture.

Elsewhere in the same book he writes:

> a deductive inference is true if and only if no *counterexample exists*. [Popper's italics.] Here a counterexample is an inference of the same form with true premises and a false conclusion, as in:
>   All men are mortal. Socrates is mortal. ∴ Socrates is a man. Let 'Socrates' be here the name of a dog. . . .

False inferences can be detected by reflection, which is mode (iii) reality testing; or pointed out by others (mode (ii), after mode (iii) testing on their part). As Popper has shown, a single counterexample is enough to demonstrate a logical inaccuracy within a theory. False predictions can be detected only by experiment: which is to say reality testing mode (i). Too many false predictions would certainly lead us to abandon a theory; since a major object of these sophisticated mental models is to enable us to predict the results in actuality of our actions, and thereby to bring about desired results rather than others. But a single unsuccessful prediction would not overthrow a theory which was the best currently available, and which yielded correct predictions much more often than not.

Thus I do not think that there is any disagreement between my own position and that of Popper: but there is a difference of emphasis. He emphasizes falsifiability, in two ways; I emphasize prediction, within the wider context of reality construction, of which theory construction is an important special case.

Reflective extrapolation

11.11   Generalization, or reflective extrapolation, of one's existing concepts is a method of reality construction used with great effect in mathematics and the natural sciences. It offers a good example of the additional power conferred by the transition from the intuitive to the reflective levels of functioning of intelligence. The process involves, first, the formation of a schema derived from examples of one particular kind: either by mode (i), or mode (ii), reality building. At this stage a person can recognize other examples of a similar kind, and apply the schema to them. The second stage consists of reflecting on this schema, and formulating its essential features in a form which is independent of the examples from which it was derived. In the third stage, new examples are sought of quite a different kind, to which the schema is applied. The new application is then tested by one or more of modes (i), (ii), (iii), as may be appropriate and possible.

The Doppler effect provides an example which, at the first stage, will be familiar to most readers. When a fast-moving vehicle goes past, we hear a sudden drop in pitch of the engine note, at the moment when the vehicle's movement changes from coming towards us to going away from us. (The effect is most noticeable when the engine has a note of fairly identifiable pitch.) Having formed this schema from examples such as passing trains, aeroplanes, cars on a motorway, it is easy to apply it to other examples of a similar kind such as fast-flying insects, whose wings emit an audible note.

Stage two consists in formulating this effect in terms of the compression or expansion of the sound waves which results from movement of the source.

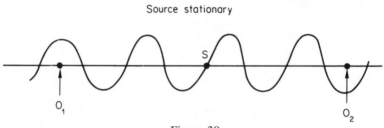

Figure 39

In Figure 39 the source S is stationary, and the frequency of vibrations will be the same for observers at O_1 and O_2. In Figure 40, the source S is moving from left to right. For an observer at O_2 on the right, the sound source is moving towards him. So it comes slightly nearer for each successive vibration, which therefore takes less time to reach him. Successive vibration, which therefore takes less time to reach him. Successive vibrations will thus be heard at shorter time intervals, and the pitch as experienced by him will be higher. For observer at O_1 on the left, the effect will be the opposite. As a further development of stage two, a mathematical model can be constructed by which, if the difference in pitch is known, the velocity of the source can be calculated.

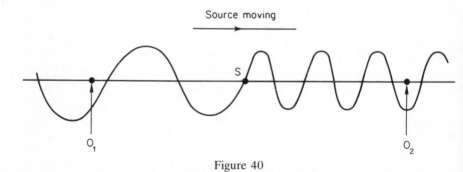

Figure 40

Stage three consists in recognizing that this principle can be applied to vibrations of other kinds, such as light. The change of frequency is now experienced as a change of colour; and a new application has been found in astronomy, whereby certain stars have been found to be moving away from us at great velocities by observing a shift towards the red (lower frequency) end of the spectrum of certain identifiable dark bands. (These are due to absorbtion of particular frequencies by the vapours of known elements.) The frequencies at which these bands occur for a stationary source are known, and the same mathematical model as for sound can thus be used to calculate the velocity, relative to earth, of the star.

Reflective extrapolation has been further discussed under the title 'Mathematical Generalisation' in Chapter 4 of Skemp (1971), pages 59–61, where other examples, both everyday and mathematical, are offered.

Intuitive and reflective levels of functioning

11.12 The change from the intuitive to the reflective levels of functioning thus enables intelligence to function in a number of more powerful ways. In addition to those discussed in Sections 11.6–11.11, all forms of mode (iii) reality construction similarly acquire additional power. For theorizing in particular, reflective intelligence is highly involved in the process of comparing predicted events with those perceived as resulting from experiment.

In the present model, this new power does not result from the addition of a new system which is absent at an age when children's thinking is restricted to the intuitive level. The delta-two system as well as the delta-one is present from birth, as evidenced by the experiment quoted in Section 7.7. That which is developed with increasing age, and which is here called for short reflective intelligence, is the ability intentionally to move the focus of consciousness from consciousness located *in* the delta-one system *of* objects existing in actuality, to consciousness located *in* the delta-two system *of* mental objects existing in inner reality. The variety and importance of the additional abilities which result serve further to emphasize the adaptive function of consciousness.

What we have been doing in this and the previous seven sections is, by means of a model, to make accessible to reflection the reflective process itself. The circles in Figure 17, Section 7.3, may now be considered as representing the fact that delta-two can perceive relationships between the schemas of delta-one and other concepts—the fact, but not the neurological processes involved, which remain inaccessible to our present knowledge.

From theory into action

11.13 What we have just been discussing is *theorizing*: the construction of theories by the three modes of reality building and reality testing already discussed, in a variety of combinations. Equally important, and perhaps receiving less attention than it deserves from pure scientists and philosophers of science, is the putting to work of existing theories. Since a theory is an important special case of a mental model built by intelligence, almost everything in this book applies in some degree. Here I will mention just three advantages of using the particularly general and abstract kind of models which we call theories,[2] before bringing together the main processes involved in putting them to work.

(i) A theory tells us what is going on beyond the observables, and thereby gives us much greater power to understand, predict, and sometimes to control events than is possible by naïve observation. Genetic theory enables us to do this with visible qualities of plants and animals; electrical theory, with pictures on television screens and sounds from loudspeakers; astronomy, with the observed movements of planets and stars.

(ii) The abstract quality of a theoretical model reduces noise, and allows us to concentrate on what is relevant for the task in hand. Some problems are often more easily dealt with by being understood as particular cases of powerful and more general theories. For example, it would be very difficult for anyone to prove that *any* triangle whose sides are in the proportion $5:12:13$ is right angled, who did not know Pythagoras' theorem and recognize this as a special case.

(iii) Another characteristic of theories is a considerable degree of independence from the particular examples and classes of examples from which they were constructed. They thereby enable us sometimes to make new paths downwards in our thinking, from the generality of the theory to *new* particular examples: to find new applications, perceive relationships we would otherwise never have looked for, and successfully do things we would otherwise never have even tried. To choose quite a simple example: who, without knowledge of the principle of Archimedes (which is the theory behind flotation) would ever think of designing a boat's hull to be built of concrete, in full confidence that it would float?

The processes by which theories are put to use are basically the same as those by which we use all our schemas, the chief difference being one of emphasis. As in theorizing, the amount of reflective activity is greater than in everyday activities. But the relation between thought and action is now reversed. In theorizing, the purpose of an experiment is to test a theory: i.e., the operand is a theory, the goal state is the best state into which we can get this theory, and the experiment is a means to this end. In application, however, we accept the theory in the state in which we find it, and use it to construct a model whereby to achieve a desired result in actuality.

A theory is not itself a model for a particular task, but something much more general: namely a schema within which can be conceptualized all the possible states within a particular universe of discourse, and relations between these states. A model for a particular task is constructed by mapping the actual situation into this schema: which is to say, by representing the given actuality is a particular example of some of the regularities already conceptualized within the schema. Often this is a two-stage process: first a verbal statement, from which the final model (mathematical, chemical, electrical) is then constructed. Abstraction takes place at each of these stages: the omission of detail which will not be incorporated in the model, but equally important, the retention of factors which may affect the outcome. Since no two actual situations are identical, the process can never be routine, and model constructing is by its nature problematic to a greater or lesser degree. The function of reflective intelligence is therefore particularly important at this stage, the goal state being a model which is optimal for the purpose involved.

The next step is to manipulate the model (again a reflective process) in ways such as making inferences, finding paths to a chosen goal, or exploring what possibilities are available starting from the given situation. The result may be a prediction, a plan for achieving a desired result in actuality, or a choice from among the possibilities. If the task is routine, there is (as we say) 'no problem'. But if it is of a kind which neither we, nor perhaps any one else, have solved before, considerable reflection may be required.

Even this is no guarantee of success, and the solution of entirely new problems—those on the frontiers of our individual or collective knowledge—usually seems to be achieved (if it is) by the combination of activities outlined in Section 10.14. These include a strong desire for a solution, leading to prolonged and concentrated reflection on the problem, followed by an interval during which conscious work on the problem takes time off. Then, if one is lucky, a new insight, perhaps even what seems to be a complete solution of the problem, suddenly comes into consciousness: after which further reflective activity is required to formulate the solution and test it mode (iii), followed by other tests in modes (i) and (ii).

There is thus a combination of reflective and intuitive processes; and while the function of the former can now to some degree be understood, the latter is by its nature more inaccessible to investigation. The resonance part of the present model suggests a speculative explanation, along the lines begun in Section 11.4. The combination of strong desire and continued preoccupation with a problem leads to continued vibration of the resonant structures by which the conceptualized problem is stored. Conscious reflection further increases the amplitude of these, and increases the possibility of a connection forming in the way already described. The interesting question is, why does the insight sometimes come after rather than during this period of reflection? To put it differently, if consciously reflecting on a problem helps, why does stopping for a while also help?

My tentative suggestion, and it is no more than that, is that during the latter period there is a partial change in the quality of the vibrations, away from the particular towards the general, the higher-order regularities; and that it is by interaction among these that a solution finally occurs. The reflective process keeps the mental realization of the problem too close to the particular details of the problem itself; and possibly also to what appear to be hopeful possibilities but which are really acting as obstacles to a solution. When by a pause in reflective activity we cease to excite the resonant structures in these particular ways, they continue to vibrate in ways by which the over-particular false trails die away. Alternative classifications can then emerge and new connections form. Mutual excitation between parts of the newly formed structure then causes a sudden overall rise in amplitude by which the new configuration suddenly rises above the threshold of consciousness. The whole situation may then in some degree be differently perceived, by being construed in terms of this new structure: which is to say, there is a new realization of the situation, and this may contain a solution of the problem.

Being able to: skill in action

11.14 The connection between *knowing how* and *being able to* is the connection between having arrived at a plan, and putting it into action. This involves directing the energies of the operators in such a way that the operand is taken along the chosen path from the present state to the goal state. A precondition for success is, of course, that this is physically within the capacity of the operators—that our muscles are strong or swift enough, that our engine is powerful enough, that our dynamo or batter is big enough. But if this precondition is not met, the remedy is usually to be found in the application of further knowledge-that and knowledge-how, as was indicated at the end of Section 6.12: which is to say, once again applying our intelligence to the problem area.

So in this section, we shall focus attention on the level of efficiency with which the director system puts the plan into action. For 'being able to' includes a wide range, from being able to follow a path only haltingly and inefficiently, to being able to follow it smoothly, efficiently, and quickly. This dimension of the plan-in-action we call *skill*.

Till now we have usually been thinking in terms of a distant goal state, with the director system taking the operand towards it through a sequence of intermediate states which constitute a path. But being on this path is another goal state which has to be maintained throughout the activity; or if lost, regained. This implies the action of a subordinate director system whose function it is to do just this.

If the path is a simple one with no sudden changes and no choice points, the path-keeping director system has an easy job. At a sudden change, however, inertia will be liable to take the operand off the path Whether this can be prevented will depend on a combination of three[3] factors:

(i)   how fast the state of the operand is changing (metaphorically or literally, how fast it is going);
(ii) how quickly the path-keeping director system can react; and
(iii) the extent to which it can anticipate.

For if the path-keeping director system derives its corrective action not from the present position of the operand but from where, without correction, it will be (say) in t seconds time, it can compare this with the position on the path at which it should be at that time and apply the necessary correction to take it there. And the faster the operand is going, the further ahead these predictions must be in space (either location, or more generally in the space of whatever 'state' means in the current universe of discourse) in order to allow the same time for the functioning of the path-keeping director system. This factor applies with particular force at choice points.

A simple example comes to hand if we turn back to Section 7.2, and think again about the two homing children, where the present conception of skill made an earlier appearance. Suppose that the path home is as shown in Figure 41, using the schema diagram this time as a road map of the locality around their home.

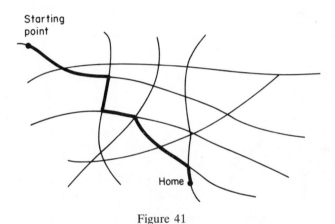

Figure 41

Consider first the visitor, who knows his way home, but not well. In terms of the present model, this means that he has a mental representation of the path, but (resonance model, Section 9.19) of a low level of sensitivity, so that the neighbourhood of concepts activated around each perceived present position as he comes to it is quite small. In other words, he relates his present position at any given time only to quite a small locality surrounding it. At the three intermediate points shown, the parts of the (mental representation of the) path which are sufficiently activated to become conscious might be something like Figure 42.

Figure 42

Only at P_2 does anticipation reach far enough forward to prepare for the necessary action at the next choice point.

Contrast this with the child to whom every part of this schema is familiar, and who has ready-to-hand paths home from almost every part of it (Figure 43).

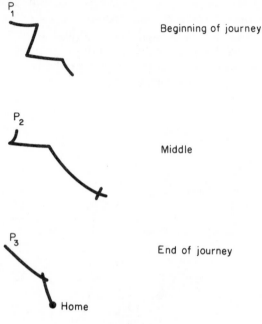

Figure 43

Wherever he is, his anticipation reaches up to and beyond the next choice point, so that he can run at full speed and still keep to the path.

And though the present example is a simple one, the principle it illustrates is general, provided that we include also the ability to anticipate relevant changes in the environment through which the path goes. For a motorist driving at speed, a medical doctor noting early signs of disease, or an accountant relating cash flow to the state of the market, one of the qualities of such an expert is his ability to predict, and to translate his predictions into skill in keeping his operand moving along the desired path. And prediction, in turn, can now be seen to depend on qualities of the relevant schema. How skilfully one is able to act is closely related to how well one knows, and how well formed are one's plans.

A-links and C-links

11.15 Once again we find that the qualities of our available schemas are crucial determinants of our success in action; and Section 11.16 will be given to an overview of these qualities. First, there is another quality to be explored which has not yet been mentioned: that of the connections within a schema.

The difference between a schema and a set of isolated concepts is that in a schema the concepts are connected; and the difference between understanding and not understanding something lies in whether it is connected to an appropriate schema or not. If the presence or absence of connections is so important, this suggests that we should give further attention to the quality of the connections themselves.

The idea of connections between concepts was first introduced (Section 9.16) to account for the fact that activation of one concept can activate, or lower the threshold for, others. This idea has been developed to include a dimension of strong or weak connections, whereby activation of a particular concept results in the activation of other within quite a large neighbourhood, or only within a small one. Recently I have become interested in another difference which is not quantitative as above, but qualitative. This is between two kinds of connection which I call *associative* and *conceptual*: for short, A-links and C-links.

Figure 44 gives some examples of associative connections.

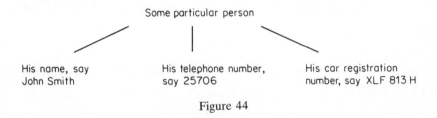

Figure 44

In Figure 44, it is not only the links marked with lines which are A-links. If we look at the interior of each concept, the links here are also A-links, e.g.:

$$2-5-7-0-6$$

Though by learning we can associate the groups of words, numerals, and letters with the person, or link the letters and numerals together to form words or other groups, it stops there. The process is that of rote memorizing, and there is no regularity which can give a foothold for the activity of intelligence.

Here is an example of a conceptual connection:

$$2-5-8-11-14-17$$

All the connections represented by the five dashes above have something in common: so much so that in this particular example one might even regard it as different occurrences of the same connection.

The same C-links connect the sets of numbers below:

$$31-34-37-40$$
$$1-4-7-10-13$$

So the above three collections of numbers are connected also with each other, because they have the same C-link.

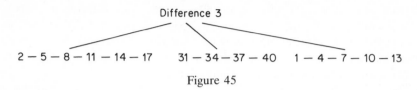

Difference 3

$2 - 5 - 8 - 11 - 14 - 17 \qquad 31 - 34 - 37 - 40 \qquad 1 - 4 - 7 - 10 - 13$

Figure 45

It is the recognition of something alike among all these connections which gives them their conceptual quality. For someone who has not recognized this, i.e., who has not formed the concept, the connections would have to be categorized as A-links.

The possession of a concept sensitizes one to recognize further examples. Thus, some one who has just read the previous passage is more likely to recognize the C-link in:

$$44–61–78–95–112$$

than some one who has not. But this is not quite the same C-link as before. And here is a third set:

$$7–15–23–31.$$

These three sets of numbers have C-links which are both alike and different.

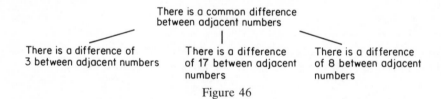

There is a common difference between adjacent numbers

There is a difference of 3 between adjacent numbers | There is a difference of 17 between adjacent numbers | There is a difference of 8 between adjacent numbers

Figure 46

Thus the conceptual quality of these C-links gives rise to higher-order concepts. These can be used as a basis for further invention, e.g.:

$$1–2–4–7–11–16$$

None of these properties is present in A-links.

Another difference is that once a C-link has been realized, we can put a name to it, communicate it, and make it an object for reflective intelligence: with all the possibilities which this opens up. But when it comes to describing any given A-link, it seems impossible to get beyond saying that it exists.

Mathematical examples were chosen to introduce the concepts of A-links and C-links because they offer useful low-noise examples to begin with. At an everyday level, the connections between different locations on a mental road map are associative; and knowing my way around in Coventry is no more help to finding my way around (say) Cardiff than knowing a man's telephone number at home is to guessing his office number. But if I am lost in a hill fog, to follow a stream in the direction of its flow is as good a course of action in Wales as it is on Dartmoor, since the connection here is a conceptual one. Languages offer a rich source of examples. For regular verbs of the same declension, the links between the infinitive and all the cases of each tense are C-links: for example:

parler	—	*je parle*
donner	—	*je donne*
aimer	—	*j'aime*
tuer	—	*je tue*

In contrast, take:

être	—	*je suis*

which is an A-link.

The examples used to illustrate the difference between A-links and C-links may well have given the impression that this difference is the same for everybody. But a connection which for some people is conceptual, may for others be associative; and we shall certainly also expect to find individual differences in ability to form, store, and use these two kinds of connection. Some persons seem able to make large numbers of A-links (e.g. shopkeepers); others have difficulty in this, but are better at conceptualizing. Moreover, even for the same person, an associative link may become a conceptual one. After vacationing for several consecutive years beside an estuary, I had formed an associative link between spring tides, high tide in the evening and morning rather than at mid-day and midnight, and either a full moon or a new moon. This changed to a conceptual link within the space of half an hour during a visit to the London Planetarium, during which the changes in the daily relative positions of sun, moon, and earth over a month were demonstrated, though without mention of tides: a change which was accompanied by the experience of an improved quality of understanding.

A feature common to mathematics and the sciences is the search for relational links. Most schemas contain both. Even in mathematics there are facts which can only be learnt associatively, such as that $\pi = 3.141\ 59\ldots$, or that the square root of 2 = $1.414\ 213\ 5\ldots$. But the larger the proportion of C-links to A-links in a schema, the better it is in several closely related ways. It is easier to remember, since there is only one connection to learn instead of many. Extrapolation is often possible and even inviting, as some will find in the case of the sequences of C-linked numbers. And the schema has an extra set of points at which assimilation, understanding, and thus growth can take place. This last needs a little more explanation. In any schema, the concepts are open to growth by the assimilation of new examples as they are encountered in experience (Section 9.12). Since a C-link is itself a particular

190

kind of concept, this is a growing point for the assimilation of new examples of
the same kind of connection. In Section 9.12 the family cat was used as
example, so let us use it again. Cat—kitten; horse—foal; bear—cub;
hen—chicken: these are all connected by the same C-link. To this C-link,
once formed, can be assimilated even such perceptually unlikely pairs as
frog—tadpole.

One more example, somewhat less obvious. A very little boy had seized his
playmate's gollywog, and would not give it back. His mother said (the names
are changed) 'David, that's Michael's *teddy*.' David, who had a much-loved
teddy bear of his own, then understood Michael's distress, and gave him back
his golly.

Qualities of a schema

11.16 The development of the concept of a schema has continued at
intervals over nine chapters (it began in Section 3.4), and will be taken no
further in the present book. The purpose of this section is to bring together
some of the main features of this important but difficult concept: difficult,
because of its high order and of great interiority. The greatest emphasis will
be on those qualities of a schema which collectively determine the
effectiveness of the director system of which it forms part.

(i)   A schema is a structure of connected concepts. The idea of a cognitive
       map is a useful introduction, a simple particular example of a schema at
       one level of abstraction only, having concepts with little or no
       interiority, and representing actuality as it has been experienced. A
       schema in its general form contains many levels of abstraction, concepts
       with interiority, and represents possible states (conceivable states) as
       well as actual states.

Factors important for effectiveness include:

(ii)   Relevance of content to the task in hand (rather obviously, but not
       always met).
(iii) The extent of its domain.
(iv)   The accuracy with which it represents actuality.
(v)   The completeness with which it represents actuality within this domain.
(vi)   The quality of organization which makes it possible to use concepts of
       lower or higher order as required, and to interchange concepts and
       schemas. (The vari-focal part of the model, linked with the idea of
       interiority.)
(vii) By a high-order schema, we mean one containing high-order concepts.
       (Clearly it will not contain *only* high-order concepts.) This determines
       its generality, and thus the extent of its domain.
(viii) The strength of the connections.
(ix)   The quality of the connections, whether associative or conceptual.

(x) The content of ready-to-hand plans, which remain integrated with the parent schema.

(xi) Penetration—the degree to which it can function in high-noise conditions.

(xii) Assimilatory power—the degree to which it can assimilate new experience.

(xiii) Assimilatory power relative to other schemas. Many breakthroughs of human thought have taken the form of the mutual assimilation of two schemas: e.g. radio astronomy, electomagnetism, algebraic geometry.

11.17 Here is a summary of the chapter.

(i) *Knowledge and belief, in the form of a schema, are the basis out of which is formed a plan which when adopted is then used by a director system to take the operand along a path from its present state to the chosen goal state.*

(ii) *Plans can also be innate, or relatively fixed as in the case of habits. But the greatest adaptability of behaviour results from the construction of a wide variety of paths to meet the needs of new situations as they arise. This is possible only if an appropriate schema is available.*

(iii) *Planning can be an intuitive or a reflective process, or a combination of these.*

(iv) *The qualities of our available schemas are crucial determinants of our success in action.*

(v) *Theorizing is another reflective process, whose goals are the optimizing of certain kinds of schema.*

(vi) *Reflective intelligence is conceptualized as a second-order activity as described in earlier chapters, but at a higher level of consciousness. It is a goal-directed activity involving on the receptor side, awareness of one's own concepts and schemas; and on the effector side, improving them in ways which may be broadly described as increasing our knowledge and ability to understand. These ways include:*

    (a) *Formulating our concepts and schemas.*

    (b) *Devising experiments by which to test the predictive powers of our schemas.*

    (c) *Revising our schemas as necessary in the light of these (and other) events.*

    (d) *Mental experiment, by which we try to optimize our plans before putting them into action.*

    (e) *Examining our schemas for inconsistencies and false inferences.*

    (f) *Generalizing our concepts and schemas.*

    (g) *Looking for connections between events and our existing schemas. This is a reflective activity in which a person is explaining to himself.*

    (h) *Increasing the number of conceptual connections within a schema, as a special case of*

    (i) *Improving and systematizing the knowledge we already have.*

192

Notes for Chapter 11

1. The great thing, then, in all education, is to *make our nervous system our ally instead of our enemy*. It is to fund and capitalize our acquisitions, and live at ease upon the interest of the fund. *For this we must make automatic and habitual, as early as possible, as many useful actions as we can*, and guard against the growing into ways that are likely to be disadvantageous to us, as we should guard against the plague. The more of the details of our daily life we can hand over to the effortless custody of automatism, the more our higher powers of mind will be set free for their own proper work.

   (James, 1890).

2. As I use the terms, there is no sharp distinction between the terms 'theory' and 'mental model'. 'Theory' is generally used for the more general and abstract kind from which a variety of particular models can be derived. Thus a theory might include all possibilities within a particular universe of discourse; a model, a more limited class of these. Up to this point I have used the term 'model' for the present theory of intelligence, to emphasize what it has in common with other mental models. Having now formulated the concept of theory in terms of the present model of intelligence, it can be seen that a theory and a mental model are essentially the same.

3. There are also other factors such as the ratio of power of operators to inertia of the operand; but here, we are concentrating on factors belonging to the director system.

CHAPTER 12

Comparison with Other Models: Likenesses and Differences

12.1 In this chapter, I shall try to show what are the main similarities and differences between my own theoretical model and those of others in the same or closely related fields. This necessarily involves the inclusion of summaries of the latter; and the difficulty of keeping a balance between length on the one hand, and trying to give clear, accurate, and fair summaries of these other theories on the other, is obvious. The difficulty is increased by the nature of my own concept of intelligence, which so greatly increases the number of other theories to which it has, or might seem to have, some relationship as to include nearly all of the field of cognitive psychology, as well as a sizeable part of social psychology. Even to try to do justice to these would require a book in itself.

To make the task possible at all, I have therefore restricted the field mainly to theories which explicitly refer to intelligence itself, and I have given most of the available space to these. Others which seem to have a fairly direct bearing on the present theory will be included towards the end of the chapter, but more briefly. And of course, references will be given by which the reader can if he wishes go back to the original sources. Where I have disagreed, I have done my best to direct my criticisms towards an accurate representation of a theory, not a 'straw' version set up only to be knocked down: as indeed I hope my own critics will do in their turn. To those who feel that I have nevertheless done injustice to their favourite theories, I apologize in advance. In such cases, the only remedy is for the reader to refer back to the original sources, and make his own comparisons.

The psychometric models

12.2 Historically the earliest group of models of intelligence was that which centred first on trying to measure it, and subsequently on investigating its nature by analytic techniques based on measurement. Probably the earliest to advocate this approach was Galton, of whom Wiseman (1967) writes that he '. . . can fairly be described as the father of experimental educational psychology', continuing: 'He believed in *measurement* as one of the basic necessities, from which facts could be produced, and hence theories evolved.' Himself of outstanding intelligence, and of distinguished family—he was cousin to Charles Darwin—he became interested in problems of individual differences in intelligence, and their distribution in the population. To investigate these he developed techniques of measurement, and of mathematical analysis, which may be regarded as the forerunners of present-day methods of psychological testing. As implied by the title of one of his books, *Hereditary Genius* (1869), he conceived intelligence as innate (his words are 'natural intellectual gift'); and as characterized particularly by versatility. Of the man of genius he writes: 'He will display an insight into new conditions, and a power of dealing with them, with which even his most intimate friends were unprepared to credit him.' In himself he offered a good example of such versatility, since he was also a geographer, an anthropologist, a statistician, and biometrician. He was among the first to study fingerprints as a method for identification; and in the field of meteorology, it was he who introduced the term 'anticyclone'.

One of the mathematical techniques pioneered by Galton, and further developed by Pearson, was that of *correlation*. Since this is the foundation for all the theoretical models derived from psychometric investigations, a brief description follows for those to whom it is not familiar. Correlation is a method for calculating a number which represents the degree of association between any two sets of measurements; more exactly, the association between their variations from the average. Since these measurements are often derived from performance at some kind of test, they are also called test scores, or simply 'scores'. A correlation value of $+1$ indicates complete association, such as we would get if one set of scores consisted of the weights of a group of people measured in pounds, and the other their weights in kilograms. If we measured their heights, and the lengths of their shadows at the same time, date, and place, the correlation would likewise be $+1$. A value of -1 also indicates complete association, but with one score increasing as the other decreases. If we chose a route from, say, London to Edinburgh, and calculated the correlation between two sets of distances of a number of intermediate places, one set being distances from London and the other from Edinburgh, the correlation between these would be -1. A value of 0 indicates complete lack of association. We would expect to obtain a value of zero (or differing from zero by an insignificant amount) if we calculated the correlation (e.g.) between the last two figures of the car registration numbers of a group of persons, and the last three figures of their telephone numbers.

Except in invented examples like these, figures of $+1$, 0, -1 are unusual. Between the heights and weights of a group of 100 male adults we would expect to obtain a correlation of the order of 0.5 to 0.7; between their heights and their average length of stride, say 0.7 to 0.9; between their heights and their lung capacities, something quite small, say 0.2; but between the difference of their chest circumferences having fully exhaled and then fully inhaled, and their measured respiratory capacity, a high correlation of the order of 0.8 to 0.9.

Spearman's 'g' model

12.3 This technique offers a method for testing experimentally the hypothesis which may be crudely stated as 'persons who are good at one thing are good at another'. Less crudely, and in the present context, the hypothesis may be re-stated: 'there is a positive correlation between the scores of a given set of persons on two given kinds of intellectual task.'

In a widely quoted paper entitled '"General intelligence": Objectively Determined and Measured', Spearman (1904) gave the following correlations between tests scores which he had obtained on the topics listed.

Table 8   Reproduced by permission of the University of Illinois Press

	Classics	French	English	Mathematics	Discrimination
Classics					
French	0.83				
English	0.78	0.67			
Mathematics	0.70	0.67	0.64		
Discrimination	0.66	0.65	0.54	0.45	
Music	0.63	0.57	0.51	0.51	0.40

Table 8 shows that the correlations between scores in classics and French are the highest of all (0.83), classics and English next highest (0.78), and so on. The major conclusion which Spearman drew was, in his own words (and italics):

> The above and other analogous observed facts indicate that *all branches of intellectual activity have in common one fundamental function (or group of functions), whereas the remaining or specific elements of the activity seem in every case to be wholly different from that in all the others.*

This common fundamental function he calls *g*, or general intelligence; so what he is saying is that ability at any particular intellectual activity can be accounted for by two factors, one being *g*, and the other a factor which is specific to that activity. The relative contributions of the general and specific factors will vary from one intellectual activity to another. In terms of test scores,

$$m_a = ag + bs$$

where m_a is an individual's test score at a particular kind (*a*) of intellectual task; *g* and *s* are given in Spearman's own words (1927) (except that for simplicity I have dropped his double suffix notation): 'm_a is the measurement or other value obtained for any individual . . . in the variable a; g is the individual's amount of g, the factor common to all the variables; and s is the individual's amount of . . . the factor specific to the variable a'.

What needs to be (but is not always) made clear is that whereas m_a is a number obtained from actual performance at a test, this is not so for g or s. Neither of these figures can be measured directly: they are statistical inferences from test scores at a variety of tasks. Though they look alike, the two sides of the equation have very different connections with actuality. The left-hand side is a test score; the right-hand side is a mathematical model by which the correlations calculated between a battery of such test scores obtained from a number of individuals can be explained. To spell this out even more clearly: g cannot be observed or measured directly, but only inferred from an individual's performance at a variety of tasks, chosen to involve the greatest contribution from g relative to that from s.

Nevertheless, there is now available a considerable body of expertise in the field of intelligence testing, developed over three-quarters of a century since Binet, in 1905, made available his method for assessing intelligence on a numerical scale. His basic idea was to find, by sampling, a set of assorted mental tasks characteristic of the intellectual ability of a child of a particular age, say 8 years old. If a child of *chronological age* 8 was found to be able to perform not only these tasks, but also those up to including the 10-year-old level, he was said to have a *mental age* of 10 years. Based on Binet's work, Terman and Merril of Stanford University published in 1916 a major revision and development known among psychogists as the Stanford–Binet scale, which has been widely used over more than half a century. This test also makes allowance for items passed at a higher age-level, or failed at a lower age-level, in assessing mental age; and converts the result into a percentage of chronological age which is called the *Intelligence Quotient*, (I.Q.). Thus

$$\text{I.Q.} = \frac{\text{mental age}}{\text{chronological age}} \times 100$$

In the foregoing example, the child whose mental age was assessed at 10 years, having a chronological age of 8 years, would be assigned an I.Q. of 125; while a child who performed equally well on the test, but had a chronological age of 12, would be assigned an I.Q. of 83. (In actual testing, the measures are in years and months.) This conversion makes it possible to compare I.Q.s of children of different ages. It is not, however, extendable in this form to adults. Thus, the first child, when he reached the age of 40, would, to obtain the same I.Q. as before, have to perform at the level of a 50-year-old; whereas in fact, the average level of performance at 50 years old is no higher for tasks of the kind included in the test. For this and other reasons, the conversion of test scores as directly obtained from the subject's performance ('raw scores') to scores on which comparisons can be based ('standard scores') is now based on comparison of an individual's performance with that of a carefully chosen sample of others of his own age range. The results are usually given in one or other of two forms: percentiles, or I.Q.s. A score at the 80th percentile is that which separates the top 20 per cent from the bottom 80 per cent; so an individual who obtained above this score would be in the top 20 per cent for his age range, and so on. Though the same name is used, standardized I.Q.s are based on the assumption that intelligence is distributed in the population according to a particular distribution, called a normal distribution. For convenience, the mean score for any given age range is standardized at 100. To compare these, let us take a child having a chronological age of 10 years. Equivalent statements about his (assessed) intelligence are that he has a standardized I.Q. of 115, and that he scores just below the 85th percentile. A person whose score was the average for his age would be assigned an I.Q. of 100, and a percentile of 50.

The foregoing is no more than an outline of how intelligence as conceived within a 'g'-type model is assessed. The technicalities involved in the construction and standardization of tests are considerable, and a considerable body of expertise has developed in the field of intelligence testing, both for use with individuals and for use with groups. But all that expertise of this kind can do is to help us make full use of the potential of a model. It cannot increase the potential of the model itself.

12.4   The successful use of a model depends on two things: the suitability of the model, and the accuracy with which actuality can be realized within this model.

What an intelligence test does is to enable us to map certain kinds of intellectual performance into a numerical scale, and the nature of this mapping will be further examined in Section 12.10. So far the term 'measurement' has been avoided, because for many people this leads to the supposition that a person's intelligence can be measured with the same accuracy as his height, weight, or basal metabolic rate. Psychometricians do not claim this: a statement such as 'This person's I.Q. is 115' is understood by them as a shorthand for 'His I.Q. is somewhere between 112 and 118'. This needs to be borne in mind, and also that these measurements (using now the conventional term) essentially describe comparisons between an individual's score and those of the sample of persons on which the test was standardized. Application of a 'g'-type model depends on the assumption that this process of measurement can be done with reasonable confidence. Making this assumption, the question now to be asked is: what are the uses to which a model of this kind can be put? As has already been emphasized, we need a variety of models according to the purposes for which they are to be used. In what ways does this model help us to explain past events, predict future events, and possibly also to control them—to achieve goals which we could not have achieved without the help of this model?

12.5 This model is essentially a comparative model, for measuring individual differences in intelligence; and a major area to which this model, with its associated techniques, has been applied is the explanation of the origins of these individual differences. This has centred around investigations of the relative effects of heredity and environment; and controversy has often become heated. Wiseman (1964) writes: 'Even to pose the question has been dangerous in certain periods of our history; and to give a particular answer has been to invite imprisonment, torture, and death. . . . It is, therefore, a social and political question first, and an educational question second.'

Since the majority of children are brought up by their natural parents, it is hard in such cases to discover whether (e.g.) the above-average measured intelligence of children from parents of above-average intelligence is to be explained by better hereditary endowment, or a better early environment, or to a combination of both: and if the last, in what proportions. This difficulty can be surmounted by the study of pairs of twins: of monozygotic twins (having therefore the same genetic constitution) raised together and those raised apart, and dizygotic twins (having different genetic constitutions) raised together and those raised apart. Correlations have been calculated for scores of intelligence, educational attainment, and physical characteristics, of sets of pairs of twins in these categories; and correlations on the same tests for ordinary siblings raised together, and for siblings raised apart. From comparisons between these correlations, a number of interesting inferences can be made. These may be summarized by two quotations from Butcher (1968). 'The most general finding has been, in practically all studies of intelligence test results in identical and fraternal twins, that identical twins are much more alike than fraternal and that a high degree of similarity persists even when they are reared apart.' . . . 'It appears therefore that environmental factors, in these studies at least, have a much more substantial influence on attainment than on intelligence, and also that this influence is particularly marked on verbal and literary attainment.'

12.6 So far as prediction is concerned, a g-type model (in conjunction with suitable tests) is likely to be helpful in finding out which persons are likely to be good at future intellectual tasks, particularly tasks of kinds which they have not yet encountered. In the United Kingdom, when the number of places available in secondary schools of the more academic kind was limited, selection for these was one of the most important uses of intelligence testing. At the time of writing, concern for social justice has taken a different form, directed towards equality of opportunity: though the meaning of the latter turns out to be elusive (*Oxford Review of Education*, 1975). As a result, intelligence tests themselves have tended to come under criticism because of their association with selection at 'eleven-plus'. So it is worth reminding ourselves that they were introduced into selection very largely on grounds of social justice. One of the pioneers in this field, Sir Godfrey Thomson, was particularly concerned with the poorer chances of able children from poor backgrounds in gaining entry to secondary grammar-type schools, and particularly of those at isolated rural schools having only one or two teachers. Given selection, he considered selection on the basis of general intelligence to be a fairer method than selection by children's present educational attainment.

But it is equally necessary to bear in mind the statistical basis of both test construction and predictions based on these. According to Vernon (1957), the efficiency of selection by a combination of tests and primary-school teachers' estimate is represented by a correlation of 0.9, which (if he is right) is remarkably high. Even so, one child in ten is likely to be mistakenly allocated.

12.7 It is perhaps in the third use of a theoretical model, that of control, that a *g*-type model is weakest. So far as the hereditary contribution is concerned, the only possibility it appears to offer is that of producing more intelligent offspring by selective breeding; or by encouraging more intelligent parents to have more children, and those less intelligent to have fewer. It is hard to see how either of these could be put into effect, even were we convinced of its desirability.

On the environmental side, this model does not tell us specifically enough to be usable what are the environmental factors which contribute to intelligence as measured, and how these might be manipulated in order to optimize the environmental contribution. Is it good teaching? If so, what *is* good teaching? Is it a home where children are encouraged to read? If so, what sort of books? Is it good meal-time conversation? Parents who talk with their children and answer their questions? A *g*-type model does not help us to penetrate beyond a common-sense level of answer to these questions.

Factor-analytic models

12.8 Since Spearman, there has been a great deal of work centred on investigating the nature of intelligence by analytic techniques based on measurement. These techniques, called factor analysis, are highly mathematical. It is, however, possible to get a good overall idea of the reasoning on which it is based with no more than an elementary knowledge of mathematics. In the preliminaries to this, which are necessary for subsequently evaluating the factor-analytic approach, we shall also come upon some important criteria of a more general kind. These apply to any theories based on measurement and to any kind of mathematical model; and are therefore of interest beyond the present context.

For those readers with the necessary mathematical background, a more detailed explanation of the techniques and my evaluation of them has also been included, in Section 12.13. This may be omitted without detriment to the general argument.

Mathematical Models in General

12.9 The starting point will be the first two sentences of a paragraph in Section 11.13:

A theory is not itself a model for a particular task, but something more general: namely a schema within which can be conceptualized all the possible states within a particular universe of discourse, and relations between these states. A model of a particular task is constructed by mapping the actual situation into this schema: which is to say, by representing the given actuality as a particular example of some of the regularities already conceptualized within the schema.

Whenever measurement is the beginning from which is then derived a theory stated in mathematical terms, the process starts one step further back. For it is now within the extensive, complex, and abstract schemas already provided by mathematics that the new theory is conceptualized; so *the relationships within the theory are mathematical relationships*. Measurement is a way of attaching numbers to observables which maps a given situation into a theory of this kind, thereby giving a model for a particular situation. For any model, the manipulations of the model will only make sense, and the predictions based thereon will only be valid, if there is proper correspondence between relationships within the model and those regularities within the observables which the model represents. And in this kind of model, the relationships are mathematical relationships.

An illustration of what can go wrong if the above principle is neglected is offered by the anecdote, no doubt invented, of a naval sick-bay attendant. To save confusing him with the long names of drugs, the medical officer simply numbered all the bottles. But one day, when he had told the attendant to give the patient a pill from bottle number nine, the attendant reported on his return that this bottle was empty, so instead he had given the patient a pill from bottle number four and a pill from number five.

It was not the arithmetic which was wrong here, but the faulty correspondence between the attendant's model and the chemical relations between the pills.

Scales of measurement

12.10 The sick-bay attendant would not have made this mistake had he realized that his officer was only using a nominal scale. This is the most primitive of the four kinds of scale, the others being ordinal, interval, and ratio scales; and the next part of the argument requires a brief explanation of these.

These four kinds of scale are sometimes described as four ways of attaching numbers to observations; but this is not quite accurate, for in a *nominal* scale it is only names of numbers, i.e. numerals, which are used as a convenient ready-to-hand set of names. An *ordinal* scale does, however, embody a mathematical relationship, that of order. The order of their attached numbers corresponds to the order of the observables with respect to some quality, such as weight, order in space or time. Performance at a given task can be interpreted by an ordinal scale; e.g., at running, by lining up the competitors, starting them simultaneously, and assigning numbers in the same order as that in which they cross the finishing line. Suppose that at the finish of a cross-country run three runners A, B, C were handed cards marked 7, 27, 47. A person who had not seen them at the finish would be able, by ordering their numbers, to deduce the order in which they had actually finished. He would also be able to make quite a good prediction of the order in which these three would finish on a similar course in the not-too-distant future. Valid manipulations of a model derived from an ordinal scale include those, and only those, which depend on the transitive property of any order relationship. This is very simple: if A comes before B and B comes before C, then A comes before C. In the race example this needs no further explanation. Interpolation is a double application of this. Suppose that another runner X showed a card marked 17. Since this is between 7 and 27, the observer can safely deduce that X finished after A and before B. But he would be mistaken if he also deduced that the time between A and X was the same as that between X and B, in spite of the fact that the intervals between their attached numbers 7, 17, 27 are equal: or that this was half the time separating B (number 27) and C (number 47). For this to be a valid inference, he would require an *interval* scale.

Temperature, measured in °C, is a good example of an interval scale. Suppose that we have a fixed quantity of water to be heated. The same amount of heat is required to raise its temperature from 7 °C to 17 °C as from 17 °C to 27 °C; twice this amount will be required to raise it from 27 °C to 47 °C; three times, from 17 °C to 47 °C; and so on. This is an inference from the model, and if you wish to test by mode (i) a prediction resulting from this inference, it is not hard to do so, provided you are willing to accept that the heat given out in each second by the element of an electric kettle stays the same. Fill the kettle; insert a thermometer so that the bulb is in the water but the stem is visible; insulate the kettle as well as possible (e.g. by a towel wrapped around), for our model is a simple one and takes no account of heat lost from the kettle to its surroundings; switch on, and record accurately the times at which the thermometer reads 7, 17, 27, 47 °C. This simple experiment, which can if you like be a 'thought experiment', will also serve as a reminder of the difference between inference and prediction. The inference is exact; the prediction is unlikely to be so, because the model is a simplification of what goes on in actuality. (For example, the insulation against loss of heat cannot be perfect; the water will not heat equally fast all over, and the thermometer records temperature at one point only.) Also, our measuring instruments or observations are not exact. But it is, for our present purposes, of importance to distinguish between these experimental errors, and inferential errors resulting from using a faulty model. It is the latter with which we are concerned at the moment.

Valid inferences from models based on an interval scale are all those resulting from addition and subtraction. In the last example, we used inferences based on results such as $17 - 7 = 10$ and $27 - 17 = 10$, and $47 = 27 + 10 + 10$. But it would be invalid to infer, from $30 = 3 \times 10$, that a lump of metal at 30 °C contains three times as much heat as it does at 10 °C. This is because even at 0 °C there is still heat left in it—it can be cooled to ten, twenty, thirty degrees below 0 °C, and beyond. On an interval scale, zero does not correspond to 'nothing at all' of what we are measuring—it is just a starting point chosen for convenience.

A *ratio* scale is an interval scale with a true zero. Mass is such a scale: and there is indeed three times as much iron in a lump whose mass measures 30 grams as there is in a lump whose mass measures 10 grams, for in a lump whose mass measures 0 grams there is no iron at all. Temperature measured in degrees Kelvin (°K) is another example of a ratio scale, for at 0 °K a body contains no heat energy at all. Multiplication and division are valid operations on a model based on a ratio scale. Also addition and subtraction, and ordering: for each of the scales described—nominal, interval, ordinal, ratio—includes the categories before it. Thus a ratio scale is also an interval, an ordinal, and even a nominal scale. ('Which weight is this?' 'It's the 2-kilogram weight.')

12.11   From these simple examples, it can be seen that the first requirement for making valid inferences, when using any kind of mathematical model, is to know which kind of scale it is based on. So this question must now be asked about intelligence tests.

Every intelligence test consists, in one form or another, of a number of questions to be answered, or tasks to be done. These are scored either right or wrong, or by awarding varying numbers of points for completely right or partially right answers. In some, the person tested may take as much time as he wants; others are timed overall, or by sections; and in a few, such as the Wechsler scales, additional points are awarded for completing tasks more quickly. Whatever the details, the result is a certain number of points known as the person's raw (i.e. unprocessed) score.

This score can only be an ordinal or an interval scale, since a ratio scale would require that a zero score signified zero intelligence. To claim that it is an interval scale is to make an assertion of the following kind: that if A, B, C score respectively 30, 20, 10 points then A is more intelligent than B by the same amount as B is more intelligent than C. In such a form, this assertion is as vulnerable as it would be to say that if A, B, C can jump heights respectively of 3, 6, 9 feet, then the differences in high-jumping ability of A and B, B and C are the same.

A more sophisticated argument in favour of an interval scale is supported y many psychometricians. Briefly, it is this. Those physical qualities of a human population which can be measured by ratio scales, such as height and weight, are found to be scattered around an average value in a way which is very widespread throughout nature, and is called a normal or Gaussian distribution. If intelligence has a physiological basis, it is reasonable to assume that it too follows this distribution. By suitable techniques of test construction and conversion from raw scores to scaled scores, tests and ways of scoring them can be produced which also follow a normal distribution. These tests, they infer, yield an interval scale. A fuller version of this argument can be found in Vernon (1960). Butcher (1968), however, considers that ' . . . a good intelligence test properly used and constructed certainly yields something more than a mere rank order, but something less strong than a physical measurement of temperature.'

The applications for which intelligence tests are generally used, such as selection, only require the assumption of an ordinal scale; for all that is required here is to put the candidates in order of merit. In factor-analytic techniques, however, extensive use is made of multiplication and division. Here is the first weakness of factor analysis.

2.12   The mathematics of factor analysis is highly technical. It is, however, possible to get a sound idea of the general method independently of the mathematical details, and this will be the aim of the present section. In Section 12.13, the mathematical argument will be given in more detail.

We will start again with a group of 100 children, but pretend now that although we suspect that they may be of varying ages, we have no information about their birth dates, and therefore no way of measuring their ages. Indeed, our concept of age itself is still at a rudimentary state.

However, it is very clear that they vary greatly in height and weight, and also in muscular strength, lung capacity, speed of running, how high they can jump, how far they can jump, and in other such ways. It is also evident that these vary together: that the taller children are also heavier, stronger, can run faster, and so on. That is to say, there is a positive association between all of these. To explain this, we can choose between two kinds of hypothesis:

(i)   That it is due to a single common factor. On this hypothesis, an individual's score of a particular kind (e.g. height, running, jumping) can be explained by this general factor, in combination with one which is specific to that particular test. (This corresponds to Spearman's approach already described.) We do not know for sure what this general factor is; and even if we suspect that this general factor is something which we can put a name to (in this case, age), we do not know the children's birth dates and in our present state of knowledge have no way of obtaining these. So we proceed to verify our hypothesis indirectly. First, we calculate all the possible intercorrelations between these scores, such as that between height and weight, height and strength, strength and speed, etc. These give a table of intercorrelations called the *correlation matrix* On the 'general factor' hypothesis, there will be certain relationships o proportionality within this table. It is unlikely that our experimental dat: will satisfy this criterion exactly; but if they do so nearly enough, we ma; feel justified in concluding that they support the hypothesis.

This common factor still cannot be observed or measured directly. W: can only estimate it indirectly from the other measurements, and work ou what combination appears to give the best estimate. Since we also do no: know for sure what it is, we choose whatever name we consider mos: appropriate. On the basis of our original conjecture, we might call it age but we might also equally well call it 'growth', or even, more cautiously 'general physical development'.

(ii) An alternative approach would be to hypothesize that several factors ar: involved, which we might tentatively identify as age, nutrition athleticism. This would give a three-factor model. To verify this by th: methods of factor analysis, which are mathematical, requires thi hypothesis to be stated as a mathematical model; and the model used b; factor analysts is a *weighted sum*. In this model, supposing that we coul: measure an individual's scores in these three factors, then his score fo: height could be obtained by adding these scores together in differen: amounts, thus:

$$(\text{height}) = c_1 \times (\text{age}) + c_2 \times (\text{nutrition}) + c_3 \times (\text{athleticism})$$

where (height), (age), etc., stand for *measures* of height, age, etc., i.e. fo: numbers; and c_1, c_2, c_3 are also numbers representing the contributions o: (age), (nutrition), (athleticism), to (height). Likewise for the othe: scores:

$$(\text{speed}) = d_1 \times (\text{age}) + d_2 \times (\text{nutrition}) + d_3 \times (\text{athleticism})$$

and so on.

This goes far beyond the assumption of a ratio scale of measurement, which is implied by the multiplication signs. It assumes that the ways in which age, nutrition, athleticism interact in actuality (the children's physical bodies) correspond to addition in the mathematical model. A single counterexample will suffice to call this strongly into question. Put (nutrition) equal to zero in the second of the above equations, and assume that (age) and (athleticism) are not zero. Then the left-hand side of the equation, (speed), will not be zero: whereas in actuality, we would expect a completely non-nourished child to be unable to run at all.

The method by which the multi-factor hypothesis is developed further uses the same intercorrelation matrix as has been described already. (Spearman's model can in fact be treated as a special case.) By factorizing this matrix, not just one set of equations can be obtained, but an infinite number. This is because a matrix can be factorized in as many ways as we like, in rather the ame kind of way as the number 24 can be factorized not only as 2×12, or $\times 8$, or 4×6, but also as 5×4.8, or 3.2×7.5, etc. There is also some egree of choice whether a small number of main factors is chosen, each mportant for a large group of tasks, together with additional group factors of nore specific influence; or whether to choose a larger number of primary actors. The first of these approaches was favoured by many British sychologists, whose two major group factors are verbal–educational and patial–mechanical. Prominent among the American school is Thurstone, ho in contrast identified seven factors: spatial ability, perceptual speed, umerical ability, verbal meaning, memory, verbal fluency, inductive easoning. These are by no means the only proposed structures for human ntelligence. Guilford proposes 64 factors in his model. A review of these and thers may be found in Butcher (1968), Chapter II.

2.13 (*May be omitted.*) The mathematical argument on which factor nalysis is based has as its starting point a set of multiple regression equations. Let $z_1, z_2, \ldots, z_i, \ldots$ be scores dependent on, and therefore predictable om, the n variables $x_1, x_2, \ldots x_n$. Then (using standard scores throughout)

$$z_1 = a_{11}x_1 + a_{12}x_2 + \ldots + a_{1j}x_j + \ldots + a_{1n}x_n$$

$$z_2 = a_{21}x_1 + a_{22}x_2 + \ldots + a_{2j}x_j + \ldots + a_{2n}x_n$$

$$\ldots$$

$$z_i = a_{i1}x_1 + a_{i2}x_2 + \ldots + a_{ij}x_j + \ldots + a_{in}x_n$$

In the case of multiple regression, $z_1, \ldots, z_i$ and $x_1, \ldots, x_n$ are scores which ave actually been obtained, from a suitable sample of persons; and there are nethods for calculating the coefficients a_{ij}. The equations then provide a nethod for predicting the z-scores of other individuals if we know their -scores.

The problem of factor analysis is to do this in reverse. Given a set of -scores for every individual in a suitable sample, which evaluate the perform-ance of these individuals in tests of various abilities, the aim is to be able to xplain these scores by a set of equations like the above, in which the $_1, \ldots, x_n$ represent scores at certain (as yet hypothetical) more basic bilities. These x-scores are not available, nor is it known how many x will be equired. But certainly we shall want $n < i$, since the aim is to simplify. The nethods for calculating the coefficients a_{ij} directly also depend on knowing hese x-scores. Factor analysis is a method for obtaining them indirectly.

All it has to start with is the set of z-scores, for all the individuals in the ample. From these, it is straightforward (though it was very time-taking until omputers became available) to calculate and tabulate all possible intercorre-ations of the form r_{pq}, where r_{pq} is the correlation between z_p and z_q for this ample. So in the algebra which follows, the r's and z's can be replaced by xperimental data; the a's and x's are as yet unknowns. Starting with the first two regression equations,

$$r_{12} = \frac{1}{N} \sum z_1 z_2$$

$$= \frac{1}{N} (a_{11}x_1 + \ldots + a_{1n}x_n)(a_{21}x_1 + \ldots + a_{2n}x_n)$$

summed over all pairs of values of z_1 and z_2 for individual subjects within the sample, i.e., over all pairs of sets of values of $x_1, \ldots, x_n$.

Notes (i) $z_1, x_1, \ldots, x_n$ are *different variates*. Our notation does not include separate individual values thereof, since this would require triple suffixes.

(ii) $r_{12} = \frac{1}{N} z_1 z_2$ because we are using standard scores, for which $\sigma = 1$.

Continuing,

$$r_{12} = \frac{1}{N} \sum (a_{11}a_{21}x_1^2 + \ldots + a_{1n}a_{2n}x_n^2)$$

$$+ \frac{1}{N} \sum (a_{11}a_{22}x_1x_2 + a_{12}a_{21}x_1x_2 + \ldots$$

$$+ a_{11}a_{2n}x_1x_n + a_{1n}a_{21}x_1x_n + \ldots)$$

In the first of these sums, we have $\sum x_i^2 = N$ (because all the x are standard scores).

The second of these sums is a complicated one, consisting of all possible pairs like $x_s x_t$ with their appropriate coefficients. However, *if and only if* there is zero correlation between x_s and x_t, the sum $\sum x_s x_t = 0$. (Reminder: standard scores are deviation scores.) So, *if and only if* there is zero correlation between every possible pair $x_s x_t$, the whole of the second sum vanishes. The whole of factor analysis depends on this condition being satisfied, for it is only by the vanishing of this complicated and inconvenient second sum that the algebra which follows becomes possible. On this assumption,

$$r_{12} = a_{11}a_{21} + \ldots + a_{1k}a_{2k}$$

and in general

$$r_{pq} = a_{p1}a_{q1} + \ldots + a_{pk}a_{qk}$$

A more compact notation is now possible:

$$r_{pq} = \sum_{j=1}^{k} a_{pj}a_{qj}$$

(Note: Two considerations have been omitted from the above, namely the effect of errors of estimates, and variables whose effect is specific to any one of the z. This would make the equations

$$z_1 = a_{11}x_1 + \ldots + a_{1n}x_n + c_1 s_1 + d_1$$

where s_1 is the factor specific to z_1, and d_1 is the error of estimate.

But by definition, s_1 has zero coefficient in all the other equations, and d_1 is random so it has zero correlation with any x. So the terms involving s_1 and d_1 vanish when summed, and the result is as already stated.)

The problem is now that of solving the $\frac{1}{2}n(n-1)$ equations obtained by putting $p,q = 1, \ldots, n \quad (p \neq q)$ in

$$r_{pq} = a_{p1}a_{q1} + \ldots + a_{pn}a_{qn}$$

having on the left-hand side the $\frac{1}{2}n(n-1)$ obtained correlations r_{pq}, and on the right-hand side the nk unknowns $a_1, \ldots, a_{nk}$. Provided that $k < \frac{1}{2}(n-1)$, the number of equations will be greater than the number of unknowns, and in this case there can be an infinite number of solutions. There should be no difficulty in meeting this condition, since by giving more tests the value of n can be increased as desired. The value of k is largely open to choice: and this choice determines the number of factors in the final model.

The solution, though theoretically possible, would in practice be excessively difficult but for the help of matrix algebra. For let R denote the (square) matrix of obtained intercorrelations, i.e.

$$R = \begin{pmatrix} r_{11} & r_{12} & \cdots & r_{1n} \\ r_{21} & r_{22} & \cdots & r_{2n} \\ & & \cdots & \\ r_{n1} & r_{n2} & \cdots & r_{nn} \end{pmatrix}$$

The diagonal terms here represent the correlations of the tests with themselves, e.g., between parallel forms of the same test, or between two administrations to the same sample.)

Let

$$A = \begin{pmatrix} a_{11} & a_{12} & \cdots & a_{1k} \\ a_{21} & a_{22} & \cdots & a_{2k} \\ & & \cdots & \\ a_{n1} & a_{n2} & \cdots & a_{nk} \end{pmatrix}$$

Then the complete set of equations can now be written

$$R = AA'$$

Where A' is the transpose of A. This can be recognized as equivalent to the earlier form

$$r_{pq} = \sum_{j=1}^{k} a_{pj} a_{qj} \quad (p,q = 1, \ldots, n)$$

having now removed the restriction $p \neq q$.

It will be recalled that R is known. So the factor-analytic problem can now be stated as that of solving the matrix equation $R = AA'$.

Details of various methods for doing this, and criteria for choosing a preferred solution out of the infinite number of possible solutions, have filled a number of volumes. It is, fortunately, not necessary to follow through these complexities of detail in order to bring to light the conditions which would have to be satisfied for this model to be a valid one. This we are now in a position to do.

The most important requirement is that *every factor has to be independent of every other factor*. Without this, the condition that there is zero correlation between every possible pair $x_s x_t$ is not satisfied, and as was emphasized earlier the whole of the algebra of factor analysis depends on this. Psychologically it seems most unlikely, e.g., that each of Thurstone's seven factors (spatial ability, perceptual speed, numerical ability, verbal meaning, memory, verbal fluency, inductive reasoning) is independent of all the others. Mathematically the requirement can be satisfied provided that the factors extracted are 'orthogonal', which is the geometric equivalent of zero correlation. Those factor analysts who permit 'oblique' factors are therefore departing from mathematical conditions which are essential for the validity of their model.

Spearman seems to have been almost alone in the clarity with which he stated this requirement, both in his psychological formulation of the independence of the general factor g and the specific factors $s_1, s_2, \ldots$, and in the corresponding mathematics by which he was able to test whether this criterion was satisfied by the obtained test scores.

My next point of disagreement with the multi-factor models is on the nature of the relationship between whatever factors are involved. To know that an electric lightbulb consists of so much glass, so much metal of this kind and that, and so much inert gas, is but a small part of what would be an adequate description. The most important thing is how they are put together: and the multi-factor models do not tell us this.

Moreover, what they do tell us is almost certainly wrong. For however the contributory factors of intelligence interact, it is almost certainly not in the way represented by a weighted sum, and this is what a regression equation is. This point will be argued further in Section 12.14, after we have been re-joined by those who have omitted this section.

12.14 Of these and the other models which have resulted from factor analysis, the same three questions as were asked of the 'g' model must now be repeated. How well do they enable us, at better than common-sense levels: to achieve certain kinds of aim; to co-operate in certain kinds of way; and to go on creating knowledge in a certain area?

In their practical applications, the answer to the first question has to be: very little, beyond some development of the applications to selection in the form of aptitude testing.

From a theoretical viewpoint, the same question can be put in the form: if we accept any of the factor-analytic models as knowledge-that, what knowledge-how can be derived?

For comparison, let us take a simple mathematical model in everyday use:

$$d = t \times s$$

where d stands for distance in miles, t for time in hours, s for uniform speed in miles per hour. Since this uses multiplication, the first check we make is whether distance, time, and speed, are measured in ratio scales. Yes, they are: so we can continue with confidence. What kinds of knowledge-how can be derived? In the model as it stands, a driver who knows his usual average speed can infer how far he will go in a given time, and thereby predict approximately where he will be at different times on a long journey: approximately, because he is replacing uniform speed by average speed, so the model is not exact. He can plan where he will stop for lunch, and if his calculations tell him that he will be passing through a large city at rush hour, he can alter his time of departure. In case this seems too simple, here are some other applications. If we know the velocity of sound in air, and time the interval between seeing a flash of lightning and hearing the thunder, we can infer how far away the storm is. Two such observations, and we know whether it is getting nearer or further away. Echo-sounders use the same mathematical model to measure depth, by timing how long sound takes to travel to the bottom of the water and, by reflection, back to the ship. Radar uses the same mathematical model, with reflected radio waves.

An important feature of a mathematical model is that it can be manipulated, according to the established operations of mathematics. In the present case we can obtain

$$t = \frac{d}{s} \quad \text{and} \quad s = \frac{d}{t}$$

and each of these is as varied in its applications as the first form.

For brevity, only one example of co-operation will be given. The first form of the model is the basis for the whole of the exercise of railway timetabling, which involves co-operation between large numbers of persons.

What new knowledge does it lead to? This question has two kinds of answer. Echo-sounding would never have been developed but for the existence of a mathematical model which said it would work. Once it has been, it yields much greater and more detailed knowledge of underwater contours. This is new knowledge of actuality. But there has also resulted new theoretical knowledge: for it poses the question, by what mathematical model(s) can we represent varying velocity, or velocity at a particular instant of time? His pursuit of an answer to this question led Newton to the development of his 'method of fluxions', now known as the calculus, which is one of the most powerful of tools in the whole of mathematics.

The foregoing is offered as an illustration of the kind of power and versatility which we are entitled to expect from a good mathematical model, even such a simple one as this. How well do factor analytic models compare?

Here we resume the discussion which was begun in Section 12.12. For simplicity, take just three factors instead of Thurstone's seven: the principle is not changed. A multi-factor model takes the form of a weighted sum.

$$z_1 = a_1x_1 + a_2x_2 + a_3x_3$$

$$z_2 = b_1x_1 + b_2x_2 + b_3x_3$$

$$z_3 = c_1x_1 + c_2x_2 + c_3x_3$$

etc.

This states that the measures z_1, z_2, z_3, .. of a person's performance at various categories of task 1, 2, 3, . . . can be explained by, and predicted from, their scores x_1, x_2, x_3 in three basic abilities. Each category requires different contributions from x_1, x_2, x_3, so these are respectively multiplied by suitable numbers to give the right weighting to each ability. These multipliers, or weightings, appear in the equations as a_1, a_2, a_3 for the first kind of task, b_1, b_2, b_3 for the second, and so on.

My first and greatest objection to the model is that it is additive, and common sense denies that this is how abilities combine, whether they are primary abilities, secondary, or tertiary. Suppose that the task is to master an advanced psychology text written in Russian. For this, ability at psychology and at Russian are clearly necessary: let us suppose that they are equally necessary. A weighted-sum model would then be:

$$z_1 = 0.5p + 0.5r$$

where p and r represent (measured) ability at psychology and Russian respectively, and z_1 predicted score at psychology-in-Russian. So if someone scored the maximum possible at psychology, but zero at Russian, this model predicts that he still would score half the maximum possible for the combined task. Given such an obvious counterexample, this by itself would at least call the model seriously into question.

Secondly, the objection has already been made that by the use of the operation of multiplication on the test scores, ratio scales of measurement are assumed: whereas interval scales are the best that can be claimed.

Thirdly: if the weighted-addition model were valid, meaningful manipulation should be possible. For example,

$$0.5p = z_1 - 0.5r$$

which is equivalent to

$$p = 2z_1 - r$$

stating that a person's performance at psychology can be estimated if one knows his performances at psychology-in-Russian, and at Russian alone.

Suppose now that he scored zero at psychology-in-Russian, but performed well in Russian alone. Then this model predicts that his measured ability in psychology would be *negative*.

The fourth objection is that the mathematical techniques involved in factor analysis, which were described in Section 12.13, require the assumption that the factors are independent. This goes far beyond just saying that they are different: it is saying that if they could be directly measured, the correlations between these measures (for the group of persons under investigation) would be zero. To give a physical example, it would be analogous to saying not just that height and weight were importantly different qualities of a person's physique, but that if we measured a group of subjects, there would be zero correlation between their heights and weights.

It is only in Spearman's model that this requirement is clearly recognized, and evidence adduced in support of the assumption that it is satisfied. In the others, it is not considered; and were it to be, there is no reason to think that it would be satisfied. Thurstone's factors, for example, are spatial ability, perceptual speed, numerical ability, verbal meaning, memory, verbal fluency, inductive reasoning. Granted that these are different abilities, can we accept the assumption that if these could be measured directly, there would be zero correlation between each and every pair? If we cannot accept this as a reasonable assumption to be used as a starting point, then evidence is required in support. Such evidence is not forthcoming.

Cumulatively, these objections to the factor-analytic model appear to me as conclusive.

12.15 It is, however, not with the early conceptions of the psychometricians that I am in disagreement. Spearman's well-known formulation of intelligence as 'the eduction of relations and correlates' accords well with that part of my model which emphasizes the merits of conceptual rather than associative connections (Section 11.15). Thorndike's 'the power of good responses from the point of view of truth or fact' could have been developed into reality testing mode (i). Binet's 'the faculty of adapting oneself to circumstances', and Galton's description of the man of genius who 'will display an insight into new conditions, and a power of dealing with them . . . ', are the same as I have made my own starting point: for example, (Section 1.8) 'the invisible asset of adaptability.' With goal-directedness and model building as starting points, I have shown in Chapter 3 and elsewhere that ability to abstract follows as a necessary consequence. Compare this with Terman's 'the ability to carry on abstract thinking'—not quite the same, but entirely compatible. Abstraction is also a major feature of intelligence tests.

It is natural to ask why much of the undoubted talent which has been applied to the study of intelligence has pursued what is now beginning to be perceived as a side issue, relative to what should have been the main direction of enquiry. Part of the answer must be sought in the overall climate of scientific thinking at the time, during which psychology was seeking to establish itself as a scientific discipline. The highly successful natural sciences emphasized, as they still do, the importance of observation and, to give precision to observation, measurement. So it is not surprising that the pioneers of scientific psychology chose these as their own starting point. In so doing, however, they were taking over the tools of the natural sciences rather than the job which has to be done by any science, namely the building and testing of theoretical models. When the latter followed, the models which they produced were largely influenced by the tools which had already been developed, rather than the other way about.

It is therefore not with the starting points of the psychometric models of intelligence, but the ways in which these have been developed, that I differ; and with the fact that unfruitful lines of thinking have been persisted in for so long. In some respects one might be pardoned for suggesting that they had gone backward; for the early pioneers did not make statements like the following:

> To object to this procedure by arguing that the I.Q. cannot be regarded as interchangeable with intelligence, or that intelligence cannot really be measured, or that I.Q. is not the same as intelligence is to get bogged down in a semantic morass. *It is equivalent to arguing that a column of mercury in a glass tube cannot be regarded as synonymous with temperature.* . . . (Jensen, 1970, my italics.)

After more than 70 years since the publication of Spearman's historic paper, if this line of thinking had been going to develop the properties of a good theoretical model, it should have shown signs of doing so before now.

Piaget's conception of intelligence

12.16   This section has to begin with an explanation of what might be called 'the author's Piaget problem'. This is the near-impossibility of giving, in a space which is short enough to be in balance with the rest of the book: (i) an adequate summary of Piaget's theory as it relates to intelligence; (ii) a critique; and (iii) a comparison with the model constructed by myself. The size of the problem is well illustrated by Flavell (1963), who encountered it when engaged in writing a graduate text on theories of child development. His intention was to include a one-chapter summary of each theory; but when he tried to do this for the theory of Piaget, he was gradually forced to the conclusion that what he needed to do was to write a book-length exposition of Piaget's work alone. It took him seven years, and it runs to almost 500 pages. This was due not only to the fact that the volume of publications from Piaget and his immediate collaborators is very great; he is also difficult to understand. As Flavell writes (1963) 'One often has to work hard to understand what Piaget has to say, and he does not always succeed in the end.' Butcher (1968) refers to 'his dense and aphoristic style'. The reader will be able to form his own judgement about this from the passages quoted hereafter.

Like Flavell, I have had to make a policy decision: but in the present case, it went in a different direction. In this I was much helped by being differently situated from Flavell in two ways. First, there now exists not only Flavell's own very substantial contribution, but also a succession of other accounts of Piaget's work, including a number of shorter ones such as Isaacs (1961), Beard (1969); and also summaries in general texts such as that of Butcher (1968, pp. 182–98).

There seemed nothing to be gained in duplicating the huge amount of work which authors such as the above have done; particularly since they have remained basically in agreement with Piaget's overall position, whereas I have been moving steadily away from it. In 1955 I was one of a relatively small number of university teachers in the English-speaking countries who included Piaget's work in their courses on developmental psychology. My efforts to understand Piaget's ideas then, in order to be able to explain them as clearly as possible to my students, set in motion some lines of thinking which I might not have started along otherwise. And it is mostly in this respect that I echo Bruner, Olver, and Greenfield, who wrote (1966, p. 185) 'we too are in his debt', but continued 'though in the end we have been led into other paths and, on some crucial points have been forced to bring his theoretical account into serious question.'

Secondly, the present goal is a different one from Flavell's. Since this is not a book on developmental psychology, it is not necessary even to try to summarize Piaget's contributions in this area, which are very considerable. By restricting our attention to his theoretical model of intelligence, the task immediately becomes of manageable size; for this is formulated by him in a relatively short space.

One problem still remains, which arises out of the difficulty of Piaget's style which has already been mentioned. This makes the task not only one of condensation, but of clarification: so that the writer is summarizing not always what Piaget wrote, but what the writer thinks Piaget meant by what he wrote. This is sometimes unavoidable; but if there is to be also a critique, then in fairness to Piaget the latter should be addressed so far as possible to what he wrote himself, and not to the writer's own, or any one else's, interpretation thereof.

So in the section which follows, I shall give, in Piaget's own words, his theoretical model of intelligence. To minimize the possibility of distorting his meaning by quotation out of context, I have tried to identify those passages which contain Piaget's summarizing formulations, and to give these at some length. These are followed by my own comments: the two being cross-referenced by Roman numerals. To enable any reader who so wishes to check the context, page references are also included. The quotations are all from *The Psychology of Intelligence* (1950), the English translation of *La*

Psychologie de L'Intelligence, first published in France in 1947, and are reproduced by permission of Routledge & Kegan Paul Ltd, London.

12.17 Early in the first chapter can be found a passage which reveals where, from a shared starting point, we almost immediately begin to diverge.

> (p. 7) This view means, right from the start, an insistence on the central role of intelligence in mental life and in the life of the organism itself[i]; intelligence, the most plastic and at the same time the most durable structural equilibrium[ii] of behaviour[iii], is essentially a system of living and acting operations[iv]. It is the most highly developed form of mental adaptation[v], that is to say, the indispensable instrument for interaction between the subject and the universe when the scope of this interaction goes beyond immediate and momentary contacts to achieve far-reaching[vi] and stable[vii] relations.

(i) I entirely agree. (ii) Piaget's use of the term 'equilibrium' is one which I find hard to grasp in the present context. Its basic meaning is (*Concise Oxford Dictionary*) 'State of balance (lit. & fig.)'. It is therefore important that I do not give my own conjectures about what I think he might mean, but rather choose other passages from which the reader can form his own conclusions. (iii) If he really means what he writes, 'equilibrium of behaviour', then the difficulty is increased; for one of the things on which I would expect the widest agreement is that intelligence refers not to behaviour but to certain kinds of mental activity which one infers from observable behaviour. (iv) Mental or physical operations? Looking back to (iii) would suggest that he means behaviour, but (v) suggests the more acceptable interpretation that he means mental operations. (vi) Certainly intelligence is one of the ways in which behaviour comes to be directed in relation to far-reaching considerations, but it is certainly not 'the indispensable instrument'. Behaviour controlled by innate systems can also fit this description, for example, the migration of birds, eels, salmon; the cycle of nest-building and courtship, mating and nurture, in birds and even sticklebacks. (vii) This depends on what he means by 'stable', so we shall need to see whether this emerges: possibly in connection with his meaning of 'equilibrium'.

> (pp. 7 & 8) If intelligence is adaptation,[viii] it is desirable before anything else to define the latter.[ix] Now, to avoid the difficulties of teleological language[x], adaptation must be described as an equilibrium between the action of the organism on the environment and vice versa. Taking the term in its broadest sense, 'assimilation' may be used to describe the action[xi] of the organism on surrounding objects, in so far as this action depends on previous behaviour involving the same or similar objects. In fact every relation between

a living being and its environment has this particular characteristic: the former, instead of submitting passively to the latter, modifies it by imposing on it a certain structure of its own.[xii] It is in this way that, physiologically, the organism absorbs substances and changes them into something compatible with its own substance[xiii]. Now, psychologically the same[xiv] is true, except that the modifications with which it is then concerned are no longer of a physico-chemical order, but entirely functional, and are determined by movement, perception or the interplay of real or potential actions (conceptual operations, etc.)[xv]. Mental assimilation is thus the incorporation of objects into patterns of behaviour, these patterns being none other than the whole gamut of actions capable of active repetition[xvi].

(viii) Yes, but as before he does not here distinguish between innate adaptation of a species and learnt adaptation of an individual, that is, between phylogeny and ontogeny. (See Chapter 1). (ix) I agree. (x) This is where his path and mine most sharply diverge. Teleology (*Concise Oxford Dictionary*: 'Doctrine of final causes, view that developments are due to the purpose or design that is served by them') is a concept which has caused difficulty to many. This is understandable, since for most people a cause is something which is necessarily antecedent to whatever events may result from that cause: so a cause which comes after an event is a contradiction in terms. The concept of goal-directed activity removes this difficulty, because the mental act of setting a goal is indeed antecedent to the behaviour which ensues. Thus it makes perfectly good sense to say 'I am putting on my outdoor shoes *because* I have decided to go for a walk'. To me, the difficulties introduced by Piaget's alternative are far greater than those which he seeks to avoid. (xi) He means both physical and mental action, as appears a few lines later. (xii) I agree. (xiii) Not just compatible with its own substance, but sometimes part of it; for as Walter de la Mare has put it: 'It's a very odd thing – As odd as can be – That whatever Miss T eats Turns into Miss T'. By understating what goes on in physiological assimilation Piaget paves the way for the greater inaccuracy of (xiv). Psychological assimilation is far from the same, for in this case the environmental objects themselves remain unchanged. What happens is that they are *classified* in terms of an existing concept, so that perceptually or conceptually they are construed as sufficiently like the other members of the class to be equivalent for some particular purpose. This psychological assimilation, unlike physiological assimilation, is reversible. What is more, the same object can be assimilated to a variety of concepts according to the goal: a chair can be used to sit on, stand on, as a present, or for taming lions. (xv) This might seem to be what Piaget is now saying, were it not that he still states that the object is modified, which it is not. To classify an object is not the same as modifying it. (xvi) It is not the actions themselves which are important, but the goals to which they are directed. An important feature of the kinds of behaviour from which we infer intelligence is the ability, not just to repeat the same actions, but to replace these with a variety of others which achieve the same result.

(p. 8) Conversely, the environment acts on the organism and, following the practice of biologists, we can describe this converse action by the term 'accommodation', it being understood that the individual never suffers the impact of surrounding stimuli as such, but they simply modify the assimilatory cycle by accommodating him to themselves[xvii]. Psychologically, we again find the same process in the sense that the pressure of circumstances always leads, not to a passive submission to them, but to a simple modification of the action affecting them[xviii]. This being so, we can then define adaptation[xix] as an equilibrium between assimilation and accommodation[xx], which amounts to the same as an equilibrium of interaction between subject and object[xxi].

This passage is consecutive with the one just discussed. (xvii) Since the following sentence begins with the word 'Psychologically', one may reasonably infer from this that the sentence under discussion refers to physiological accommodation. This would parallel the previous paragraph in which Piaget first describes physiological assimilation, and then psychological. So one may reasonably assume that the term 'stimulus' is used here with a physiological, not a psychological, meaning. Beyond this, I fear that I can be of little help to the reader in understanding what this sentence means. (xviii) That changing circumstances lead to a modification of the action by the organism, I entirely agree. It is a central feature of my own model; but with this crucial addition, that the modification is such that the same goal state is achieved. (xix) This might refer to both physiological and psychological adaptation, or to the latter only. Provided that it includes the latter, this does not matter. (xx) and (xxi) These, taken together with (viii) and (ix), lead to a formulation of Piaget's conception of intelligence. In his own words (p. 11):

intelligence constitutes the state of equilibrium towards which tend all the successive adaptations of a sensori-motor and cognitive nature, as well as all assimilatory and accommodatory interactions between the organism and the environment.

Since the passages quoted are from a book first published in 1947, it might be suggested that this is an early formulation which Piaget later changed or further developed. But Piaget was born in 1896, and took his doctorate in 1918 at the age of 22; so he was 51 when *Le Psychologie de L'Intelligence* was published. It was not one of his early works. Moreover, in 1966 (first publication in French) and 1969 (English translation) he published with Inhelder *The Psychology of the Child*; which they describe in the preface as 'a synthesis, or a summing up, of our work in child psychology'. On page 58 of this book is the sentence: 'Intelligence constitutes an equilibration between assimilation and accommodation.' So 29 years later, the formulation is the same. That this is the core of Piaget's model is also the interpretation of Flavell (1963, p. 67), who heads a section of his own book: 'The assimilation–accommodation model as a theory of intelligence'. I must frankly admit that I have been unable to discover how this can help us to understand, predict, and sometimes to control events: which is the function of any theory.

12.18 Two other important differences between Piaget's conception of intelligence and my own can be seen from the following passages. (Unless otherwise stated, these are all from *The Psychology of Intelligence*.)

> (p. 10) we can say that behaviour becomes more 'intelligent' as the pathways between the subject and the objects on which it acts cease to be simple and become progressively more complex.

My view would be that the functioning of intelligence is evidenced as often by progress towards greater simplicity as towards greater complexity. For a simple example, take the idea of putting a point on a wood screw, which neatly combined into one the operations of making a hole in the wood and screwing in the screw. At a much more advanced level, consider the theory of Darwin, which unifies by a small number of powerful ideas the enormous complexity of different species and their adaptations; or Newton's gravitational theory, which concentrates into one mathematical equation the relationships by which the orbits of all the planets can be explained and predicted. This simplicity is of a very different kind from naïvety. For me, it is one of the hallmarks of a great thinker, as against just a clever one.

An even more important disagreement is with Piaget's view that any behaviour, or mental state, can in itself be described as intelligent. That he adopts this viewpoint is indicated by other passages:

> (p. 9) If we undertake to define intelligence, which is certainly important for determining the field which we shall be studying under this heading, it is sufficient that we be agreed on the degree of complexity of distant interaction which we shall call 'intelligent'.

And from *The Psychology of the Child*:

> (p. 4) What one actually finds is a remarkably smooth succession of stages, each marking a new advance, until the moment when the acquired behaviour presents characteristics that one or other psychologist recognizes as those of 'intelligence'.

In my own model, intelligence cannot be inferred from a behaviour in itself, but only from *changes in behaviour* towards better functioning. It is not characterized by any particular state, but by an ability to progress from one state of functioning to a better. It is not (p. 11) 'that state of equilibrium towards which tend all the successive adaptations . . . ', but that by which the process of adaptation takes place. And in my model, intelligence is present at birth, and the kind of learning characteristic of the activity of intelligence makes its appearance soon after.

12.19 When the concept of reflective intelligence was first introduced (Section 11.6), I acknowledged that this term was borrowed from Piaget, and noted also that my model was not the same as his. So it may be useful here to give these two together, for comparison.

Piaget (1947, p. 121):

> There are thus three essential conditions for the transition from the sensori-motor level to the reflective level. Firstly, an increase in speed allowing the knowledge of the successive phases of an action to be moulded into one simultaneous whole. Next, an awareness, not simply of the desired results of action, but its actual mechanisms, thus enabling the search for the solution to be combined with a consciousness of its nature. Finally, an increase in distances, enabling actions affecting real entities to be extended by symbolic actions affecting symbolic representations, and thus going beyond the limits of near space and time.

Skemp (the present book, Section 11.17(vi)):

> Reflective intelligence is conceptualized as a second-order activity as described in earlier chapters, but at a higher level of consciousness. It is a goal-directed activity involving on the receptor side, awareness of one's own concepts and schemas; and on the effector side, improving them in ways which may be broadly described as increasing our knowledge and ability to understand. These ways include:
>
> (a) Formulating our concepts and schemas.
> (b) Devising experiments by which to test the predictive powers of our schemas.
> (c) Revising our schemas as necessary in the light of these (and other) events.
> (d) Mental experiment, by which we try to optimize our plans before putting them into action.
> (e) Examining our schemas for inconsistencies and false inferences.
> (f) Generalizing our concepts and schemas.
> (g) Looking for connections between events and our existing

schemas. This is a reflective activity in which a person is explaining to himself.

(h) Increasing the number of conceptual connections within a schema, as a special case of

(i) Improving and systematizing the knowledge we already have.

Though these two conceptions are not the same, it seems to me that in this case they are not opposed, but rather that 'they fit where they touch'. So I do not feel that confusion is likely to result from my using Piaget's term 'reflective intelligence', which is a good one.

Some possibility of confusion does however arise in connection with the term 'schema' (plural, either 'schemata' or more recently 'schemas'). The term has been widely used by psychologists both before and after Piaget: and its usage in British psychology was reviewed at length in a four-part article by Oldfield and Zangwill (1942 and 1943). In early translations of Piaget, the term 'schema' is used for the same idea as is later translated as 'scheme'.

It is hard to identify Piaget's usage with confidence. Flavell writes (1963, p. 52):

What is a schema? As we have seen to be the case for other theoretical concepts, Piaget does not give a careful and exhaustive definition of the term in any single place; rather, its full meaning is developed in successive fragments of definition spanning several volumes . . . A preliminary and somewhat inadequate definition may be the following. A *schema* is a cognitive structure which has reference to a class of similar action sequences, these sequences of necessity being strong, bounded totalities in which the constituent behavioural elements are tightly related.

(Flavell follows with six pages of careful analysis of Piaget's usage of the term, and to this source I recommend the reader who wishes for greater detail.) Hunt (1961, p. 112) likewise refers to: 'these structures, which are observed as repeatable and generalisable pieces of behaviour termed *schemata* . . . .' And later, a concise definition became available from Piaget and Inhelder (1969, p. 4, footnote): 'A scheme [= schema in earlier translations] is the structure or organisation of actions as they are transferred or generalized by repetition in similar or analogous circumstances.'

Piaget's concept of a schema is thus closely linked with action. In my own model, a schema is a conceptual structure existing in its own right, independently of action. From it a wide variety of plans for action can be derived, not only for similar circumstances, but to achieve similar goals in quite new circumstances; and further, to conceive new goals and devise new plans for achieving them. These plans too can exist independently of action, as well as being used to direct action.

A schema integrates the knowledge gained from past experience; and one of the functions of reflective intelligence in my own conception of it (though not in Piaget's) is by reflecting on one's memories of past actions and events, to improve the organization of one's existing schemas. Another important difference is that in my own model, a schema is an important means for the acquisition of new knowledge, in a variety of ways which have already been described.

Piaget's developmental psychology

12.20 There can now be seen to be very little resemblance between my own model of intelligence as a second-order, goal-directed activity, and that of Piaget which rejects teleology and is based on equilibration. Another contrast is between Piaget's conception of intelligence as a stage of mental development, reached after a succession of earlier stages, and my own as that mental function which brings about these changes, from the earliest onwards. Yet paradoxically, it is here that the nearest to a relationship can be found between his theory and my own. For it is the investigation and description of these stages which form the core of Piaget's developmental psychology. In particular, he has made us aware that some of the differences between the thinking of children and that of adults are qualitative and not quantitative, and has formulated the main characteristics of these stages. A description of them is not possible within the objectives which have been set for this part of the present chapter, but an analogy may be helpful. In most ways, a kitten (once its eyes are open) is very much like a smaller version of a cat, both physically and behaviourally; whereas a tadpole bears no resemblance to a smaller version of a frog. Looking at a kitten and a cat together, one has no difficulty in accepting that one is an early form of the other: whereas to look at a tadpole and a frog, one would never guess that the former would grow into the latter, or that the latter was the adult stage of the former, unless one had either observed the transitional stages oneself, or had had them described by someone who had made these observations.

The physical differences between children and adults are in the 'kittens and cats' category, and lead easily to the unthinking assumption that in their mental processes too children resemble adults, being more limited and less efficient in their thinking but qualitatively much the same. This assumption is made easier by the fact that it is largely true of their speech—though more limited in vocabulary and sometimes less grammatical, it is otherwise very like that of adults.

This, is, however, not the case for their underlying mental processes: for the levels of abstraction at which they can think and the kinds of inference which they can make. In these areas, the differences between children's thinking and that of adults are more like the differences between tadpoles and frogs than those between kittens and cats; and it is to Piaget that we owe our present awareness both that this is the case, and also of the main characteristics of the various stages of mental development.

This fulfils an important need of teachers, as will be discussed in Chapter 14: that of knowing the present mental state of the learner, and matching the teaching to this. Piaget's descriptions of these successive states are, however, global descriptions. He does not, for example, show how by reflective analysis of a concept, a teacher can choose and group together suitable examples by which to help a learner form the concept more quickly and reliably; nor how by further analysis, a teacher can find out what lower-order concepts a learner requires to have available before a particular higher-order concept can be formed. This limits the detailed applications of his model to processes of learning and teaching. Nevertheless, Piaget has greatly helped to sensitize and improve our perceptions of the ways in which children think; and has remedied a common error, of treating them as if they were, in their mental processes, similar to adults but less efficient and experienced. This important contribution must be fully acknowledged.

OTHER RELATED MODELS

Hunt: Intelligence and Experience

12.21 As has already been noted, one of the indirect contributions of Piaget has been as a stimulus to the thinking of others, even though some of these may have been stimulated into other than Piagetian lines of thinking. One who has built a substantial amount of his own thinking on a Piagetian beginning is Hunt (1961): though it must be emphasized that Hunt also developed ideas from many other sources, and has made considerable contributions of his own. A substantial excerpt from Chapters 8 and 9 of this work can be found in Wiseman (1967). The excerpts which follow are from Chapter 7 of Hunt (1961), (pp. 267, 268, 269).

> Although Piaget often remarks on the importance of basing educational practice on the natural phases of the child's interaction with the environment, and in a sense the work of his group is concerned with the problem, Piaget only hints at the principle that environmental circumstances force accommodative modifications in schemata only where there is an appropriate match between the circumstances that a child encounters and the schemata that he has already assimilated into his repertoire. He fails to formulate the principle directly or to clarify it. In a sense, this principle is only another statement of the educator's adage that 'teaching must start where the learner is', but it is poorly understood. . . .
>
> Even though it be poorly understood, this principle appears to be of tremendous import for both theory and practice. On the side of theory, it is related to the discrepancy theory of positive interest and fearful avoidance proposed by both Hebb (1949) and McClelland & Clark (1953), to Festinger's (1957) notion of cognitive dissonance, and to the concept of 'critical periods' in development suggested by

Fuller and Scott. It has significance for both motivational and intellectual development. On the side of practice, this notion of a proper
match between circumstance and schema is what every teacher must
grasp, if he is to be effective. . . . It would appear that where there is
some common ground between them, any discrepancy between central processes and circumstances beyond the limits of an organism's
capacity for accommodation evokes distress and avoidance, while
any discrepancy within the limits of an organism's capacity for
accommodation is a source of pleasurable interest or curiosity.

The foregoing is entirely consistent with the model developed in this book
and particularly Chapters 9 and 10. Very little paraphrasing is required to
make possible a reciprocal assimilation between the two formulations

As becomes clear from the second excerpt, what Hunt means by 'an
appropriate match' is not a perfect match requiring no expansion of existing
concepts, but a discrepancy small enough to be assimilated to an existing
concept, but large enough to result in expansion of that concept. In circumstances of this kind, an individual is, in my own formulation, in a frontier zone
of his domain, but not so far out that he feels mentally lost. The new experience is not quite understood yet, but understanding seems possible. Consciousness is heightened (Chapter 2) and the individual experiences the situation as one in which he has good hope of expanding his domain; a very
general goal state. 'Pleasurable interest' indicates a willingness to enter a
situation of this kind, for the opportunity to enlarge an existing schema is an
opportunity for mental growth and improved survival probability. 'Curiosity'
goes further, for it describes an inclination to seek out situations of this kind.

In contrast, an individual who is confronted with a situation which is not
only outside any of his domains, but also beyond the limit of what can be
brought into one of these either by expansion of an existing concept, or by
extrapolating from an existing schema, is mentally lost, as described in Section 10.1. This explains the feelings described by Hunt as distress, and by me
as anxiety. Such a situation is an anti-goal in my terminology, which coincides
with Hunt's 'evokes . . . avoidance'.

What Hunt's formulation suggests, therefore, is that the frontier zone of an
individual's conceptual domain constitutes an interest zone which in some
ways is more attractive than the established domain; and such that a learner
feels confident that he can expand his domain to include it. This is a very
general formulation, and in this form would be difficult to put to work; as
Hunt himself points out, in a passage closely following the one just quoted.
'Unfortunately such statements have only intentional meaning, for neither
what-is-discrepant-from-what nor capacity for accommodation have definite
enough operational meaning to permit verification.' This results partly from
the use of Piaget's global approach, rather than one based on a detailed
conceptual analysis. The latter does enable a teacher to know (not with cer-

tainty but at a level far better than guesswork) what, at a given state of development of his schemas, a learner is likely to find interesting.

In this necessarily brief section, I have tried to show one of the regions where a reciprocal assimilation is possible between Hunt's approach and my own. There are others, and the reader who finds the time to read the whole of Hunt's penetrating and scholarly study will find himself well rewarded. Overall, though he has much to say on the subject which is pertinent and useful, I have not been able to find in his work a specific model for intelligence which is clearly enough separable from others to be easily compared.

Hebb's Neurophysiological Model

12.22 Those who are familiar with the neurophysiological model of Hebb (1949) will at once have seen a close correspondence between this and the resonance model suggested in Chapter 9 of the present work. A central feature of Hebb's model is the *cell assembly*, which is a closed circuit of nerve cells in which a nerve impulse from the first cell fires the second, the second likewise fires the third, and so on, and the last of which fires the first. Such a circuit, once established, will continue to be active in this circular fashion independently of input from outside. The time a nerve impulse takes to get once round the circuit will depend on both the number of nerve cells involved, and the total length of the axons (transmitting nerve fibres) in the circuit; so any particular cell assembly will have a natural frequency of its own.

My own model was not derived from Hebb's, but had its origins some years earlier during six years of war service with the Royal Signals, when I developed a considerable acquaintance with the phenomenon of resonance as used in telecommunications. But I was considerably emboldened to develop it as a possible theoretical explanation for memory and perception after I had learned, by reading Hebb, that there existed a feasible neurophysiological basis for it. In Section 9.19 I introduced an additional hypothesis that repeated excitation of particular tuned structures increases their sensitivity for future occasions. Hebb has suggested that whenever one nerve cell fires another, some kind of change occurs which increases the capacity of the first cell to fire the second. This nearly corresponds to my hypothesis, but not quite; for Hebb's suggestion would have the effect that once circular firing had been set up at all within a cell assembly, it would gradually increase in amplitude or in frequency, according as whether the increased capacity of the first cell to fire the second has the effect of increasing the amplitude or decreasing the latency of the latter's response. In fact, stored memories, left to themselves, tend rather to decay than to build up. Nevertheless, Hebb does again seem to offer the possibility of a neurophysiological basis for my own hypothesis.

The starting points of the two models thus correspond, though they are not the same, for Hebb's is a neurophysiological model whereas I have emphasized that I am concerned with the functions of intelligence, not with its physical basis. (Note also that Hebb's *is* a model: it is a description of what might very well be the neurophysical explanation of certain observables, and not of actual observations which do explain these observables.) Not surprisingly, their development has been in different directions; Hebb's neurophysiological, and mine towards possible explanations of perceptual constancy, higher-order concepts, and (tentatively) towards rationality itself.

Intelligence A and Intelligence B

12.23 Hebb (1949) has also pointed out that there are in current use two meanings of the word 'intelligence', which he calls 'intelligence A' and 'intelligence B'. (In the following excerpt, the italics are Hebb's.)

> From this point of view it appears that the word 'intelligence' has *two* valuable meanings. One is (A) an *innate potential*, the capacity for development, a fully innate property that amounts to the possession of a good brain and a good neural metabolism. The second is (B) the functioning of a brain in which development has gone on, determining an *average level of performance* or comprehension by the partly grown or mature person. Neither, of course, can be observed directly; but *intelligence B*, a hypothetical level of development in brain function, is a much more direct inference from behaviour than *intelligence A*, the direct potential. (I emphasize that these are not two parallel kinds of intelligence, coexistent, but two different meanings of 'intelligence'.)

Although Hebb's model is specifically linked with the brain and its functioning, the terms 'intelligence A' and 'intelligence B' have come to be used in a more general way; corresponding respectively to intelligence (genotype), the innate potential, and intelligence (phenotype), the result of interaction between genotype and environment. Vernon's view (1960) that: 'Intelligence B depends not only on the total number and complexity of schemata, but also on the degree to which we are able to differentiate or break them down and keep them flexible' accords very closely with my own, as expressed in Section 11.5. Here I pointed out that 'When particular plans are over-practised, their connections with their integrating schema may weaken past recall. The advantages of routinizing may then be outweighed by lack of adaptability, since all that is left is a set of fixed habits.'

12.24 How does Hebb's distinction apply to my own model? On the one hand, I have taken the position that intelligence is a capacity for a particular kind of learning, dependent on the combination of a teachable direction system delta-one and a higher-order director system delta-two acting on delta-one. This is present at birth, and its activities can be inferred from observable behaviour very early in life. This suggests that I have been using the term 'intelligence' to refer to the genotype: in nearly but not quite the same sense as Burt's 'innate general cognitive ability' (Burt, 1955), for what I am referring to is a general potential for *acquiring* cognitive ability.

But in any given universe of discourse, ability to learn depends greatly on a person's existing available schemas in that universe; and one's adaptability depends on the quality of their organization, from which by intuitive or reflective plan-making we can derive from them appropriate plans of action for a wide variety of circumstances. I have also emphasized that intelligence is not a quality to be inferred from a particular stage, but from ability to progress from one mental state to another. This would include both the activity of reflective intelligence on existing schemas to produce new plans; and also further development (including improved organization) of these schemas. This cluster of abilities clearly describes a phenotype.

The following imaginary experiment may help the discussion by bringing it to a lower level of abstraction. Supposing that we started with monozygotic triplets, and sent the first to a school where he learnt mathematics, science, but no languages other than his own; the second to a school where he learnt French, German, Latin, but no maths or science; while the third was not sent to school at all, but spent his childhood segregated from all but a minimum of contact with the environment. If all three were then entered for a course in engineering, the first would learn most quickly. At a course in Italian or Spanish, the second would do best; while the third would compare unfavourably with the other two in almost every way. Would we say that the first child was more intelligent in the first situation, while the second child was more intelligent in the second situation, and the third was stupid all round? Or would we say rather than the first *demonstrated* more intelligence in the engineering course, the second demonstrated more in the language course, while the third was unable to demonstrate intelligence in either of these situations: but (using our special knowledge of their shared genetic constitution) that all three were of equal intelligence, which the first two demonstrated in different ways, while the third had been given no chance to develop his innate potential at all?

In the first case we would be using the term 'intelligence' for the phenotype alone, in the same way as we say that a person is tall or short without considering it necessary to mention specifically that this is influenced by the quality and quantity of early nutrition. In the second case we would be using the term 'intelligence' for the genotype, which is by definition both independent of environmental factors and also much more difficult to deduce from observables, particularly since genotypes are seldom delivered in matched triplets. There have been those such as Burt, who not only preferred to use the term intelligence for the genotype, but believed that it could be measured with reasonable confidence. Without fully accepting this, there are certainly physical observables (such as eye colour) in which the phenotype is much more closely determined by the genotype than others (such as height);

and similarly there are tests (such s those which measure ability to perceive abstract spatial relationships) in which performance is much less dependent on environmental factors than others (such as vocabulary). However, the majority of psychologists would be more likely to share the viewpoint of Vernon (1960): 'We would prefer, however, to apply it to the ability which can be observed in daily life, at school or at work and which is sampled fairly effectively by our tests; and this is the product of heredity and upbringing.'

My own view is that Hebb is right in emphasizing that 'the word "intelligence" has *two* valuable meanings', and that when necessary we should specify which one we are using. In relation to my own model, unless stated otherwise, 'intelligence' refers to intelligence B, the phenotype: emphasizing once again that the term applies not to an ability to do, but a particular kind of ability to learn. Since this is very much dependent on the relation between a person's available schemas and what has to be learnt, the kind of evidence needed from which to make inferences about a person's intelligence will differ greatly according to their individual and cultural background. In other words, phenotypic intelligence (B) is always relative to an assumed environment: that from which regularities were abstracted in the past and incorporated in an individual's schemas, and that in which he will have to make future adaptations. These environments cannot be entirely the same, and they may be very different.

Miller, Galanter, and Pribram's 'Plans and the Structure of Behaviour'

12.25 An approach which in some of its starting points has much in common with my own is that of Miller, Galanter, and Pribram (1960). Rejecting (like myself) the school of thought which continues to use various forms of stimulus–response model to explain human behaviour, they write:

> Arrayed against the reflex theorists are the pessimists, who think that living organisms are complicated, devious, poorly designed for research purposes, and so on. They maintain that the effect an event will have upon behavior depends on how the event is represented in the organism's picture of itself and its universe. . . . A human being—and probably other animals as well—builds up an internal representation, a model of the universe, a schema, a simulacrum, a cognitive map, an Image.

Immediately after the above passage they quote Bartlett's (1932) description of the term 'schema': a conception which, as has already been acknowledged, has been a major influence on my own thinking. But they do not fully accept the viewpoint of the cognitive psychologists either.

> The crux of the argument, as every psychologist knows, is whether anything so mysterious and inaccessible as 'the organism's picture of

227

itself and its universe' or 'an active organisation of past reactions', etc., is really necessary. Necessary, that is to say, as an explanation for the behaviour that can be observed to occur.

In their search for a suitable model, they also, like myself, find cybernetic ideas to be very relevant. Two central features of their model are the plan, and the feedback loop.

A plan is any hierarchical process in the organism that can control the order in which a sequence of operations is to be performed. (Their italics.)

And a little later:

The interpretation toward which the argument moves is one that has been called the 'cybernetic hypothesis', namely, that the fundamental building block of the nervous system is the feedback loop.

As a model of the latter they introduced their now well-known Test–Operate–Test–Exit unit, TOTE for short, pictured in Figure 47.

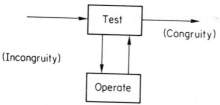

Figure 47 Reproduced by arrangement with Holt, Rinehart and Winston, New York, from *Plans and the Structure of Behavior*, by Miller et al., 1960.

There are, however, considerable differences of emphasis between the model proposed by Miller, Galanter, and Pribram, and that offered in the present book; and also in the direction and extent to which our respective models have been developed. Their development centres around the plan, whereas mine gives much attention to what they call the image and I call a schema. They elaborate the hierarchy of TOTE units; I elaborate the director system itself: compare the diagram above with Figure 12. In their discussion of the transition from *knowing how* into *being able to*, they emphasize the integration of subordinate TOTE units into a smoothly executed sequence of operations: but make no mention of anticipation, which for me is a major factor. For them, 'Probably the major source of new Plans is old Plans'. For me, it is an appropriate schema, out of which new plans are produced as required, intuitively and reflectively. Greater differences become apparent when one recalls the importance attached in my own model to the formation

228

of concepts and their connection into schemas, to reality testing and the building up of knowledge structures, to consciousness and to emotions; and the relation between goal-directed behaviour and survival.

In spite of these differences, the approach of Miller, Galanter, and Pribram shares with my own not only some of our starting points, but also a concern with the same kinds of problem. Beyond this, there is an underlying common attitude which shows itself at a number of points, and which may be exemplified by juxtaposing their query: 'How is it possible to recognize man's unique accomplishments without violating the concept of evolutionary continuity from animals to man?' with my own conception of man as an evolutionary breakthrough (Section 1.10). As with the approaches of Hunt and of Hebb, I regard that of these three co-authors as entirely compatible with my own, and as in some ways supplmentary to it.

Feedback

12.26 This is also a convenient point in which to compare the conceptions of *feedback* as used in other models (including the TOTE model), and in my own. Again, there is no essential conflict: the differences are as before in the ways in which they have been developed. From the basic TOTE unit, 'more complicated Plans . . . can be similarly described as TOTE units built up of subplans that are themselves TOTE units.' In this hierarchic development the basic TOTE unit stays the same, as in their example reproduced in Figure 48.

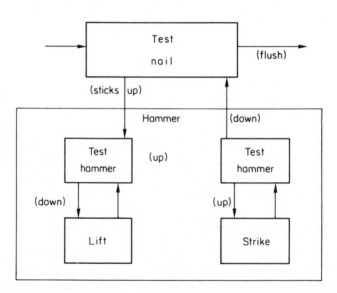

Figure 48. '*The hierarchical plan for hammering nails*'. Reproduced by arrangement with Holt, Rinehart and Winston, New York, from *Plans and the Structure of Behavior*, by Miller et al., 1960

Annett *et al.* (1974) give the following explanation and diagram
(Figure 49) as a starting point:

> The results of human action are *fed back* to the organism so that the
> action may be modified in extent or kind to achieve more effectively
> the goal which initially motivated performance.

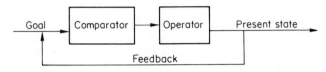

Figure 49. Reproduced by permission of the Open University

As an example of how this may be elaborated, they offer the following:

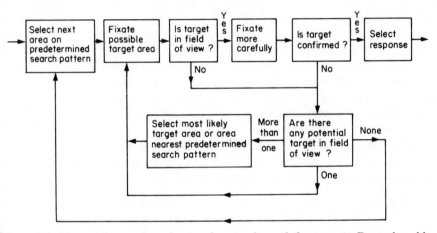

Figure 50. *Suggested control mechanism for visual search for a target.* Reproduced by
permission of the Open University

My own elaboration takes a different direction. One difference is that the
director system is differentiated from that which provides the physical power.
This takes account of the variety of director systems which share the same
operators. Another important difference arises from the incorporation of the
environment into the feedback circuit. In the simple kind of feedback loop,
such as that by which the output of an amplifier is stabilized (automatic
volume control, or AVC), part of the amplifier's own output is fed back
electrically to an earlier part of the circuit in such a way as to reduce the
amplification (negative feedback). The effect is thereby to stabilize the
output. But where feedback takes place via the environment, there has to be
some kind of sensor which selectively abstracts from the environment the
right information. Both present state and goal state have to be internally

represented before the comparator can perform its function: and here is the beginning which in my model leads to concept formation, the building up of schemas, and so on.

The reader will also notice that up to this point I have not used the term feedback. For it is not the environment which feeds back information: it is the organism which actively and selectively gets data from the environment. And the conversion of this data into meaningful information, by which the organism can direct its behaviour, depends on the realization of the input sense-data within an appropriate schema. The term 'feedback' thus has stimulus–response connotations which do not fit well into any information-processing kind of model; still less into my own. So my avoidance of the term has been deliberate.

* * * * * * * *

12.27 At this stage it becomes necessary to recall the first section of this chapter, and the difficulties of deciding where to bring the present review of other models to an end. Whatever criteria were adopted, it was inevitable that the eventual drawing of a finishing line would be somewhat arbitrary and subjective. Much has still been omitted which is interesting and relevant, but the inclusion of which would have turned a single chapter in a book of one kind into a whole book of a different kind—a fate which the present author was anxious to avoid. To these other contributors to knowledge and to their adherents, I can only apologize, and repeat that these omissions are regretted but, in pursuit of the present goal, necessary.

In this chapter I have been comparing other models with my own, from a viewpoint which by its nature cannot be altogether impartial. The balance can be redressed somewhat by referring back to 3.4.

> We have different models of different parts of the environment. . . . And even of the same part of the environment, we use different models for different purposes and activities. A road map is not much help to a climber. A tailor and a medical doctor will be interested in different qualities of the same person. . . .'

The present model thus predicts and justifies the construction and use of an assortment of models, according to different purposes and interests: and would discourage claims on behalf of any one model, including itself, that it is the only good one. Impartiality is not however to be regained thus easily; for it must also be pointed out that while my own model thus explains the emergence of psychometric models in a society largely preoccupied with who is better than whom, the reverse is not the case.

12.28 In the present chapter, a number of other models have been outlined and compared with that developed in the present work. These include:

(i) *Psychometric models, including those based on factor analysis.*

i) *Piaget's model of intelligence (but not his developmental psychology).*

ii) *That part of Hunt's contribution which related to matching of environmental circumstances and existing schemata.*

v) *Hebb's neurophysiological model.*

/) *Miller, Galanter, and Pribram's cybernetically based model.*

CHAPTER 13

Roles

The social environment

13.1   In the process of planning as described in Chapter 11, there was a tacit assumption that the environment remains much the same while the operand is progressing along the chosen path from its present state to its goal state. This was a useful simplification for getting started, but holds good only in a static environment, not a changing one. One category of environmental change is fairly easy to take care of. This includes physical changes which are time-dependent: where the oncoming car will be at the time when one is overtaking, whether it will be dark when we get there. There are also changes caused by physical consequences of one's own actions: the engine warms up as we drive, the boat goes backwards away from us as we try to climb out. At an everyday level we learn to predict these fairly easily. For more complex examples, we apply the natural sciences.

Difficulties of a new kind arise whenever the environment is itself goal-directed, the putting of one's plans into action changes the environment in which others are doing the same, and their actions are modified as a result, necessitating further adjustment of one's own actions. The situation then arises which was described earlier in Section 8.3, where it was asked: 'In view of the aforesaid complexity of possible interactions, how do we manage ever as well as we do?' To this question we now return.

13.2   Again, in Section 8.12 I referred to 'the complexity and *unpredictability* of free-for-all interactions between any but a very small number of director systems'. It is this unpredictability which is at the core of the problem. We can only plan our actions successfully if we know what will be their effect. For this, we require a mental model which includes the operand itself, and also those parts of the environment which affect the outcome. We now have very good models for predicting the effects of our actions on the inanimate parts of our environment, as evidenced from the success of natural sciences and technology. This part of the environment is not goal-directed, so the present difficulty does not arise. But where the operand (which may be our own body) and relevant parts of the environment consist of other persons,[1] no model for directing our own behaviour will be a good one which does not take account of the fact that a major part of what goes on is goal-directed. This is one of the themes of this whole book: and its present development is that an adequate model of our *social* environment has to be that of a complex structure of director systems.

13.3 When we see a stranger for the first time—as happens whenever we go outside our own homes—we cannot possibly know what goal state he is currently pursuing, short-term or long. Much of the time we do not interact: we co-exist. But as soon as we step onto a bus (or even signal it to stop), enter a shop, or go to the bank, we cannot avoid interacting with persons who may be complete strangers. So how do we get on as well as we do for much of the time? By trying to answer this question, both generally and in simple particular cases, we may hope to find out what it is that goes on when we do interact successfully but does not happen when we don't. For although an intuitive level of functioning may be adequate for small-scale interactions and those of a routine kind, increases in scale and novelty require the adaptive potential of a clear, reflective awareness of what we are doing and how we are doing it, whereby we may be able to modify, expand, and generalize. This is one of the ways in which intelligence can be brought to bear on social interaction: not in quite the same ways as it has been brought to bear on the physical world, since this can lead to 'the thingifying of people', but in ways which take account of their wants and emotions, and relate them to our own.

A first step in this process of making accessible for analysis, discussion, and possibly experiment, is to realize it in terms of an appropriate schema (Section 10.2, last paragraph but one). Such a schema may readily be available, as in Section 10.9, example (ii) (a); or it may first be necessary to build one, as in the examples given just after in (ii) (c). In the present case, the building of an appropriate schema has been going on throughout Chapters 1–11, and the present problem can now be formulated as a particular case within the theoretical model which has been built up. This special case is called a *role*.

Role theory has been developed at length within the discipline of sociology, and a number of books have been written about it, as well as chapters in other books. The present chapter is not offered as an alternative approach to these, but rather as a conceptual bridge showing how the present model and some of the sociological ones may be linked, and as indicating another area to which the present model can be applied.

Co-operative role pairs

13.4 The simplest kinds of role come in pairs, such as passenger/bus-driver, customer/shop assistant, patient/doctor. In these pairs, each person knows approximately what the other will do as a result of his own actions: not exactly, in terms of every detail of the physical actions; but more importantly, in terms of the goals to which these actions are directed.

When a passenger offers a coin to the driver on entry (we assume it is a 'pay-as-you-enter' bus), he does not know exactly what the driver will do. But whether the driver takes the coin and gives change, takes the coin and gives no change, or asks for another two pence; whether he then hands the passenger a ticket, or presses a button causing a ticket to emerge from a machine—none of these actions will come as a surprise. And whichever of these the driver does, the passenger knows what to do on his side. Likewise at other stages of the journey, and for the other role pairs mentioned. Nor should the everyday character of these actions cause us to lose sight of the complexity of the role structure into which we step every time we go downtown. The complexity is great, and great also would be the chaos without the role structure.

In terms of the ideas developed in earlier chapters, a role involves a new kind of director system which we have not considered before. It is a *director system which contains a model of someone else's director system*, that of the role partner. A passenger, by having a model of the director system by which the conductor is directing his actions can predict—not exactly, but well enough—what the conductor will do as a result of his own actions as a passenger. This is a major contribution towards solving the predictability problem with which this chapter began. It also requires on the part of the passenger an awareness of what the driver's expectations are of himself. As before, these expectations are not of the exact details of his actions, but in terms of his schema for performing these, his goal structure and plans. Applying this also reciprocally to the bus driver, we get the following formulation, generalizing now from the present example to the general case of a role pair A and B.

A's director system (e.g. as a passenger), is a complex one containing:

(i)   parts relating to the inanimate enironment (e.g. the director system by which he climbs aboard the bus);

(ii) a schema for directing his actions in relation to B (the bus driver); containing as an essential part

(iii) a model of the director system by which B (as a driver) directs his actions towards himself, A (as a passenger).

And reciprocally B's director system (as a bus driver) contains:

(i)   parts relating to the inanimate environment (e.g. the director system by which he drives the bus);

(ii) a schema for directing his actions in relation to A (the passenger); containing as an essential part

(iii) a model of the director system by which A (as a passenger) directs actions towards himself, B (as a bus driver).

The aim of the above formulation is not to introduce complication into a simple everyday situation, but to help towards a conscious realization of some

f the complexity which is already there, within as simple a model as is
dequate for purposes already mentioned.

3.5 Roles may come in more than pairs, but as here conceived they cannot
ome in less. The first essential of a role pair has now been formulated: that it
a pair of director systems, each of which contains a model of the other. The
econd is that *these are largely independent of which persons are occupying
these roles*. We need not get to know the bus driver in order to be taken to
enilworth, nor the shop assistant in order to make our purchase. Although
e may usually go to our family doctor, when he or we are on vacation we can
et treatment from a doctor we have never seen before. The same is true,
eciprocally, for each role pair. Without this second feature we would lose the
redictability conferred by the first.

This is not to say that the person occupying a role makes no difference at
ll. For a start, the knowledge and skill necessary for the performance of some
oles, such as surgeon, airline pilot, professional musician, may be beyond the
bility of some to achieve. And given the necessary technical skill, personality
nters into role performance. The printed notes may be the same, but some
an play them more beautifully than others; and even in such everyday roles
s bus driver, ticket collector, shopkeeper, it is noticable that some persons
xecute what is basically the same behaviour with more grace and skill than
thers. Long-term roles may also be chosen because they fit in with certain
spects of personality.

This does not contradict the earlier statement, that if you know the person's
ole you do not need to know the person. A role is that which is constant
etween different people in the same situation, whereas individual
ersonality is that which is constant for the same person in different
ituations. (The latter was well put by an old Somerset countryman, many
ears ago: 'Whatever 'e d' do, 'e d' do well.') So there is a spectrum of
elationships, from those in which the relative contributions to behaviour
hich come from role and from personality are in the main role-determined
o those which are mainly personality-determined. Ticket collector/rail
assenger is a pair in the former category, brother and sister the second. The
nore completely persons are strangers to each other, the more they depend
n role-governed behaviour for their interactions; while in ongoing
elationships, time is available to get to know them as persons. One can
ecome friends with a ticket collector whom one meets daily.

3.6 The examples we have thought about so far are co-operative role pairs,
nd we shall stay with this kind for the present. This recalls our attention to
he minimal requirements for co-operation which were discussed in
ection 8.9. These are matching schemas; goal structures which are
ompatible and plans which are complementary; and a shared
oding/decoding system for the exchange of information. How important the
ast is will, however, vary according to how well-defined the roles are; and it is

striking the success with which one can get around in a foreign country t
which one has never been before, and where one speaks none of the languag
beyond 'Please', 'Thank you', and 'Excuse me', provided that the rol
structure is reasonably like that which one already knows.

Matching schemas entails the strengthening of a requirement which wa
touched on in Section 13.4, where we noted that 'it also requires on th
part of the passenger an awareness of what the driver's expectations are c
himself'. This awareness has to be reasonably accurate, which entails
satisfactory match between the passenger's conception of the driver'
expectations of him, and what the driver's expectations are in the reality o
the driver. And the other way about. Thus, if the passenger expects the drive
to stop at the bus stop as a result of seeing him waiting there, whereas th
driver expects the passenger to raise his hand if he wants him to stop (ther
being several different services over this route) there is insufficient matcl
between their plans, and the co-operation necessary to get the passenge
aboard the bus fails. Referring back to the general case at the end of 13.4
there has to be a match between part (ii) of A's director system and part (iii
of B's director system, and between part (iii) of A's director system and par
(ii) of B's. Where the roles are not sufficiently well defined, discussion anc
possibly also negotiation may be required to bring about this match. Until thi
has successfully taken place, there will be role confusion.

Complementary plans, in this example, include such simple details as: th
passenger waits at a labelled bus stop, and the driver stops only at these. Th
driver opens the door, the passenger climbs aboard. And so on. In th
doctor/patient role pair, the patient opens his mouth, the doctor examines hi
throat, and so on. We do not need to spend time here.

Compatible goal structures is a weak requirement, satisfied even unde
conditions of co-existence. For co-operative role pairs there is a stronge
criterion, that the interaction is positive-sum. Each both gives and gets: not by
a bargain newly struck each time, but in its essentials predictable, anc
independent of the individuals concerned. An essential part of every role is a
set of rights and privileges on the one hand, and a set of responsibilities anc
obligations on the other. Staying with the bus example just a little longer
among the passenger's rights are: to have the bus stop for him to get on anc
off, to be taken to his chosen destination, to have reasonable questions (such
as those about his journey) answered, to occupy a seat if one is available. His
obligations include: to pay his fare, not to distract the driver while driving, tc
obey reasonable instructions of the driver such as those about dogs anc
baggage, not to try to alight except at regular stops. The driver's rights
include: to be given the fare for the journey, not to be distracted while
driving, to have reasonable instructions obeyed. And among his obligations
are: to stop when requested to allow passengers to get on and off, at regular
stops; to take only the correct fare, to drive with due care and attention, tc
answer reasonable questions (like 'Does this bus stop at . . . ?'). Each has
other rights and obligations too: the driver has a right to receive a salary, the

assenger has an obligation to refrain from smoking in a non-smoking area. but these relate respectively to the employed/employer roles and to the assenger/passenger roles, not to the role pair under discussion.

From the examples given it will also be noticed that some of the rights of ne correspond exactly to the obligations of the other: to pay the fare/receive ne fare, to be taken to his chosen destination/to stop the bus on request at egular stops. Other obligations are such as enable the other party to fulfil the obligations of his side: not to distract the driver while he is driving/to drive with due care and attention. These belong to the general category of omplementary plans, and these in turn are the means by which the ositive-sum relationship is maintained.

There are also discretionary areas of behaviour, belonging to the role but ot so strictly determined by it as those mentioned so far. A driver who sees a assenger running towards a bus stop may wait to let him on, or he may not. Ie may wait to see that a frail and elderly passenger is seated before ccelerating away from the bus stop, though he is not strictly obliged to do so. hese are some of the areas mentioned earlier, in which personality enters nore strongly into role performance. And they are also areas in which redictability is reduced. However hard we may run and wave, we do not now with any reliability whether the bus driver will wait for us.

Predictability as an independent requirement

3.7   Role behaviour by one is not only, as we have seen, largely dependent or its success on complementary role behaviour by the other: often it is also onditional on this. A customer in a shop who departs from an essential eature of this role by neglecting to pay will quickly find himself in quite a lifferent role, that of a shoplifter. This is as one would expect. There are lways two sides to a bargain; and beyond the exchange of benefits in a articular bargain, it is also important in general to be able to rely on people keeping their bargains.

But the requirements of taking up and keeping within a role go beyond this, n a way which is harder to explain at a common-sense level. Once when we stopped at a motorists' cafe, the waitress sat down at our table while she was aking our order. Afterwards I wondered why I had felt just a little put out, since she was in no way departing from her obligations—she looked after our needs efficiently and cheerfully, nor infringing any of our rights—there were plenty of seats. Very likely her feet were tired, and indeed I felt ungracious that it had made any difference to me at all.

An explanation becomes available as soon as we recall that a key feature of role behaviour is predictability. Although there may be some areas of discretion, if the mis-match between A's model of B's role behaviour, and the schema which B is using, is too great, A will begin to lose confidence in his ability to predict the effect of his actions on those of B, and the success of the co-operation within that particular role pair is threatened. It is also important to know what role someone is occupying: and the less well we know him, the more we depend on correctly identifying this. (The polite stranger at the door: is he a salesman, a new neighbour, a canvasser in the current elections or a plain-clothes detective? We are cautious in our responses till we know. So when someone behaves in a way which does not quite fit the role model to which one has assigned them—when a waitress acts in one respect like another customer—the detail itself may be small and unimportant, but not so the principle which is breached.

As well as needing others to behave predictably by staying within the role they are enacting, we are also aware of this need in others directed towards ourselves. In an unfamiliar social situation, which is to say one which we are not easily able to realize in terms of known roles, we wonder what we are supposed to do, what is expected of us. In such a situation we are sensitive even over-sensitive, to the expectations of others; and we may feel ourselves to be irrationally concerned with whether we are meeting these expectations beyond the needs of the rights and obligations of the situation, or even of everyday courtesy and friendly human relations. The present model helps us to understand why we feel this way. Beyond this, it helps us to penetrate beyond trivialities such as 'Should I wear a tie? A formal suit?' by relating these questions to an underlying theory. It may even help us to reach more rational decisions about whether and when we will conform to irrational expectations of others.

Behaviour construed in terms of roles

13.8 Since a role is a particular case of a schema, the general principle developed in Chapter 10 applies to it: that we construe, interpret, understand a person's behaviour in terms of the role we attribute to them. This has two aspects. First, we may compare their performance with our own conception of a satisfactory, good, or excellent performance. In a recent television series, a young doctor prescribed for an undernourished patient a series of good meals. The patient naturally thought him an excellent doctor, but his senior partner thought otherwise. Note that he was within the discretionary area, though perhaps only just. There was no suggestion that the behaviour was outside the role of a doctor, as might have happened had his treatment gone outside what was the accepted medical practice of the time. To do this is always dangerous for any professional person, for by thus stepping outside his prescribed role, he loses an important part of his privileges, namely the support of his professional colleagues and possibly even the law if anything goes wrong.

The other aspect is that behaviour may be acceptable within one role, which is not so in another. Flinging another person to the ground is acceptable in a game of rugby or American football, but not in ordinary daily life. Killing an enemy is legal only for soldiers. Making a person unconscious by inhalation of gas is acceptable from an anaesthetist, but not from a burglar. At a more everyday level, requesting money from a passenger is appropriate for a bus driver but not from a private motorist. What makes the behaviour acceptable in the above cases is that within the appropriate role we relate it to a goal structure which is also implicitly accepted if we allow a person's occupation of that role. In other cases, it may be accepted simply because it has come to be part of the expected behaviour of the role, whether it serves any other purpose or not. In England a barrister in court, and a judge, wear wigs of a style which would be considered ridiculous in the street.

13.9 The quality of our understanding of another person's actions will thus sometimes depend on how good a conception we have of the role from which these actions are derived. A superficial role-model will make possible only superficial understanding, a more penetrating model will make possible deeper understanding. Roles which we have learnt by enacting them ourselves, we can understand from the inside; and in these and other cases where we know not only what the role partner does, but also why he does it, we are in a better state to relate our own actions effectively to theirs. In the case of roles we never occupy ourselves, our models are more likely to be superficial, embodying more of what is done and less of why it is done, and distinguishing less clearly between the essential and the unimportant, and between the observable actions and the underlying schema and goals.

But it is over-optimistic to assume that roles which we learn to occupy are necessarily well understood as a result. Even when these are consciously and deliberately taught, what is learnt is as likely to be the action rather than the reason for it: as when a parent gives coins to a child so that he can buy the tickets. But as often as not, we learn roles not by being taught them but by finding ourselves in them, and discovering (sometimes the hard way) what is expected of us.

It has already been noted that in an unfamiliar social situation, we are sensitive to the expectations of others. 'Doing the wrong thing' is an anti-goal state, 'doing the right thing' is a goal state, both of a very general kind; 'right' and 'wrong' here taking on the meaning of conforming or not conforming to these expectations. These conditions take the learning into a different universe of discourse from that to which the role properly belongs, and favour the learning of a set of poorly understood actions rather than that of a schema, goal structure, and plans from which these actions could be derived, and in relation to which they could be well understood.

Consciousness, and enactment of role behaviour

13.10 To what degree are we conscious of the roles we occupy, and enact? During a day, one person occupies a number of different roles; and to the degree that these are familiar, he can enact them routinely at a low level of consciousness. This gives the advantage of routinizing, first mentioned in Chapter 2. If every time a person got on a bus he had to puzzle out anew whom he paid and how much, and likewise for every other situation he entered, by the end of the day he would be mentally exhausted. But we can and do enact routine roles such as passenger on a bus, customer in a cafeteria while talking or thinking about something quite different. This frees con sciousness for attention to the novel or problematic: such as what is on the menu today, and whether we can afford it (in cash or calories, according to one's personal situation).

We need to be clear what is meant by this. It is not that a person waiting for a bus is largely unaware of its approach, but that he does not while doing so reflect 'What am I doing, and why?' Consciousness of a role is consciousness in a delta-two system *of* a delta-one system, in this case of the special kind of delta-one system which forms one side of a role pair. It is an activity of reflective intelligence, and may involve not only reflective awareness but other reflective operations as well.

To occupy different roles in succession is not usually difficult. Where prob lems may arise is in situations which evoke two roles (or more) at the same time. These may be combinable, or they may co-exist, or they may be in conflict. Thus a policeman easily combines his roles as agent of the law, and breadwinner for his family; and passes easily from his former role to that of a father when he gets home. But if, while on duty, he find his own son in an act of vandalism with a gang of other lads, these roles are in conflict.

Role conflict is a major topic within the subject of role theory, and an important one from a sociological viewpoint. It is equally important from an individual viewpoint as a possible source of inner conflict and consequent unhappiness. The contribution of the present chapter is a penetrating one on a narrow front: that the best hope of a satisfactory solution lies in the activity of reflective intelligence. Where, as in the case of role conflict, there is opposi tion between two complex director systems within the same person, then it is here that the problem lies, and on these that consciousness needs to be focused. Two factors which help to make this possible are a well-developed reflective intelligence as such, which is a very individual matter; and the availability of a suitable model, towards which the present chapter is offered as one contribution among many.

This is a first step only, and reflection may combine with intuitive processes in reaching a solution, as described in earlier chapters. The simplest kind of solution is the overriding of one role by another; the most difficult is a resolution of the conflict by some kind of synthesis; and compromise comes in between. It is not within our choice to avoid conflicts, of this kind and others Where we do have some choice, with the help of reflective intelligence, is in trying to resolve these creatively rather than destructively; and in some cases self-creatively rather than self-destructively.

Other categories of role

13.11 As a means for first introducing the concept of role in relation to the present model, examples were used in which simplification was gained at the expense of generality.

One of these was in confining our attention to pairs, often of short duration. Many roles, however, are not one-to-one relationships, but one-to-many or many-to-many. They may also be longer lasting, perhaps over months and years. A role structure of this kind forms an organization: a business, an amateur operatic society, a university. A culture is similar in kind, but somewhat looser in both structure and conception: one may talk of an advanced technological culture, of teenage culture, or of our own cultural heritage. A complex culture contains both individuals and organizations, in a variety of role relationships.

So far as organizations are concerned, the basic characteristics of roles still apply as already formulated, and summarized at the end of this chapter (Section 13.16). Since expertise in the more difficult roles takes time to achieve and has often to be bought at the expense of expertise in another, role specialization is likely to be positive-sum for an organization as a whole. Likewise for a culture. In the exchange of goods, services, and expertise, giving and getting may be directly reciprocal, as when one pays a decorator to paint one's house; or more circuitous as when one's refuse is collected by dustmen who are paid by the local council out of taxes levied on householders. But unless a positive-sum relationship exists overall, one may surmise that the organization will not hold together indefinitely, particularly in the face of competition.

Imposed roles and elective roles

13.12   A person's occupation of any role involves some loss of freedom, as an inseparable part of the package. It includes the acceptance of certain obligations and responsibilities, in exchange for what he gets in the way of rights and privileges. It also includes conforming to other expectations which may be irrelevant to these. Much of a person's behaviour within a role is thus determined by the role and not by his own free choice.

But in all of the earlier examples, two major freedoms remain: to assume the role or not, and to remain in it or not. In the latter case, one may not be free to leave it at whatever moment one wants. Notice is required in most jobs, especially if they form part of an organization. But this too is part of an obligation known in advance as part of the role; and in exchange there are corresponding rights.

We must now consider another class of situations which resemble the kind of role we have been considering in many ways, but which differ in one particular which is so serious that for the present I shall postpone the decision whether to call them roles at all. This difference is that *one side in each pair lacks this freedom of choice* whether to enter or leave.

Examples of such pairs are: master and slave (one of the oldest); baron and mediaeval serf; prison officer and convict; army officer and conscript; schoolteacher and child of compulsory school age. It comes as a shock to find the last pair in such company:[2] so much so that I propose to leave it on one side for the present, and return to it in a later chapter after we have used the other examples to try and abstract some general principles.

In each of the above examples, the second named is on the wrong side of a power relationship. And the first not only exerts his power to make the other do what he wants, but also to keep him from escaping from that situation. Slaves who tried to escape were mutilated, tortured, or killed. Serfs were treated in much the same way. Convicts are physically confined. Deserters from an army are court-martialled and may be shot.

This difference is a particular case of the very general one between categories 1 and 2 of Table 4 in Section 8.6; the present examples all being in category 1. The privileges are nearly all on one side (though not quite all: conscripts have quite a number of rights, and even convicts have some); the obligations are mostly on the other. Nevertheless, a number of the other characteristics of roles still apply: most notably, that a person's behaviour is determined by the role, and not by his free choice. This implies the criterion which was introduced first in Section 13.4: that each knows what to expect from the other. The slave knows what to expect from his master, the conscript what to expect from his officers. And the one in power knows what to expect from the other, largely because he has the power to require it, and often also because he trains the other efficiently to fulfil his duties. All the other criteria of roles which were described in Section 13.6 now follow, except their co-operative nature as embodied in the mutuality of rights and obligations. Each must have a model of the other's director system as related to the role. There have to be goal structures which are compatible and plans which are complementary—these are ensured by being imposed almost entirely from one side. And there has to be a shared coding/decoding system for the exchange of information.

If the second in each pair has no rights, he will feel no obligations, and obey only out of fear. But the last line of Table 4 reminds us that 'these conditions will be effective if and only if B knows of, or believes in them'. The power may be factual or fictional, provided that B believes in it: as we shall remind ourselves in the next chapter. But most often it is factual, and in some cases the side in power may inflict punishment on one of the other side simply to make sure that the others know this.

The second's choice is mostly restricted to choosing between anti-goals. Of the alternatives, he may prefer obedience to punishment. He may even decide 'If you can't beat them, join them' and work the system. Convicts can earn remission of sentence and parole; conscripts can gain promotion; even slaves sometimes served their masters so well that they were eventually given their freedom. But this is their only kind of choice. They cannot choose to leave the system, except by incurring risk of anti-goals which are usually worse.

With this single difference, albeit a very important one, all the other criteria for roles still apply. I propose, therefore, that we also call the second set of examples roles, marking the difference between the two kinds by calling them *imposed roles* and *elective roles*.[3] These terms do not correspond entirely to the difference between categories 1 and 2 in the table. Both sides in category 2, but also the side in power in category 1, are elective roles, since a person need not take up the role of an army officer or prison officer if he does not wish. If we want a term which includes both sides in category 1, that is, roles which are elective on one side but imposed on the other within a power relationship, we may refer to them as type 1 role pairs, and the other sort as type 2.

It should be noted that type 1 roles are *within* a power relationship. A power relationship is not itself a role, but can be used to make one party take up a variety of roles which may be very different. Slaves acted as secretaries, gladiators, concubines; conscripts may be radio operators, gunners, clerks. On the other side, though it may be necessary to be in a position of power before electing to take on a role, it is more often the case that the power is conferred by social confirmation of the role. It would be virtually impossible to sustain the role of one master *vis-à-vis* a number of slaves, or one officer *vis-à-vis* a batallion of conscripts, without the backing of the rest of a social structure which legitimates (or once legitimated) these roles.

We may also note that certain kinds of imposed role are inflicted on all individuals within a particular class. Thus, in particular historical periods and societies, all captives left alive were automatically made slaves; all children of serfs were born as serfs; all able-bodied males of a certain age became conscripts.

Intelligence and role occupation

13.13 Power and authority are closely related, and the present line of thinking could easily lead to discussion of these in contexts such as organizations, management, politics. In Chapters 14 and 15 we shall consider these inasmuch as they enter into the teacher–learner relationship: particularly the authority of position, the authority of knowledge, and personal authority. But this is a book about intelligence, so for the rest of this chapter I want to examine further how intelligence can be brought to bear on social interaction in the present context of roles, and particularly of co-operative roles.

Two salient features of these we have seen to be the positive-sum aspect, and the predictability aspect.

The first of these is embodied in the rights and obligations of each role. In role pairs, one finds that A's rights from B match rather closely with B's obligations to A, and vice versa. This is not necessarily so in larger organizations. A person may receive his salary from one source, and discharge his obligations to another; and we have already seen (Section 8.7) that over a period, interactions of this kind can be positive-sum to a high degree. The extent to which this will be so will depend partly on the viewpoints adopted by the members of the organization. A restricted viewpoint would be for each individual, or group of individuals, to try to maximize the rights and minimize the obligations of the roles they occupy. One sees this in many negotiations. A more intelligent approach—more intelligent because integrating more of the relevant factors—would be to try to maximize the positive-sum aspect, on the basis that 'what is good for the firm may well be good for me too'. This does not require total unselfishness, which few of us are able to achieve. Rather, it means alternating between a close-up viewpoint centred on one's individual role, and a wide-angle viewpoint taking in the whole situation, on the vari-focal model described in Section 9.2. It also means realizing the present situation within a model which is extended in time, backwards in the events leading to the present state and forwards to take in long-term goals; and plans for achieving these.

13.14 The predictability requirement is closely linked with independence of role behaviour from the individual who is enacting it. This is necessary: we could not get through our day if we had to get to know personally every individual with whom we interact. But it means that every entrant to a role is under constraint to act as expected. Departures will often be signalled as unwelcome even if they do not affect the role-occupant's fulfilment of his obligations, or the positive-sum aspect in general. Even a person who was not a stickler for convention might nevertheless look askance at a doctor who came to his bedside in patched jeans and an open-necked shirt, however clean.

It was also suggested earlier that roles, or at least some aspects of them, may be learnt largely in this way. Thus not all the features of role behaviour may derive from the matching schemas, each containing a model of the other's director system, which were described in Section 13.4. Some may have been acquired simply on the basis of 'what is expected'.

The result of these in combination is that a role occupant may never bring reflective intelligence to bear on why he acts as he does; and even if he were to do so, he might have difficulty in making changes. So some parts of role behaviour may not have been considered intelligently, ever, by anyone. This opens wide the possibility that some of it could be unnecessary, or even misdirected.

It does not follow from this that the advantages of routinizing and predictability have to be foregone; but rather that all roles should at least sometimes be reflected on, by someone.

Freedom within a role structure

13.15 While this chapter was being discussed in draft form with a seminar group of postgraduate students, one of them made an unexpected contribution to the exchange of ideas, in the form of a personal reminiscence. When a student, and a theological student at that, preparing for the ministry, he used to depart from his expected behaviour within the role of passenger on a bus by sticking used tickets into the hatband of the trilby hats of passengers sitting in front of him. As well as enlivening our discussion, this also raised the question of why he used to 'break out' in this small way, and why others do so more drastically.

We have already noted the loss of freedom which is inseparable from the occupancy of any kind of role. In the case of voluntary, short-term roles, this is usually no great matter, and outweighed by the advantages of acting within the role. In the case of imposed roles, however much a person may want to break out, it is part of such a role that he cannot do so except with difficulty and by incurring risk. The examples of these which we have considered so far have been of an evident and drastic kind. But there is another set of roles, less obvious, perhaps less drastic, but which we find ourselves constrained towards occupying; not of our own free and conscious choice, but simply by being born at all into a particular family, locality, culture, nation, and time in history. Some of these roles are identifiable: child (*vis-à-vis* parents), school-child, employee, taxpayer. Others, such as membership of a peer group, also impose constraints on behaviour; though these may be harder to formulate. This interlaced network of roles is, as we have already seen, supportive as well as constraining. But by some the constraints are felt more strongly than the supports. This may be well founded on fact, as in the case of badly paid workers on an assembly line, or of persons living under a tyrannical political regime. But others too may feel themselves as confined within a set of roles which, though not imposed overtly and under duress, are equally not of their own free choice. These persons may come from middle and upper classes, with advantages of affluence, social position, and schooling: yet they feel themselves as prisoners within society. Others, on reading this chapter, may even construe it as leading to this view: as implying that as individuals in society, we have in fact small freedom to be ourselves; but that our behaviour, and thereby in course of time our personalities, are determined mainly by the roles in which we are placed.

The present argument has in fact been leading away from the latter way of thinking, though paradoxically by first becoming aware of it. Freedom within a role structure increases greatly, and often suddenly, when we realize that we have it. By reflecting intelligently on the roles in which we find ourselves, we move towards greater consciousness and understanding of these in relation to the roles of other persons. We can also compare our own conception of our roles with how others appear to conceive them; and discover which behaviours are central to the role, and which are discretionary areas; possibly even that the latter are greater than we had realized. As long as we occupy and enact our roles unreflectively and near-automatically, our freedom is diminished. But by the activity of reflective intelligence, we can become less automatic and constrained by our roles, more creative and self-determined in how we occupy and enact them. We can put ourselves in a position, though not of completely free choice, of greater freedom: not as puppets of our roles, but as intelligent actors thereof.

The present model also indicates that if too many people spend too much time challenging the system, it cannot work at all; and it would have to be a very bad system to be worse than chaos. The benefits of routinizing the process of co-operation are considerable. So one needs a balance between preserving a role structure as it is, and critically examining it: between stability, and the possibility of change for the better.

13.16 In the present chapter, the concept of roles has been introduced and discussed in relation to the present theoretical model, as a partial answer to the question: 'In view of the aforesaid complexity of possible interactions, how do we manage even as well as we do?' Its main features are as follows:

(i) *When two persons are in a role-pair relationship, their behaviour is directed by corresponding director systems, each of which contains a model of the other.*

(ii) *To the extent that a director system belongs to a role, it is independent of which individuals occupy it.*

(iii) *One of the functions of a role is to make possible greater predictability of behaviour. Conformity to expectations of others may therefore extend beyond what is necessary for successful interaction in terms of complementary plans.*

(iv) *We construe the behaviour of others in terms of the roles which we perceive them as occupying. If this does not match their own conceptions, there will be role confusion and difficulties of co-operation.*

(v) *Occupation of roles may be imposed or elective, and these characteristics are often associated with certain roles in themselves.*

(vi) *Freedom within a role structure may be increased by the conscious activity of reflective intelligence.*

Notes for Chapter 13

1. More generally, other organisms of all kinds. The present chapter concentrates on persons.

2. However, just before sending the manuscript of this book to the publishers, I came upon the following passage by another author who—like myself—does not regard herself as a de-schooler. (She is Reader in Psychology at Edinburgh University.)

> When we make laws which compel our children to go to school we assume collectively an awesome responsibility. For a period of some ten years, with minor variations from country to country, the children are conscripts; and their youth does nothing to alter the seriousness of this fact. Nor is it altered by the intention, however genuine, that the school experience should be 'for their good'.
>
> I am not among those who advocate what has come to be known as 'deschooling society'. I believe that we need schools—and never more than now. But the justification of a long enforced period of national service is not something we can treat lightly. (Donaldson, 1978, p. 13).

3. Sociologists also use the terms 'ascribed roles' and 'allocated roles', but I think that 'imposed' and 'elective' are clearer.

CHAPTER 14

The Teacher–learner Relationship

The Problem

14.1 The number of those who believe that all is not well with our educational institutions has lately increased from a few lonely pioneers such as Rousseau, Dewey, Neill, Holt, and Goodman, to a chorus including (at the time of writing) the British Prime Minister and the Secretary of State for Education and Science. Not so long ago, critics of compulsory schooling were regarded as a lunatic fringe. Now, a senior university teacher of education (Richmond, 1975)[1] can truthfully write that 'some of the best minds in the business now share a sense of profound disillusion with the established system of education and all it stands for'. Both the former and the latter groups alike quote Einstein:

> It is, in fact, nothing short of a miracle that the modern methods of instruction have not yet entirely strangled the holy curiosity of inquiry; for this delicate little plant, aside from stimulation, stands mainly in need of freedom; without this it goes to wrack and ruin without fail. It is a very grave mistake to think that the enjoyment of seeing and searching can be promoted by means of coercion and a sense of duty. To the contrary, I believe that it would be possible to rob even a healthy beast of its voraciousness, if it were possible, with the aid of a whip, to force the beast to devour continuously, even when not hungry, especially if the food handed out under such coercion were to be selected accordingly.[2]

Side by side with these criticisms of educational institutions, there continues a firm belief in the value of education in itself, both to individuals and to the community. This view is also implicit in most of the present volume, from Chapter 1 onwards (e.g. Sections 1.11 and 1.12); and especially at the end of Section 10.3:

> We can now see how a positive-sum system of relationships of great value can develop within a community where there is a suitable

balance between the achievement of completely new understanding the hard way by particular individuals; the building up of knowledge by learning from those who already know; the exchange of expertise in many ways; and the raising of our overall level of general knowledge. These processes together provide a collective level and extent of knowledge, and thereby potential for understanding, which is one of the major differences between advanced and primitive cultures.

So what is wrong, and why? Where lies the discrepancy between education as we feel strongly (though perhaps rather vaguely) it should be, and education (or what goes under that name) as it is? And why?

To the question 'What is wrong?', two answers can be given in brief. Firstly, the teaching itself is often inefficient. There are still children who reach secondary schools unable to read, despite six years of instruction in primary schools. And the teaching of mathematics is such that many—probably a majority[3]—acquire a lifelong dislike for the subject, together with lack of confidence in their ability to understand it. These are two of the most important subject areas. As for the others, how many adults voluntarily continue to study subjects which they were taught at school, other than those necessary for their employment or professions? Secondly, the system itself is being run with increasing difficulty, as evidenced by the fact that stress in teachers is now a common topic for articles in the educational press.

Some answers to the other question 'Why?', will be offered in the remainder of this chapter, and in the next.

14.2 At the heart of the matter is the continuing lack of a satisfactory theory on which to base either the activities of learners and teachers, or the institutions within which these activities are organized. For as I wrote in the preface, quoting Dewey (1929), 'Theory is in the end . . . the most practical of all things'; and as was emphasized in Chapter 10, the more we need to penetrate beyond what is easily observable, the more we need the help of a good theory. All teachers build up their own stores of empirical knowledge, and have abstracted from these some general principles on which they rely for guidance. But while their knowledge remains in this form it is still largely at the intuitive level within individuals, and cannot be communicated. They lack a shared schema in terms of which their own experience can be formulated, made accessible to reflection, and communicated: so that the results of individual learning are not integrated into a unified body of knowledge which can be made available for use by newcomers to the profession. Every new teacher has to learn mostly from his own mistakes.

The present chapter, and the next, are not offered as a complete educational theory, but as a beginning from which such a theory can be developed. Hitherto, the theoretical studies of those training to become teachers have been based mainly on the history of education, philosophy of education, psychology of education, sociology of education: four distinct subject areas derived from four distinct parent disciplines. From these they have been left to form their own synthesis, and their own applications to the practical problems of teaching.

This makes as much sense as it would to confine the theoretical studies of future medical practitioners to the history of medicine, philosophy of medicine, psychology of medicine, and sociology of medicine. All of these can be justified as important and relevant to the profession of medicine: but unless these doctors also learnt medicine itself, as a central discipline to which all these others relate, their future patients would suffer.

Unfortunately, as Wilson (1975) has convincingly argued, there is no central discipline or theory of education; and as a result, children do suffer. The present chapter, and that which follows, provide a beginning from which such a theory can be developed: for intelligent learning, which is what this book is all about, is certainly at the heart of education however we may conceive it. In this chapter the model will be used for an analysis of the teacher–learner relationship itself: that is, of the intrinsic factors—what goes on within the learner, within the teacher, and the interaction between the two. In the next chapter the model will be applied more widely to examine how situational factors affect the relationship, and the learning which takes place within it.

Before embarking on this, however, it must be emphasized that the positive-sum interaction described in the passage just quoted from Section 10.3, and the snowball effect described in the last paragraph of Section 1.11, are neither of them necessarily dependent on teaching. What is important is *the availability of opportunities for accelerated learning*; and whether being taught is necessarily an opportunity of this kind, and especially being taught within a situation of compulsory school attendance, is one of the questions which must now be asked seriously.

Intelligent teaching and learning

14.3   The term 'teach' is used for a wide variety of cases; ranging from brief informal situations such as that in which one person teaches another how to make bread, to institutionalized processes extending over years, such as those by which professional teachers teach a body of academic and professional knowledge. Teaching also includes teaching-not-to: parents teach their children not to hit each other when cross, not to use bad language, not to use the roadside as a toilet.

All kinds of teaching have this in common, that they are *an intervention in the learning process*. This learning process is inaccessible to direct observation by an outside person such as a teacher, in the same sort of way as one's digestive processes are inaccessible to direct observation by a medical practitioner. In both these cases, a person who intervenes without any clear picture of what is going on inside is as likely to do harm as good.

One can begin to realize the complexity of the interactions by noting that at least four director systems are involved, two in the learner, and two in the teacher. There is the teachable delta-one director system of the learner, and his own delta-two director system by which learning takes place. Part of the task of the teacher is to collaborate with the learner's delta-two: not to try to replace it, nor to confuse or disrupt it by the wrong kind of intervention. Part of the task of the student is to make use of the help made available by the teacher, and this itself may need to be learnt. The teacher likewise has a delta-one director system whose function is to teach the student, whose operand is delta-one within the student, and whose goal state is a certain state of ability to function of the latter. Also within the teacher is a delta-two system by which, in the present universe of discourse, he learns to teach. We need, moreover, to remind ourselves that what for simplicity we think of as a single director system is usually a complex of director systems behaving as a unity (in the same kind of way as the navigating officer, helmsman, and power steering of a ship function as a unity to direct the course of a ship along a chosen path). So even the four-director-system model just outlined is a considerable simplification. But this, we recall, is one of the features of a model: to reduce the complexity of what goes on enough to make it possible to think about.

14.4 Though the present emphasis is on intelligent teaching and learning, there are overall four categories.

(i) *Sub-intelligent learning from sub-intelligent levels of teaching.* Examples: animal training of the more primitive kind, army training as performed by a typical drill sergeant. The teacher here has only a crude empirical model of the learning process.

(ii) *Intelligent learning from sub-intelligent levels of teaching.* A superb historical example of this is offered by the mathematician Gauss as a schoolboy. His teacher, to keep the class occupied while he took things easy, set them the task of adding together all the numbers from 1 to 100. But Gauss arrived at the answer in a minute or two. (Hint: pair the first and last numbers, then the second and last but one, and so on inwards, thus:

$$1 + 100 = 101, \qquad 2 + 99 = 101, \qquad 3 + 98 = 101, \qquad \text{and so on.}$$

How many such pairs are there?) Having available a mathematical schema rather than a set of rote-memorized habits, young Gauss was able to devise a new and highly successful plan by which he was able to reach the set goal much more easily than his classmates.

(iii) *Intelligent teaching directed towards sub-intelligent levels of learning.* An example of this is provided by a method of curing dogs which chase sheep. A sheep is raised from birth, not with other sheep but with dogs, so that during its critical period of learning it acquires dog-like rather than sheep-like behaviours. When the offending dog tries to chase this particular sheep, the sheep instead of running away chases the dog, which quickly gives up its bad habit. To devise such a method required on the part of its inventor an accurate theoretical model of animal learning, from which he was able to devise a plan of action to meet the needs of the particular situation.

(iv) *Intelligent teaching directed towards intelligent learning by the learner.* This will be our main topic for the remainder of the present chapter.

14.5 On the side of the teacher, the requirements for this last process fall into two main categories.

(i) A theoretical model of all the processes of human learning. Particularly, of course, of intelligent learning: but he also needs to know about more primitive modes of learning. These are not described in this book, and are only briefly referred to at all under the collective description 'sub-intelligent learning'. Without knowledge of the whole spectrum of human learning, however, a teacher will not know when intelligent learning needs the support of more primitive kinds, or when it is being inappropriately replaced by more primitive kinds. Also, he will be unaware of, and so unable to deal appropriately with, whatever meta-learning takes place

(ii) A theoretical model of the processes by which he can interact with the delta-two system of the learner, for the co-operative activity of taking the learner's delta-one systems to states of better functioning.

Learning to teach at a professional level involves:

(a) acquiring the models described in requirements (i) and (ii), in an explicit form which is accessible to reflection;
(b) consciously applying these to the particular subject matter which he wants to help the learner to learn;
(c) developing a repertoire of routine plans by which his conscious attention can be largely freed to deal with the succession of non-routine situations which are almost inevitable during a teaching and learning situation, these plans still remaining integrated within an overall schema based on (a) and (b);
(d) regularly reflecting on his own activities as a teacher, so that he learns intelligently from his experiences by continuing to assimilate these to an expanding schema;
(e) in addition to the foregoing, if he is a professional teacher within a teaching institution such as a school, it is very desirable that he has a model of his role as a teacher which matches reasonably well with those of his pupils and of his colleagues. And if, as is all too likely, this condition cannot be met, then a grasp of the applications of Chapter 13

to his situation *vis-à-vis* his pupils will at least help him towards understanding what is going wrong.

14.6 So far as (a) is concerned, we may hope that requirement (i) has now been in some degree satisfied, though here restricted to intelligent learning. Requirement (ii) is a difficult one. We shall make a start in Section 14.7.

In the present section, (b) will be given a little more interiority. To fill the interior more completely would be to write a book on the teaching of some particular subject such as reading, or physics, or drama. This is an enterprise at the T_2 level, where T_1 stands for a professional teacher, and T_2 stands for someone who teaches T_1. Long-term, T_1 must take some of this on himself as part of (d); but it is a time-taking and arduous exercise, and T_1 needs both to be set on the path by being shown how it can be done, and also helped along it by making use of the contributions of others.

This task is essentially an application of Chapters 9, 10 and 11 to the subject which is to be taught. Part of Section 9.13 is worth repeating here, with four words newly italicized.

We have now examined a number of factors which affect the process of concept formation and the progressive development of schemas. A person who has already acquired particular concepts can manipulate these factors in ways which will greatly help others to acquire them too, *if he knows how*. What is difficult is to form these concepts for the first time without such aids, under conditions such as are encountered in everyday life and in scientific research: high noise; random encounter at irregular and often long time intervals; not knowing which experiences belong together as contributors; high levels of abstraction; and often too a shortage or absence of others who have enough knowledge in the same area to engage in useful discussion.

The first stage, as a preliminary to manipulating these factors for the benefit of the learner, is deep reflection on the subject matter—the concepts and schemas to be acquired within a particular field of knowledge—in order to become aware of its structure, both within and between concepts. One has to find out which concepts are prerequisite for others: which primary concepts are necessary for which secondary concepts, and which higher-order secondary concepts are entirely dependent for their formation on which lower-order concepts. Also, what are the other interconnections between concepts, and which of these are A-links and which are C-links. This task is a demanding one whatever the subject matter, both in itself and also because it often leads to unwelcome discoveries. Things which one thought one understood, one finds that one did not—the connections were either muddled, or absent. Here is another reason why it is not always easy to engage in this activity while also teaching the subject matter, for it is disconcerting (to say the least) to become aware of serious gaps in one's understanding of a topic the evening before one has to give a lesson on it.

The next stage is to use the results of the above to structure the subject matter which is to be taught and learnt in the form of a schema, possession of which is one of the goals of learning. In constructing such a schema, and in choosing from among the possibilities, it is necessary to bear in mind both short-term and long-term goals. Quick results can be achieved by teaching, not schemas, but a collection of isolated habits, rules for arriving at the right answers in a limited class of examples. These are completely lacking in adaptability, like a traveller who memorizes sentences in a foreign language from a phrase book. Here we frequently encounter serious discrepancies between the learning goals as conceived by the teacher, and those which are achieved by the learner. The following examples were all related to me by teachers or parents who encountered them at first hand; and they cannot be regarded as rare or exceptional. The first was related to me by a father, himself a lecturer in a college of education. His young son came home from school and said that he now knew his seven-times table. 'Good', said the father. 'Can you tell me what are seven threes? Seven fives?' The child answered these correctly, so the father asked him: 'You are seven little boys at a party, and you have four balloons each. How many balloons altogether?' 'I don't know, daddy. We haven't done balloons.' Next: a boy adding a column of numbers, which required 'carrying'. He told my colleague 'I always carry the smaller number.' 'Why?' 'Because it's lighter.' Another child could subtract correctly in one classroom, but not in another. The reason turned out to be that he always started from the end nearer the piano. A university lecturer in mathematics heard from his younger brother (aged 10) that he was learning about sets at school. Interested, he asked 'What did you learn about sets?' All the boy could say was: 'Sets must have a capital letter.' Another college lecturer, this time in education, visited a school where children learning about time had been provided with rubber stamps of a clock face. They could draw in the hands at the correct position for a specified time, and say what the time was if the hands were drawn. But when he asked them questions such as 'Where are you, or what are you doing, at (say) half past four in the afternoon?' the children did not know. Similar examples can be found in almost every subject.

Good teaching certainly requires that the goal of learning is a schema, not a set of rote-memorized facts. Excellent teaching requires, beyond this, an ability to compare the merits of alternative schemas, both for present use as a source of plans (*knowledge that* as a source of *knowledge how*) and also as a tool for future learning by the assimilation of new concepts (knowledge on which to build further knowledge). To do this a teacher has to know beyond what he is teaching, so that he can consider which schemas will be applicable to future learning, and which will have to be restructured or replaced. Here is a simple mathematical example: the reader is invited to seek others in areas with which he is familiar. If multiplication is learnt as repeated addition, this schema has to be replaced as soon as the learner comes to multiplication of fractional numbers. But if multiplication is learnt as the composition of two operations (doing an operation, and then doing a second operation on the result of the first), this schema can be applied to all number systems right through to imaginary and complex numbers. This basic schema will also be applicable later in other areas, such as the composition of any two functions. And if properly taught, it is only marginally more difficult to acquire at the outset.

Having decided on the schema which is to be the goal of learning, the next task is to replace the haphazard learning conditions of everyday life as already described (high noise, random encounter at irregular and often long time intervals, not knowing which experiences belong together as contributors, high levels of abstraction) with their opposites. This is to say that examples have to be chosen and grouped together from which the learner can abstract the concept to be learnt: if necessary, physical examples first for the formation of primary concepts, followed by groupings of primary concepts from which secondary concepts can be abstracted, and so on. These examples have to be carefully chosen so that they have in common the concept to be abstracted, other attributes varying so that these do not become abstracted, and mistakenly incorporated into the concept. (What is wrong with Figure 51 as an example from which to abstract the concept of parallel lines?

Figure 51

It comes from one of the better-known mathematical texts used in the UK.) Likewise the order of concepts to be learnt in this way has to be carefully planned, to ensure that the necessary lower-order concepts are available from which the successively higher-order concepts are to be formed. Using again the example of invisible exports (Section 9.8), before this could be abstracted from examples such as insurance, banking, tourism, a sequence of lower-order concepts would have to be built up, starting with examples of over-the-counter purchases, for cash, of physical objects. The reader who cares to complete the above example will find it a useful exercise, as a way of somewhat consolidating his own schema for understanding what is involved in a conceptual analysis followed by a planned sequence of groups of examples. The teacher analyses, so that the learner can re-synthesize. For any subject area, the task is great: how great is only likely to be realized by those who have attempted it themselves. An application of this approach to the field of mathematics can be found in Skemp (1971); and a similar overall approach characterizes the study of man described by Bruner (1966). But attempts of any kind to teach subject areas in this way are scarcer than presentations in which no thought seems to have been given to the matter at all. In history, for example, there seems small chance that one learner in a thousand will acquire historical concepts of any generality or penetration, such as might help him to understand events of his own times, from the mass of factual material about kings and queens (with their dates), invasions, battles, and conquests which they are required to memorize and reproduce. In my own case, it was not until many years after I had left school that I began to discover what history, geography, chemistry were really about: or even, as a necessary preliminary, to realize the superficiality of what I had been learning under these names, which is to say the lack of higher-order concepts and unifying schemas.

The result of the foregoing exercise, if properly done, will be a plan for making possible the learning, in weeks, months, or years, of conceptualized and structured knowledge which has taken mankind years, decades, or centuries to acquire for the first time. Such a learning plan takes the form of a partially ordered schema, in which order is important, but there is no unique order which is the only right one.

Though the hardest part has now been done, the exercise is not complete. What remains, however, is relatively straightforward. At each level of the process of successive abstraction, before concepts at one level can serve as examples for the derivation of concepts of the next higher order, they need to be consolidated. So additional material is required for this purpose.

It has also be emphasized that what can be routinized needs to be routinized, so that conscious attention is freed for the novel and problematic. Examples are thus needed for the development of a repertoire of ready-to-hand plans for tasks which recur.

The purpose of the first kind of repetition is to make the superordinate concepts increasingly independent of particular examples. Provided that the examples are well chosen, with plenty of variability and increasing noise, there should be no danger of this kind of practice degenerating into rote memorizing. Practice of the second kind does, however, carry with it the danger than the particular parts which are being thus practised become separated from their underlying schema; so losing the adaptability which is one of the main attributes of intelligent learning. At each level it is therefore necessary also to include examples of a different kind: problems which cannot be solved entirely by routine processes, but which require the construction of new plans from the parent schema. Pupils need to know which kind of examples they are doing, for which learning goal—consolidation, routine skills, schema maintenance, or formation of new concepts.

The teacher's function

14.7   The process described in the long section just concluded is only a beginning, though an important one. A state of knowledge which has taken successive generations many hundreds of years to reach, often by paths more difficult and circuitous than they need have been,[4] is to be reached within a single generation. Not only the final state, but also the many possible ways of getting there, have to be considered. And since what has to be mapped consists, not of tangled forests and waterless deserts, the objects of physical exploration, but of complex and interconnected mental states, it is an activity of reflective intelligence: in its own way no less arduous. This is the work of the map-makers and pathfinders who follow the early explorers. After these come the guides, with their parties of travellers.

The preparatory work described in Section 14.6 is thus necessary for making possible the process of accelerated learning referred to in Section 14.2, but it does not ensure it. Only by the activity of the learner can this come about; and this activity may or may not be helped by a teacher. The last part of this sentence is double edged, and this is deliberate: for we must continue to bear in mind that the interventions of a teacher, though they may be helpful, are not necessarily so.

And to say this does not imply ill will on the part of the teacher. It results from difficulties which are intrinsic to a teacher's function, which are not yet fully realized, still less overcome; and also from factors which are external to this function but which may greatly affect it.

For purposes of the present section, we will assume that the teacher's function is to help the learner to learn something which he could not learn unaided, or to learn it more quickly, or to learn it better. In the guide analogy, he is taking the traveller to a destination which he could not reach unaided; or he is taking him there more quickly and comfortably; or he is helping him to find the best place to stay among a wide range, some much better than others, within the general area of his chosen destination. But since this is a mental journey, the guide does not know with any great reliability what is the present location of the traveller, nor in which direction he is heading. So it is not altogether surprising if sometimes a traveller gets lost, temporarily or beyond rescue: for he has not been there before, and has no map.

The general requirements for successful co-operation between two director systems were discussed in Chapter 8. Minimally, these are compatible goal states, and plans which are complementary. Long-term co-operation requires an overall positive-sum set of relationships between their goals, and widely shared conceptual structures.

The discussion which led to this formulation was based on examples where the operand is something in actuality, accessible to perception. Co-operation between a teacher and a learner encounters a new difficulty: for here, the operand is itself a director system, that within the learner which we are calling delta-one. The two director systems which have to function as one are delta-two within the learner, and a delta-one system within the teacher. Between them they have to contribute all the necessary components of a single delta-two, each contributing what the other lacks; in the same kind of way as the driver and co-driver described in Section 8.8, but under conditions which make unified functioning much more difficult. From one side or the other, in varying contributions, there has to be:

(i) Some way of knowing the present state of the learner's delta-one. The learner has direct access to this, but not an appropriate schema within which to realize it. The teacher has an appropriate schema, but no direct way of perceiving this delta-one. How much the learner can contribute will depend on how well he can perceive his own delta-one. Otherwise, the teacher has to infer the present state of the learner's delta-one from observing it in action.

(ii) A plan for taking the learner's delta-one from its present state to its goal state. The teacher may decide on the path, but it is the delta-one within the learner which has to be directed along it. So together they are like a traveller with a guide who cannot accompany the traveller on his journey, but has to direct him from afar by radio. And it is likely that the guide has the only copy of the map on which the route is marked.

(iii) There also needs to be some way of identifying the obstacles which the learner is likely to encounter on his way towards the goal state. Again, the learner is well aware that there is a difficulty, but he may be unable to say what it is. He just knows that he is 'stuck', or seems to be slipping backwards. To be able to diagnose learners' difficulties of this kind is one of the major contributions which a teacher can make.

(iv) We must never forget the emotional factors discussed in Chapter 2 and Chapter 7. The learner is at the frontier of his domain, or outside it; whereas the ground is familiar to the teacher. So understanding of the emotional stresses of learning, and ability to give the kind of support which is needed, is another of the contributions which a teacher needs to make to the joint task.

Conditions for co-operation between teacher and learner

14.8 The minimal requirements for co-operation, of compatible goal states and plans which are complementary, may seem easy to satisfy. The learner wants to progress in his learning, the teacher wants him to do so. As part of his plan, the teacher chooses an exercise which is not too difficult for the learner's present state of knowledge, but which if he does it successfully will take him a further step along the path. The learner's degree of success in the task is the only way the teacher has of knowing whether the learner has reached a given point, and is ready to go further. So if the learner has done badly, the teacher will point out where he has gone wrong, and perhaps set a further task to be done.

But is this how it is construed by the learner? Consider the following example. A colleague told me that his 12-year-old son learnt his homework well, but forgot it as soon as he had been tested on it. Why might this be? Perhaps the boy had a bad memory? Could anything be done to help?

In such a case, whatever explanation is offered cannot be more than a guess. But an appropriate model helps one at least to guess intelligently, and sometimes to test one's guesses if there is opportunity. My conjecture here was that the goal set by this child was to perform as well as he could in next morning's test, and thereby to get a good mark; and also, to avoid having to do extra work which he construed as a punishment. He did not share the long-term goal set for him by his teacher: possibly he did not even conceive it. So, if he achieved the short-term goal, that was an end to it. Some support for this explanation is given by the fact that the boy was a successful performer in school plays and operatic performances, for which he remembered his part well for as long as was necessary.

A parallel example is offered by another child, the older members of whose family used to converse in French when they did not want him to know what they were saying. At school he was taught both French and Latin: but his learning of French progressed very much faster than his Latin!

Successful long-term co-operation is only to be expected if there is a reasonably good match between the overall goal structures of learner and teacher. And it is the long-term goal which is most important, for the intermediate goals will then be construed alike by both, as successive steps forward along the path. This is much more likely to take place—possibly it can only take place—if the long-term goal is chosen by the learner rather than the teacher. Since the learner may not be able clearly to conceive a state which he has not yet reached, his formulation of this goal may sometimes necessarily be imprecise. This does not affect the main argument, which is that if the long-term goal is chosen by the learner and agreed by the teacher then the intermediate goals can be chosen by the teacher, and will be agreed by a learner who trusts his teacher's knowledge and good faith. These short-term losses of freedom for the learner are more than compensated by his free choice of the main goal. In contrast, if it is the teacher who chooses the long-term goal, he necessarily has also to choose the short-term goals which will take the learner towards it; and the learner has little freedom at all. The teacher may have in mind a long-term benefit for the learner, but how the learner construes the situation is much more uncertain. It may well be in quite a different universe of discourse, related more closely to whatever constrains him to accept the teacher's choice of learning tasks, than it is to the teacher's reasons for choosing them. A mis-match between their overall goal structures is therefore much more likely in such conditions, and likewise in the plans; for the goal which is set will necessarily determine what learning takes place, and how. For example, a task often given to children is to estimate, and then check the accuracy of their estimate by measuring. The learning goal as conceived by the teacher is for the children to become good at estimating. But not surprisingly, many children measure first and then write a plausible estimate. Their goal state is a page of good results, and this is what they have learnt to achieve.

Relational learning and instrumental learning

14.9   A subtle mis-match which may occur between the goals of learner and teacher is one between the building up of schemas, and the learning of a set of fixed plans (see Section 11.5). This mis-match can occur either way round; and in the field of mathematics, where I first became aware of it, it can now be identified as one of the major sources of difficulty for both learners and teachers. (Skemp, 1976.) The distinction is however entirely general; and once it has been conceptualized (for which mathematics is a useful source of low-noise examples), once can become aware of it in a wide variety of contexts.

Instrumental understanding, in a mathematical situation, consists of recognizing a task as one of a particular class for which one already knows a rule. To find the area of a rectangle, multiply the length by the breadth. For a triangle, calculate half times the base times the perpendicular height. If the figure is a parallelogram, multiply the length of one pair of parallel sides by the perpendicular distance between them. If it is a trapezium, multiply half the sum of the lengths of the parallel sides by the perpendicular distance between them. The kind of learning which makes this possible, which I call instrumental learning, is the memorizing of such rules.

Relational understanding, in contrast, consists primarily in relating a task to an appropriate schema. If there is also a ready-to-hand plan, so much the better. It is an economy of effort to have available a set of these for tasks of the kinds which are encountered more often. But if there is not, one is not at a loss. One can devise a plan for the particular task in hand; or one can adapt an existing plan, or combine parts of two such plans. If he has an appropriate parent schema, someone who does not know the rule can still calculate the area of a given trapezium by dividing it into a triangle and a parallelogram, or into two triangles and a rectangle, or even into three triangles. If he wants he can also, by any of the above paths, arrive at the general rule for finding areas of trapeziums.

Another advantage of relational understanding is that it reduces the likelihood of talking nonsense. Here is an example, authentic, though hard to believe, from a teacher who was teaching area to a class new to him. Suspecting that they had little understanding of what they were doing, he asked them: 'What is the area of a field 20 cm by 15 yards?' The reply was '300 square centimetres'. He asked 'Why not 300 square yards?' 'Because area is always in square centimetres.'

To prevent a repetition of such errors, the teacher might give the learners a new rule to learn, that both dimensions must be in the same unit. This shows up another weakness of instrumental learning, that it usually leads to a multiplicity of rules. These become an increasing burden on the memory;

whereas in relational learning, which is the building up of a schema, the model predicts that mutual excitation within the network of connected concepts makes the schema as a whole more easily retained in memory than isolated, rote-memorized material. This prediction has been confirmed experimentally (Skemp, 1962).

As an everyday example of the same distinction, take a driver starting a car on a cold morning. He has learnt, instrumentally, that the way to do this is (having switched on the ignition) to pull out the choke and press the starter button, keeping his foot off the accelerator pedal until the engine fires. If this plan succeeds, as it usually does, well and good. But if it does not, he cannot devise alternatives. Suppose that he seeks assistance from another driver who has available a schema representing what goes on, out of sight, under the bonnet. The first thing the latter will probably do, having diagnosed the fault as 'over-choked' (too much petrol vapour and too little air) will be to push the choke in, and gently press the accelerator pedal right down, before pressing the starter button. This will doubtless surprise the other, since this plan appears to be exactly the opposite of the one he knows. The purpose is of course to reduce the petrol and increase the air intake, until a mixture is obtained which will fire.

Where the tasks fall into a small number of classes, sufficiently alike within each class for the same plan to serve, instrumental learning is quicker than learning a schema. But this only holds good if the number of fixed rules to be learnt is small. Paradoxically, in a schema there is more to learn but less to remember: more to learn, because higher-order concepts are involved, and more connections; but less to remember because once learnt it forms a cohesive whole, from which an indefinitely large number of particular plans can be derived.

14.10 In any learning task, the most obvious immediate goal of the learner is to give a right answer, and that is what the teacher wants too. But in relational learning, the right answer is wanted not in itself but as an indication that the right ideas have been acquired—that part of a schema has been learnt. In instrumental learning it is the other way about—the right answer is the goal, and the rule a means for getting to it.

So there can be two kinds of match, and two kinds of mis-match, between the goal structures of learner and teacher. If the learner's goal is building up a schema, then he will construe the succession of exercises set by the teacher as steps toward this long-term goal. If he cannot understand at a particular stage, he will ask the kind of question which a teacher will be pleased to hear if he has a matching goal structure. 'Good question', he will say, and try to give a clear explanation. But a teacher who himself has only instrumental understanding will answer in terms of a rule, either reiterating it or showing where the rule was not correctly used. If the learner persists in wanting to know the reasons behind the rule—not just how, but why—such a teacher may well (consciously or unconsciously) feel threatened, and discourage this kind of questioning.

If a learner and a teacher both have instrumental goals of learning, their overall goal structures will match—if acquiring a collection of separate plans can be called a structure. If, however, the teacher's conception of the learning goal is the building up of a schema, the explanations he gives for the purpose of relating the current exercise to this schema, which exists in his own mind but not in that of the learner, will not relate to anything within the goal structure of the learner. Such learners will have no interest in their teacher's careful explanations about *why*, for what they want is some kind of rule *how* by which they can get the right answer. When something like this is reached, they latch on to it and forget the rest.

14.11   There are three other advantages of a teacher–learner relationship in which the goal structures of both are relational. The first is that it evokes the activity of reflective intelligence in the learner, and favours its development. For the teacher's explanations, and still more so discussions on a level of reciprocity between learner and teacher in which it is accepted as equally appropriate for each to challenge the inferences of the other, are addressed to questions such as 'Why is this the case?'; 'Why do you say that?'; 'How can this be connected with that?' In all such cases the object of scrutiny in both learner and teacher, from which questions arise and by which answers are constructed, are matching schemas: the teacher's being more extensive and developed, but the learner's closely matching a sub-schema within that of the teacher, and thus within the body of knowledge constituting the discipline. Examining, working on, enlarging, and improving the quality of these schemas is one of the central functions of reflective intelligence.

The second advantage is that continuing development of an existing schema seems to be capable of becoming a goal state in itself, independently of any other goals such as may be reached by plans derived from it. This becomes particularly evident in pure scientists and pure mathematicians, who just want to know more, to understand better, and who pay little or no attention to any practical uses to which their new knowledge may be put. But there is observational evidence, and now a little experimental evidence too, that this is true also for children of school age.

When first I became aware of this, it was an empirical observation, for which I could offer no explanation. The present model, however, makes it clear that any activity which results in the enlargement of a domain, or increased expertise within a domain, is likely to be pro-survival. An earlier discussion (Section 7.5) has shown also that a learning process does not have to be pro-survival every time to be naturally selected, only more often than not. Relational learning gives increased long-term adaptability, in future situations which may be unforeseen and even unforeseeable at the time when the learning takes place. It is like money in the bank: useful for so wide a variety of purposes that even though we do not always know in advance what we will use it for, we like to acquire it.

The third advantage follows from the second, but bears more directly on the teacher–learner relationship. It was argued in Section 14.8 that successful co-operation is much more likely to take place if the long-term goal is chosen by the learner rather than by the teacher. In the less favourable condition where the teacher first chooses the long-term learning goal, there is always the possibility that if the teacher is able to get the learner started on the path of relational learning, then for the reasons given above the learner may himself begin to develop a taste for it. In cases where this does happen, what may have begun as a teaching situation of the less favourable kind may undergo a substantial improvement. It has to be admitted, however, that it will take an excellent teacher to bring this about.

The distinction between relational learning and instrumental learning is a very general one. It relates to qualitative differences in learning which are independent of the subject matter, are deep rather than superficial, and thus can only be diagnosed, not directly observed. They can be identified most easily in low-noise examples such as mathematics, physics, chemistry, biology, where the underlying conceptual structure is strong relative to the detailed content, and its presence or absence is therefore easier to discern. But once the distinction has been conceptualized, one can begin to discern either relational or (regrettably, more often) instrumental learning taking place in almost every subject area: which is to say, intelligence being called into action strongly, or hardly at all.

Meta-learning and meta-teaching

14.12   The subject of meta-learning was introduced in Section 7.12, where it was described as learning which takes place as a result of what is intentionally (and therefore consciously) being learnt, but in a different universe of discourse from this, and often unintentionally and unconsciously. If the learner's difficulties result from earlier meta-learning, then this will have to be remedied before progress can be made. And since they will be particularly hard for the learner himself to identify, here is where the help of a good teacher is almost essential.

One of the commonest obstacles of this kind results from a person's having meta-learnt that he is bad at learning some particular topic. This is meta-learning, because it is learning about his own ability at a particular topic, not learning about the topic itself: though clearly these two are closely related. Some years ago, it was part of my job to teach elementary statistics to first-year psychology students. Here I knew in advance that at least half of them would have meta-learnt that they could not do mathematics, so I decided to try to change this self-conception, which was mostly inaccurate, before starting on the main topic. Asking them to bear with me for a little,

hile we looked at something of which they would not immediately see the
relevance, I produced a map of the London Underground network. Though
they did not know it, this provides an excellent embodiment of some of the
basic concepts of topology. We then discussed what kind of a representation
of the actual railway system this was: what properties had been abstracted and
were embodied in the model, such as connectivity, order; which were not,
such as distance, direction; what changes we could make in this map which
would not affect its use, and what changes would matter. Of course they had
no difficulty with this, and found it quite interesting as an exercise in thinking
about what I would now call the construction of models. At the end, I
explained that we had been studying together a branch of mathematics called
topology, and that this was usually studied at university level rather than at
school because it was regarded as difficult. (In fact it soon becomes so: it is
only the early stages which are so easily grasped.) I went on to explain that the
purpose had been to try to convince those of them who thought they couldn't
do mathematics that this was not the case: so please would they now try to
believe that if we studied statistics together, they could make headway?

   This I would now call meta-teaching, since the object was not at this stage
to teach them any statistics, but to try to remove an obstacle to this from a
different universe of discourse, namely their self-conceptions of their own
abilities to learn this kind of subject. To what extent it was successful I do not
know, since only a controlled experiment would have given this information.
Another interesting question is whether the chance of success had I made my
intentions known to the students would have been the same, or greater, or
less. At the time, I thought that if they knew that what we were discussing was
mathematics of some kind, this would have aroused negative expectations in
many from the outset, and would have prevented this approach from
succeeding. But there is also an ethical question: is it right to try to do good by
stealth? In this case my conscience is easy, because by coming to me to learn
statistics, there was not only an implicit acceptance of my ability as a teacher,
but of my good faith. Nevertheless, it is a question which always has to be
considered, and in each case the onus of proof, if only to himself, is on the
doer.

   A meta-learning which all too many persons have undergone at some time
is that saying one doesn't understand, asking questions, seeking an
explanation, results in further discouragement such as being made to look
stupid, or told they should have paid proper attention. If the questions were
genuinely intended as a request for help in understanding, this kind of
meta-teaching is so clearly harmful and long-term in its effects that I have
coined a word for it: *torting*. An example of good meta-teaching in this area
was given some years ago at a conference on mathematical education
Fielker, *c*. 1967). A teacher said: 'If a boy says something I disagree with, I
ask him to explain his reasons. Sometimes we all learn something. Sometimes
he makes a start, then breaks off and says "Oh, I see", and then he has taught
himself something.'

14.13 In this chapter, we have begun to see some of the complexities of the teacher–learner relationship, which are such that a teacher's intervention can inhibit the learning process as well as help it if he does not have a clear understanding of what he is doing. This is hardly possible without the help of a good theoretical model, towards which the present chapter is offered as a contribution. Its main points are:

(i) *Teaching is an intervention in the learning of another person. A necessary though not sufficient, condition for intelligent teaching is to have a theoretical model of the processes of human learning at both intelligent and sub-intelligent levels of learning. This model should include an understanding of the differences between relational learning and instrumental learning; and also of meta-learning.*

(ii) *Preparation for intelligent teaching includes an analysis of the subject matter in order to become aware of its conceptual structure; so that it can be taught in a way which enables the learner to re-synthesize this structure in his own mind as a schema.*

(iii) *Co-operation between a teacher and a learner involves co-operation between the delta-two system of the learner and a delta-one system of the teacher, the operand being a delta-one system within the learner which the teacher cannot directly either observe or act on.*

(iv) *Successful co-operation of this kind is by its nature difficult, but is more likely to succeed if it is the learner who has chosen the long-term goal of learning.*

Notes for Chapter 14

1. He is Reader in Education at the University of Glasgow.
2. This widely quoted passage can most easily be found on page 69 of Jeremy Bernstein's biography *Einstein* (Bernstein, 1973). He gives as its source Schilpp (1949), page 100.
3. On three separate occasions, I asked a group of postgraduate students numbering around a hundred how many of them felt anxiety or dislike towards mathematics. On a show of hands, the number was between 70 and 80 per cent on each occasion. A very similar percentage was obtained when the same question was put to a group of assorted adults at a parent–teacher evening in a local primary school.
4. An absorbing account of this process in the context of cosmology has been given by Koestler (1959).

CHAPTER 15

Schooling and Education

Stress in schools

15.1   Despite the continuing efforts of a large body of experienced and for the most part dedicated teachers, the situation in many of our schools (though with notable exceptions) is causing increasing concern, and reports of stress in teachers have become frequent. Under a headline 'Why comprehensive heads are weary and worried', a responsible national newspaper[1] reports the results of a large number of interviews with comprehensive school heads, the interviewer herself[2] being a retired head teacher. Replies such as 'I hate the job, but I'll do it to the best of my ability' are by no means atypical. Another: 'I am absolutely weary—not of good ideas, but of the conflict of ideas . . . '. And even: 'I sit on my bed, first thing in the morning, trying to think of some reason for not coming here'. (Jackson, 1976.)

Professional organizations do not hide their concern. In England the National Association of Schoolmasters and the Union of Women Teachers have jointly published a study entitled *Stress in Schools* (Casey *et al.*, 1976) from which the following quotations are taken.

(p. 24): 'It is not the physical aspects which cause difficulty, as these are not too extreme, so much as one's requests being ignored and verbal abuse.' A teacher, describing the problems of one of his colleagues (also p. 24): 'The fact that I used the adjoining classroom made me aware that he was being subjected to all manner of taunts, insults and threats of violence.' (p. 25): 'It tends to become a question of survival for both sides.' Psychosomatic disorders are reported. (p. 44): 'The response to stress in my school has taken many forms, some, alas, with serious medical complications, such as a very quiet mathematician, whose frustration had always been suppressed, until in his mid-forties he suffered a coronary. Others have shown inexplicable body rashes or have lost weight.' Not surprisingly, these are particularly common among students on teaching practice. (p. 45): 'I developed a nervous rash on my arm.' 'I lost my voice.' 'I lost weight and had a permanent slight lump in my throat probably due to an increase in my smoking.' Summarizing his conclusions from a survey of the reports of a total of 810 teachers from a wide spectrum of institutions—infant, junior, and secondary schools, a college of education, and a university department of education—Dunham[3] writes: 'More teachers are experiencing stress. Severe stress is being experienced by more teachers. These are the two major conclusions of my survey of stress in schools. . . . Stress can no longer be dismissed as a short term characteristic of adjustment problems.'

A remarkably similar picture is given by a survey carried out by the Swedish Union of Teachers.[4] Of the 500 teachers included in the survey, one in three said that they would not choose the same career again; and this rose to half among teachers of 13- to 16-year olds. At every level, about four in every five teachers felt under stress.

As Hannam, Smyth, and Stephenson (1976) have shown, teachers in their first year have a particularly hard time. (p. 69): 'I would think "My God, I just can't go in tomorrow".' (p. 68): 'Why should I feel so awful all the time?' (p. 100): 'I think perhaps the worst aspect of teaching is that one has to spend so much energy absorbing aggression'.

Nor is it only the teachers who are under stress. John Holt, now prominent among the de-schoolers, came to his present position via a discovery that 'Even in the kindest and gentlest of schools children are afraid, many of them a great deal of the time, some of them almost all the time. . . . Why is so little said about it? Perhaps most people do not recognize fear in children when they see it. They can read the grossest signs of fear . . . but the subtler signs of fear escape them.' (Holt, 1956.) A medical officer (Dann, 1974) also writes of tension in schoolchildren, instancing children who need sleeping tablets or tranquillizers in order to deal with the stresses of school.

15.2 Given that the persons involved are very like, and indeed often the same persons as those who work together harmoniously and enjoyably in other situations, it seems inescapable that the causes lie in the institutions themselves. Some, like Illich (1971), take the view that the only possible remedy lies in the abolition of these institutions. Ten years after the publication from which the earlier quotations were taken, Holt has now come to believe that 'Education, with its supporting system of compulsory and competitive schooling, all of its carrots and sticks, its grades, diplomas and credentials, now seems to me perhaps the most authoritarian and dangerous of all the social institutions of mankind.' (Holt, 1977.)

While regarding these as 'radical extremists', Richmond (1975) agrees that 'Much the same verdict has been reached by educationists who do not necessarily share the ideology of the deschoolers.' And a professor of educational research, in a valedictory address to his associates, declares: 'I think it is time to take a critical look at institutionalised education without necessarily letting the pendulum swing to the other extreme and requiring complete "deschooling".' (Husén, 1974.)

Through other paths, I find myself in the same position, though with a different emphasis and perspective. If we accept that the present situation is urgently in need of change, it is hard to see how any genuine understanding of the problem can be reached, or how progress can reliably be made towards a better state of affairs, in the absence of an appropriate theoretical framework. Given also that joint action is needed by many persons and categories of persons if things are to get better, it is hard to see how co-operation of the extent and duration required can be achieved and maintained if the requirements for co-operation described earlier in the present book are not satisfied. These include (see Section 8.18) an overall positive-sum set of relationships between their goals, and widely shared conceptual structures within the universe of discourse involved. Unless and until these requirements are satisfied, change is as likely to be for the worse as for the better.

The purpose of this chapter is therefore to continue with the application of the present model to the teacher–learner relationship, with increasing attention to situational influences which affect this relationship and the learning which takes place within it.

Apart from the increasing amount of empirical evidence which points to the need for an analysis of this problem situation, the logic of the present enquiry also leads directly to this area. And though some of the (still tentative) answers may be unexpected, the questions themselves should not be. One of the characteristics of any good model is that it leads one to ask questions which one might not otherwise have thought of. And a central feature of the present model, introduced as early as Section 1.2, is that of goal-directedness. Combine this with the discussions on consciousness (Chapter 2) and of the conception of learning itself as goal-directed (Chapter 7), and questions immediately arise such as whether the learning is intentional, and whether the goals of learning are chosen by the learner or by the teacher. The discussions of roles in Chapter 13 raise further questions about the extent to which the teacher-learner relationship is role-governed in a particular case. And all of these will lead eventually back to the question of whether, and if so in what ways, these factors affect the teacher's ability to function in the ways discussed in Sections 14.7 and 14.8.

Intention

15.3 Teaching implies intention on the side of the teacher, but this may be either present or absent in the learner. A parent may successfully teach his child to speak grammatically by correcting him when he does not: but the child need not necessarily intend this, nor need the learning itself be conscious. To say that an action or activity is intentional means that the choice of a goal is conscious and deliberate, as in the case of an adult who decides to learn a foreign language. The presence or absence of intention is one of the important qualities in relation to which we construe the behaviour of others: such as 'Did she intend to poison him?; 'His remark was kindly intended'.

The intention to learn, or its absence, is of course independent of whether or not a teacher is involved. To mark this distinction on the side of the learner, I propose that we use the terms *'student'*, *'study'* in cases where intention is present, or where we believe it to be. Thus 'Jimmy has learnt to talk' (no intention implied); but 'Catherine is studying chess'. This usage includes students of all ages, and learning goals of all kinds. We would thus refer to a five-year-old as studying swimming as well as to a thirty-year-old studying for his doctorate. This is a slight extension of everyday usage, where the word is used mainly for academic subjects. Its purpose here is to call attention to the common factor of intention, and especially to whether this is present or absent, in the context of learning.

Power relationships and co-operative relationships

15.4 Whether the goals of learning are *chosen* by the teacher or by the learner is not the same question as who *sets* the goals of learning, for no one can set a person's goals but himself. A learner can and does set learning goals of his own, without a teacher being involved either before or during the learning process.

But if a teacher is involved at all, the nature of the relationship which has led to his involvement is one which may greatly affect the teacher–learner relationship itself.

The conditions under which one person sets his goal in accordance with information from another were discussed in Section 8.6. The same four categories apply with equal force when the goals are learning goals; and reference back to Table 4 reminds us that two of these are power relationships, and two are co-operative relationships.

For category 1(a), the term *supervisor* is convenient. This is already in general use for people who tell others what to do in a setting of work or employment, such as department stores, factories, building sites. The term as here used is neutral. People accept the directions of a supervisor in exchange for benefits, often in the form of payment. Nevertheless, the relationship is asymmetric: the supervisor can give or withhold a variety of benefits (choice of lunch hour, more interesting or agreeable jobs, favourable reports to superiors). The various ways in which subordinates are protected against misuse of his power by a supervisor is proof that this power is there. And the protections are of comparatively recent development: not so the power.

For category 1(b), the term *taskmaster* is as old as history, and so too is the relationship. Slavery is its extreme form, serfdom was little better, and those who directed the wage slaves in factories and sweatshops of many countries merit the same description. In some cases the distinction between a supervisor and a taskmaster may be somewhat blurred, particularly if factors of personality are superimposed on the relationship. A strict supervisor, a not-altogether-brutal taskmaster, may sometimes appear as alike. But usually the distinction between 1(a) and 1(b) becomes clear on reflection. Does the power of A derive from his unilateral ability to make possible goals, or to impose anti-goals? If the alternative for B, if he does not do as A tells him, is a less attractive job, or reduced likelihood of promotion, the category is 1(a) and A is B's supervisor. If B is an agricultural worker and the alternative is to be thrown out of his tied cottage, or if he is a soldier on a drill square and the alternative is some form of military punishment, the category is 1(b) and A is B's taskmaster.

For clarity, we have chosen extreme examples, in which the situation is likely to be interpreted in the same way by a majority of those who view it from the outside. In other situations, and particularly when viewed from the inside, interpretation may not always be so easy; and two B's *vis-à-vis* the same A may construe their relationships differently. The present aim is to conceptualize this particular distinction as clearly as possible in relatively straightforward situations, before trying to apply it in the more difficult context of teacher–learner relationships.

Even in this context, supervisor and taskmaster are not just sub-categories of teacher, for one person may tell another to learn something without helping him to learn it. This help may come from another source, or it may not be received at all. Someone who requires another to learn assigned portions of a text and subsequently to reproduce this in similar or modified form is not a teacher, but either a supervisor or a taskmaster. In my own school days, I had at least as many of the latter two categories as I did teachers. More accurately than I then realized, they were called 'schoolmasters'.

Very often, however, the same person does both. For the combined activity of deciding what someone else is to learn, and teaching it, the word 'school' (used as a verb) is appropriate. This accords with everyday usage, though few of those who use it have thought through its implications. The *Concise Oxford Dictionary* defines it as follows: 'discipline, bring under control, deliberately train or accustom to, induce to follow advice'. A power relationship is clearly implied, and the meaning is equally clear. It also brings sharply into question the common assumption that the terms 'schooling' and 'education' are interchangeable.

Though the distinction between categories 1(a) and 1(b) of the power relationship is important, to avoid multiplying our terminology the term 'school' will be used for both. A teacher who is in either of these relationships towards a learner will be called a 'schooler'. In such a situation, the learner may not intend to learn, or even know that he is being taught. Schooling does not only take place in schools, and a child's earliest schoolers are not professional teachers at all, but usually his own parents. Eating decently at table, toilet training, the use of 'please' and 'thank you', and the multiplicity of what constitutes acceptable social behaviour, are all examples of schooling, together with the many precautions and avoidances necessary for survival – how to cross roads safely, not going with strangers, not playing with matches. Reading and writing are important contributors for survival in most contemporary cultures, and the teaching of these is one of the earliest tasks of institutionalized schooling, often after parents have made a beginning.

These examples show that much of the schooling which children undergo is useful and necessary to them, and this is independent of whether they like it or not. A little boy who rides his tricycle in the road has to be taught not to do this, for his own survival. If his schemas do not include concepts such as being killed, or crippled, he will be unable to understand an explanation in these terms of why he must not. In any case the short-term and clearly realized attractions of tricycling on this wide smooth surface are likely to outweigh his distant and vague conceptualizations of these anti-goal states. So a parent might tell the child something he is able to realize, such as, that if he rode his tricycle on the road again, it would be taken away from him for the rest of the morning; and use his power relationship to enforce this. This comes into the category of necessary schooling, for the benefit of the child, whether or not he sees it that way at the time. What he is later required to learn at school, however, goes far beyond this, and we shall return to consider institutionalized schooling later.

The burden of the present section is not that schooling is a good or bad kind of teaching, or that it is either necessary or unnecessary. It may be any of these, in particular cases. The purpose has been to define the category in terms of the present model, so that we can analyse the effects of this and other such factors on the teacher–learner relationship.

15.5   In the second pair of categories, 2a and 2b, the goals of learning are set by the learner himself. If this is by his conscious intention, he is thus a student (as the term has already been defined). If, further, he freely seeks the help of a teacher, and the teacher agrees to give this help, the relationship is clearly so different from that of schooler (whether supervisor or taskmaster) that it must be distinguished by the use of a different name. For this I propose *mentor*.

Within a student–mentor relationship, the intention may take a wide variety of forms, loose or strict. The mentor may not intervene at all except when the student asks for his advice. He may go beyond this, actively encouraging the student to explore freely, to enlarge his self-awareness, to 'do his own thing'. A teacher of painting I used to know worked like this. Or he may set the student exercises to do, and correct and criticize these: thereby guiding the student along a path which has been carefully planned beforehand, as in Section 14.7. Sometimes he may look like a taskmaster, as when his students are athletes preparing for a competition. A schoolteacher was amazed to see some of his more unruly pupils, after school, smartly obeying every order from a drill sergeant. But these had joined the Cadet Force of their own free choice, and in the present formulation the sergeant was in the relationship of a mentor. Though this is somewhat different from the kind of image normally evoked by the word, nevertheless these boys were studying how to become cadet soldiers, and had freely sought the help, not perhaps of this particular teacher, but one of this category. And under these conditions the boys were willing to accept discipline of a kind which earlier in the day would have caused open rebellion.

This example will serve also as a reminder that the form of words used may often disguise whether the teacher–learner relationship is in category 1 or category 2. From the upper side of a power relationship, a request, however politely worded, has the force of a command. 'For homework I would like you to do Exercise 17.' And perhaps because within a mentor–student relationship it is less likely to give offence, a mentor's instructions need not be worded so delicately. '*Point* those toes', calls the ballet teacher sternly. 'Jane, you landed like a sack of potatoes'.

Schools

15.6 The third of the extrinsic factors which affect the teacher–learner relationship is whether or not it takes place within an institution existing for that purpose. If it does, then it is role-governed, since any organization is a structure of roles. Some of the questions which then arise are:

(i) Is the role of the learner elective or imposed?
(ii) Who chooses the goals of learning?
(iii) How do the participants conceive their own roles, and those of each other?
(iv) Do their role-models match?
(v) Is there role conflict?

There are of course many kinds of institution which exist for the purpose of teaching and learning. These go under names such as schools, colleges, universities, polytechnics, academies, and a few more. There is a particular group of these which is distinguished from the others by one major fact: that those who attend them as learners do so under compulsion. In most countries of the world, including the UK, other European countries, Scandinavia, the USA, Russia, China, school attendance is compulsory for children between certain ages, starting in the UK at 5 and continuing until 16. Since these children not only have to attend, but for many of them these schools are the only institutions of learning which they do attend, this particular learning situation is a major feature in their childhood and adolescence. So it is on the effect of this factor on the teacher–learner relationship that the present section will centre: as elsewhere, necessarily limiting ourselves (though with difficulty) to features which relate to intelligent learning and to the present theoretical model.

For these learners, question (i) is now answered: their role is imposed. When the children in form 2B go to their history lesson at 11.15 a.m., not they but the society in which they live has decided that they will be in school: a decision which is backed by the force of law. Question (ii) is also answered, for it is in this case the deputy head teacher (who draws up the timetable) who has decided that they will be doing history. And either their own teacher, or perhaps the senior history teacher who plans the syllabus, has decided that the lesson will be about the battle of Waterloo. At no stage have the children themselves made a choice.

For this role, which is an imposed role of learner in a school which they must attend, I propose the term *pupil*. This is but a slight narrowing and sharpening of its everyday meaning. The role partner is a *schoolteacher*. As the terms will used here, the emphasis is on the roles themselves, with a minimum of presuppositions about the effects on teaching and learning which result from putting persons into those roles. What effects these are is one of the questions now to be asked.

15.7 The first point at which the present model identifies a source of trouble is failure even to recognize that a situation of this kind requires to be role-governed. 'Sometimes the new teacher is shaken in his faith that good relations with individual children are essential. . . . One of the important factors in establishing good working relations with a class is simply time. Both teacher and pupil have to become familiar with each other's ways. It is rarely possible simply to jump in and expect things to go smoothly from the start.' (Hannam *et al.*, 1976, p. 98.) But on the present model, the relation between one schoolteacher and thirty to forty pupils at a time, perhaps a hundred pupils within a day, and the converse relation between one pupil and half a dozen teachers, with a changeover at the end of each school period, cannot by its nature be an individual and personal one. Unless it is role-governed, the individual and discretionary areas of behaviour expand into the whole of the situation. And since the situation is not of the pupils' own choosing, they may do almost anything. Hence the distressed surprise of a new teacher, ill prepared by his expectations for the situation which arose. 'things got out of hand in the lesson . . . they really got a riot built up. And that shouldn't have happened—according to what I have been told, the relationship should be such that when I turn my back they carry on doing what they should be doing.' (The same source, p. 97.)

15.8 If we now accept that the schoolteacher–pupil relationship must be role-governed if it is to succeed, it is hard to think of any imposed role which more directly affects the daily lives of so many persons at a formative stage of their lives than that of being a pupil. One might reasonably expect that the roles of schoolteacher and pupil would therefore be well defined and agreed: as are those of lawyers, medical doctors, police, firemen, and others whose roles vitally affect the welfare of others. The development of a clear understanding of these roles is an important part of preparation for their professions. But this is far from the case with those preparing to be schoolteachers. These conceive their functions in a wide variety of ways: to prepare children for life, to educate them, to initiate them into certain disciplines of study, to help them to pass examinations, to develop self-discipline in pupils, to develop the potential of each individual pupil.

Strong role expectations from outside also include arousing pupils' interest, 'motivating' them to learn. But as has been argued at length in Sections 8.13 and 8.14, this conception is confused and confusing; as becomes apparent if we replace 'teachers should motivate pupils to learn' by 'teachers should make their pupils want to learn'. To the extent that teachers accept this particular role expectation, they are adding to their problems. Overall, the conceptions of their own future roles which are held by students preparing to be teachers are closer to that of mentor than of schooler, and this is inconsistent with the facts of the situation.

For a teacher's role-conception of herself as a mentor implies that of the pupils as willing learners. The following teacher was unable to see the inconsistency between this conception and the relationship implied by the words 'make them . . .'. The restriction of her thinking to her own goals is also apparent. 'I thought my job was to make them think and make them reason . . . all those lovely ideas I have had, you see. I wanted to use them, especially if I had spent three hours the night before preparing some great beautiful thing.' (Hannam *et al.*, 1976, p. 62.)

In contrast, pupils' conception of their teacher's role is usually closer to that of a schooler: usually the taskmaster kind. 'Teacher's job is to control us and if you can't control us you are not a good teacher.' (The same source, p. 62.) Even those who are enjoying a lesson, and would accept a teacher in the role of supervisor, expect this. 'Miss, can't you shut them up? Get the slipper out and hit them' (The same source, p. 79.) Given a mixture of willing and unwilling pupils, she has to be a taskmaster for the latter to maintain reasonable working conditions for the former.

Eventually the teacher just quoted conformed to her pupils' expectations.

> I walked over and went wham, which isn't me, I hated doing it but it was just that I'd got so frustrated. It was the most effective thing I have ever done. They liked it and they respected me then and some of the others said 'We wanted to do work but because so-and-so was playing around we couldn't and when you hit him it stopped him and meant that we could do our work.' (The same source, p. 63.)

Though the foregoing quotations are from reports by teachers in their first year, the surveys cited at the beginning of the chapter are evidence that the problems are continuing ones. 'Those who stay on pay a high price for survival. . . . It seems to us that schools can and ought to be better places to work in than they commonly are.' (The same source, p. 221.) Can they? That the problems result from the situation in which they are placed rather than from the personalities of the individuals concerned is shown by our last extract from this particular collection.

> The youth tutor and I took a bunch of the kids away youth hostelling for the weekend. I was a little worried as the crowd going were most

of the rowdy fifth form lot. They were so different! They weren't being confined against their will in a classroom and they showed a degree of responsibility which, in school, would have been impossible for them. (The same source, p. 205.)

Survival in the classroom, for schoolteachers and pupils

15.9   The emotions aroused by the situation in which they find themselves can be intense for both teachers and pupils, as has been seen both from the surveys and from the verbatim quotations; and the use of the word 'survival' in a classroom context is increasing. Usually this is meant metaphorically, as in the answers of a group of teachers in their first term to an older teacher who asked them what was their main objective. They replied 'Just to survive'. (Sadler, 1977.) But not always. Under the headline 'Why teaching is a dying profession', the *Times Educational Supplement* recently published an article opening with the statement: 'Deaths among male teachers approaching the end of their careers have more than doubled in the past 10 years while the number qualifying for a breakdown pension has more than trebled.' (Hodges, 1976.)

The present model offers a clear explanation for the emotions involved, and shows that they are indeed concerned with survival in ways which are not metaphorical, but which relate to survival both in a person's inner reality and in actuality.

For many schoolteachers now find themselves in the position which was described in Section 6.6. Despite their best efforts, they fail to achieve the goal states which they have set for their appropriate operands; in this case, learning-goals for their pupils. Many of these pupils do not even perform the kinds of action which would begin to take them towards the learning goals chosen by the teacher, such as paying attention to the lesson, doing work which is set, refraining from conversations with other pupils which are irrelevant to what is being taught. In such conditions a teacher is no longer viable as such, and within his own inner reality, with respect to his own self-conception as a teacher, he is failing to survive. The feelings which result have been substantiated from many sources, of which I have given only a few. They are those summarized in Section 6.6 as 'ranging from loss of confidence to personal disaster'.

On the child's side, to the extent that he does try to satisfy the teacher's expectations of him as a pupil, he is putting himself emotionally at risk and this also is directly predictable from our model.

A domain is that region within a universe of discourse where a director system can function; that is, enable a person to reach the set goal (provided the task is also within his physical capacity, which in the cases we are considering it is). Within his domain, a person feels confident and secure; outside it, he feels frustrated, or anxious, or both.

In a competitive situation, the choice of universe of discourse may have a major influence on the outcome. Suppose that A is good at chess but weak at backgammon, whereas B is weak at chess and good at backgammon. If the game is chess, A will feel confident, for he is within his domain and B is not; and vice versa. Thus the one who chooses the game can be confident of winning.

In school lessons, the universe of discourse is always chosen by the teacher; and likewise the starting points within that universe. So the teacher is always well within his domain, the pupils in the frontier zone of theirs, or outside it. As long as they have to accept the teacher's choice of universe, the pupils are thus liable to find themselves outside their own domains.

> everyone seemed in a relaxed frame of mind, so I said ' . . . What do you think what goes through your mind, when the teacher asks you a question and you don't know the answer?' It was a bombshell . . . all said the same thing, that when a teacher asked them a question and they didn't know the answer they were scared half to death. I was flabbergasted—to find this in a school which people think of as progressive; which does its best not to put pressure on little children . . . which tries to keep children from feeling that they're in some kind of race. (Holt, 1965.)

A learner is of necessity, for much of the time, outside his domain at the delta-one level, or in its frontier zone. His consequent insecurity needs to be compensated by feelings of security from another source, and this is part of the contribution of a teacher to the joint learning task. This is easy in a student–mentor situation; much more difficult, perhaps impossible, in a pupil–schooler situation. The first pair may be compared to a learner-swimmer who has entered the water of his own free choice because he wants to learn to swim, and who ventures out of his depth on his own initiative with a good swimmer keeping close beside him. The second pair is like a learner-swimmer who has been forcibly taken into the water by someone who himself likes swimming and is good at it, and considers it to be for the pupil's own good that he too should learn to swim. It will make little difference that the teacher may be a nice fellow, speaks reassuringly, and offers help in learning to swim. The pupil wants to be on dry land, in some situation of his own choice, not another's. If he had wanted to learn to swim, he'd have asked. And it is these situational factors which are likely to dominate pupils' emotional reactions, even in schools such as that which John Holt has described.

Small wonder that much of a schoolteacher's effort has to be spent in preventing his pupils from scrambling out of the water, so to speak: from changing the universe of discourse to others in which they are as expert as the teacher, perhaps more so.

The authority of a teacher

15.10   Unless the learner accepts the authority of a teacher, the teacher cannot function as such. But unless both teacher and learner know and indeed agree which kind (or kinds) of authority are involved, there is no less likelihood of failure.

Paterson (1966) distinguishes three kinds of authority. These categories are quite general, and are particularly relevant to the teacher–learner situation. He calls them: *structural authority*, which is authority of position; *sapiential authority*, which is authority of knowledge; and *personal authority*, which derives from an individual's personality and its relationship to the goals of the enterprise and to the personalities of the others in the group.

In the teaching situation as in general, these three kinds of authority have this in common: that to say 'B accepts A's authority' is equivalent to saying that B sets his goal states as he is told to do by A. But between the three, there are important differences in B's reasons for doing so, and in the present section we shall consider what these reasons are.

Structural authority, or positional authority as it may also be called, derives from a role. This may be within a role pair, or within a small or large organization. A power relationship is not necessarily implied, provided that the role is occupied by mutual agreement. Thus while they are aboard a bus, passengers accept the positional authority of the driver—though only in matters belonging to his role. But a power relationship is likely to depend on position to sustain it: the powers of a magistrate, of a policeman directing traffic, of a cabinet minister or senator, of a sergeant-major, depend on the back-up of a sufficient number of the others in that society to ensure that his orders are obeyed. And when a person is no longer in the position, he is out of power.

Authority of knowledge remains quiescent until another person has need of it, and requests it: which puts it in sharp contrast to positional authority. A doctor, or a lawyer, or a television engineer, stays out of our lives until we need expertise which he has and we have not. And even when we have asked for his help, we are free to use it or not: to undergo the operation, to sign the contract, to replace our old television set with a new one, or not to do so. If we do reject their advice, such persons might then ask us to go elsewhere for their particular form of expertise. But this is part of the reciprocal nature of the relationship: one needs not ask for authorative advice if he does not want it, and the other need not give it (or continue to give it) if he construes its rejection as diminishing his authority in this sphere.

Personal authority is much the hardest to define. Paterson calls attention to the suitability of particular kinds of personality for particular roles. It is also related to strength of personality, but is not the same. Charm, 'personal magnetism', charisma, all increase a person's power to influence and persuade others: but someone can have personal authority without these, and he can have all of these without personal authority. It seems to derive from an intuitive recognition of an individual's worth as a person, appreciation and respect for what one perceives, even in some cases veneration. But while it remains intuitive it remains inaccessible to reality testing, and so it is open to error. At its most authentic, personal authority has been a quality of the great leaders of history, moral, artistic, intellectual: possibly too in other fields such as political and military. But a person with a deep conviction of his own merits may induce others to accept this valuation of himself; and this conviction may be supported by lack of the self-criticism which would favour the development of genuine merits. So the same characteristics which make personal authority the hardest to define also make it the hardest to recognize surely.

Knowledge in itself, and positional authority, are by no means incompatible. A person's expertise in appropriate areas may well be one reason for giving him a particular position of authority. But once this has been done, the possibility of role confusion is introduced: for positional authority is a type 1 relationship, while authority of knowledge a type 2 relationship. As was explained in Section 8.6, instructions deriving from positional authority, however politely worded, are in fact orders; whereas instructions deriving from the authority of knowledge, however bluntly given, are advice. Paterson gives a clear example of this confusion in a management situation. The general manager of a company insisted that he had never given an order. Referring to a particular instance, Paterson asked him 'Wasn't that an order?' 'No!' the manager replied. 'I merely told him what I wanted done'. But as Paterson goes on to comment, 'There was no question that when the general manager said to the production superintendent that he wanted something done, the superintendent reacted to this communication as a command. If the production superintendent had not interpreted this communication as a command and had chosen to act in a way that the manager did not want, there would have been trouble of some kind.'

Another difference of importance for our present analysis, which Paterson also emphasizes strongly, is that positional authority is not vested in an individual as himself but in a position: which is to say, a role within an organization, large or small. Authority of knowledge, in contrast, is vested in the person himself by virtue of his own knowledge.

15.11 The authority of a teacher can thus be either that of position or of knowledge, and we have seen that these kinds are not only different but largely incompatible. A teacher whose authority is positional is a schooler. His relationship with his pupils is a type 1 relationship, for they are not there of their own choice. Their role is imposed, not elective. The teacher commands, the pupils obey. In contrast, a teacher whose authority is that of his own personal knowledge is a mentor. His students seek his help of their own free choice, within a type 2 (co-operative) relationship.

The problems of a *schoolteacher* arise largely from the fact that he has to try to be both, with resulting role conflict and role confusion. Situationally he is a schooler, and this too is how pupils for the most part conceive his role. But what he wants to be is a mentor. This, at least, is the conception of a teacher which leads most new entrants to join the profession. Role confusion results from the difference between the teacher role as conceived by would-be mentors on the one hand, and by pupils and disillusioned colleagues on the other. Role conflict results from his trying to be both mentor and schooler together.

A further source of anxiety has been identified, in discussion with probationary teachers, as what may be called the 'grey area'. Where behaviour is role-governed, there is always some discretionary area, which may be small or large. But all of a person's behaviour in any given situation should be identifiable as one or the other. That which is not role-governed should be truly discretionary.

It has already been argued (Section 15.7) that a schoolteacher's behaviour needs to be much more clearly role-governed, simply because so many different teachers have to interact with so many different pupils. This lack of role definition leaves a large 'grey area' which these new teachers felt to be neither role-governed nor discretionary. If part of their behaviour was determined by the role (such as calling the register), at least they knew what they were required to do. If it was truly discretionary, then they were free to use their own initiative and intelligence. But within these grey areas, they felt that they were not free to use their own discretion; yet it was not clear to them what they were supposed to do. They were in a situation in which others had expectations of them, and in which it mattered whether or not they fulfilled these expectations. Yet they did not know just what these expectations were. This added yet another source of anxiety.

15.12 The power attached to positional authority is given to a person by the organization as a whole, and possibly also by the wider society within which the organization exists. For example, a police sergeant has structural authority both from his rank within the police force and from the authority given to the force as a whole by parliament. If a schoolteacher's role is to be that of schooler, whether supervisor or taskmaster, then he needs to have sufficient power to fulfil this role. As a supervisor (category 1(a)), this would mean that there were important goals of the pupil which the teacher could help the pupil to reach. For the more academically able pupils, these could be examination successes leading to better career prospects, possibly via higher education. For the others, however, there is little that the schoolteacher offers which the pupils genuinely want to learn—that is, which they would learn of their own free choice. This puts the teacher into the role of a taskmaster; but without sufficient power to enforce his commands effectively, as has been argued at much greater length than here by Musgrove (1971).

In the schoolteacher–pupil relationship, pupils may *consent*, or *submit*, or *rebel*, according to whether they construe their teacher's role as that which we have described as a supervisor, as a strong taskmaster, or as a weak taskmaster. And in a class of wide-ranging abilities and background, there are likely to be found pupils who behave in each of these three ways, and who need different treatments perhaps almost simultaneously. What is not possible within the imposed role of a pupil is whole-hearted co-operation; and in some ways this is the saddest result of all.

Even in a role-relationship which on one side is imposed, there are usually rights and obligations on both sides. If a pupil has, or seems to himself to have, mostly obligations and few rights, then he is less likely to consent than if (as he sees it) there is a fair exchange of rights and obligations. For a minority group, teaching which makes possible academic success for the pupil on one side, good behaviour and reasonably diligent work by the pupil on the other, seem to provide such an exchange. For another minority group, sport provides a similar exchange. But in many schools as they are today, the majority of children have little that they perceive as rights worth having, and in exchange for which they are willing to accept obligations.

A fair objection to the foregoing paragraph would be that pupils today certainly do have rights, though mostly of a negative kind. For example, they are no longer liable to be stood in the corner, or caned just for giving a wrong answer. Such rights cannot, however, appear as anything very substantial to pupils who do not realize that fifty years ago these were common occurrences. Again, the right to be at school rather than in a factory or a coal mine can be seen as no small benefit by those who take a historical perspective. But it can hardly be perceived as such by pupils who have no realization of the evils of child labour.

15.13 The present state of affairs in many of our schools must not be regarded as an unavoidable consequence of the institutionalizing of learning. For learning as for many other activities, an institutional setting can offer many advantages, including continuity, the availability of shared resources too expensive for individuals alone, the attraction of funds from outside, specialization and the exchange of expertise, and the company of those with similar interests. An institution for learning can be highly positive-sum for those who participate, and can help to actualize for the community as a whole the potential provided by human intelligence. Even as things are now, there are schools where pupils receive more good than harm.

So having identified some, at least, of the causes of the present predicament, the next step is clearly to explore possible alternatives. Given that learning is a natural activity, particularly vigorous in children but operative at all ages, it begins to seem obvious that, as Einstein said in the passage already quoted, 'It is a very grave mistake to think that the enjoyment of seeing and searching can be promoted by means of coercion and a sense of duty.' What the learner most needs is *opportunities for accelerated learning*, as was emphasized in Section 14.2; and these an institution for learning is particularly well able to provide. At such an institution, teachers are but one kind of resource among others such as libraries, studios, workshops, laboratories, sports centres, depending on what is to be learnt. But the most important factor is freedom: freedom of the learner to choose what he wants to learn, and freely to seek the help of the institutions, including that of its teachers, to enable him to learn it quicker, better, or in some cases to learn it at all. This in my view implies also freedom not to do so. Though many will disagree with the last, in the present model compulsion forces the teacher–learner relationship from type 2 to type 1, and is the root from which all the other problems stem. Wars are fought for freedom, and I believe this to be the underlying cause of most of the small 'guerilla wars' which go on in many schools today.

If this view is accepted, it is also reasonable for both the institution and its individual teachers to require of a learner that if he chooses to learn a particular topic, he follows a planned course of instruction, performs certain tasks, and fulfils certain other obligations in exchange for the right to receive their help. If he finds the benefits provided not to his liking, he must be free to withdraw: not necessarily unconditionally, but under conditions known in advance and accepted as part of the obligations.

Under such conditions, the relationship between a learner and a teacher is clearly that between student and mentor. Co-operation in learning is by its nature more difficult than one in which the operand is external, and is open to direct perception by both; as was explained in Section 14.3. It therefore needs the most favourable conditions possible if it is to succeed, and a mentor–student relationship offers hope of providing these. For the only person who has direct access to the operand is the student, since the operand is a delta-one system within himself. The only person who can directly set the learning goal is also the student. So what is required is a situation in which the student's delta-two system gets whatever help it needs to perform the function which ultimately only it can do: for it is only the student's own delta-two system which can act on his delta-one.

Once the learner comes to the teacher, everything else falls into place. The student wants the help offered by the mentor, and from what is offered he takes what he needs. That which he is not yet ready for and cannot immediately use, he should be free to leave on one side till he is ready for it. On the side of the mentor, his task is to teach, and encourage. It is not necessary for him to persuade or coerce. If a student is progressing well unaided, and is not likely to fall into bad habits which will later be hard to change, the mentor may do well not to intervene: for there are times when the least teaching is the best teaching, and simply to know that help is available when needed is the best help.

The benefits of the foregoing relationship apply equally whether it is outside or within an institution. But under the right conditions, an institution can offer the additional advantages which have already been described; and these can apply to the mentors as well as to the students.

Such conditions may sound utopian; but they can and do exist in principle, since universities, colleges, polytechnics, academies of music, schools of art and design, are attended voluntarily by learners over the age of compulsory school attendance. For some students they exist also in reality. But to the extent that learners, and perhaps their teachers, also carry over attitudes and role conceptions from their long periods of compulsory schooling, the mentor–student relationship is distortingly construed in terms of earlier schooler–pupil relationship, and some of its benefits are lost. This is one of the reasons why a 'mature student', one who returns to college or university after a period during which he has had time to shed some of his conceptions about institutionalized learning, is often such a joy to teach.

Education as a combination of schooling and entelechy

15.14 The terms 'education' and 'schooling' are used by many as if they meant the same. This has been partly the result of more liberal intentions towards the children involved: who nevertheless remain in a schooling situation, as shown by the foregoing analysis.

One result is that the term education itself has become associated with all the present defects of schooling. Another is that what goes on in schools is now assessed relative to people's conceptions of education, which is usually thought of as something rather splendid though ill defined. Because schooling is not education, it falls short of people's expectations by more than it would if it were judged simply as schooling. So schooling and education, whatever these may be, both suffer by the confusion.

It is easier to say what one means by schooling than by education. Schooling has here been defined as the combined activity of deciding what someone else is to learn, and teaching it, within a power relationship. Power is not necessarily misused, and the examples given towards the end of Section 15.4 have already made the point that some of the schooling which children undergo, both at home and in schools, is useful and necessary. It is equally clear that there is schooling which does nobody any good, the learners or their teachers. In the present section we shall distinguish between these kinds of schooling, and also make a start with trying to distinguish between schooling and education.

The chief characteristic of schooling is the goal-directed activity of the teacher, not that of the learner. On the side of the teacher, it is intentional; while the learner may not even be conscious that it is happening. Its overall purpose is to make sure that children learn what is necessary for them to fit into society while they are growing up, and when they are adult.

They soon learn that certain things are expected and perhaps required of them, including obedience to their parents, and to others who at the time are looking after them. They learn what is acceptable behaviour and what is not, both as sharply defined by law and as generally accepted within the community. In due course they are sent to school, where the goals set by their schoolteachers are usually consistent with those of their parents. Parents want their children to be successful in life, and in particular to become able to provide for their own food, clothing, and shelter by earning a living when they are grown up. Talcott Parsons also points out that the school is one of the agencies by which children are prepared for their adult roles. 'That is to say, it is an agency through which individual personalities are trained to be motivationally and technically adequate to the performance of adult roles.' (Parsons, 1959.)

A child is not consulted about any of this. His role as a learner is an imposed role, and the authority of the schoolteacher over him is positional authority. It will, however, make a difference whether children (albeit unconsciously) perceive their teachers as in category 1(a) or 1(b); as deriving their power from the ability to make possible goals, or to impose anti-goals. In the former case, they are more likely to consent to their schooling; the more so if the values and expectations of their supervisors match well with those of their families. In the latter case they will perceive their teachers as taskmasters, taking power from anti-goals such as work to be repeated, detention, possibly ridicule. Obedience to the commands of these will be construed as submission.

As has already been pointed out, teachers are under-powered for their roles of taskmasters relative to what is expected of them in the way of keeping pupils diligently at their tasks. So it is hardly surprising that teachers try so far as possible to put themselves into the category of supervisor, and to gain their pupil's consent by persuading them of the benefits they can get from learning what they are set. This may be true in the case of the brighter pupils, for whom examination successes leading to higher education and a career in a profession, business, or industry, are a genuine possibility. But for the many, it is an exaggeration of the facts of the situation which in other conditions would be open to accusations of dishonesty.

Accepting that some schooling is both useful and necessary, it does now seem clear that it will be best for learner and teacher alike if what is taught under these conditions is restricted to the minimum of that which the learner must learn, for his own good and that of society; which in the absence of schooling he might not learn; and which therefore must not be left to the free choice of the learner. Just what comes into this category is still open to debate; and it is a debate for another time, since this is a book about intelligence, not about schooling. But the moment that this criterion is applied, it becomes obvious that much more is being taught in situations of compulsory schooling than can possibly be justified in this way. Hodgkin (1977) suggests that the major part of schooling (*as here defined*) might well be completed by the age of twelve. This would fit it into the pre-adolescent period of children's development, when they are biologically more dependent and thus more amenable to schooling. This is certainly not to imply that children up to twelve should receive only schooling, since their appetite for self-chosen learning is also very active during this period. Nor is it implied that they should be free to leave school at this age, in the sense of no longer attending any institution for learning. This is a different and more complex question altogether, since there is still need of some schooling during adolescence. But this might well be regarded as a period during which the learner's role becomes predominantly that of a student. It should also be noted that this suggestion refers to the roles of these young persons as learners. As members of the school community they are subject to positional authority, in the same way as members of any other organization.

15.15 While there are some who use the term 'education' interchangeably with 'schooling', or as a more honorific name for it, there are others who use these terms in contradistinction. For the latter, education means everything that ought to happen in schools, but usually does not: or something of this kind.

I have much sympathy with the latter viewpoint, and for some time used these terms in a similar way myself, until I found that it led to two difficulties. The first was failure of communication with those who use 'education' in the first way, who are still in a majority. If one is trying to present a new viewpoint to these, it is not a good beginning to try to attach a different meaning to a word for which they already have a well-established meaning, whether one thinks this to be a good meaning or not.

The second difficulty arose out of the earlier emphasis that self-chosen learning, which is one of the main criteria for education in the second sense, does not necessarily require formal teaching, nor even teaching at all. So the verb 'educate' in this sense has to be intransitive. We would have to say that a child engaged in serious play, a university student in a library, a research scientist alone in his laboratory, were all *educating*. To which the vast majority would ask 'educating whom?' since as a verb 'educate' is currently used only transitively. It would not be sufficient to say that the university student (and the others) is educating himself, because this is still a transitive verb used reflexively. And the essence of my present position is that this other activity, which at present lacks a name, is essentially not something which someone does *to* anyone else, or even *to* himself. He just does it, alone or in company, possibly with help from a teacher; but at the centre of the activity is the learner, and it can sometimes be a lonely activity, taking him away from and possibly ahead of his fellows.

To convey this new emphasis (for it can hardly be claimed as an entirely new idea) it eventually seemed best to use a word which was either altogether new, or at least unusual enough to call attention to the fact that one was saying something different. After a search, I now propose *entelechy*. My *Concise Oxford Dictionary* gives for this: 'n. (philos.). Realization, the becoming or being actual of what was potential . . . '. The word is not widely used outside philosophy, and the dictionary meaning as quoted (leaving out some of the alternatives given) is sufficiently open to allow further development as and when we discover more clearly what meaning we want to attach.

For it is at present easier to say what education (in the widest sense) is not,

284

than what it is. For a longish period I would have joined those who would say that it is not schooling. The introduction of the concept of entelechy, even i its present rudimentary form, now makes possible an alternative formulatioι which not only now seems to me more accurate, but also reconciles the tw opposing camps. Certainly education is not *only* schooling, and if it is onΓ schooling it is not education. Likewise, if it includes much unnecessar schooling, and little or no opportunity for entelechy, it is not education. Bι some parts of schooling are necessary prerequisites for entelechy. On thι positive side, this includes (in our own society) learning to read and writι And on the negative side, it involves keeping out of trouble—learning whɑ one is required to do and not to do, to be left free to get on with one's ow entelechy. So I now include schooling as a necessary contribution t education in its wider meaning.

The formulation which I now offer, based on the present model and iι application to the present problems in our schools, is this. *Education is αι appropriate combination of schooling and entelechy.* This still leaves opε several questions. One of these is 'What is an appropriate combination?', an beyond a strong contention that it involves much less schooling and mucι more entelechy than it does at present, I must postpone further debate on thι to another occasion. Entelechy, on the other hand, will be one of the mai topics of the next (and last) chapter of the present book. If it is to be regarde as the more important part of education, however, it would be unsatisfactor to end this chapter without a brief preliminary formulation.

Schooling properly includes that which children need to know for thι survival of themselves and of the society in which they must take their plaɑ when adult, and which cannot be left to their own inclination whether or nɑ they learn. It relates to the first part of what living involves—just survivinɡ Entelechy belongs to the other half of what life is about—finding out what w are here for, finding our own goals in life, finding how to achieve these, an trying to do so. It is a quest for whatever makes life worth living.

What comes next?

15.16   In a discussion of the present chapter with a group of experience teachers, one of them said: 'This speaks directly to me as a teacher. This ι how it is.' On this there was general agreement. But of Chapter 16, he weι on to say:[5] 'The book as a whole is like a fault diagnosis chart. I'm still lookinɡ for the end of it, "Take such and such a spanner and do this". That's what I'ι still looking for, and when it didn't come I was thinking "Where is it? It muɩ be in here somewhere".' Another, agreeing, said: "I thought it [Chapter 1€ would be very much a pulling together and spelling out in clear terms for thι layman the implications for educational practice on the shop floor. Obviousl the implications are here.' A third, who had particularly enjoyed Chapter 1€ said that there had already been a lot of hints about wider horizons, and thι was what Chapter 16 was about. A fourth, agreeing, said 'I think what sums it up for me is the sub-heading of 16.2, "From survival to being".'

In the ensuing discussion, it was generally agreed, first, that readers should be prepared for a change of direction in Chapter 16; and second, that some kind of answer was needed for the many others who would ask: 'So what do we do?' The first has I hope now been done, and the rest of the present section will be a response to the latter.

To answer that question adequately would require, not a closing chapter to this book, but another book, and one of a different kind. The present book provides a theoretical basis for the kind of changes which need to be made; but the working out of these in detail, and the bringing of them into effect, will require the co-operative effort of a group of people bringing to bear a variety of experience and expertise.

There are, nevertheless, a number of implications of the new model which can be derived immediately. One consequence of reading this book, and particularly Chapter 14 and this chapter, is that a teacher construes events in the classroom differently. He realizes more clearly what is going on, and even if he cannot yet do much to change it, this will still make a great difference to the effect on his self-image—to survival in his inner reality. And until people realize situations within an appropriate model, they have not taken the first step towards successful action.

Another benefit of having an appropriate theory is that it enables a person to penetrate noise, in the technical sense. He can see through a confusion of detail to identify whatever underlies these events, and is thus able to recognize and deal with causes rather than effects. This is one of the marks of an expert. He does not just react to events as he is overtaken by them, but he is ahead of events in his own thinking, and is thus much better able to control them.

Given that an increasing number of voices are calling for change, a unified educational theory will enable these as individuals to perceive more clearly, and perhaps to begin to agree, what changes are required and how to bring them about. And one thing the present model emphasizes is that until teachers are using a shared conceptual structure, they will not be able to co-operate with any measure of success. At present the efforts of individuals do not combine in a positive-sum relationship, and each classroom teacher fights a lonely battle. A shared conceptual structure is also needed so that teachers can speak with one professional voice to politicians (local and national), administrators, and the many who consider themselves as experts on education.

It is towards this state of affairs that the present model is offered as a contribution—towards provision of the missing foundations, rather than efforts to shore up a shaky edifice. And to the question, fairly asked, 'Which spanner do I apply where?', it offers the answer: 'In your job, instrumental understanding is not enough; so even if I knew the answer I would be reluctant to give it you. Relational understanding is what I am offering, and with the help of this you can become master of your profession.'

15.17 In this chapter, attention has been focused on factors which are extrinsic to the learner–teacher relationship as such, but which have important effects on this relationship, and on the learning which takes place within it.

(i) Factors which have been discussed include:
  (a) *the intention or otherwise of the learner*;
  (b) *whether the relationship is a power relationship or a co-operative relationship*;
  (c) *whether or not the relationship is within an institution, and is therefore role-governed.*
(ii) *Teaching within a power relationship is called schooling. If it is also institutionalized, the learners occupy the imposed role of pupil; and the schoolteachers can be either supervisors or taskmasters.*
(iii) *Within a co-operative relationship, in which the learner freely seeks the help of a teacher, the participants are called student and mentor, whether or not this takes place within an institution.*
(iv) *Some of the stresses which are experienced by both teachers and pupils result, firstly, from failure clearly to realize that the relationship needs to be role-governed to a much greater degree than it is. Secondly, from role confusion and role conflict between the possible roles of learner and teacher.*
(v) *A related source of a schoolteacher's problems is lack of acceptance by pupils of his authority. This authority may be of position, of knowledge, or personal. But he is given insufficient power for effective positional authority; his authority of knowledge is unwanted by many pupils while personal authority is not possessed by all.*
(vi) *Until professional teachers share a unified educational theory, they will find it very difficult to co-operate successfully in bringing about the changes which are needed in our educational institutions.*

Notes for Chapter 15

1. *The Observer*, 30 October 1977.
2. Miss Audrey Jackson, formerly head teacher of Leeds Girls' High School. Her full report is published by Leeds University Department of Psychology (Counselling and Career Development Unit).
3. All the passages quoted are from the section by Jack Dunham: 'Stress Situations and Responses'.
4. Quoted in the *Times Educational Supplement*, 28 October 1977, in an abstract by Mike Duckenfield.
5. This and the following quotations are transcribed verbatim from a tape recording of the seminars.

CHAPTER 16

Beyond Survival

16.1 The new theoretical model of intelligence offered in this book has throughout been closely related to survival. This emphasis was necessary to explain how our own species has outdistanced all others on this planet in the ceaseless competition for survival, by an evolutionary breakthrough: the invisible asset of adaptability. It was also necessary in order to push the concept of intelligence beyond the boundaries within which it has become confined by 'I.Q.' and an overemphasis on measurement. But this emphasis on survival may itself be seen as too narrow by some; and as early as section 4.8 the question was asked: 'Is this all that life is about?'

What is the purpose of life—not just of our own lives, but of all life—is clearly a question far outside the realm of the present book. On the other hand, an individual life which has no purpose beyond that of day-to-day existence, and the accumulation of material wealth, would be thought by many (including myself) to be incomplete. For such persons, to find some goal in life, or better still to find what seems to be the right goal for one's own particular life, is part of what makes life itself meaningful.

The aim of this chapter is not to try to answer questions such as these; but rather, to offer some suggestions as to possible directions of thinking in which answers might be found. In so doing, however, it is important for me to make clear that these suggestions have a different status from the rest of the book. The fifteen chapters preceding this are closely related to existing knowledge, some of it specialist, but much of it easily available to everyday observation and reflection. A new synthesis has been offered, and sometimes new conclusions have been drawn; but in these I have tried not to go beyond what is capable of being verified by reality testing in one or more of the three modes which have been described. Much of the present chapter does go beyond these limits. It is not within the traditional scientific approach exemplified by the natural sciences, nor within the expanded scientific approach which the present model suggests as necessary for the life sciences. This does not imply any disparagement of the scientific approach, which I believe to be one of man's major achievements. It is simply to accept that there are other approaches which are also valuable. And the present model itself has stressed the importance of creative imagination, both as a necessary part of scientific thinking and also in its own right. Where imagination explores, science may afterwards follow.

From Survival to Being

16.2 The three modes of reality construction which have been distinguished from Chapter 4 onwards, and which are summarized in Table 7 (Chapter 10) relate to survival in three different aspects. Mode (i) relates directly to survival in actuality—in the physical world. Mode (ii) relates to survival by co-operation with others, and also to survival as a co-operator with others—to survival socially. But we also have to survive in our own inner realities. We have to survive in our physical bodies, and with our fellow humans; but there is also an inner self which may need seclusion to find itself. Survival in all three of these ways needs a balance between action and reflection, company and solitude.

Though different, these three aspects of survival are interdependent. In getting the bare necessities of life, we face one set of difficulties which are intrinsic in our physical environment—heat and cold, drought and flood, seasonal but perishable food supply; and another set of difficulties arising out of the fact that we strive for these necessities in competition with other species. Co-operation has been a major factor of our success in overcoming these difficulties, and in achieving our present degree of mastery over both our physical environment, and other species. And long-term co-operation, as we saw in Chapter 8, requires a shared schema. The realms within individuals' inner realities which determine how they perceive actuality, and from which they make plans to deal with it, have to match if long-term co-operation is to be possible. It is partly with bringing about this match that mode (ii) reality construction is concerned.

But not entirely. The building and testing of knowledge about actuality is a slow and difficult process; so co-operation in the building up of these shared schemas, as well as in action based on them, has been a major factor of our success in science and technology. Thus, both for individuals and collectively there is a shift inwards of the operands and goals of activity. From trying to bring about goal states in actuality which contribute to our survival, we move to seeking knowledge whereby to improve those director systems which function in actuality. From the activities of delta-one systems directing physical operations, we move to the activities of delta-two systems directing delta-one systems towards states of better functioning, and having enlarged domains. This opens the door to the pursuit of knowledge for its own sake; and though it does not follow that everyone will go through this door, many have done so.

This path constitutes an open-ended goal state. The more we know, the more we realize that we don't know. This is a natural consequence of the expansion of our schemas: for as was pointed out in Section 10.2, some problems do not exist for us until they can be realized by one of our available schemas. Until we know that raising the temperature of a liquid increases the amount of a solid which can be dissolved, we do not begin to wonder why this has the opposite effect on gases. And the search for an explanation entails a considerable expansion of our knowledge about how molecules of the same and different substances arrange themselves in space, in relation to each other; of the inter-molecular forces which determine these arrangements; and of the kinetic theory by which the nature and effects of heat are explained. But this is the stuff of which the physical universe is made. From asking questions like 'Why does hot tea dissolve sugar more easily than cold tea, whereas warm fizzy drinks lose much of their fizz?, we may progress to answers which themselves pose further questions, but which at every stage reveal more general regularities in our physical environment. And not just our local environment: for so far as we can tell, these same regularities are to be found in the remotest parts of the universe to which the range of our sensors can be extended.

Where does this knowledge, when we have got it, have its existence? The position taken, from Chapter 3 onward, is that it exists in our inner realities. So by the expansion and deepening of our knowledge of the universe, in an important respect we are expanding and deepening our inner selves. The road outwards also leads inwards; and by very different paths, science and mysticism converge towards a common goal: that of understanding the universe. The scientist's path leads through wanting to 'be able to', based on 'knowing how', towards ever expanding 'knowing that'. This path can be retraced, and many increases in scientific knowledge lead quickly to new technology. The mystic's path, in contrast, is by an expansion of inner consciousness, leading (if he is successful) to an understanding of the universe by direct apprehension. This path is not retraceable in the same way as that of the scientist; for though his consciousness returns to that of everyday life, the mystic is not able to carry back the knowledge he had during his state of self-transcendence easily, if at all. Nevertheless, some of the greatest scientists perceive the relationship as a close one. Here again is Einstein:[1] 'The most beautiful emotion we can experience is the mystical. It is the sower of all true art and science.'

I do not propose here to develop this particular line of thinking more than one step further, since this has been done elsewhere by those better able to do so than myself.[2] My purpose in introducing it has been to suggest one possible direction of thinking which is consistent with the present model, and which can be pursued in distinguished company.[3] This leads from the concept of *surviving*, as existing continuously over a period of time, to that of *being*, as having existence independent of time.[4] It is this state of being which is experienced in its purest and most intense form by mystics, and in this experience their consciousness turns away from actuality, deeply and extensively into their inner reality. Nevertheless, changes may thereby take place which are favourable to their behaviour in actuality. William James writes 'Yet the unseen region in question is not merely ideal, for it produces effects in this world. When we commune with it, work is actually done upon our finite personality, for we are turned into new men, and consequences in the way of conduct follow in the natural world upon our regenerative change.' (James, 1901–2) Three-quarters of a century later, this same view is supported by the adherents of transcendental meditation.

Intelligence as creative and self-creative

16.3 Intelligence is creative both in actuality, and within our inner realities: and creation must take place first in thought before it can be manifest in action. When these have happened, the person is no longer quite the same as he was before. Edison after his successful conception and actualization of the phonograph, Michelangelo after he had finished carving his David, a seven-year-old after he had written his first book[5]—these were no longer quite the same persons as they had been before. In creating these new objects in actuality, each of these also brought into existence a self which a short time before had not been able to do so. I am also indebted to a painter friend[6] for bringing to my awareness the interaction—he called it a dialogue—between the artist and his painting. What he has painted so far speaks back to him, so that the artist both shapes and is shaped by his painting. Such an interaction is characteristic of many creative activities, inventive as well as artistic. Sometimes the whole conception is formed, virtually complete in the mind, before being actualized; sometimes it proceeds by stages, the actualization of each stage providing a new focus and support for mental activity (not necessarily conscious) preliminary to the next.

Activities of this kind are importantly different from the performance of routine plans, or even the constructing and putting into action of new plans from existing schemas. One difference is that which has already been described, for the performance of that which he can already do leaves the person himself no different from what he was before. Another is in the greater risk taken, for until the thing has been done, the person does not know if he can do it. If he cannot, then at best he has lost an investment of time and effort which may be considerable; and at worst he feels in this respect a failure: his self-image is diminished.

Another sense in which intelligence is self-creative results from the fact that each concept is a potential growing point for the schema of which it forms part: for it sensitizes its possessor to new regularities in actuality. Beyond this, a schema may suggest further questions to be put to actuality, and thus be an agent of its own further expansion. This is not the case for sub-intelligent forms of learning, such as habit learning. A schema, itself the product of intelligent learning, thus increases a person's ability for further intelligent learning in that realm of thought. And by assimilation to itself, a schema extends to the newly learnt knowledge those qualities of internal organization which have been distinguished as also characterizing intelligence. These were described at length in Chapters 10, 11, and 12.

16.4 The close relevance of intelligent learning, as here described, to *self-actualization* as it has been conceived by Maslow, is well shown by the following passage.

> So-called learning theory in this country has based itself almost entirely on deficit-motivation with goal objects usually external to the organism, i.e. learning the best way to satisfy a need. For this reason, among others, our psychology of learning is a limited body of knowledge, useful only in small areas of life and of real interest only to other 'learning theorists'. This is of little help in solving the problem of growth and self-actualization. Here the techniques of repeatedly acquiring from the outside world satisfactions of motivational deficiencies are much less needed. Associative learning and canalisations give way more to perceptual learning, to the increase of insight and understanding, to knowledge of self and the steady growth of personality, i.e. increased synergy, integration and inner consistency. (Maslow, 1968, pp. 38–9.)

The concept introduced at the end of the last chapter under the term 'entelechy' is clearly so like that which Maslow is describing that it is reasonable to ask whether we should not now replace the term 'entelechy' by 'self-actualization'. The latter is a good term, and has been current since 1968, so if I want to introduce another then it is for me to show why this is desirable.

Part of the need results from the particular meaning which we have given to 'actual', as existing in physical actuality. While it is not suggested that the self does not have physical existence, there are those who would wish to leave open the possibility that it exists also in some other way. 'Entelechy', introduced in Chapter 15 as 'Realization, the becoming or being actual of what was potential', is open in this way: for it allows us to include both self-realization and self-actualization in the process of entelechy.[7] Maslow also refers to 'the gap between human aspirations and limitations (between what the human being *is*, and what he would *like* to be, and what he *could* be). . . . That serious concern with this discrepancy could revolutionize psychology, there is no doubt in my mind.' (Maslow, 1968, p. 10.) Entelechy, as here conceived, is concerned with just this discrepancy, and with whatever kinds of activities are directed towards reducing the difference between present self and desired self. Beyond this, it involves also the possibility of growth in the conception of the ideal self; and it includes growth of what is a conceivable self as one kind of growth of a present self.

The concept of entelechy is thus taking shape as a goal-directed activity in which intelligence is concerned with successive states of the self of which it is part. These states refer to both that which a person does, and what he is; for he may become better by what he does, but also he may do better as a result of what he has become.

16.5   There is a difference to be reconciled between the ways in which 'self' has been used in Sections 16.3 and 16.4. In the former, when intelligence was described as 'creative and self-creative', the term was being used reflexively to mean that intelligence was in certain ways creating itself. Section 16.3 was directly related to the conception of intelligence as a combination of a second-order director system delta-two acting on a teachable director system delta-one. In Section 16.4, however, 'self' was used with Maslow's meaning of 'self as a person'. This takes us into a new area, that of personality theory; which is one of notorious difficulty to psychologists.

Each delta-one director system in the present model relates to a particular realm of thought and action. Thus we also have a wide variety of delta-ones relative to activities as various as cooking, managing our finances, gardening, writing a book, taking a shower. So far we have not discussed whether the model requires each delta-one to have its own separate delta-two, or whether a single delta-two operates on them all. (This question will be taken up again in Section 16.13.) But whichever delta-one is in action, we are still recognizably the same person—not just physically, but in our active and cognitive styles. What is being built up by the process of intelligent learning is not just a collection of isolated delta-ones, but also something which embodies regularities common to all of these. This something is not just a set of common factors, so much as a superordinate system of which each delta-one forms part, which integrates these, and which also gives them a common style: in the same way as we can recognize the same composer's style in each of his individual compositions. Is this superordinate system a delta-two? Is it a delta-three which can contemplate (and possibly change) delta-one and delta-two? The model here is incomplete; nor was it, at the outset, intended even as a first step towards a theory of personality. It can now be seen as open-ended in this direction, particularly towards approaches such as Maslow's. And it is worth noting that this integrative activity of intelligence is in accordance with the well-known findings of Terman and Oden (1959), that children of above-average intelligence grew up into adults who were better adjusted and more stable in both their personal and their professional lives.

Outer freedom and inner freedom

16.6   Freedom has been an important feature of the present model from Section 8.6 onwards, where I wrote: '*So it is hardly surprising that being able to choose and pursue one's own goals is itself a goal state which is widely sought. We call it freedom.*' The kind of freedom discussed in the rest of that section was in relation to the absence or presence of a power relationship influencing the choice of goals. But there are other constraints on a person's freedom. Some of these arise straightforwardly out of the fact that freedom in choosing one's goals necessarily refers to a particular universe of discourse, that to which this goal state belongs. So the advantage of a particular goal state may be outweighed by disadvantages inseparable from it in other universes of discourse. This may appear as a reduction of freedom of a kind; but only within the restricted viewpoint of a particular universe of discourse. The full exercise of one's intelligence requires the vari-focal approach described in Section 9.2, in this case spanning all the ways in which the goal state may be advantageous or disadvantagous. From this wider viewpoint a person may try to reach a balanced judgement, and a final choice of which goal to set, which will be influenced by individual values and preferences. The constraints here arise from force of circumstance. Thus a person, or a family, may not be free at a particular time both to buy a new car and to take an expensive holiday; but provided they are in a position which allows them to make their own choice between these two goal states, then in this wider sense they are still free.

Ability to take a wider view, to include both a greater number of universes of discourse and a longer future of likely consequences, is thus one of the ways in which intelligence can contribute to freedom.

The super-ego

16.7 Our main concern here is, however, with an internal limitation on freedom of choice the conception of which, though it will be reformulated in terms of the present model, has been taken directly from Freud. So let him introduce it in his own words (or rather, those of his English translator).

> There is hardly anything that we separate off from our ego so regularly as our conscience and so easily set over against it. I feel a temptation to do something which brings me pleasure, but I refrain from doing it on the ground that 'my conscience will not allow it'. Or I allow myself to be persuaded by the greatness of the expectation of pleasure into doing something against which the voice of my conscience has protested, and after I have done it my conscience punishes me with painful reproaches, and makes me feel remorse for it. I might simply say that the function which I am beginning to distinguish within the ego is the conscience; but it is more prudent to keep that function as a separate entity and assume that conscience is one of its activities, and that the self observation which is necessary as a preliminary to the judicial aspect of conscience is another. And since the process of recognising a thing as a separate entity involves giving it a name of its own, I will henceforward call this function in the ego the 'super-ego'. (Freud, 1949, lecture xxxi.)

This fits so closely into the present model that it hardly requires rewording. Freud has already partly replaced the term 'conscience' by 'super-ego', but retains conscience as one of its functions. In view of the religious connotations which the term 'conscience' has for many, I think that its use is best avoided altogether in the present context. The Freudian 'ego' corresponds to the totality of an individual's delta-one systems, particularly having regard to their overall integration as already described in the discussion of a possible meaning for 'self' (Section 16.5). So the terms 'self' and 'ego' have as nearly the same meaning as is possible having regard to their different derivations.

If, following Freud, we accept that there is some kind of separate entity which needs to be recognized and given a name, what kind of existence are we thereby attributing to this super-ego? Just the same kind as that of the rest of the present model, or indeed of any other mental model. To conceptualize the observable behaviour of compass needles at different locations near a strong bar magnet, we use a model consisting of a set of 'lines of force'. To conceptualize our ability to organize our behaviour in ways conducive to the achievement of particular goals, I have proposed the use of a model called a director system. It is also a matter of common experience that we often restrain the functioning of our director systems—we may want to do something, but something else within us does not allow us to do it. We do not strike, or verbally attack, those who arouse our anger; we restrain ourselves from making sexual approaches to whoever happens to arouse our desire; we do not steal objects we would like to own. And this, even when we could do so with impunity. It is also a matter of experience that when we do act against this internal prohibition, we feel bad about it afterwards. To conceptualize this, Freud introduced the super-ego. In the present context this is simply another model which has good explanatory power, and which has the additional advantage that it fits neatly on to the present model of intelligence.

Reformulated in these terms, the super-ego can be regarded as a director system in one way like delta-two, in that it has a delta-one for its operand; but in another way very unlike, in that its function is not facilitating but limiting. Whereas delta-two acts on a delta-one in such a way as to enlarge its domain, and to improve the functioning of delta-one within its domain, the super-ego is (in Freud's words) 'set over against it'. The super-ego restricts the choice of goals which delta-one may set, either by forbidding certain goals altogether, or if unsuccessful in this, then by the knowledge that there will be feelings of guilt afterwards, with the result that the goal will certainly seem less attractive. This guilt is equivalent to self-punishment—punishment of the self by the super-ego.

The super-ego is thus in a power relationship towards the ego, more of type 1(b) than 1(a); for its power over the ego's choice of goals comes more from the super-ego's power 'to punish me with painful reproaches, and make me feel remorse' than to provide positive reward.

16.8 Whereas the delta-one and delta-two combination is innate, representing our inborn capacity for intelligent learning, the super-ego is not. Very young children follow what Freud calls the pleasure principle without self-restraint; and those whom we call psychopaths continue to do so throughout their lives. By most people, however, a super-ego is acquired by learning, and is fully established by about the age of seven; though consolidation and further development may continue for a number of years afterwards. In the present model, it has been seen as a learnt second-order director system, having one or more delta-ones for its operand, but acting on them in ways which are not only very unlike the delta-two of reflective intelligence , but which we shall later see to be antagonistic.

For further understanding of the effects of the super-ego, it is necessary to turn our attention to the circumstances which lead to its establishment. Freud relates the formation of the super-ego closely to the period of the Oedipus complex. This makes our willingness to accept this concept largely dependent on our acceptance of Freud's theories about psychosexual development during infancy. Here I shall offer an explanation which is alternative to Freud's in that it does not necessarily depend on the Oedipus complex. But it is closely based on that of Freud, and remains consistent with his model, as can easily be verified.[8] Moreover, it can, if desired, be applied to the Oedipus complex as a special case.

The explanation which follows is somewhat condensed,[9] to preserve a fair balance between the topics of this chapter. It takes as its starting point the concept of *ambivalence*, having opposite feelings towards the same person or object. And in particular, it hinges on the ambivalence of a very young child towards his[10] mother. Initially, his mother is the source and provider of all good. But as soon as the babe-in-arms becomes a crawler and then a toddler, prohibitions of many kinds begin to be necessary; for the child's mobility gives him access to many things which are dangerous to him—fire, electrical outlets, sharp instruments, boiling kettles—and to which he is dangerous—valued but breakable objects of all kinds. The main source of these prohibitions is his mother, who by frustrating his desires becomes an object for his anger; and the vehemence of a small child's anger can be great, as evidenced by his going scarlet in the face, his contorted expression, and his angry cries. Even before this stage, his mother is sometimes a source of frustration as well as of pleasure, at such times as she does not satisfy his needs as quickly as demanded by the urgency of his desires.

Loving and being angry with the same person is a state of mind so painful that it has to be alleviated by some means. Objective means are not available to the child, because of his helplessness and dependency. Of the subjective means available, we shall consider only that which leads to super-ego formation. If he could divert either his love or his anger to some other person, the conflict would be resolved. But his love for his mother, and his need for her, are too great for this to be diverted elsewhere. So it is his anger for which another object has to be found; and this object is himself, or rather those acts or wishes of his own which are objectionable to his mother.[11]

This retroflection of aggression also solves the external conflict between his own wishes and those of his mother. By now regarding these wishes as bad, and by the threat of mental self-punishment if he indulges them, these wishes become prohibited internally instead of externally. His behaviour conforms to parental requirments in this respect; and since his mother is no longer the source of these particular prohibitions, his ambivalence towards her is resolved and she is restored as an object of unmixed love. This way of dealing with a difficult problem—perhaps the most difficult which a small child normally encounters—is so successful that it is likely to be repeated on every occasion when prohibition of its desires by his mother (and in due course father, and other authority figures) arouses frustration, anger, and thereby ambivalence. Each time this happens, the super-ego gains in strength, and is thereby more able to enforce its internal prohibitions.

Though this method is (in most persons) very successful in adapting to this recurrently difficult situation—a particularly human problem arising from our prolonged dependency as infants and children—the price paid for this adaptation is high. It is the alienation of desires which, though they may be objectionable to parents and others, are nevertheless parts of the self; such as curiosity (including sexual curiosity), aggression, getting dirty, making a noise, and most generally doing as one wishes rather than as one is told. Though these may be primitive in their early forms of expression, they could by learning develop into useful parts of an integrated personality. Another part of the price paid is the creation internally of an entity which is alien to the self, and in opposition to it: in Freud's words already quoted, 'set over against it'.

The super-ego is an internalization of the schooling function of the parents, and its relation towards the rest of the ego is an imitation of the power relation of the parents towards the child. It is, however, a distorted imitation, in two important ways. First, as Freud has pointed out, the severity of the super-ego may far exceed that which parents have used towards the child during its upbringing. This is easily explainable on the present model, since this aggression does not come from the parent, but is the child's own aggression, resulting from the frustration of its desires, turned back towards itself.[12]. If indeed the parents are loving, and show more affection to the child than severity, this could sharpen the effect of the child's ambivalence; for it is even harder for him to tolerate hostility towards a much-loved and loving parent. Secondly, the super-ego resembles a composite image of his parents as perceived by a child during the period from the first few months of life up to five or six years old. So it is larger than life, more powerful; and as has already been noted, it incorporates only (in Freud's words) 'their preventive and punitive functions, while their loving care is not taken up and continued by it.'

To summarize so far, the terms of my own model: the super-ego is a delta-one which has changed its operand. Originally it has harmful, angry, destructive wishes towards the mother; but for the reasons described, its operands have become other delta-one systems, those which embody what are now conceived as 'bad' wishes within the child. And although the super-ego may assume pathological forms, both the circumstances leading to its formation and the nature of the super-ego itself seem to be almost inevitable consequences of our prolonged dependency during childhood.

16.9   Once established, the super-ego has no less than five long-term effects.

(i)   the first has already been described: a divided self.
(ii)   it affects learning.
(iii)   it affects morality.

(iv) it affects attitudes towards, and relations with, authority.

(v) it is an enemy of entelechy.

(i) This division of the self is likely to be permanent, unless wholeness is restored by conditions which most people do not experience. These will be discussed in Section 16.12.

(ii) The super-ego acts as an internalized schooler, mainly of the taskmaster kind. It is thus antagonistic to the function of intelligence; for the first demand of a taskmaster (internal or external) is obedience, whereas the goal of intelligence is learning, directed towards the continual increase of understanding. These learning processes, by which the 'bad' delta-ones might develop from their primitive states to socially acceptable forms, require freedom to experiment, to make mistakes, to discover consequences of action, to talk about, and to reflect one—all the modes of reality construction which have been described and discussed. But the super-ego disallows all of these. Its continued action leads not only to inhibition of the forbidden acts, but their being rejected as acceptable parts the self, and may result in their repression from consciousness altogether. Once this last has happened, they become inaccessible to conscious reflection and thereby to the learning, up-dating, adaptive function of reflective intelligence. This offers an explanation, based on the adaptive function of consciousness which was introduced as part of the model in Chapter 2, of the infantile nature of the wishes which can sometimes re-emerge into consciousness, particularly with the help of methods such as those used in psychoanalysis and the various forms of therapy derived from it. But this infantile quality is now an additional reason for their being unacceptable as part of the self, unless the person concerned is able to accept and thereby perhaps to understand them—this being one of the main functions of the therapist. In the absence of such help, the probable outcome is continued rejection and possible re-repression.

(iii) The actions prohibited by the parents, and thus the wishes inhibited by the super-ego, are normally those which are not only disapproved of by the parents but are generally regarded as anti-social. The schooling function of the parents is largely directed towards inculcating in the child behaviour acceptable not only to themselves but to the culture in which the child is growing up—not lying, not using rude words, not stealing, not investigating the anatomy of playmates of the opposite sex. From this point of view, the formation of a super-ego could be regarded as an internalization of moral standards. But this, if it can be called a morality at all, is one based on obedience enforced externally by fear and internally by guilt. Since fear and love are antagonistic, it is difficult for the kind of morality based initially on the super-ego to develop later into that based on love for one's fellow beings.

(iv) We recall, from Section 4.5, that day-to-day experience is construed by the concepts and schemas which it activates. Sensory input and the activated concept fuse into a perception of something which we *project* into the environment and regard as 'out there'. The super-ego, like any other director system, includes its own characteristic schema; so a person's perception of all those in authority, be they teachers, customs officials, foremen, managers, or police officers, will include a projection of his own super-ego. Those with severe super-egos will perceive these authorities as more powerful and threatening than they are in fact.

This effect can also be explained in terms of role perception. In Chapter 12 we saw that a role includes a model of the corresponding opposite role. When a person encounters someone in a role which carries positional authority, the super-ego becomes part of his model of this role. This certainly helps to maintain 'law and order', but for the wrong reason. In a well-constituted organization or society, positional authority should overall be facilitative, nor restrictive: which is another way of saying that it should help to make the total interaction positive-sum. The job of the police is to make life safer and more free for honest citizens; more difficult only for thugs, swindlers, and the like. To the extent that this both is the case and is so perceived, people will in general co-operate with authority according to their respective roles. But the more that a person's perception of authority is overlaid by a projection of his own super-ego, the more he will feel himself to be on the wrong side of a power relationship, and the more his attitude will move away from willing co-operation towards resentful obedience.

Since life would become chaotic, and individual freedom diminished rather than increased, by a state of affairs in which everyone pursued his own goals without regard to the needs of others, obedience to duly constituted authority is a necessary and useful part of schooling. It comes into the category of things which, for the good of society and themselves, cannot be left open to children's own choice whether they learn or not. But this aspect of schooling is more likely to be successful if it is based on the conscious learning of well-understood roles than on the unconscious projection of an irrational super-ego. Learning of the former kind is accessible to conscious reflection; learning of the latter kind is assimilated to the existing super-ego, and results in its further development both in power and domain.

The ill-effects of an over-developed super-ego will if anything be greater when this is projected on to a person whose authority is that of knowledge. This leads the learner to confuse a mentor with a taskmaster, and puts him in quite the wrong frame of mind. Following the instructions of a mentor is for building up concepts, enlarging schemas, increasing understanding, enlarging the learner's domain in a particular realm. This activity is conducive to intelligent learning and relational understanding.[13] Following the same instructions from someone who, even mistakenly, is construed as a taskmaster, is to satisfy the requirements of someone in a power relationship towards the learner. Learning of this kind is an act of obedience, and is conducive to instrumental understanding.

If the learner is in the imposed role of pupil (Chapter 15), the teacher may already be trying to combine the roles of both schooler and mentor, which is a bad start because these are incompatible. Situationally, the best choice which is open to the teacher is that between supervisor and taskmaster—between learning based on consent by the pupil, and that based on submission. In the ormer case, there still remains a moderate chance of relational learning of he subject matter. In the latter, the likelihood of instrumental learning is great: for the goal of learning has been shifted to that of satisfying the equirements of the teacher.

In the student–mentor situation, and with reasonable possibility also in the pupil–supervisor situation, 'right' and 'wrong' answers mean 'good' and 'bad'; and ignorance is a cause for fear. Let us look again at a passage already quoted in Section 15.9

all said the same thing, that when the teacher asked them a question and they didn't know the answer they were scared half to death. I was flabbergasted—to find this in a school which people think of as progressive; which does its best not to put pressure on little children; which does not give marks in the lower grades; which tries to keep children from feeling that they're in some kind of race. (Holt, 1965.)[14]

Such fear would be understandable if the teacher did in fact behave like a taskmaster, punishing ignorance with a leather strap. But the teacher who wrote the above wished nothing but friendliness towards his pupils, as evidenced not only by this passage but the whole of the book from which the above was taken.

For many years I have been asking myself why intelligent children act unintelligently at school. The simple answer is, 'Because they're scared'. (Holt, 1965, p. 59.)

Why are they scared? And why does this adversely affect the functioning of intelligence? To the intuitive conclusions of this sensitive teacher, the present model offers at least part of an explanation. These children are scared because they project their super-egos on to their teacher, even though in this case he is a kindly one. And they learn badly because of the conflict already discussed between the ways in which the two director systems, delta-two and the super-ego, act on a teachable operand delta-one; and because the confusion between the schooler and mentor roles of a teacher is compounded by the intrusion of the super-ego into the perceived situation.

Let me again emphasize, as will be necessary at intervals to try to avoid misunderstanding, that I am not advocating the abolition of schooling, which I believe to be a necessary component of education. What is needed is first, a clear distinction between this and the entelechy component; and second, for schooling to occupy much less time, and for both this and other forms of teaching to be done more effectively and more efficiently by the application of greater theoretical understanding on the part of the teacher. This section suggests that some understanding of the nature of the super-ego is a necessary part of a professional teacher's theoretical equipment.

(v) Reasons in support of the last statement, that the super-ego is an enemy of entelechy, depend on further discussion of the concept of entelechy and the conditions which favour it. This is the subject of the next section.

Entelechy and Love

16.10 For those to whom this heading suggests a departure into realms of high-sounding but nebulous surmise, may I begin by offering some answers? This section is concerned with trying to find out what may lie beyond those goal states which collectively contribute to survival, and beyond survival itself: with the question 'Having succeeded in keeping ourselves alive, what then?' As I wrote at the end of Section 15.15, 'Entelechy belongs to the other half of what life is about—finding out what we are here for, finding our own goals in life, finding out how to achieve these, and trying to do so.' If these are not important questions, what are?

A fair objection to this would be that these are indeed important questions, but that a book about intelligence is not the right place to try to answer them, and that they may well be unanswerable. To this, I would agree that these questions are not answerable generally or completely. Each person has to find his own answers, and ready-made answers may be self-defeating. If someone does not want even to try, that is his privilege. It may be that he is not yet ready; but my view would be that to whatever extent entelechy is taking place at all in a person, he is seeking answers to these questions; though his search may not be conscious as such, and the questions not explicitly formulated. If this is so, then I suggest that a book which tries to make the functioning of intelligence more accessible to consciousness is at least one of the appropriate places in which to consider such questions. Extrapolation from an existing model is one of the ways in which knowledge may be increased. Certainly, the resulting ideas have to be tested, by one or more of the three modes of reality testing: but they cannot be tested before they have been conceived. And if also the model can indicate what are likely to be favourable conditions in which individuals may seek their own answers to these questions, this might turn out to be its most helpful form of contribution.

As a beginning, I propose the following formulation. Not everyone may agree with it, but by making the concept accessible to conscious reflection and discussion, it also becomes open to improvement and further development.

Entelechy is a continuing process by which the ego finds and creates itself, discovering as it goes along both the means and the goals. This is as much a process of artistic creation as one resembling science or technology: but it may need knowledge of all these kinds, in the same way as does the creation of a bronze statue of two dancing figures, looking as light as air but actually weighing several tons. The joy and grace of the dancers have their existence in reality—first the inner reality of the sculptor,[15] and then that of those who view his work. But their physical expression in bronze required the mastery over actuality of an expert in a number of different domains, co-ordinated and integrated by the higher-order function which we call the ego.

The present model suggests that if entelechy is a process of creation of the inner self, then it can usefully be considered in relation to the three modes which have already been distinguished in relation to reality building and reality testing. In learning what is necessary for survival in the physical world, the ego also grows and evolves. Beyond this, a person who learns hang gliding, surf riding, mountaineering, or skin diving is not only enlarging his domains, but in so doing is growing new parts of himself; and so in a less spectacular but equally real way is a child who learns to swim or to ride a bicycle. There is also the social or interpersonal self necessary for survival in co-operation with others, and growing by personal interaction of many kinds. And there is the self of one's inner being, often needing solitude to become aware of itself.

16.11 Situations which favour entelechy include those described earlier as 'Opportunities for accelerated learning', and which an educational institution at its best would be so well able to provide—libraries, laboratories, workshops, studios, sports halls; and also mentors.

It also requires freedom in the use of these opportunities, without which they cease to be opportunities. Entelechy depends on both outer and inner freedom: freedom to explore, to make mistakes, and to seek answers to questions of one's own choosing, since these represent the current growing points of one's schemas. The advocates of 'discovery learning' are rightly aware of this, but they have failed to realize that within a schooling situation, what goes by this name is often misleading to the point of fraudulence. For their teacher has already decided what it is that the pupils should discover, so these children have two tasks instead of one: both to discover what their teacher intends them to discover, and to discover it.

Outer freedom can be greatly supported by a well-ordered society, and also by smaller organizations, including primary schools at their best. Freedom also includes free time. In society, for example, this includes time left over from the demands of making a living; and in school, freedom from the ever-encroaching, ever-intruding homework with which many teenagers are burdened. No doubt it was of an apocryphal school that we heard that 'everything which was not compulsory was forbidden' (Worsely, 1955); but I know of some not far removed from this description. Within proper limits, however, schooling can support freedom; both for individuals in equipping them to earn a living, and opening a wider choice in how they do it; and in contributing to a well-ordered society in which respect for the law is based on understanding of the need for it, and awareness of the democratic processes by which it can be changed.

Inner constraints on freedom are harder to recognize, one of the most perversive in its effects being a harsh and punitive super-ego. Why it is so inaccessible to reflective intelligence, by which it might be updated in accordance with the requirements of an intelligent morality based on reciprocity, is something which has long needed explaining: since this inaccessibility is one of the major hindrances to psychotherapy. A tentative explanation can be derived from the model of super-ego formation proposed earlier in this chapter. As there described, it is to avoid criticism of his parents that a child turns his hostility back on to himself, making instead the offending delta-ones the object of attack. Because the super-ego is modelled on the parent, it is thereby conceived as immune from criticism. Even constructive, rational criticism seems to be excluded; for at the time when the super-ego was established, the child's ego was too undeveloped to be capable of this, and subsequent encounters with authorities of power often continue to reinforce the pattern, by disallowing questions: 'Just do as you're told'.

Another feature of the super-ego which may contribute to its immunity from criticism is that, like the parents on whom it is modelled, it is conceived by the person concerned as essential for his survival. Originally the parents were so in actuality; and the super-ego was at the time of its formation the solution to an otherwise intolerable mental conflict, which made it essential for a different reason. Moreover, when once it was well established, it had (though at a cost) the useful function of keeping the child from doing things which would get it into trouble with parents and others in charge of him. So it may well be that a person continues to cling to his super-ego because he continues to conceive it—irrationally and unconsciously—as essential for his survival.

Unfortunately, this is in the long term far from being the case; for the internal activity of a harsh super-ego is opposite in its effects to that of reflective intelligence, and when the super-ego and delta-two are in competition for the same operand, the former may inhibit the latter. Intelligent correction of errors requires consciousness to be focused on this area, with the purpose of increasing understanding and adaptability. The super-ego, however, punishes errors by feelings akin to guilt, such as stupidity, inadequacy. Intelligent learning requires the kind of exploratory activity described earlier, which a person will be afraid to do if mistakes are likely to result in punishment, whatever the source.

More generally, the projection of the super-ego into actuality has the result that the world, and especially the people in it, are perceived as more threatening, more restrictive, than they are in fact. There is thus a corresponding effect on outer freedom. From being less free to think, a person becomes less free to act, and fails to perceive some of the choices which are open to him. In Bruner's terms, he is defending rather than coping.[16] On the other hand, a person with a well-established ego can achieve entelechy in what would for others be very unpromising situations. This is even better than just coping—it is converting a stumbling block into a stepping stone. A harsh super-ego is thus an enemy of entelechy; whereas the better integrated an ego already is, the better it is able to grow. This follows directly from the properties of a schema, as described in Chapter 9.

16.12   How can wholeness be restored to a divided self? The logic of the present model points directly to the same answer as has been given by many others, out of a wide variety of rationales, doctrines, and convictions: it is by love. But the emphasis of the present model will be that love needs to be combined with understanding: with understanding of the nature of the problem, of the conditions favourable to healing, and of the fact that ultimately it is only the person's own restorative forces which can do the work.

An important contribution towards understanding the problem is given by Maslow's distinction between two kinds of love, which he calls 'B-love (love for the Being of another person, unneeding love, unselfish love) and D-love, (deficiency-love, love need, selfish love)'. (Maslow, 1968, p. 42.) The latter is related to what Maslow calls deficit motivation, and although I have given up using the term 'motivation' for the reasons given in Section 8.15, the distinction he makes is a good one. 'Deficiency' is also perhaps not the best term, since this kind of need can also be a surplus. The oxygen level of one's blood, or the total water content of one's body, can be either too high or too low; and the innate director systems which in these examples are called homeostatic have the function of returning their operands to goal states which are optimal for bodily functioning, and keeping them there. 'Maintenance needs' is a more satisfactory term. The examples just given are relative to physical needs, others being nutrition, shelter, physical safety. We have maintenance needs also relative to survival in inner reality, such as acceptance within certain social groups. These needs structure our perception of both objects and persons. The hungrier we are, the more an apple is perceived as something to eat, and less as possibly also something to paint, as a tree's means of propagation, and simply as an apple. And as Maslow writes, (1968, p. 36): 'This dependency colours and limits interpersonal relations. To see people primarily as need-gratifiers or as sources of supply is an abstractive act.' In terms of the present model, persons are perceived as members of an equivalence class: and thereby less as their unique selves. I do not, however, go so far as Maslow when he refers to 'waiters, taxicab drivers, porters, policemen or others whom we *use*' (his italics) (Maslow, 1968, p. 36). As was explained in Chapter 12, role relationships are essential in our daily lives, and can be positive-sum. Even the relationship between a psychotherapist and a patient is role-governed to an important extent. But the overall point he makes is a good one, and here I would go further than he does. For to the extent that feelings towards another person are derived from what we need from them, this is so different from unneeding love that one begins to wonder whether the former should be called love at all. His 'D-love' is a need *for* love, not a need *to* love. In his own words, (1968, p. 41) 'It is a hole which has to be filled, an emptiness into which love is poured.' So hereafter I shall use 'love' only with the meaning of Maslow's 'B-love'.

Maslow describes ten attributes of (B-) love, of which I give the following four. (His numbering is retained.)

3. The B-love experience is often described as being the same as, and having the same effects as, the aesthetic experience or the mystic experience.

4. The therapeutic and psychogogic effects of experiencing B-love are very profound and widespread. Similar are the characterological effects of the relatively pure love of a healthy mother for her baby, or the perfect love of their God that some mystics have described.

9. The truest, most penetrating perception of the other is made possible by B-love. It is as much a cognitive as an emotional–conative reaction . . .

10. Finally, I may say that B-love, in a profound but testable sense, creates the partner. It gives him a self-image, it gives him self-acceptance, a feeling of love-worthyness, all of which permit him to grow. It is a real question whether the full development of the human being is possible without it. (Maslow, 1968, pp. 42–3.)

The need of the baby and young child *for* this kind of love is great, and it is when, and to the extent that, his receiving of it is interrupted by the schooling function of his parents that the division of the self begins—super-ego against ego, 'bad' wishes rejected as parts of the self. Restoration of wholeness in a person is greatly helped by being loved in this way, at any time in life: but the sooner the better, since there is less to undo. Much of the help comes from the freedom to be oneself, to experiment and make mistakes, and to experience oneself consciously as one is, as a starting point for the re-integrative function of reflective intelligence and the re-commencement of entelechy. Here again the present model is in agreement with Maslow, who writes 'Even in principle, many of the tasks of self-actualisation are largely intrapersonal, such as the making of plans, the discovery of self, the selection of potentialities to develop, the construction of a life-outlook'. (Maslow, 1968, p. 38.)

Intelligence, ego development, and being

16.13   The model described in this book has been developed to remedy what I regard as the deficiencies of earlier conceptions of intelligence, and of stimulus–response models for the understanding of behaviour. This last chapter has been included both as an acknowledgement of some of the limitations of the present model as it has been developed so far; and also to show that these are not inherent in the model (as are, for example, the limitations of the factor-analytic model). Another feature of the present model is that it is reflexive: it points to itself as a necessary consequence of the model-building function of delta-two. I shall end by suggesting that it is also reflexive in another way, namely that the present conception of intelligence points in the direction of further expansion of itself.

Discussion of the basic pro-survival function of intelligence led directly to the concept of the domain of a director system (Chapter 6), and to the expansion of this domain as, in general, favourable to survival in actuality.

While a set of fixed plans is satisfactory for routine situations, adaptability within a domain is greatly improved by the construction of well-connected schemas; from which plans can be constructed as required to meet the demands of new situations which arise in actuality, and also to enable us to achieve new goals conceived for the first time in our own imaginations (Chapter 11). Thus the continuing improvement of the survival function of intelligence leads to 'knowing that' as the best long-term basis for 'knowing how,' and thereby to knowledge as a goal in its own right: derived from, but transcending, the original survival function.

The wide variety of operands and goal states which contribute in many different ways to survival has led to the concept of intelligence as also building up an increasing number of delta-ones, each related to a particular realm, and each acquiring an increasing domain within that realm. But since (as we saw in Chapter 8) the functioning of each of these may support or inhibit the functioning of any of the others, survival also demands the development of a director system whose operands are the set of delta-ones, and whose goal state is the overall optimizing of their functioning. This system, which we can conceive as a particular delta-two, is distinct from the delta-two which in our model represents reflective intelligence. Indeed, it could include the latter as one of its operands, calling it into action as and when required. (In that case we might want to regard it as a delta-three.) It corresponds (as we have already seen) to the 'Ego' of Freudian psychology, as also to the 'I' of everyday thinking: hence now the capital letter. It is very different from the super-ego, which has in the present chapter been conceived, not as a delta-two at all, but as a retroflected delta-one.

This line of argument suggests that while the director system corresponding to the Ego may be conceived of as innate (like reflective intelligence), the overall organization into which it integrates the individual delta-ones is of relatively slow development: since it necessarily comes after the building up of these delta-ones themselves. One of the most valuable aids to Ego-development which early nurture can provide—and which offers an outstanding example of the power which understanding can add to love—is therefore not only to love a child (which cannot be done to order) but also to ensure that he knows himself to be loved, which can. It is also possible for a parent by skilled management to minimize her schooling function in early years; and thus help Ego development to keep ahead of super-ego development, and in time to absorb it.

The above argument also suggests that this overall organization is likely to be a highly individual matter, which is entirely consistent with the conception of the Ego as unique to an individual; and that since the constituent delta-ones are as important as the integrating delta-two (or possibly delta-three), we should now expand our model of the Ego to include not only this superordinate director system, but also all the delta-ones which belong to its integrated structure.

A well-developed Ego is a valuable asset for survival. One reason for this has already been given—the overall optimizing of the contributions from individual delta-ones. Another is the better variety and organization of delta-ones which can be brought into service for a particular need. In addition, awareness that this is the case gives such a person a confidence in his own abilities, a self-image, which is itself a substantial contributor to success.

Beyond this, it can be argued that not only is such an Ego a valuable asset for survival, but that entelechy, which is the bringing into being of such an Ego, is of all activities the most closely related to survival. For if there is not a self *to* survive, above and beyond something that goes through the day-to-day motions which keep alive a physical body, with what meaning of the word is a person surviving? Survival in actuality is certainly prerequisite, and maintenance needs have to be assured if entelechy is to be possible. But given this, there are many, including myself, who would contend that survival in actuality is a vehicle for the creation and survival of a self in reality: for finding and making one's real self.

16.14   The mouth originally evolved for eating, the lungs for oxygenating the blood; but now we use them also for speaking, singing, and playing wind instruments. The present model embodies the belief that intelligence has evolved largely as a result of competition for survival, and that this is still one of its major uses. But this does not imply that it has no other important function. The model does, however, suggest that these may only become clear in retrospect; that sometimes we may only find out where we were going after we have got there.

In a model centred around goal-directed activity, this appears as a paradox. But it is a direct consequence of the principle described in Chapter 10, that experience takes its meaning from the schema by which it is realized. We could only have a very limited understanding of the balance wheel of a watch unless we could relate it to its function within the watch as a whole; and the watch itself takes most of its meaning from its function in helping us to catch trains, meet people, go for lunch when it is ready, and in general to time our own activities in co-operation with those of others. Everything we do takes its full meaning from a wider schema than that belonging to its own domain. In the case of intelligence we have been able to understand one of the functions of intelligence in relation to a schema which integrates ideas about survival, evolution, goal-directed activity, and the building and testing of schemas: that is, by looking backwards over what it has already achieved as a breakthrough in evolution. It now seems that we may expect the emergence of other functions; but also that their meaning will only become clear in relation to schemas under construction, or still to be constructed. Intelligence is reflexive in yet another way, since it is in process of constructing part of its own future meaning.

16.15 This chapter is different in both character and intention from the fifteen before it; so instead of a summary, let a poet provide the closing words.[17]

> And what you thought you came for
> Is only a shell, a husk of meaning
> From which the purpose breaks only when it is fulfilled
> If at all. Either you had no purpose
> Or the purpose is beyond the end you figured
> And is altered in fulfilment.

Notes for Chapter 16

1. From Frank (1947), pp. 340–1.
2. As an introduction I recommend Campbell (1975). I am also indebted to this source for reference 1.
3. Such as Einstein, William James, Schrödinger: I confine my examples to scientists.
4. Compare: 'There never was a time when I was not, nor you, nor these rulers of men. Nor will there ever be a time when all of us shall cease to be'. (Bhagavad-Gita, Chapter 2, verse 12, translation by Maharishi Mahesh Yogi, Penguin, Harmondsworth, 1969). And 'Before Abraham was, I am'. (St John's Gospel, Chapter 9, verse 58.) These can only refer to survival in being, not in actuality.
5. 'All About Lions', by Peter Skemp (1970) (Unpublished).
6. Terry McGlynn, of Stockport.
7. This was not necessarily intended by the writer of this definition: it is my own good fortune that the new meaning I wish to develop fits so well into this definition.
8. See Freud (1949), lectures XXXI and XXXII.
9. It omits reference to identification, and it also omits clinical evidence by which this explanation can be supported and expanded.
10. Here and in what follows, 'he' always means 'he or she'. I deplore the lack of a pronoun with this bisexual meaning, since I could not bring myself to refer to the child as 'it'.
11. This is where Oedipal wishes can be regarded as a special case by those who accept Freud's account.
12. This is substantially the same as Freud's account. See Freud (1949), pp. 141–142.
13. See Section 14.9; and also Skemp (1976).
14. See p. 50, and also the whole of part 2: 'Fear and failure'.
15. I am thinking of David Wynne's 'The Dancers' (1971). This may be seen in Cadogan Place Gardens, London; Hilton Head Island, South Carolina; and Chicago, Illinois.
16. See 'On Coping and Defending', which forms Chapter 7 of Bruner (1966).
17. Lines 10–15 from 'Little Gidding' (Eliot, 1944).

Bibliography

Annett, J., Morris P., Holloway, C., and Roth, I. (1974). *Human Information Processing Part 1*, Open University Press, Milton Keynes.

Bartlett, F. (1932). *Remembering*, Cambridge University Press, Cambridge.

Beard, R. M. (1969). *An Outline of Piaget's Developmental Psychology for Students and Teachers*, Routledge and Kegan Paul, London.

Bernstein, J. (1973). *Einstein*, Fontana/Collins, Glasgow.

Biggs, E. E. (1972). 'Investigational methods', in *The Process of Learning Mathematics* (Ed. L. R. Chapman), pp. 232–3, Pergamon, Oxford.

Bower, T. G. R. (1974). *Development in Infancy*, Freeman, San Francisco.

Bower, T. G. R., Broughton, J. M., and Moore, M. K. (1971). 'The development of the object concept as manifest by changes in the tracking behaviour of infants between 7 and 20 weeks of age', *J. Exper. Child Psychol.*, **11**, 2.

Bowlby, J. (1953). *Child Care and the Growth of Love*, Penguin, Harmondsworth.

Bruner, J. S. (1966). *Towards a Theory of Instruction*, Chapter 4, 'Man: a course of study', Harvard University Press, Cambridge, Massachusetts.

Bruner, J. S., Olver, R. R., and Greenfield, P. M. (1966). *Studies in Cognitive Growth*, Wiley, New York.

Burt, C. (1955). 'The evidence for the concept of intelligence.' *Brit. J. Educ. Psychol.*, **25**, pp. 158–177.

Butcher, H. J. (1968). *Human Intelligence, its Nature and Assessment*, Methuen, London.

Campbell, A. (1975). *Seven States of Consciousness*, Gollancz, London.

Casey, T., Simpson, S., Dunham, J., and Gilling-Smith, D. (1976). *Stress in Schools*, National Union of Schoolmasters/Union of Women Teachers, Hemel Hempstead.

Dann, T. C. (1974). 'Personal view', *Brit. Med. J.*, **2**, 438.

Dewey, J. (1929). *Sources of a Science of Education*, Liveright, New York.

Donaldson, M. (1978). *Children's Minds*, Fontana/Collins, Glasgow.

Eddington, A. S. (1928). *The Nature of the Physical World*, Dent, London.

Eliot, T. S. (1944). *Four Quartets*, Faber, London.

Erikson, E. E. (1950). *Childhood and Society*, Penguin, Harmondsworth.

Emlen, S. T. (1975). 'The stellar orientation system of a migratory bird', *Scientific American*, **233**, no. 2, 102–11.

Festinger, L. (1957). *A theory of Cognitive Dissonance*, Evanston, Illinois.

Fielker, D. (*c.* 1967). Personal communication, during a conference at the London Teachers' Residential Centre, Stoke d'Abernon.

Flavell, J. H. (1963). *The Developmental Psychology of Jean Piaget*, Van Nostrand, Princeton.

Frank, P. (1947). *Einstein, His Life and Times*, Knopf, New York.

Freud, S. (1913). *The Interpretation of Dreams*, Allen and Unwin, London and Macmillan, New York.

Freud, S. (1922). *Beyond the Pleasure Principle*, Hogarth, London.

Freud, S. (1949). *New Introductory Lectures on Psycho-Analysis*, Hogarth, London.

Galton, F. (1869). *Hereditary Genius*, Macmillan, London.

Galton, F. (1883). *Inquiries into Human Faculty and its Development*, Macmillan, London.

Gibson, J. J. (1950). *The Perception of the Visual World*, Houghton Mifflin, Boston.

Haldane, J. B. S., and Huxley, J. (1927). *Animal Biology*, Clarendon, Oxford.

Hannam, C., Smyth, P., and Stephenson, N. (1976). *The First Year of Teaching*, Penguin, Harmondsworth.

Hebb, D. O. (1949). *The Organisation of Behaviour*, Wiley, New York.

Hodges, L. (1976). 'Why teaching is a dying profession', *Times Educational Supplement*, 12 November 1976.

Hodgkin, R. (1977). 'The exploded school', *Times Educational Supplement*, 14 October 1977.

Hollands, R. (1972). 'Ruth', *Mathematics Teachers' Forum*, **41**.

Holt, J. (1965). *How Children Fail*, Pitman, London.

Holt, J. (1977). *Instead of Education*, Penguin, Harmondsworth.

Hunt, J. McV. (1961). *Intelligence and Experience*, Ronald, New York.

Husén, T. (1974). *The Learning Society*, London, Methuen. (Quoted in Chapter I of Richmond, 1975.)

Illich, I. (1971). *On the Necessity to De-School Society*, UNESCO, New York.

Isaacs, N. (1961). *The Growth of Understanding in the Young Child: A brief introduction to Piaget's work*, Educational Supply Association, London.

Jackson, A. (1976). *Heading for What?* Counselling and Career Development Unit, Dept of Psychology, University of Leeds.

James, William. (1890). *The Principles of Psychology*, Holt, New York; and Macmillan, London.

James, W. (1901–2). *The Varieties of Religious Experience,* first delivered as the Gifford Lectures in Edinburgh, and currently available in the Fontana Library, Glasgow. The quoted passage is from pp. 490–1.

Jensen, A. R. (1970). 'Can we and should we study race differences?', in *Compensatory Education: A National Debate* (Ed. J. Hellmuth), **3**, *The Disadvantaged Child*, Brunner-Mazel, New York.

Jung, C. G. (1964). *Man and his Symbols*, Aldus, London.

Koestler, S. (1959). *The Sleepwalkers*, Hutchinson, London.

Lack, D. (1943). *The Life of the Robin*, London University Press.

Lorenz, K. R. (1952). *King Solomon's Ring*. London, Methuen.

Maslow, A. H. (1968). *Towards a Psychology of Being*, 2nd edn, Van Nostrand, New York.

Miller, G. A., Galanter, E., and Pribram, K. H. (1960). *Plans and the Structure of Behaviour*, Holt, Rinehart and Winston, New York.

Musgrove, (1971). *Patterns of Power and Authority in English Education*, Methuen, London.

Oldfield, R. C., and Zangwill, O. L. (1942 and 1943). 'Head's concept of the schema and its application in contemporary British psychology', Brit. J. Psychol., **32**, 267–86; **33**, 58–64 and 113–29; **43**, 143–9.

Oxford Review of Education (1975). Vol. I, No. 1. This whole issue is given to the theme: Equality and education.

Packard, V. (1975). *The Hidden Persuaders*, Longmans, Green, London. (Also 1960, Penguin, Harmondsworth.)

Papousek, H. (1969). 'Individual variability in learned responses in human infants', in *Brain and Early Behaviour* (Ed. R. J. Robinson), Academic Press, London.

Parsons, T. (1959). 'The school class as a social system: some of its functions in American society', *Harvard Educational Review*, xxxix, 297–318. Reprinted in Halsey, A. H., Floud, J., and Anderson, C. A. (Eds) (1971), *Education and Society* The Free Press of Glencoe.

Paterson, T. T. (1966). *Management Theory*, Business Books, London.

Piaget, J.(1950). *The Psychology of Intelligence*, Routledge and Kegan Paul, London.

Piaget, J. (1955). *The Child's Construction of Reality*, Routledge and Kegan Paul London.

Piaget, J., and Inhelder, B. (1969). *The Psychology of the Child*, Routledge and Kegan Paul, London.

Polya, G. (1945). *How to Solve it: a New Aspect of Mathematical Method*, Princeton University Press.

Popper, K. (1976). *Unended Quest*, Fontana, London.

Richmond, W. K. (1975). *Education and Schooling*, Methuen, London.

Rosenblueth, A., Wiener, N., and Bigelow, J. H. (1943). 'Behaviour, purpose and teleology', *Philos. of Science*, **10**, 18–24.

Rosenzweig, S. (1944). 'An outline of frustration theory', in *Personality and the Behaviour Disorders* (Ed. J. McV. Hunt), pp. 379–88, Ronald, New York.

Ross Ashby, W. (1956). *An Introduction to Cybernetics*, Chapman and Hall, London.

Rutter, M. (1972). *Maternal Deprivation Reassessed*, Penguin, Harmondsworth.

Sadler, J. (1977). Private communication.

Schilpp, P. A. (1949) (Ed.). *Albert Einstein: Philosopher-Scientist*, The Library of Living Philosophers Inc., Evanston, Ill.

Skemp, R. R. (1962). 'The need for a schematic learning theory', *Brit. J. Educ Psychol.*, xxxii, 133–42.

Skemp, R. R. (1971). *The Psychology of Learning Mathematics*, Penguin, Harmondsworth.

Skemp, R. R. (1976). 'Relational understanding and instrumental understanding', *Mathematics Teaching*, **77**.

Spearman, C. (1904). '"General intelligence": objectively determined and measured', *Amer. J. Psychol.*, **115**, 201–92.

Spearman, C. (1927). *The Abilities of Man*, Macmillan, London.

Spitz, R. A. (1945). 'Hospitalism', in *The Psychoanalytic Study of the Child*, Vol. 1, (Eds O. Fenichel and others), International Universities Press, New York.

Tennyson, A. (1885). *Works*, Macmillan, London.

Terman, L. M., and Oden, M. H. (1959). *The Gifted Child Grows Up*; *twenty-five years' follow-up of a superior group*, Stanford University Press.

Tinbergen, N. (1951). *A Study of Instinct*, Clarendon Press, Oxford.

Trivers, R. L. (1971). The evolution of reciprocal altruism, *Quart. Rev. Biol.*, **46**, 35–57.

Vernon, P. E. (Ed.) (1957). *Secondary School Selection*, Methuen, London.

Vernon, P. E. (1960). *Intelligence and Attainment Tests*, University of London Press.

Vygotsky, L. S. (1962). *Thought and Language*, M.I.T. Press, Cambridge, Mass.

Wiener, N. (1948). *Cybernetics*, pp. 13–14, Wiley, New York.

Wilson, J. (1975). *Educational Theory and the Preparation of Teachers*, National Foundation for Educational Research, Windsor.

Wiseman, S. (1964). *Education and Environment*, Manchester University Press.

Wiseman, S. (Ed.) (1967). *Intelligence and Ability*, Penguin, Harmondsworth.

Wolberg, L. R. (1948). *Medical Hypnosis*, Grune and Stratton, New York.

Worsely, T. C. (1955). Personal communication.

Glossary

This includes both technical terms (e.g. 'schema') and everyday words to which a particular meaning has been given (e.g. 'realize').

Abstract (verb). To select regularities appropriate to the needs of a particular director system, either directly from what is encountered in the environment, or from other concepts.

Activate. A concept is said to be activated when it is an object of conscious attention; or when sensory input matches a particular concept, leading to recognition; or when (even unconsciously) it is affecting the functioning of a director system.

Actuality. The physical world; also, the kind of existence which we attribute to the physical world.

Actualize. To bring into physical existence.

Adaptability. The ability to achieve goal states, and thereby to survive, in a changing environment.

Ambivalence. Feeling opposite emotions, such as love and hate, towards the same person or object.

Anti-goal state. A state which we try to avoid or prevent, usually because it has a negative contribution to survival.

Assimilation. The emphasis in our experience of actuality towards what is like an existing concept.

Associative link (*A-link*). A kind of connection between concepts, discussed in Section 11.15.

Assumed environment. An environment sufficiently like that in which natural selection or learning took place for a director system to function.

Behaviourist. An approach to psychology which restricts itself to the study of observable behaviour.

Being. The kind of existence which may be attributed to our inner selves.

Belief. Something which we accept as a fact without having tested it against our own experience of actuality.

Capable (of operators). Able to bring the operand to a goal state, assuming that the energies of the operators are rightly directed.

Capacity (of operators). The set of states within which the operators are capable.

Coexist. Neither to support nor to hinder.

Cognitive. Having to do with knowledge or belief, as against emotion or desire.

Cognitive strain. Difficulty of maintaining organized awareness.

Command. Unilaterally to choose the goal of another, and require him to set it.

Comparator. That part of a director system in which is represented the difference between the present state of the operand and the goal state.

Component. One of those items of information which collectively specify the state of an operand.

Conceivable states. States for which we have available concepts, and which therefore we can imagine.

Concept. A mental entity which embodies certain regularities of experience, and may be changed in the light of further experience. (This may be experience of actuality, or mental experience.)

Conceptual structure. A set of connected concepts.

Conceptualise. To embody in a concept.

Conceptual links (C-links). A kind of connection between concepts, discussed in Section 11.15.

Conditioned reflex. A primitive learnt behaviour, first systematically investigated by Pavlov.

Confidence. Knowledge of (or belief in) ability to achieve a goal state.

Conflict. Reciprocally obstructing.

Construe. To interpret by a particular concept or conceptual structure.

Co-operate. Reciprocally to help.

Cybernetics. The name given by Norbert Wiener to the theory of control and communication in machines, animals, and man. (From the Greek *kubernetes*, meaning 'steersman'.)

Delta. A particular kind of director system, by which learning is explained in terms of the present theory.

Delta-one. A teachable director system whose operand is in the physical environment.

Delta-two. A director system which has a delta-one as its operand.

Differentiation. Forming new classes within existing conceptual groupings.

Director system. That which directs the ways in which the energies available to the operators are applied so as to change the state of the operand from its present state to a goal state.

Domain. The set of states within which (and only within which) a director system can *function*, i.e., can take the operand to its goal state and keep it there, provided that the operators are *capable*.

Education. A combination of *schooling* and *entelechy*.

Ego. The 'I' of everyday thinking. In Freudian psychology that which mediates between the demands of instinct, of the external environment, and of the super-ego. In the present model the ego is conceptualized as a particular delta-two, together with an organization of delta-ones which are integrated and co-ordinated thereby.

Established domain. That part of its domain within which a director system functions with certainty, or at least a very high probability, of success. (As contrasted with *frontier zone*.)

Entelechy. A continuing process by which the ego finds and creates itself, discovering as it goes along both the means and the goals.

Expansion (of a concept). Increasing the number and variety of experiences which can be *realized* in terms of this concept.

Expert. One who has well beyond the minimal requirements for survival in a given *prohabitat*.

First-order system. A director system whose operand is something in the physical environment, i.e., something in actuality. A *delta-one* is a first-order system, but first-order systems can also be innate.

Freedom. Being able to choose and pursue one's own goals.

Frequency (of a vibration). The number of complete repetitions per second.

Frontier. The boundary of a domain.

Frontier zone. A region (set of states) within which a director system can function, but not with complete dependability.

Function (verb). A director system *functions* if it takes the operand to its goal state and keeps it there. (This assumes adequate power from the operators.)

Functional equivalence. Interchangeability with respect to the achievement of a particular goal state or with respect to the functioning of a particular director system.

Generalization. A simpler but less precise term for *reflective extrapolation*.

Goal. Short for *goal state*.

Goal-directed. This term may be applied to an operand which is being taken to a goal state, to an operator whose energies are so applied by a director system as to bring this about, or to the two together. It may also be used to describe the activity itself.

Goal-seeking. May be applied to a system which combines director system, operators, and operand: such as an organism, or a goal-seeking machine.

Goal state. A state to which the state of the operand is changed, and at which it is kept. This is not generally a unique state, but one within an interval or region.

Habitat. The total environment in which an organism is *viable*.

Help (verb). Intentionally to *support* the activity of.

Hierarchy. An organization in which superordinate members command, and subordinate members obey.

Imagine. To bring into mental existence without reality testing against actuality.

Inference. A logical process within a particular schema by which, if we know that A is true, we know or believe that B is also true.

Inhibit. If an activity of A results (intentionally or otherwise) in a decrease in the probability of B's achieving B's goal state, then we say that A (or A's activity) inhibits B (or B's activity).

Innate. Inborn. Strictly this includes both genetically determined characteristics, and those which result from other pre-natal conditions. As used in this book, the emphasis is on the former.

Innate releaser. A term used by ethologists for a genetically determined perceptual classification which results in action.

Inner reality. Our mental realm; the quality of existence which we attribute to this realm.

Intention. A consciously set goal state.

Intuitive. In which consciousness is centred at a delta-one level, without reflection.

Intelligence. An advanced kind of learning, by which director systems are built, tested, up-dated, and improved in their internal organization.

Interiority. The quality or dimension of a concept by which, on closer examination, further detail can be found.

Involuntary. Not subject to intentional control.

Learning. The construction and/or improvement of director systems within the lifetime of an individual.

Love. I use this in Maslow's second sense, that of 'love for the being of another person, unneeding love, unselfish love'. In terms of the present model it can be formulated as an unconditional desire for the survival of another person.

Mentor. A teacher whose help is freely sought and given.

Meta-learning. If while consciously learning X, a person also learns Y, which is in a different universe of discourse, we say that he meta-learns Y relative to X.

Meta-teaching. Teaching with the intention of bringing about meta-learning.

Model. A conceptual representation. (A physical 'model' may serve to evoke and/or support this.)

Mutualism. A positive-sum system without an *organizer*.

Noise. Irrelevant input which has to be ignored in relation to the functioning of a particular director system.

Object-concept. The very basic kind of concept by which we recognize an object as having continued existence independently of our perception of it, and as being (or not being) the same thing that we have seen before.

Obstruct. Intentionally to *inhibit.*

Oedipus complex. In Freudian theory, a son's psychosexual desires towards h mother.

Open goal state. A goal state which is represented by a rather general concept, so th although we recognize it when achieved, we do not have a clear mental representatic of it in advance.

Operand. That which is changed from one state to another by the combined activity a director system and operators.

Operators. That which actually does the work of changing the state of the operan

Organizer. A director system whose operands are other director systems, and who goal state is a positive-sum interaction between them.

Organization. A state of affairs as described in the definition of *organizer,* with th additional requirement that the organizer intends this.

Organism. Something alive.

Path. A sequence of states, both in actuality, and as represented within a direct system.

Perception. The process by which a person becomes aware of present actuality, and so doing structures and classifies it.

Perceptual learning. The development of concepts which, when activated by senso input, result in new perception.

Plan. A path from a present state to a goal state, together with a way of applying th energies available to the operators in such a way as to take the operand along this pat A plan is thus one essential part of a director system.

Positive sum. An interaction in which the overall sum of every participant's gains survival contributions is greater than the overall sum of their losses.

Power relationship. One in which a person can unilaterally choose the goals another, and can require or induce him to set them.

Prediction. A sophisticated kind of expectation of events in actuality, involvin (i) realizing actuality within a model; (ii) inferences within the model; (iii) projectic of the result into actuality.

Primary (of a concept). Formed directly from sensory experience of actuality.

Prohabitat. Those features of a total habitat whose presence is necessary for particular complex of goal-seeking activities to take place.

Projection. A process by which objects and/or qualities which exist in inner reali are regarded as if they were in the physical environment. This may happen conscious or unconsciously.

Proportion. A set of equivalent *ratios,* such as $2:3, 4:6, 6:9, 10:15, \ldots.$

Pupil. A person in the imposed role of learner in a school (or similar institutio which he must attend.

Ratio. A pair of numbers representing a comparison. For example, if two perso walk at speeds respectively of 3 m.p.h. and 4 m.p.h., the ratio of their speeds is 3 (read as '3 to 4'). If they now travel in cars respectively at 30 m.p.h. and 40 m.p.h., t ratio of their speeds is $30:40$. These two ratios are equivalent: we say that they belor to the same proportion.

Reality. I use this interchangeably with *inner reality.*

Reality construction. The combined process of reality building and testing.

Reality testing. Testing our concepts and conceptual structures by one or more three modes: (i) against expectations of events in actuality; (ii) by comparison with th realities of other persons; and (iii) for consistency with other knowledge and beli within our own realities.

Realize. To represent within an appropriate conceptual structure, and thereby make available for use by a director system. The term may be applied either actuality, or to the utterances of another person; and sometimes also to things in one own inner reality.

Recognize. To realize as belonging to a known class-concept.

Re-construct (a schema). To take it to pieces, partially or completely, and then to re-build it in an improved form, in response to the requirements imposed by reality testing.

Reflective. In which consciousness is centred in delta-two; the objects of consciousness being concepts, schemas, plans, or activities, in delta-one.

Reflective extrapolation. A powerful and sophisticated method of reality construction from existing concepts, described in Section 11.11.

Region. A set of states. This can conveniently be represented in a diagram by a loop enclosing a (spatial) region of neighbouring points.

Resonance. A process by which a system having a natural frequency of vibration can be made to vibrate by the cumulative effect of small impulses, accurately timed in their application to match this natural frequency.

Role. A director system which contains a model of someone else's director system, that of the role partner.

Schema. A conceptual structure.

School (noun). Used in the everyday sense.

School (verb). The combined activity of deciding what someone else is to learn, and teaching it.

Schooler. A teacher who schools, as defined above.

Schoolteacher. A teacher in a school which pupils have to attend.

Secondary (of a concept). Formed from other concepts.

Self. The present model does not attempt a definition of this, but an approach to a possible formulation is discussed in Section 16.5.

Sensor. Something by which a director system is sensitive to the *state* of an operand.

State (of an operand). A relationship between the operand and its environment. This relationship may be described by the value of a single observable, or it may need a 'package' made up of several observables. The latter are called *components* of the state.

Student. A learner in whom there is intention to learn.

Study (verb). To learn intentionally.

Supervisor. One who, within a power relationship of category 1(a) (as described in Section 8.6), chooses the goals of another and induces him to set them.

Super-ego. An internalization of the schooling function of parents and other authorities, particularly that by which a person restrains actions and suppresses desires which have been found unacceptable to these.

Support (verb). If an activity of A results (intentionally or otherwise) in an increased probability that B achieves a particular goal state, we say that (this activity of) A supports (that of) B.

Survival. Continuing in existence as such, though not necessarily in exactly the same form.

Symbol. A primary concept, which activates and is activated by another concept which is the meaning of the symbol.

Taskmaster. One who, within a power relationship of category 1(b) (as described in Section 8.6), chooses the goals of another and requires him to set them.

Teachable (of a director system). Which can be changed towards a state in which it functions better.

Theory. An advanced conceptual structure within which can be represented a wide variety of actualities of some particular category. In this way, models for particular situations and tasks can be constructed, and used to direct action in ways more powerful than are possible without the use of the theory, because they take account of qualities of the environment which are inaccessible to simple observation.

Torting. Meta-teaching which is harmful and long-term in its effects.

Universe of discourse. A set of conceivable states, together with all the other concepts by which these are connected, together with all those which are generated by this co ceptual structure. More simply, it is a set of related concepts which together form particular subject matter; or, the set of all states currently under consideration.

Vari-focal. A way of describing the different ways in which the same concept schema can be viewed, from a simple entity to a complex and detailed structure.

Viable (of an organism). Able to survive, because capable of achieving its goal state

Index

318

LB1051 .S565 1979
Skemp, Richard R.
Intelligence, learning, and
action : a foundation for
theory and practice in
education

Skemp, Richard R.

Intelligence,
learning, and ac-
tion

MERCYHURST
COLLEGE LIBRARY
ERIE, PENNSYLVANIA 16501

16546.

SEP 18 2007

DEMCO